Oracle BPM Suite 12c Modeling Patterns

Design and implement highly accurate Business Process Management solutions with Oracle BPM Patterns

Vivek Acharya

BIRMINGHAM - MUMBAI

Oracle BPM Suite 12c Modeling Patterns

First published: September 2014

Production reference: 1220914

Published by Packt Publishing Ltd.
Livery Place
35 Livery Street
Birmingham B3 2PB, UK.

ISBN 978-1-84968-902-1

www.packtpub.com

Cover image by Artie Ng (artherng@yahoo.com.au)

Credits

Author

Vivek Acharya

Reviewers

Cyril Brigant

Haitham A. El-Ghareeb

Jaideep Ganguli

Ramakrishna Kandula

Max Pellizzaro

Surendra Pepakayala

Acquisition Editor

Nikhil Karkal

Content Development Editor

Rikshith Shetty

Technical Editors

Menza Mathew

Akash Rajiv Sharma

Copy Editors

Roshni Banerjee

Dipti Kapadia

Karuna Narayanan

Stuti Srivastava

Project Coordinator

Kinjal Bari

Proofreaders

Simran Bhogal

Mario Cecere

Maria Gould

Paul Hindle

Chris Smith

Indexers

Mariammal Chettiyar

Monica Ajmera Mehta

Rekha Nair

Tejal Soni

Graphics

Ronak Dhruv

Valentina D'silva

Abhinash Sahu

Production Coordinators

Melwyn D'sa

Manu Joseph

Cover Work

Melwyn D'sa

Disclaimer

The views expressed in this book are my own and do not reflect the views of Oracle Corporation or the company (or companies) I work (or have worked) for.

The information in this book is written based on personal experiences. You are free to use the information in this book, but I am not responsible and will not compensate you if you ever happen to suffer a loss/inconvenience/damage because of/while making use of this information.

This book is designed to provide information on BPM Patterns only. This information is provided and sold with the knowledge that the publisher and author do not offer any legal or professional advice. In case of a need for any such expertise, consult with the appropriate professional.

This book does not contain all the information available on the subject. Every effort has been made to make this book as accurate as possible. However, there may be typographical and/or content errors. Therefore, this book should serve only as a general guide and not as the ultimate source of subject information.

Furthermore, this manual contains information on writing and publishing that is current only up to the printing date.

About the Author

Vivek Acharya is an Oracle BPM and Fusion Middleware Applications
professional and works for Oracle Corporation, USA. He has been in the world of
design, development, consulting, and architecture for approximately 10 years. He is
an Oracle Certified Expert, an Oracle Fusion SOA 11g Implementation Specialist, and
Oracle BPM 11g Implementation Specialist. He has experience working with Oracle
Fusion Middleware and Fusion Applications. He loves all the things associated
with Oracle Fusion Applications, Oracle BPM/SOA, Cloud and SaaS, predictive
analytics, social BPM, and adaptive case management. He has been the author
for a couple of books, has an interest in playing the synthesizer, and loves travelling.
You can add him on LinkedIn at `http://www.linkedin.com/pub/vivek-acharya/15/377/26a`, write to him on `vivek.oraclesoa@gmail.com`,
or reach him at `http://acharyavivek.wordpress.com/`.

Acknowledgments

First and foremost, I would like to thank God. I could never have done this without the faith that I have in Him, the Almighty.

No one walks alone, and when one is walking the journey of life, you begin to thank those who joined you, walked beside you, and helped you along the way.

Many thanks to mom, papa, and my brother, Alankar; you all have been supreme. You have nurtured my learning and have always stood by me when things were odd or even. Thanks to my in-laws for giving wings to Richa.

Huge thanks to my wife, Richa, for inspiring me at every step, supporting my efforts, and encouraging me through the long journey. Thanks for having patience with me when I was facing yet another challenge in my life that reduced the amount of time I spent with you, and your sacrifice of all those weekends and vacations.

I would like to express my gratitude to Bill Swenton for all his support. I would like to take this opportunity to thank all those with whom I have worked in the past and those who have inspired me in one way or the other. Many thanks to Dean Welch, Vijay Navaluri, Prakash Devarakonda, Sebastiaan Dammann, Monique Albrecht, Nader Svärd, and Jugni for inspiring me.

Thanks to the reviewers who worked on this book. I would like to thank Rikshith Shetty, Binny Babu, Navu Dhillon, Larissa Pinto, Anthony Albuquerque, Menza Mathew, Akash Rajiv Sharma, and all the members of the Packt Publishing team for editing and polishing the book.

Last but not least, I beg forgiveness from all those who have been with me over the course of all these years and whose names I have failed to mention.

About the Reviewers

Cyril Brigant is an application architect specialized in BPM modeling and SOA Architecture. He has been involved in various workflow projects and SOA initiatives for the last 10 years in various Enterprise environments. At the European Commission, DG RTD, he was in charge of modeling the Enterprise architecture and SOA governance. He has recently joined the CMA CGM Group to bring his expertise for an ambitious project to rebuild the complete information system based on the top-down approach.

Haitham A. El-Ghareeb is an Associate Professor at the Information Systems Department, Faculty of Computers and Information Sciences, Mansoura University, Egypt. He is a member of many distinguished computer organizations, reviewer for different highly recognized academic journals, contributor to open source projects, and the author of different books.

Haitham is interested in e-learning, Enterprise architecture, information architecture, and software architecture, especially in Service-Oriented Architecture (SOA), Business Process Management (BPM), Business Process Management Systems (BPMS), Information Storage and Management, Virtualization, Cloud Computing, Big Data, and in collaboration with Information Systems and e-learning organizations and researchers.

Haitham holds a Master of Science degree (in 2008) from the same faculty that he is currently working for. His thesis was titled *Evaluation of Service Oriented Architecture in e-Learning*. This thesis was highly recognized and has been published as an international book under the same title (ISBN-13: 978-3-83835-538-2). He holds a PhD degree (in 2012) from the same faculty. His PhD dissertation was titled *Optimizing Service Oriented Architecture to Support e-Learning with Adaptive and Intelligent Features*, which was highly recognized and has been published as an international book under the title, *Optimizing Service Oriented Architecture to Support e-Learning*, *LAP Lambert Academic Publishing*, (ISBN-13: 978-3-84731-187-4).

Haitham is the author of the book, *Enterprise Integration Opportunities and Challenges*, *LAP Lambert Academic Publishing*, (ISBN-13: 978-3-65937-179-0). For an updated list of Haitham's activities and research articles, please consider the following websites:

- Haitham's personal website: `http://www.helghareeb.me`
- Haitham's blog: `http://blog.helghareeb.me`
- Haitham's channel on YouTube: `http://video.helghareeb.me`

Jaideep Ganguli has more than 20 years of experience in developing software solutions for several domains, including financial services, e-government, criminal justice, and wireless application services. Over the last 10 years, he has delivered several Enterprise-scale solutions based on WebLogic, JEE, Oracle BPM, SOA Suite, ADF, and WebCenter. He is a Certified Implementation Specialist with Oracle WebCenter Portal 11*g* and Oracle BPM 11*g*.

Currently, Jaideep is one of the cofounders and partners of Fusion Applied (`www.fusionapplied.com`). Fusion Applied offers top-notch Oracle Fusion Middleware-focused consulting and training.

Jaideep holds an MBA degree from Johns Hopkins University and a BS in Electronics Engineering from Mumbai University, India.

He can be contacted at `http://www.linkedin.com/in/jaideepganguli/`, or you can e-mail him at `jaideep@fusionapplied.com`.

I'd like to thank my wife, Rajeshwari, for her patience and support and my partners, Vivek Chaudhari, Vikram Bailur, and Sanjib Rajbhandari, for their encouragement and technical expertise.

Ramakrishna Kandula has an experience of 10 years in the IT sector and 7 years with Fusion Middleware technologies. He has worked on different projects in SOA and BPM Suites with various clients.

He completed his graduation with a Bachelor's of Technology degree in Electronics and Communication, in 2003.

He has received many accolades and awards in his career from client and internal organization recognition events for key implementations and innovative approach design.

He has designed and implemented many B2B and EAI architectures for different business implementations, which have also become role model architectures for many other implementations.

He has technically reviewed *Oracle BPM Suite 11g Developer's Cookbook*, *Packt Publishing*.

You can e-mail him at ramakrishna.rpkandula@gmail.com.

Max Pellizzaro, with over 15 years of working experience, has been working as a software/IT consultant in complex projects within different industries: automotive, telecommunication, and entertainment and media. Within the projects he has been involved with, he has developed experience throughout all the phases of a project's life cycle: collecting user requirements, designing software solutions, leading software development, and designing monitor tools for the on-going production environment. In his last organization, Max was the leading architect of Center of Excellence of Oracle Technology. His main activity was to understand clients' needs to help him drive the design and prototype of Oracle Solutions.

Max loves technologies; even in his day-to-day jobs, he mainly deals with Oracle technology. His passion has brought him to learn other technologies such as mobile development, game development, and 3D development.

Max has contributed to the review of other books on XML technology and open source frameworks.

Surendra Pepakayala is a seasoned technology professional and entrepreneur with over 16 years of experience in the US and in India. He has a broad experience in building enterprise software products for both startups and multinational companies.

After 11 years in the corporate industry, Surendra founded an enterprise software product company based in India. He subsequently sold the company and started Cloud computing, Big Data, and Data Science Consulting practice.

Surendra has reviewed drafts, recommended changes, and formulated questions for various IT certification literature/tests, such as CGEIT, CRISC, MSP, and TOGAF.

www.PacktPub.com

Support files, eBooks, discount offers, and more

You might want to visit www.PacktPub.com for support files and downloads related to your book.

Did you know that Packt offers eBook versions of every book published, with PDF and ePub files available? You can upgrade to the eBook version at www.PacktPub.com and as a print book customer, you are entitled to a discount on the eBook copy. Get in touch with us at service@packtpub.com for more details.

At www.PacktPub.com, you can also read a collection of free technical articles, sign up for a range of free newsletters and receive exclusive discounts and offers on Packt books and eBooks.

http://PacktLib.PacktPub.com

Do you need instant solutions to your IT questions? PacktLib is Packt's online digital book library. Here, you can access, read and search across Packt's entire library of books.

Why subscribe?

- Fully searchable across every book published by Packt
- Copy and paste, print and bookmark content
- On demand and accessible via web browser

Free access for Packt account holders

If you have an account with Packt at www.PacktPub.com, you can use this to access PacktLib today and view nine entirely free books. Simply use your login credentials for immediate access.

Instant updates on new Packt books

Get notified! Find out when new books are published by following @PacktEnterprise on Twitter, or the *Packt Enterprise* Facebook page.

Table of Contents

Preface	**1**
Chapter 1: Flow Control Patterns	**9**
Sequence flow pattern	**10**
Working with the sequence flow pattern	12
Elucidating the sequence flow pattern	14
Getting ready for executing use cases	**14**
Exclusive choice and simple merge pattern	**16**
Working with exclusive choice and simple merge pattern	18
Knowing about the exclusive choice pattern	21
Elucidating the simple merge pattern	22
Multichoice and synchronizing merge pattern	**22**
Demonstrating multichoice and synchronization with the OR gateway	23
The working of multichoice and synchronization pattern	26
Structured synchronizing merge pattern	26
Local synchronizing merge pattern	27
The parallel split and synchronization pattern	**28**
Parallel split pattern	28
Synchronization pattern	29
Conditional parallel split and parallel merge pattern	**32**
Working with conditional parallel split and merge	33
Antipattern – the conditional parallel split and merge	35
Multimerge pattern	**36**
Exploring multimerge	38
Discriminator and partial join pattern	**40**
Structured discriminator pattern	41
Structured partial join	42
Working with a complex gateway to implement the discriminator and partial join pattern	43

Testing a process by failing the complex gateway exit expression	44
Testing process as success by the complex gateway exit expression	44
Complex synchronization pattern	**45**
Canceling discriminator pattern	46
Canceling partial join pattern	47
Summary	**48**
Chapter 2: Multi-instance and State-based Patterns	**49**
Multiple instances with prior design-time knowledge pattern	**50**
Executing the multi-instance subprocess with prior design-time knowledge	51
Multiple instances with prior runtime knowledge pattern	**54**
Demonstrating MI with prior runtime knowledge	55
Understanding how MI with prior runtime knowledge work	57
Multiple instances without prior runtime knowledge pattern	**57**
Working on MI without prior runtime knowledge	58
Testing the use case	60
Static partial join for multiple instances pattern	**62**
Testing the use case	64
Understanding how static partial join for MI works	66
There's more	66
Canceling partial join pattern	**66**
Dynamic partial join for multiple instances pattern	**67**
Working with dynamic partial join	68
Understanding the functionality behind partial join for MI	69
Structured loop pattern	**69**
Working with structured loops	70
Demystifying do-while	70
Demystifying while-do	72
Arbitrary cycle pattern	**72**
Exploring arbitrary cycle	73
Understanding the functionality of the arbitrary cycle	76
Trigger patterns	**76**
Transient trigger pattern	76
Persistent trigger pattern	77
Implicit termination pattern	**78**
Amalgamating implicit termination in the process flow	78
Explicit termination pattern	**79**
Learning how explicit termination works	79
Cancelation patterns	**80**
Cancel multi-instance task pattern	80
Summary	**83**

Chapter 3: Invocation Patterns   85

Web service pattern   86
Asynchronous request-response (request-callback) pattern   87
Request-response pattern   90
One request, one of the two possible responses pattern   92
Two request a pattern   94
Exposing the BPM process using Receive and Send Tasks   97
Loan Origination over Send and Receive tasks   97
One-way invocation pattern   99
Implementing one-way invocation using a timer   100
Implementing one-way invocation using an e-mail   102
The Loan Origination process over e-mail   103
Testing the flow to instantiate a process over e-mail   105
Publish-subscribe pattern – initiating the business process
through an event   105
Loan origination over an event   107
Multievent instantiation pattern – process instantiation
over multiple events   111
Loan origination over multiple event occurrence   111
Human task initiator pattern – initiating processes through
human tasks   113
Loan origination via the human task form   114
Testing the process   116
Guaranteed delivery pattern – process instantiation over
JMS – Queue/Topic   117
Loan origination over JMS – Queue/Topic   119
Creating JMS resources   120
Creating the publisher process   124
Developing the consumer process   124
Testing the process   126
Understanding multiple start events   128
Summary   129

Chapter 4: Human Task Patterns   131

Learning about human tasks   133
Milestone pattern   136
Modeling in a human task versus a BPMN process   139
Routing pattern   139
Task assignment pattern   140
List builder pattern   142
Absolute or nonhierarchical list builders   143
Hierarchical list builders   144
Rule-based list builders   145

Parallel routing pattern   **147**
  Getting ready to test sample use cases   147
  Parallel routing pattern with name and expression list builders   148
  Parallel routing pattern with approval group list builder   152
  Parallel routing pattern with lane participant list builder   153
  Parallel routing pattern with rule-based list builder   154
  Parallel routing pattern with management chain   156
Serial routing pattern   **158**
  Serial routing pattern with list builder – name and expression   158
    Participant identification type – users   158
    Participant identification type – groups   159
    Participant identification type – application role   159
  Serial routing pattern with list builder – approval group   159
  Serial routing pattern with list builder – management chain   160
  Serial routing pattern with list builder – job level   160
    Modifying participant lists using list modification   162
    Substituting participants using list substitution   162
  Serial routing pattern with list builder – position   163
  Serial routing pattern with list builder – supervisory   164
  Serial routing pattern with list builder – rules   165
Single routing pattern   **165**
  Single approver pattern with list builder – name and expression   166
  Single approver pattern with list builder – approval group   166
  Single approver pattern with list builder – management chain   166
Notify/FYI pattern   **166**
  FYI approver pattern with list builder – job level   167
  FYI approver pattern with list builder – name and expression   167
Task aggregation pattern   **167**
Dispatching pattern   **170**
Escalation pattern   **171**
Rule-based reassignment and delegation pattern   **172**
Ad hoc routing pattern   **173**
Request information feature   **175**
Reassignment and delegation pattern   **177**
Force completion pattern   **178**
  Enabling early completion in parallel subtasks   180
Routing rule pattern   **180**
Deadlines   **182**
Escalation, expiry, and renewal feature   **186**
Exclusion feature   **190**
Error assignee and reviewers   **190**
Notifications   **192**

Configuring driver properties and attributes	193
Configuring the notification definition	194
Content access policy and task actions	**196**
Enterprise content management for task documents	**197**
Summary	**199**
Chapter 5: Interaction Patterns	**201**
Defining use cases to demonstrate interaction patterns	**202**
The BackOffice process	202
The Loan origination process	203
The CatchFraudDetails and Feedback processes	203
Conversation pattern	**207**
Asynchronous interaction pattern	**211**
Interacting with an asynchronous process using the Message Throw and Catch events	213
Interacting with an asynchronous service using the Message Throw and Catch Events	216
Enabling external services interaction	217
Interacting with an asynchronous process and service using Send and Receive Tasks	219
Attaching boundary events on Send and Receive Tasks	221
Interacting with a process defined with Receive Task as a start activity	222
Synchronous request-response pattern	**224**
The business catalog	226
Subprocess interaction patterns	**227**
Reusable process interaction pattern	229
Use case scenario for reusable process interaction pattern	231
Embedded subprocess interaction pattern	**232**
Interrupting a boundary event	234
Boundary event on an activity	234
Event-driven interaction pattern	**236**
Defining an event-based interaction pattern scenario	238
Summary	**240**
Chapter 6: Correlation Patterns	**241**
Correlation mechanism	**242**
Types of correlations	242
Components of correlation	243
Configuring the environment	244
Defining correlation properties	246
Defining correlation keys and configuring the correlation definition	247
Understanding the correlation behavior	249

Message-based correlation pattern	**250**
Testing the message-based correlation pattern	256
Cancel instance pattern	**258**
Understanding the components	259
Testing cancelation pattern	261
Restart instance pattern	262
Testing the Loan Origination process to restart a loan	263
Testing the restart scenario	264
Update task pattern	**266**
Demonstrating the update task functionality	268
Query pattern	**268**
Testing the query pattern	270
Suspend process pattern	**272**
Suspend activity pattern	**274**
Cancel activity pattern	**275**
How a boundary event based activity correlation works	276
Testing the cancelation pattern on an activity	277
Summary	**278**
Chapter 7: Exception Handling Patterns	**279**
Classifying exceptions	**280**
Business process state	**281**
Reassigned Exception Handling Pattern	**284**
Allocated Exception Handling Pattern	**285**
Changing the Boundary Catch Event from Interrupting to Noninterrupting	289
Force-Terminate Exception Handling Pattern	**292**
Force-Error Exception Handling Pattern	**293**
Force-Complete Exception Handling Pattern	**295**
Invoked Exception Handling Pattern	**296**
Invoked State Exception Handling Pattern	**297**
Continue Execution Exception Handling Pattern	**299**
Force-Terminate Execution Exception Handling Pattern	**302**
Force-Error Execution Exception Handling Pattern	**303**
Allocated state – External Exception Handling Pattern	304
Implementing Allocated state – External Exception Handling Pattern	306
Allocated state – Internal Exception Handling Pattern	309
Implementing Allocated state – Internal Exception Handling Pattern	309
Reallocated Exception Handling Pattern	313
External Exception Handling Pattern	**314**
Process-Level Exception Handling Pattern	**314**
Implementing Process-Level Exception Handling Pattern	315

Testing Process-Level Exception Handling Pattern	317
System-Level exception handling pattern	**318**
External Triggers	**318**
Summary	**319**
Chapter 8: Adaptive Case Management	**321**
Defining adaptive case management	**322**
Case	323
Case management	323
Dynamic case management	323
Mechanism of adaptive case management	324
Process versus case	325
Case management offerings	325
The building blocks of adaptive case management	327
Exploring ACM use case scenarios	**329**
The building blocks of the Insurance Claim use case	332
Testing the use case	333
Case stage	**336**
Event pattern	**338**
Milestone pattern	**341**
Case interaction pattern	**344**
Localization feature	**345**
Holistic view pattern	**346**
Ad hoc feature	**348**
Ad hoc inclusion of stakeholders	349
Ad hoc inclusion of activities	349
Ad hoc inclusion of documents	350
Association of a case with subcases	350
Ad hoc inclusion of rules and activities	351
Summary	**352**
Chapter 9: Advanced Patterns	**353**
Strategic Alignment Pattern	**354**
The Value Chain Model	357
The Strategy Model	361
Mapping goals to an organization	363
Defining KPIs in a BPMN project	363
Defining KPIs in a BA project	365
Defining KPIs in a child Value Chain Model	365
Defining KPIs in the master Value Chain Model	368
Publishing report data	370
Capturing the business context	**372**

Emulating Process Behavior	377
The Debugger feature	381
Round Trip and Business-IT Collaboration	383
Summary	392
Appendix: Installing Oracle BPM Suite12*c*	**393**
Installing JDK	393
Installing BPM suite	394
Configuring the default domain	397
Enabling the demo user community	399
Custom domain creation	402
The BPM/SOA configuration	407
Summary	412
Index	**413**

Preface

This book demonstrates the perceptible regularity in the world of BPMN design and implementation while diving into the comprehensive learning path of the much-awaited Oracle BPM modeling and implementation patterns, where, the readers will discover the doing rather than reading about the doing and this book, *Oracle BPM Suite 12c Modeling Patterns*, effectively demonstrates the doing. The scope of this book covers the patterns and scenarios from flow patterns to strategic alignment (goals and strategy model)—from conversation, collaboration, and correlation patterns to exception handling and management patterns; from human task patterns to asset management; from business-IT collaboration to adaptive case management; and much more.

This book will demystify various patterns that have to be followed while developing a professional BPM solution. The patterns such as split-join, multi-instance, loop, cycle, termination, and so on, allow you to drill into basic and advanced flow-based patterns. The integration, invocation, interaction, and correlation patterns demonstrate collaboration and correlation of BPM with other systems, processes, events and services. The human interaction pattern section leaves no stone unturned in covering task modeling, routing, dispatching, dynamic task assignment, rule-based assignments, list building, and other advanced topics. The chapter on Exception Handling Pattern is a comprehensive guide to model and implement exception handling in Oracle BPM implementation and design. The chapter on Adaptive Case Management offers detailed information about patterns handling unstructured data and unpredictable scenarios. The adaptive case management features and patterns will empower you to develop a milestone-oriented, state-based, rule-governed, content outbid, event-driven, and case management solution. Also, the witness patterns bring enhanced and dynamic business-IT collaboration. Experience the magic of strategic alignment features, which brings together the requirement and analysis gaps and makes the organizational activities very much in-line with the goals, strategies and objectives, KPIs, and reports.

This is an easy-to-follow yet comprehensive guide to demystify strategies and best practices to develop BPM solutions on the Oracle BPM 12c platform. All patterns are complemented with code examples to help you better discover how patterns work. The real-life scenarios and examples touch many facets of BPM, whereas solutions are a comprehensive guide to various BPM modeling and implementation challenges. Each pattern pairs the classic problem/solution format, which includes signature, intent, motivation, applicability, and implementation, where implementation is demonstrated via a use case scenario along with a BPMN application with each chapter.

What this book covers

Chapter 1, Flow Control Patterns, covers the basic flow control patterns in BPMN. This chapter offers an exemplary and comprehensive exposure to flow control patterns that are helpful in modeling and implementing BPMN solutions. During the course of modeling from "As-Is" to "To-Be" process, a process analyst models, designs, drafts, and publishes a sequence of activities and their flow control. This chapter starts off by showcasing the essentials of flow control patterns. This chapter explains converging from conditional and unconditional sequence flow to simple and parallel split and merge; later, the flow in this chapter expands to multi merge and transitioning patterns. Then, there is a comprehensive guide to patterns such as the partial join and discriminator patterns.

Chapter 2, Multi-instance and State-based Patterns, discusses a set of patterns that will demonstrate how processes can handle batch jobs and simultaneously spawn multiple work item instances in a process. This chapter simplifies the usage of loop characteristics while showcasing multi-instance perspectives. This chapter emphasizes on developing solutions for use cases with multi-instance requirements with design time and run time knowledge. This chapter further covers iteration patterns by demonstrating structured loop and unstructured looping mechanism. Then, implicit and explicit termination patterns will showcase the termination pattern.

Chapter 3, Invocation Patterns, gives an insight into the various discrete mechanisms to initiate processes and this chapter covers various patterns that illustrate these discrete invocation patterns. Process interfacing offers other processes, services, and external systems to communicate with BPM processes. This chapter uncovers process interfacing with queues, services, and processes by exposing different operations which external systems can interact with.

Chapter 4, Human Task Patterns, discusses the patterns and features that offer formalized best practices and solutions for the commonly occurring issues and challenges that allow process analysts, developers, and designers to build solutions to bring in human intuition in the process. This chapter discusses various task flow patterns and also demonstrates working with complex task flow. This chapter also demonstrates the inclusion of business rules to build a dynamic participant list. This chapter covers patterns that allow you to explore the feasibility to build a participant list statically, dynamically, or based on rules. The task assignment patterns section demonstrates how tasks are assigned statically, dynamically, or based on rules to the participants. The ad hoc assignment patterns, delegation patterns, and escalation patterns give depth to the chapter. The various other advanced features such as exclusion, notification, ECM integration, access policy, and so on are covered in detail along with elaboration on routing patterns, delegation, and so on.

Chapter 5, Interaction Patterns, discusses how processes interact and integrate with other systems, processes, and services and how these interactions are facilitated by various interaction patterns. This chapter includes various patterns that help to communicate with other processes, systems, and services. This chapter focuses on patterns that facilitate collaborative interaction of process with other processes, service, events, and signals.

Chapter 6, Correlation Patterns, showcases patterns that offer solutions to scenarios where processes need to be interrupted on the fly and sometimes need to be cancelled. The solution to a scenario where a task needs to be changed and/or updated in an in-flight process or cases such as querying an in-flight process. This chapter also uncovers all those patterns that need to interact with an in-flight process and also will explain how we can relate processes and associate a message with the conversation that it belongs to. The much awaited 12*c* features include suspending process and activities. These are elaborated in the chapter along with various other patterns to cancel, update, and query a process or activity.

Chapter 7, Exception Handling Patterns, focuses on demystifying various Exception Handling Patterns. This chapter focuses on exception classification, exception propagation, exception handling mechanism, and fault management framework. This chapter explains the strategies of how exceptions are handled in Oracle BPMN with detailed coverage of the fault management framework. We will examine the handling of exceptions in tasks, subprocess, and processes while covering different categories of faults. We will also cover modeling for exception handling and various modeling best practice while taking care of exception handling. Though the chapter is focused on exception handling patterns, it covers various exception handling mechanisms, their implementation, and usage in Oracle BPM.

Chapter 8, *Adaptive Case Management*, focuses on the case management framework that enables building case management applications, which comprise business processes, human interaction, decision making, data, collaboration, events, documents, contents, rules, policies, reporting, and history. This chapter demonstrates the inclusion of human intuition, empowered case, knowledge workers, collaborative decision-making, enhanced content management, and social collaboration. This chapter elaborates on Oracle Adaptive Case Management solution and in the course of learning it, one can explore various patterns and features that enable designers, developers, and analysts to model case management solutions and bring in agility, true dynamism, collaborative decision making, and a 360-degree holistic view of the case. This chapter also covers milestone patterns, case framework, event patterns, localization, case states, case interaction patterns, holistic view, and ad hoc features.

Chapter 9, *Advanced Patterns*, covers patterns in analysis and discovery category, where alignment patterns demonstrates features such as analyze, refine, define, optimize and report, and business processes in the enterprise. Alignment patterns highlight how IT development and process models can be aligned with organization goals while performing alignment, learning enterprise maps, strategy models, value chain models, KPIs, and reports. This chapter will also show how to create different reports based on the information documented in the process such as RACI reports, and so on. This chapter heavily focuses on demonstrating round trips and business IT collaboration, which facilitates storing, sharing, and collaborating on process assets and business architecture assets. This chapter also focuses on creating a collaborative ecosystem for business and IT and a detailed analysis of PAM methods to emulate the process behavior.

Appendix, *Installing Oracle BPM Suite12c*, gives us a brief introduction to the technology used in the book and also lists the steps to install Oracle BPM. Perform the steps given in this appendix to install Oracle BPM 12*c* to implement the use cases demonstrated for each pattern in this book.

What you need for this book

To explore modeling and implementation patterns and various features of BPM 12*c* through recipes in this book, you need the following software installed in your development environment:

- JDK 1.7.0_15 or higher
- Oracle BPM Suite Downloads 12*c* (12.1.3)
- Oracle Database XE (11*g*)

The detailed steps to set up the environment are included in *Appendix, Installing Oracle BPM Suite12c*.

The important considerations that should be taken care of are as follows:

- Tool/IDE JDeveloper 12*c* to develop solutions should be a part of the 12*c* BPM installation
- The installation document (*Appendix, Installing Oracle BPM Suite12c*) contains two methods to install the database; follow the one that suits your development requirements the most. It's a quick installation guide.

Who this book is for

This book is an invaluable resource for enterprise architects, solution architects, developers, process analysts, application functional and technical analysts, consultants, and all those who use business process and BPMN to model and implement enterprise IT applications, SaaS, and cloud applications. The primary focus is to showcase BPM patterns which are generic and can be read by anyone allied with any BPM offering. Hence, if you are associated with BPMN, you can relate to this title.

Conventions

In this book, you will find a number of styles of text that distinguish between different kinds of information. Here are some examples of these styles, and an explanation of their meaning.

Code words in text, database table names, folder names, filenames, file extensions, pathnames, dummy URLs, user input, and Twitter handles are shown as follows: "This is a static approval group defined in the BPM workspace with users (Christine, salesrep, Jim, and Kim)."

A block of code is set as follows:

```
If Discount < 10% then
Process performs other activity and process ends.
Else-if Discount > 50%
Accept Quote task is revisited by salesrep user.
Else-if Discount > 10% and Discount < 50%
Sales Manager Approval task is initiated.
```

New terms and **important words** are shown in bold. Words that you see on the screen, in menus or dialog boxes for example, appear in the text like this: "Now, click on the sequence flow with the **Deal** or **Terms Reject** tag and check its properties."

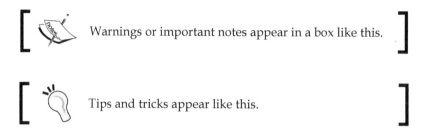

Warnings or important notes appear in a box like this.

Tips and tricks appear like this.

Reader feedback

Feedback from our readers is always welcome. Let us know what you think about this book—what you liked or may have disliked. Reader feedback is important for us to develop titles that you really get the most out of.

To send us general feedback, simply send an e-mail to feedback@packtpub.com, and mention the book title via the subject of your message.

If there is a topic that you have expertise in and you are interested in either writing or contributing to a book, see our author guide on www.packtpub.com/authors.

Customer support

Now that you are the proud owner of a Packt book, we have a number of things to help you to get the most from your purchase.

Downloading the example code

You can download the example code files for all Packt books you have purchased from your account at http://www.packtpub.com. If you purchased this book elsewhere, you can visit http://www.packtpub.com/support and register to have the files e-mailed directly to you.

Errata

Although we have taken every care to ensure the accuracy of our content, mistakes do happen. If you find a mistake in one of our books—maybe a mistake in the text or the code—we would be grateful if you would report this to us. By doing so, you can save other readers from frustration and help us improve subsequent versions of this book. If you find any errata, please report them by visiting http://www.packtpub.com/submit-errata, selecting your book, clicking on the **errata submission form** link, and entering the details of your errata. Once your errata are verified, your submission will be accepted and the errata will be uploaded on our website, or added to any list of existing errata, under the Errata section of that title. Any existing errata can be viewed by selecting your title from http://www.packtpub.com/support.

Piracy

Piracy of copyright material on the Internet is an ongoing problem across all media. At Packt, we take the protection of our copyright and licenses very seriously. If you come across any illegal copies of our works, in any form, on the Internet, please provide us with the location address or website name immediately so that we can pursue a remedy.

Please contact us at copyright@packtpub.com with a link to the suspected pirated material.

We appreciate your help in protecting our authors, and our ability to bring you valuable content.

Questions

You can contact us at questions@packtpub.com if you are having a problem with any aspect of the book, and we will do our best to address it.

1
Flow Control Patterns

A pattern is a generic solution to a recurring problem. Patterns describe a problem and its solution, which can be adopted in discrete situations. Patterns are adorned best practices that deliver a reusable architecture outline. **Business Process Management** (**BPM**) is widely adopted for process transparency, process intelligence, business empowerment, and business alignment. While designing business processes, we are not just automating and managing processes; it's more about how an enterprise adapts to a comprehensive view of business processes.

This chapter offers an exemplary and comprehensive exposure to flow control patterns, which are helpful in the modeling and implementation of Oracle BPM 12c solutions. During the journey, it will walk you through various BPM patterns based on real-life examples. The book offers projects to download with each chapter; these projects allow you to design, model, and analyze the patterns discussed in each chapter. Hence, it offers an interactive way to learn and implement BPM patterns. It allows you to fill the gaps and offers content that allows you to use BPMN to its full potential.

Process analysts, architects, and process developers deal with process modeling, define and design process models, and implement them. While performing process modeling and implementing them, they constantly deal with varied common challenges. Process modeling and BPM patterns offer techniques to solve repeatable issues, enhance the process-modeling approach, improve process modeling and implementation quality, and offer great productivity.

This chapter covers the basic and advanced flow control patterns in Oracle BPM. Perceptible regularity in the world of process control flow is demonstrated here. During the course of modeling from the "As-Is" to "To-Be" process, a process analyst models, designs, drafts, and publishes a sequence of activities and their flow control. This chapter starts off the book by showcasing the essentials of flow control patterns. Flow control patterns capture the various ways in which activities are represented and controlled in workflows. Implementing these patterns gives Oracle BPM the capability to handle the widest range of possible scenarios to model and execute processes.

This chapter will focus on the flow control patterns in the following points:

- Sequence flow pattern
- Exclusive choice and simple merge pattern
- Multichoice and synchronizing merge pattern
- Structured synchronizing merge pattern
  - Local synchronizing merge pattern
- Parallel split and synchronization pattern
- Conditional parallel split and parallel merge pattern
- Multimerge pattern
- Discriminator and partial join pattern
  - Structured discriminator pattern
  - Structured partial join pattern
- Complex synchronization pattern
  - Canceling discriminator pattern
  - Canceling partial join pattern

Sequence flow pattern

One of the fundamental steps in the BPM process modeling is to build a process model (diagram) which enables a shared understanding between participants on a process flow pattern. The process participants are not going to discuss each and every page of the document, neither will a collaborative, iterative process improvement or approach succeed with a group of people sitting and walking through documents. However, this group will be interested in a process model (diagram) and discuss the flow, sequence, and process patterns visible through the process model. This makes sequence flow patterns of paramount importance, as each and every activity is related to the other. In a process diagram, this relationship is created and managed through sequence flows. The following table summarizes the details of the sequence flow pattern:

Signature	Sequence Flow Pattern
Classification	Basic Flow Control Pattern
Intent	Offers sequence routing.
Motivation	The fundamental constituent to weave process components and demonstrate dependency and state transition between tasks/activities.
Applicability	The sequence pattern enforces a transitive temporal ordering to process activities. In business terms, sequences denote a strong dependency between activities and cater to strictly separating process involvement at organizational boundaries. They define the behavior of a business process.
Implementation	Widely adopted in most of the modeling languages including Oracle BPMN.
Known issues	Difference in acceptance.
Known solution	Usage of tokens in process instances.

The sequence is the simplest pattern and is implemented through a graphical sequence of actions, as graphical form is used for the sequencing of patterns. In BPMN, the model elements that are to be executed in sequence are connected with sequence flow connectors. When activities are connected with sequence flow connectors, processing of the second activity will not commence before the first activity is completed. This pattern defines the dependency of one task on the other and governs the fact that execution of one task is dependent on the other and cannot be completed until that task gets completed. Ordering of tasks in a business process is determined by sequence flow, and it governs how the process token will flow through the process. With sequence pattern, you can create a series of consecutive tasks, which are executed one after another based on the sequence connector's connections.

Categories: The sequence flow can be categorized as follows:

- **Incoming sequence flow**: This refers to flow that leads into a flow object
- **Outgoing sequence flow**: This refers to flow that leads out of a flow object

Some activities/flow objects can have both the sequence flows, and most of the activities/objects in a process have them. However, the `start` object can only contain an outgoing sequence flow and the `end` object can only contain an incoming sequence flow.

There are different types of sequence flows which are as follows:

- Default sequence flow/unconditional sequence flow
- Conditional sequence flow

Working with the sequence flow pattern

Perform the following steps to check the sequence flow usage in action:

1. Download the application (**SalesQuoteDemo**) contained in the download link of this chapter.
2. Open **SalesQuoteProject** in JDeveloper 12*c*.
3. Open **SalesQuoteProcess**; this will open the process flow in the design area.
4. Go to **Approvers Swim lane** and click on **Exclusive Gateway** (**ApprovalsOutcome**) that works on the **ApproveDeals** and **ApproveTerms** outcomes. The process is shown in the following screenshot:

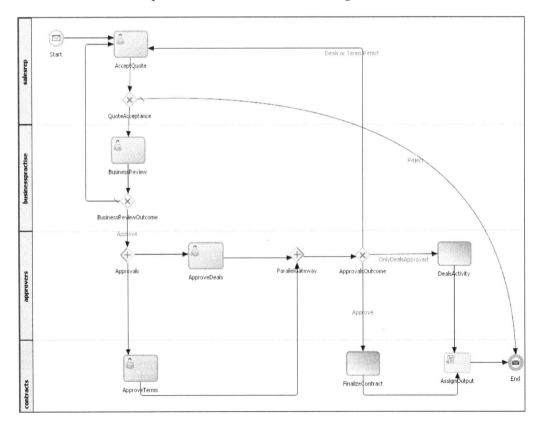

5. Click on the outgoing sequence flow with the **Approve** tag. In the properties, you will find that the type of sequence flow is **Unconditional**. This is the default sequence flow from the **Exclusive Gateway**.

6. Now, click on the sequence flow with the **Deal or Terms Reject** tag and check its properties.

7. The sequence flow type is **Condition**, and it has a conditional expression build. When this conditional expression returns `true`, the process token will take this sequence flow path. This is shown in the following screenshot:

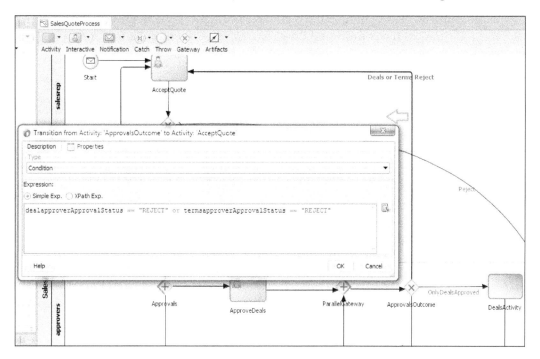

8. Click on the sequence flow with the **OnlyDealsApproved** tag and check its properties. This sequence flow is also a conditional flow with the following expression:

```
DealapproverAppr ovalStatus == "APPROVE" and
termsapproverApprovalStatus == "REJECT"
```

Elucidating the sequence flow pattern

The conditional sequence flow governs the token movement based on conditions associated with the sequence flows, where conditions are expressed using the x-path expressions. A path that is taken out of the gateways when none of the conditions specified on the conditional flow is evaluated. This is termed as default sequence flow, and it's drawn as an arrow line with a tick mark at one end.

Upon the arrival of token at the gateways, conditions associated with the drawn sequence flows are evaluated, and that sequence route is picked whose conditional evaluation returns `true`. Then, the token starts trailing this path. However, if none of the evaluations of the conditional flow returns `true`, then the default route is picked.

> Conditional sequence flows can be associated with exclusive and inclusive gateways for split.

Getting ready for executing use cases

This section talks about the steps that we will perform to get ready to execute the use cases demonstrated in this chapter. As we check **SalesQuoteProcess**, there are various human tasks. The following is the list of roles associated with the human task and users associated with the role:

Task	Role	User
Accept Quote	Salesrep	`salesrep`
Business Review	Business practice	`fkafka`
Approvers	Approvers	`jcooper`
Contracts	Contracts	`jstein`

We have to perform the following steps to execute the processes that have human task:

1. Log in to the WebLogic console and navigate to **myrealm** (embedded LDAP).
2. Click on the **User and Group** tab.
3. Verify that we have the aforementioned listed users in **myrealm**. If not, we can create users (`salesrep`, `fkafka`, `jcooper`, and `jstein`) in **myrealm**.

If we execute demo community that is installed while configuring Oracle BPM 12c, we will get users (fkafka, jcooper, and jstein). However, we can follow the preceding steps and create a user (salesrep).

4. Open JDeveloper and navigate to **Organization** in **SalesQuoteProject**.

5. Click on **Roles** and associate users to roles as listed in the preceding table. Save the changes.

Human tasks are executed with respect to organization units. Hence, we will create an organization unit and associate the users to it. We will also make sure that the organization unit is passed to the process when the process executes. Execute the following steps:

1. Log in to the Oracle BPM workspace as an admin user (weblogic).

2. Navigate to **Administration** | **Organization** | **Organization Units**.

3. Click on the **+** icon to create a root organization.

4. Enter the name of the organization as SalesOrg.

5. In the **Members** section, add the users we listed in the preceding table. To add users, we can browse the **myrealm** LDAP.

6. When users are added, we can save the changes. This process is shown in the following screenshot:

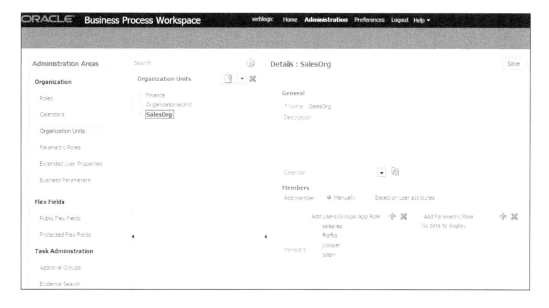

7. Go back to JDeveloper and open **SalesQuoteProcess**.

8. Click on the Message Start Event (**Start**) and open its properties.

9. Go to the **Implementation** tab and open data association.

10. On the right-hand side of data association, scroll to the predefined variable (**Organization Unit**).

11. Assign the newly created organization units, **SalesOrg**, to the predefined variable (**Organization Units**) and save the project. This is demonstrated in the following screenshot:

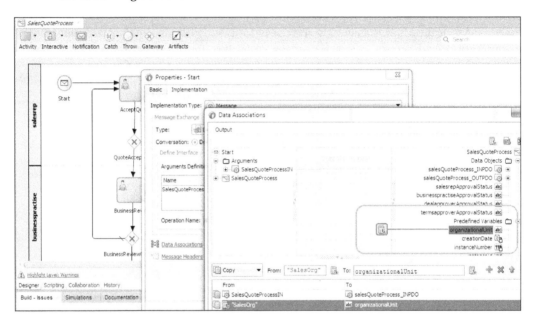

Exclusive choice and simple merge pattern

In this section, we will uncover the exclusive choice and simple merge pattern. It's also known as the exclusive choice pattern.

The control points in the process flow, where the sequence flows converge or diverge are known as gateways. There are different types of gateways, each supporting specific control logics. The gateway types are indicated with a marker in the center of the gateway symbol. Gateways can split and/or join (merge) sequence flows. You need gateways to control the process flow. A gateway is used to model decisions, merges, forks, and joins on a BPMN business process diagram. An exclusive gateway in Oracle BPMN offers simple split and merge patterns. An exclusive gateway (represented by XOR) evaluates the state of the business process and based on the condition, breaks the flow into one of the two or more mutually exclusive paths. This is how the name "mutually exclusive" got derived. The exclusive gateway splits the process into multiple paths, but the token follows only one path. The following table illustrates the details of the exclusive choice pattern:

Signature	Exclusive Choice Pattern
Classification	Basic Flow Control Pattern
Intent	Breaks the flow into one of the two or more mutually exclusive paths.
Motivation	Fundamental constituent to enable dynamic routing decision.
Applicability	Decision point in the business process where the sequence flow will take only one of the possible outgoing paths when the process is performed.
Implementation	Widely adopted in most of the modeling languages, including Oracle BPMN, as the XOR gateway.
Known issues	Enforcing accuracy in triggering an outgoing path.
Known solution	Based on the evaluation of the conditions associated with the outgoing sequence flows from the gateway, routes are determinate. In case of multiple outgoing sequence flow, it is always a best practice to associate an order of their evaluation, as this will enable the fact that in case of multiple conditions getting evaluated as `true`, the process token will route to the first sequence flow for which the evaluation is `true`.

The decision mechanisms are categorized as follows:

- **Data**: An example of data is conditional expression. The conditional expressions are evaluated at the gateway when the process token reaches the gateway. That path whose evaluation result is `true` is followed, and it can route to only one flow

- **Events** (for example, the receipt of alternative messages): An event-based XOR gateway represents a divergence point where the alternatives paths are picked based on the event that occurs at that instance in the process flow. The event could be a receipt of message or a timer event. In an event-based gateway, it's the events that determine the path to be taken and not the conditional evaluations. The process becomes dynamic as process divergence is based on the external system's interaction with the process.

Working with exclusive choice and simple merge pattern

In order to evaluate the data-decision mechanism, refer to **SalesQuoteProcess** associated with the project (you have referred to it in the *Working with sequence flow pattern* section). Check the **Approvals Outcome** exclusive gateway, as shown in the following screenshot.

There are three outgoing sequence flows from the **Approvals Outcome** exclusive gateway. Two are conditional and one is default, as we discussed in *The Sequence flow pattern* section. Hence, these sequence flow conditions are based on the values of process data, the value of the data token itself, to determine which path should be taken. An order of evaluation is associated with the **Approvals Outcome** exclusive gateway, as this will enable the fact that in case of multiple conditions getting evaluated as true, the process token will route to the first sequence flow for which the evaluation is true. The following screenshot demonstrates this process:

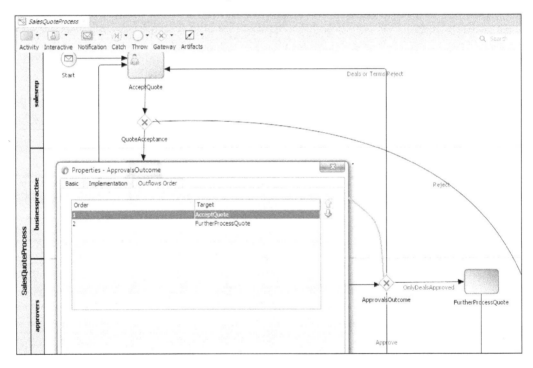

Open the **ExclusiveChoice&SimpleMerge** process in JDeveloper 12*c* to evaluate the event-based gateway.

The use case illustrated in the preceding screenshot elucidates that quote processing can happen for both, **New Quote Application** and **Existing Quote Application**. In this case, use an event-based gateway, as there are multiple types of messages or events that can start a business process. The **SalesReqApprovalTask** human task is associated with the **salesrep** role, and we already assigned a user (salesrep) to this role. Hence, when the process executes the task, it will get assigned to the salesrep user, as shown in the following screenshot:

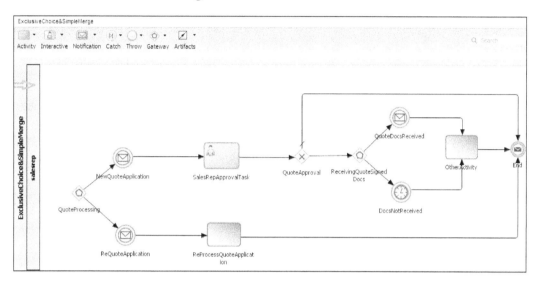

The following are the facts about the use case:

- **Quote Processing** is an initiating type of event-based gateway. **NewQuote Application** and **ReQuoteApplication** will catch the event messages. **SalesReqApprovalTask** is a task to be performed by the sales representative.

- **QuoteApproval** is the decision point based on process data which is the outcome of the user task (**SalesReqApprovalTask**) performed by the sales representative.

- **ReceivingQuoteSignedDocs** is a non-initiating event-based gateway.

- **QuoteDocsReceived** is a Message Catch Event, while the **DocsNotReceived** timer will move the token flow if documents are not received in 3 days.

- **OtherActivity** is a drafted process that performs further quote processing. The correlation key is designed and associated with all the event messages (**NewQuoteApplication**, **ReQuoteApplication**, and **QuoteDocsReceived**). This is demonstrated in the following screenshot:

When the process initiates, it would either initiate for a new quote or an existing quote. If initiated for a new quote, it would be caught by the **NewQuoteApplication** event message. If initiated for an existing quote, it would be caught by the **ReQuoteApplication** event message, as shown in the following screenshot:

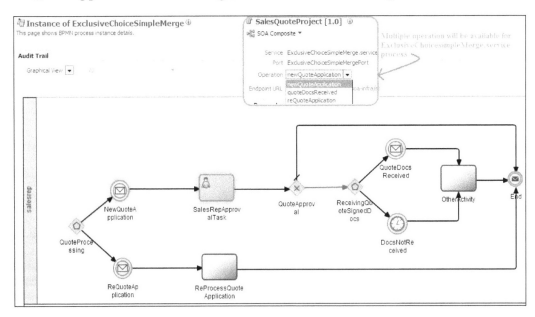

Test the process for the **NewQuoteApplication** event message by performing the following steps:

1. Open EM Console and click on the **SalesQuoteProject** project.

2. Execute **ExclusiveChoiceSimpleMerge.service** to execute the **ExclusiveChoice&SimpleMerge** process.

3. Select the **NewQuoteApplication** operation. As we can see in the preceding screenshot, **ExclusiveChoiceSimpleMerge.service** exposes multiple operations, which are essentially the event gateway's Message Catch Events.

4. Browse through the **ExclusiveChoiceSimpleMerge.xml** test data file in the project by navigating to **SalesQuoteProject | SOA | testsuites**.

5. Execute the process instance.

6. Log in to the BPMN workspace as a `salesrep` user and **APPROVE** the **SalesReqApprovalTask** task.

The **Quote Processing** event gateway initiates the sequence that has the **NewQuoteApplication** message event, and the instance reaches the **SalesReqApprovalTask** user task. Once the task is approved, we will find that the process halts at the **ReceivingQuoteSignedDocs** event gateway. The instance status will be running, and the token will stay there until a token arrives from any of the branches. Either the supporting document message will be received, or the waiting time will exceed three days.

Knowing about the exclusive choice pattern

Events receive communication, and hence, correlation needs to be defined to correlate them with the main process instance. A quote's opportunity ID is used as a correlation key. This correlation key is used in the intermediate events to correlate them with the existing process instance. With the correlation defined for the intermediate event gateway, the message will be correlated back to the original instance when it arrives at the **QuoteDocsReceived** event.

The message flow waits at the **ReceivingQuoteSignedDocs** event-based gateway, waiting for a token to arrive from any of its branches. In this case, the token can be a receipt of an event message or time. The first event triggers one of the alternatives that is an exclusion of any other path from the gateway. The event will basically pull the token from the gateway and continue to sequence flow that event.

Elucidating the simple merge pattern

We can use exclusive gateway to merge incoming sequence flows; however, there is no synchronization with other tokens that might be coming from other paths within the process flow. Simple merge combines several transitions back into a single activity. Tokens that merge at an exclusive gateway will be passed through as they are, and they would not be evaluated. Token merging at the exclusive gateway will not be synchronized. At the converging point, you would never have more than one token.

The following table illustrates the details of a simple merge pattern:

Signature	Simple Merge Pattern
Classification	Basic Flow Control Pattern
Intent	Merging two or more paths.
Motivation	Fundamental constituent to enable simple merge.
Applicability	Combining several transitions back into a single activity. At converging point, you would never have more than one token.
Implementation	Widely adopted in most of the modeling languages using XOR-Join.
Known issues	Token merging at the exclusive gateway will not be synchronized.
Known solution	Multimerge.

For example, we have an invoice payment, and there are different ways to pay the invoice, which include paying through credit card, bank transfer, or check. However, to make the payment, only one method will be used for an invoice, and once paid, the data need to be infused into Oracle E-Business Suite ERP. We would always use only one payment method. This is an ideal candidate for a simple merge using an exclusive gateway.

Multichoice and synchronizing merge pattern

We can perform simple split and merge with the gateway (inclusive gateway) offered by Oracle BPMS. It can perform token evaluation and also synchronize the token merging at the convergence. An inclusive gateway (OR) specifies that one or more of the available paths will be taken. They could all be taken, or only one of them will be taken. This capability is also termed **Multichoice**. Sometimes, you need to select a subset of alternatives from a set of possible alternatives. This is what the multiple choice (inclusive) patterns are for. The multiple choice pattern is a point in the workflow where, based on a decision or control data, one or more branches are chosen, triggering one or more paths of the process.

An inclusive OR merge is simply an OR gateway that is used to merge multiple sequence flows into one outgoing sequence flow. Each outgoing sequence flow from the gateway will have a Boolean expression that will be evaluated to determine which sequence flow should be used to continue the process. The downstream inclusive gateway is used to merge the paths created by the upstream inclusive gateway. The downstream inclusive gateway synchronizes all the alternative paths created by the multiple choice gateway. The following table shows details of the multichoice pattern:

Signature	Multichoice Pattern
Classification	Advance Flow Control Pattern
Intent	Breaks the flow into one of the two or more mutually exclusive paths.
Motivation	Fundamental constituent to enable selection of a subset of alternative paths from a set of possible alternatives.
Applicability	Decision point in the business process where the sequence flow will take one or more of the possible outgoing paths.
Implementation	Widely adopted in most of the modeling languages using the OR split.
Known issues	Ensure at least one path selection.
Known solution	Inclusive gateway splits the process at the divergence; however, process tokens can advance to multiple outgoing flows/paths. Sequence flow is picked based on the conditional evaluation where a token is generated for each flow for which the condition is evaluated as true, otherwise, a default sequence flow is picked. The solution is the default path.

Demonstrating multichoice and synchronization with the OR gateway

Download **SalesQuoteProject** from the download link of this chapter. Open the project in JDeveloper. Open the **SalesQuoteSimpleMerge** process. The process accepts **QuoteRequestData** and waits for the sales representative's approval, which will be performed by the salesrep user (we already created a salesrep user in WebLogic **myrealm** in the previous section). Deploy the process to a WebLogic server.

Let's consider an example scenario. In this business process (**SalesQuoteProcess**), after **SalesQuoteApprovalTask**, the approval request also needs to be sent to **Legal** and **Terms** for approval. Once **Legal** and **Terms** approve, other activities are performed over **Quote**.

When **Legal** and **Terms** act on the task, the gateway will merge them, and the process will move ahead. Perform the following steps to test the **SalesQuoteSimpleMerge** process:

1. Test the process from EM or use SOAPUI.

2. Enter the **QuoteRequest** elements and submit **QuoteRequest**. We can use the test data (**SalesQuoteSimpleMerge.xml**) available in the `testsuites` folder in the project.

3. We will notice that the process token is waiting at **SalesQuoteApprovalTask** to be acted upon by the `salesrep` user.

4. Log in to the BPM workspace at `http://<server>:<port>/bpm/workspace` as a `salesrep` user and approve the **QuoteRequest**.

We will find that the process token will reach both the user tasks, **Legal** and **Terms**, for approval. There will be two threads created to process the **LegalApproval** and **TermsApproval** tasks and both will be in the processing mode.

As per the process design, both these tasks will again be assigned to the `salesrep` user. You can customize the sample and associate different users for **Terms** and **Legal** approval. For the moment, log in to the BPM workspace again as the `salesrep` user and approve the legal task. You will find that in the process, the thread processing the **LegalApproval** task is completed, while the thread processing the **TermsApproval** task is still processing.

As we can check in the following screenshot, the process flow shows the point where the process token is awaiting. The audit trail on the left-hand side showcases the snapshot when the **Legal** task is approved; however, the **Terms** task is not being acted upon by the `salesrep` user. We will notice that for both the tasks (**Legal** and **Terms**), there are two separate threads for processing. Even though the **Legal** task is approved, the process token waits at the merge inclusive gateway (**MergeQuoteApproval**). Log in back to the BPM workspace as the `salesrep` user and approve the **Terms** tasks. In the right-hand side of preceding screenshot, we can witness that once both tasks are acted upon by the user, the process token converges at the inclusive gateway (**MergeQuoteApproval**), and the process moves ahead to subsequent activities. This is shown in the following screenshot:

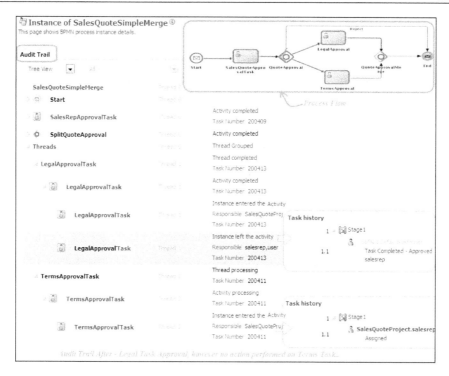

Audit Trail After - Legal Task Approval, however no action performed on Terms Task.

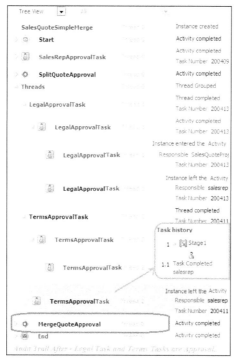

Audit Trail After - Legal Task and Terms Tasks are Approval.

The working of multichoice and synchronization pattern

The process token will diverge to that sequence flow for which the conditional expression gets evaluated as `true`, and if not, then it routes to the default sequence flow.

In the preceding sample process, the sequence flow from the inclusive gateway's divergence is **Conditional** and is based on the approval status from the **SalesQuoteApprovalTask** user task.

Run another test of the same process and reject the **SalesQuoteApprovalTask**. You will find that the token passes along the default sequence flow, as the other two sequence flows have not been evaluated as `true`.

Similar to the exclusive gateway, the inclusive gateway also splits the process at the divergence; however, the process tokens can advance to multiple outgoing flows/paths. The sequence flow is picked based on the conditional evaluation where a token is generated for each flow for which the condition is evaluated as `true`; otherwise a default sequence flow is picked. The tokens are merged at the convergence, which can be an inclusive gateway.

Structured synchronizing merge pattern

Synchronizing merge, also known as structured synchronizing merge, is implemented using the inclusive gateway in Oracle BPMS. When the inclusive gateway is used downstream, it is used to merge the paths created by the upstream inclusive gateway. The downstream inclusive gateway synchronizes all the alternative paths created by the multiple choice gateway (inclusive gateway in the upstream). The following table shows details of the structured synchronizing merge pattern:

Signature	Synchronizing Merge Pattern
Classification	Advance Flow Control Pattern
Intent	Merging and synchronizing two or more paths.
Motivation	Fundamental constituent to enable structured synchronizing merge.
Applicability	An ordered merging of all the previous activations of the divergence point and then to synchronize them.

Implementation	Widely adopted in most of the modeling languages using OR-Join. All of the tokens associated with a multichoice divergence point must reach the structured synchronizing merge before they can fire. In the case of structured synchronizing merge, there will be a single multichoice divergence point, and the structured synchronizing point will merge all the paths from that particular multichoice divergence point.
Known issues	Arbitrary loops in complex process models.
Known solution	General synchronizing merge.

Perform the following steps to execute the **SalesQuoteSimpleMerge** process from EM Console, as we did in the previous section:

1. Log in to the Oracle BPM workspace as a `salesrep` user and approve **SalesReqApprovalTask**. As per the process design, the **Legal** and **Terms** tasks will also gets assigned to the `salesrep` user.

2. Being logged in as the `salesrep` user, approve the **LegalApproval** task.

3. Check the status of the process in EM; it would be in the running state.

The following are the observations:

- Tokens wait at the merge gateways till all the tokens from the multichoice split have converged to the merge point. When all the tokens arrive, the merge gets completed, and then, the process can advance to subsequent activities/tasks.

- Inclusive gateways are used when you need an ordered execution of all the previous activations of the divergence point (inclusive gateway) and then to synchronize them using a convergence element (exclusive gateway).

Local synchronizing merge pattern

The following table shows details of the local synchronizing merge pattern:

Signature	Local Synchronizing Merge Pattern
Classification	Advance Flow Control Pattern
Intent	Merging and synchronizing two or more paths.
Motivation	Fundamental constituent to enable the local synchronizing merge.
Applicability	An ordered merging of all the previous activations of the divergence point/points and then to synchronize them.

Implementation	Widely adopted in most of the modeling languages using OR-Join. All of the tokens associated with multichoice divergence point/points must reach the local synchronizing merge before it can fire.
Known issues	Determining the number of branches that need synchronization.
Known solution	Local synchronizing merge will determine it on the basis of local data, for example, threads of the control that arrive at the merge.

The parallel split and synchronization pattern

The parallel gateways are points in the process where multiple parallel paths are defined and they are also used to synchronize (wait for) parallel paths.

Parallel gateways represent concurrent tasks in business flows, and a fork gateway is always accompanied by a join gateway, where a fork gateway illustrates concurrent flows and expresses the fact that all outgoing paths must be pursued. On the other hand, a join synchronization gateway mandates that all the concurrent paths must be completed ahead of process advancement to subsequent tasks/activities.

A fork divides a path into two or more parallel paths and this is known as an AND split. It's the point in the process flow where activities can be performed concurrently rather than sequentially. In an OR gateway, one or another path is taken; however, in an AND gateway, a single thread of execution will be split into two or more branches that can execute tasks concurrently. For example, once an employee's on-boarding process has started, then enter the employee's information in the ERP system and also start the process for the provision of e-mail IDs, stationary, desk allocation, and so on in parallel.

Parallel split pattern

The following table shows the details of the parallel split pattern:

Signature	Parallel Split Pattern
Classification	Basic Flow Control Pattern
Intent	Breaks the flow into one of the two or more paths that execute concurrently.
Motivation	Fundamental constituent to the concurrent execution of two or more paths.

Applicability	Decision point in the business process where all the outgoing paths must be pursued.
Implementation	Widely adopted in most of the modeling languages using the AND split. When many activities have to be carried out at the same time and in any order, AND splits (parallel split) can be used to fork the concurrent flow where two or more concurrent threads independently process the activities (gateways, events, and so on) that reside on the corresponding control flow branches.
Known issues	NA
Known solution	NA

Synchronization pattern

The following table shows the details of the synchronization pattern:

Signature	Synchronization Pattern
Classification	Basic Flow Control Pattern
Intent	Synchronize paths that exit a parallel split.
Motivation	To synchronize the flow from multiple parallel branches. Parallel join merge exactly one thread from each incoming branch into a single thread on the outgoing branch by converging the threads of all the parallel branches.
Applicability	Merge point to synchronize the parallel paths. The AND join to be symmetrically paired up with a corresponding upstream AND split.
Implementation	Widely adopted in most of the modeling languages using the AND join. Accepts multiple incoming sequence flow and blocks the sequence until all activities within the flows are completed; then, the flow continues. Till the concurrent tokens are not synchronized, multiple incoming sequence flows are blocked. Upon synchronization, one token is passed out of the merge gateway's outgoing flow.
Known issues	Nonavailability of a token at the AND join that got created from the AND split.
Known solution	The solution lies in how meticulously the process is modeled, and it's anticipated that the issue will not arise in a structured context.

Design consideration by modelers is taken into account if you really need parallel processing, that is, whether, in reality, the distinct branches are executed in parallel.

Navigate to **SalesQuoteDemo | SalesQuoteProject | ParallelSplitSynchronization process**. When the sales quote is initiated, it halts for quote acceptance by the salesrep user at the **ApproveQuote** user task. Once it is approved, it's reviewed by business practice, and on approval from the fkafka user, the token reaches the parallel gateway, which is the divergent fork point. Both **DealsApproval** and **TermsApproval** need to be performed in parallel, and hence, the choice was a parallel gateway to diverge the flow. This is discussed in the following bullet points:

1. Click on **Organization Unit** in the project to verify the user assignment to the roles. We will make sure that the user assignment to roles should happen based on following table:

Task	Role	User
Accept Quote	Salesrep	salesrep
Business Review	Business practice	fkafka
Approvers	Approvers	jcooper
Contracts	Contracts	jstein

2. If not already deployed, deploy **SalesQuoteProject**.

3. Log in to EM console or use any tool of choice to execute the **ParallelSplitSynchronization** process using the ParallelSplitSynchronization.xml test data available in the **testsuites** folder in the project.

4. Log in to the Oracle BPM workspace as the salesrep user and approve the **AcceptQuote** task.

5. Log in to the Oracle BPM workspace as the fkafka user and approve the **Business Practice Review** task.

6. Token has now reached the **ApproveDeal** and **ApproveTerms** task.

7. Log in to EM console and check the **Audit Trail** of the process.

We can find that a group of threads is created for each sequence flow from the parallel gateway that forks/diverges the path. This is shown in the following screenshot:

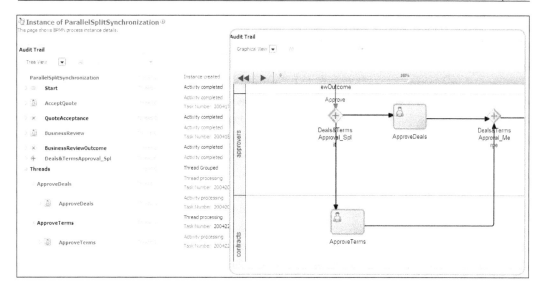

Check the process flow using the graphical view of the process in the process audit trail, as shown in the preceding screenshot. We can analyze that both the paths are processed in parallel. Execute the following steps:

1. Log in to the BPM workspace as a `jcooper` user and approve the **ApproveDeal** task. We can notice that at the convergence point, that is, at the join (merge parallel gateway), tokens will be synchronized. Hence, the process waits for the other token to reach the convergence point, which is the AND join parallel gateway.

2. Click on the process audit trail in EM for the process. We can witness that **Approve Deal** thread is completed, while the other thread for the **Approve Terms** is still processing.

3. Log in to the BPM workspace as a `jstein` user and approve the **Approve Terms** task.

4. Once both the tokens arrive at the AND join (**Deals&TermsApproval_ Merge**) the tokens are synchronized, and one token is passed out of the merge gateway's outgoing flow.

Conditional parallel split and parallel merge pattern

The conditional parallel split and parallel merge pattern is a part of advance branching and synchronization. It's similar to parallel split and merge; however, it is based on conditions, that is, it must follow a conditional transition. This process is shown in the following screenshot:

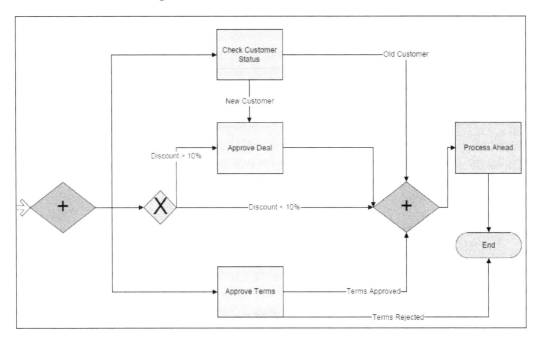

Let's consider an example scenario. When the token diverges at the first parallel gateway, it should perform conditional transition to different parallel tasks as follows:

- **ApprovalDeals** should be performed only when effective discount is greater than 10 percent; otherwise, it should converge to the second parallel gateway without requesting for the deal's approval.

- Similarly, we implement conditional parallel merge based on conditional transition. For the sake of example, let the equation of conditional transition be as follows:

    ◦ Check customer status to find if it's a new or old customer. Converge to join at the parallel gateway. If the customer is old, you would not need an approval of deals; however, request for a deal's approval if the customer is new.

- After **TermsApproval**, if the term approval request status is approved, then it converges at the join at the parallel gateway. Otherwise, the quote request can be ended, as shown in the preceding screenshot.

Working with conditional parallel split and merge

Oracle BPM does not have conditional transitions from the parallel gateway. If we try to implement a conditional transition outgoing from or incoming to a parallel gateway, it throws a **Parallel Gateway cannot have outgoing Conditional Sequence Flows** error . As we don't have a method to do conditional transition from the parallel gateway, we can still implement it in combination with the other gateway; in this case, it's the exclusive gateway (XOR). This scenario would be developed using parallel gateway in combination with exclusive gateway.

Download **SalesQuoteProject** from the download link for this chapter and open **ConditionalParallelSplit&Merge**. Check the configuration of the outgoing sequence flows from the parallel split point (**ParallelSplit**) and incoming sequence flow to the parallel merge gateway (**ParallelSplit**).

1. Open EM console and test the **ConditionalParallelSplit&Merge** process using the **ConditionalParallelSplit&Merge.xml** test data available in the **testsuites** folder in the project.

2. The test data contains the following data:

   Effective discount: 9

   Quote request status: Old

   Rest all fields can be user choice

3. Log in to the Oracle BPM workspace as a salesrep user and approve the **AcceptQuote** task.

4. Log in again to the BPM workspace as a fkafka user to approve the **BusinessReview** task.

5. Process flow will reach the fork divergent parallel gateway (**ParallelSplit**) and would initiate the parallel flow to perform the **DiscountCheck**, **ApproveDeals**, and **ApproveTerms** task, as shown in the following screenshot:

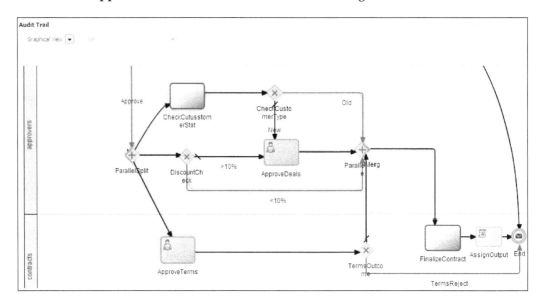

6. As the effective discount is 9, which is less than 10 percent condition on the transition flow (**<10%**), the process will flow at the sequence flow (**<10%**) pathway and halts at parallel gateway (**ParallelMerge**) to get synchronized at the join convergence parallel gateway.

7. Log in to the Oracle BPM workspace as a jstein user and approve the **ApproveTerms** task. Post approval, the token will get synchronized at the convergent point parallel gateway (**ParallelMerge**), and the process flow will move ahead.

A token gets created for each outgoing flow from the split parallel gateway, and none of the outgoing sequence flows are evaluated as the parallel gateway doesn't allow for outgoing conditional flow. However, we can use exclusive gateways to perform conditional transitions. This is not a direct offering of Oracle BPM; however, we can implement this using a combination of gateways. The parallel merge gateway waits for all the concurrent tokens to reach it. Until the concurrent tokens are not synchronized, multiple incoming sequence flows are blocked. Upon synchronization, one token is passed out of the merge gateway's outgoing flow.

Antipattern – the conditional parallel split and merge

In this section, we will demonstrate the fact that one cannot use conditional parallel split and merge by just merging some of the gateways. Process modeling needs to be performed meticulously. Hence, in this book, we are talking about patterns that offer techniques to solve repeatable issues and enhance the process modeling approach.

We will test the **ConditionalParallelSplit&Merge** process using the **ConditionalParallelSplit&Merge.xml** test data available in the **testsuites** folder in the project. However, this time, we will change the effective discount to any value greater than 10. Let the customer type be old, and keep all other fields as they are as follows:

- Log in to the Oracle BPM workspace as the `salesrep` user and then as the `fkafka` user to approve the **AcceptQuote** and **BusinessReview** tasks.

- Log in to the BPM workspace as the `jstein` user. It's the user to whom the **ApproveTerms** task is assigned. Log in and reject the task as follows:

    ○ The **ApproveTerms** task is now rejected, and the **ConditionalParallelSplit&Merge** process is modeled in such a way that if the **ApproveTerms** task is rejected, then the process should end. We can verify an outgoing sequence flow from the **ApproveTerms** task to the **TermsOutcome** exclusive gateway, which checks for task's outcome. If the outcome is **REJECT**, then the process should end.

- Check **Process Trace** and **Audit Trail** in EM console as shown in the following screenshot. We will notice the following behavior:

    Once the **ApproveTerms** task is rejected, the process moves to the **Terms Outcome** exclusive gateway and then to the message end event of the process.

    However, we can check the process trace, as encircled in the following screenshot; the process is still running.

Now, if we log in to the BPM workspace as the `jcooper` user and approve the **Approve Deals** task, then only the parallel paths will converge, and the process will move ahead. This is demonstrated in the following screenshot:

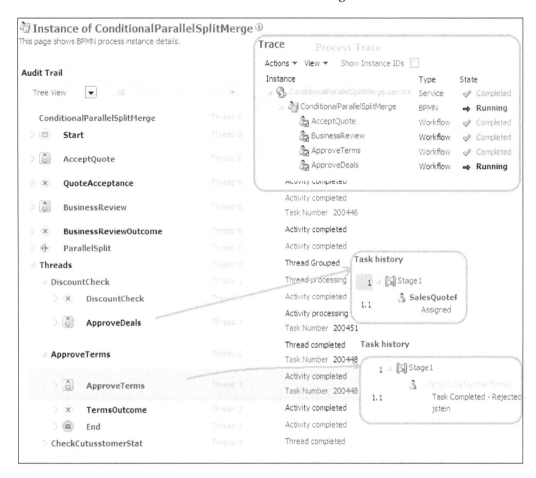

Multimerge pattern

Use the multimerge pattern to model the convergence of two or more branches into a single path. Each time an incoming branch is enabled, it results in the activation of the next activity within the process. For each multimerge gateway, there should be an associated multibranch gateway.

The following table shows the details of the multimerge pattern:

Signature	Multimerge Pattern
Classification	Advance Flow Control Pattern
Intent	Converges two or more branches into one subsequent branch and in doing so, it converges tokens of the incoming branch into one token and passes the token to the subsequent branch. The multimerge pattern allows each incoming branch to continue independently of the others, enabling multiple threads of execution through the remainder of the process.
Motivation	Offers convergence of parallel paths into a single path; however, parallel paths merging at the multimerge convergence point are not synchronized.
Applicability	Convergence point without synchronization.
Implementation	Widely adopted in most of the modeling languages using the XOR join. Accepts multiple incoming parallel sequence flow and passes the tokens as they arrive to the subsequent activity.
Known issues	Activity performed in the subsequent branch after the multimerge convergence point is not safe. With this pattern, more than one incoming branch can be active simultaneously, and this means that the activity that you are going to follow in the subsequent branch is not necessarily safe. For example, the subsequent branch performs a change in data. All the incoming parallel branches will act on the data, as the behavior of the subsequent branch is same for all the parallel flows. However, the order of the incoming parallel branches' execution is unpredictable. This behavior will make the change in data unpredictable, and hence, any subsequent process or activities will exhibit unpredictable behavior.
Known solution	NA. Workaround is to model the process flows meticulously.

Let's consider an example scenario. The requirement is to check inventory and credit in parallel while reviewing the order. However, for each branch, the requirement is to calculate the freight. In this case, when the parallel gateway diverges (fork) the flow, three tokens will be generated and processed by three different threads. Each time the incoming branch is enabled, it would result in the activation of the **Calculate Freight** activity.

However, the process will move ahead only when all the divergent paths get synchronized at the convergent point (parallel gateway) after the **Calculate Freight** activity takes place, as shown in the following screenshot:

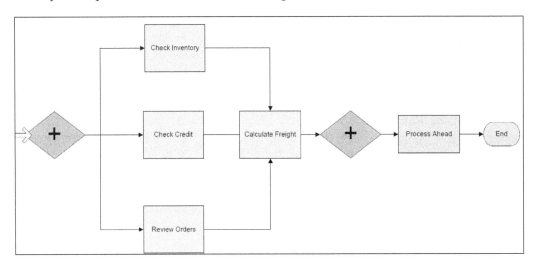

The multimerge pattern allows each incoming branch to continue independently of the others, enabling multiple threads of execution through the remainder of the process. However, with the usage of parallel gateway in Oracle BPM for divergence, it would always need either a parallel gateway for convergence or a complex gateway. This means that it would always lead to synchronization of the token, either all of the tokens (with parallel gateway as convergent point) or some of the tokens (with complex gateway as the convergent point).

Another multimerge example could be of an employee background check process. The requirement is to perform personal reference check, business reference check, and criminal background check in parallel. However, you need to notify Human Resources (HR) of the enterprise each time a branch gets activated and performs a reference check.

Exploring multimerge

Download the **SalesQuoteProject** project from the download link for this chapter and open the **MultiMerge** process. While analyzing the **MultiMerge** process, you can witness **Exclusive Gateway** before **MultiMergeActivity**. This is the XOR gateway that will enable multimerge for this scenario. Execute the process with the **MultiMerge.xml** sales quote data available in the **testsuites** folder in the project.

The following are the key values being passed as input to the process:

- Customer type: **OLD**
- Effective discount: `10`

The following screenshot demonstrates two states of the process. The left-hand side showcases the state when the **Approve Deals** task is approved by the `jcooper` user. However, the `jstein` user has not acted on the **Approve Terms** task. This showcases that the **MultiMergeActivity** activity was executed, but both the time and process didn't move ahead, as all the threads need to be synchronized at the **ParallelMerge** parallel gateway.

The right-hand side of the screen shows the **Audit Trail** process after the **ApproveTerms** task was approved. We can clearly witness that multiple threads are enabled for the process branch execution. You can witness different threads that process each parallel branch, the **XOR exclusive gateway** multimerge point, and the (**MultiMergeActivity** activity getting executed for all the branches, as demonstrated in the following screenshot:

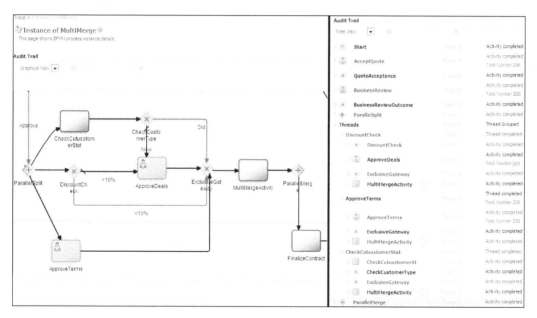

You can witness that each merging branch at **Exclusive Gateway** has its own thread, and they are parallel processing. However, the **Exclusive Gateway** multimerge convergence point will get executed for each parallel branch that has its own token. You can check in the above screenshot that the AND split (**ParallelSplit**) will split the token in three parallel paths. However, each parallel path will execute the **Exclusive** multimerge convergence point, and all the parallel tokens will get synchronized at the AND join (**ParallelMerge**). Hence, the **MultiMergeActivity** activity will also get executed three times. The XOR gateway that acts as multimerge will pass the tokens, as they arrive to the subsequent activity.

Discriminator and partial join pattern

This section will cover the advance flow control patterns such as structured discriminator pattern and structured partial join pattern. The scenario for this section is about employee request for resources such as machine, e-mail ID, batch ID, and so on at the time of on-boarding. These resources will be credited to the employee only when their request for the resource gets approved by their manager. Another scenario is as per the following process screenshot. If the credit check fails, then there is no need to perform inventory check and order review. This is shown in the following screenshot:

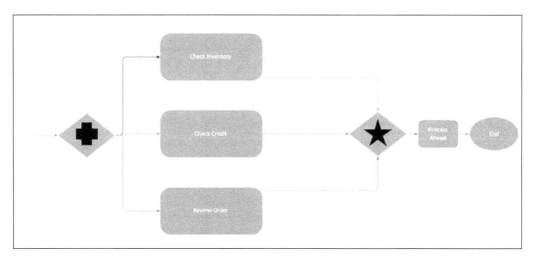

To achieve this, you need a mechanism to set a trigger or an indicator in the converging point. When conditions related to the indicator meet, the synchronize activity in the process instance will be immediately released, and the BPM engine will automatically remove the instances struck in **Check Inventory** and **Review Order**. Then, the process instance converges at the convergence point and continues on through the rest of the process.

Structured discriminator pattern

The structured discriminator describes a convergence point in the business process that waits for one of the incoming branches to complete before activating the subsequent activity. All other incoming branches will be omitted after they are completed. Until all the incoming branches are complete, the discriminator is not reset. Once all the incoming branches are completed, the discriminator is reset. Structured discriminator construct resets when all incoming branches have been enabled. Upon completion, the first branch out of the given number of branches triggers a downstream activity. A token will be generated for all other branches. However, all the remaining tokens that were generated from the parallel split will eventually arrive at the discriminator, but they will be blocked and hence, will also not be able to trigger the subsequent branch.

The following table shows the details of the structured discriminator pattern:

Signature	Structured Discriminator Pattern
Classification	Advance Flow Control Pattern
Intent	A convergence point in the business process that awaits one of the incoming branches to complete before activating the subsequent activity.
Motivation	When the first branches gets completed, the subsequent branch gets triggered, but completions of other incoming branches thereafter have no effect on the subsequent branch.
Applicability	One out of M joins. It's a special case of M out of N Join, that is, structured partial join.
Implementation	Widely adopted in most of the modeling languages using the complex join. Structured discriminator occurs in a structured context, that is, there must be a single parallel split construct earlier in the process model with which the structured discriminator is associated, and it must merge all of the branches that emanate from the structured discriminator.
Known issues	Nonreceipt of input on each of the incoming branches means there might be cases when some of the incoming branches might not have input.
Known solution	Canceling the discriminator pattern will look for the first token to be received at the incoming branch, and upon the receipt of the first token at the incoming branch, all other branches will be skipped. The branches that are not yet commenced will be aborted, and the discriminator will get restarted.

Structured partial join

The structured partial join is an "N out of M Join" pattern. In this pattern, an AND split (parallel gateway) or a multichoice (inclusive gateway) pattern produces a number of tokens on parallel branches (known as runtime). From the total number of "m" tokens, a subset "n" token will trigger synchronization and produce a single token for the outgoing edge. The remaining (m-n) tokens are suppressed, and they would not be able to trigger any subsequent branch. The following table shows the details of the structured partial join pattern:

Signature	Partial Join Pattern
Classification	Advance Flow Control Pattern
Intent	A convergence point in the business process of "m" branches into one subsequent branch only when "n" incoming branches are enabled, where "n" will be less than "m".
Motivation	The convergence point will trigger synchronization and produces a single token for the outgoing edge, only when a defined threshold is reached. In case of N out of M joins, N is defined as the trigger for the convergence point (complex join gateway). Once the trigger is fired and a single token is produced for the outgoing edge, then completion of the remaining incoming paths will not have any impact and they will not trigger any subsequent path.
	Convergence point will reset only when all the active incoming branches are enabled.
Applicability	For "N" out of "M" joins, the convergence point will trigger synchronization when the defined threshold "N" is reached.
Implementation	Widely adopted in most of the modeling languages using the complex join.
	Join should happen in a structured fashion, means at the convergence point. The complex join gateway must be associated with either a single parallel AND split gateway or a multichoice inclusive gateway. Once the partial number of paths is active, subsequent paths can be followed. Hence, there will be no requirement to wait for other incoming paths to complete
Known issues	NA
Known solution	NA

Working with a complex gateway to implement the discriminator and partial join pattern

Oracle BPM offers a complex gateway to implement the structured discriminator and structured partial join pattern. Parallel split is performed by a parallel gateway named **Approvals**, shown in the following screenshot. Synchronization will be performed at the **ApprovalsMerge** complex gateway. Perform the following steps to test the scenario:

1. Download **SalesQuoteProject** from the download link for this chapter and open the **PartialJoin** process.

2. To implement the "N out of M join" pattern, click on the **ApprovalsMerge** complex gateway and check its properties.

3. In the properties, we can witness that **Abort Pending Flow** is unchecked, and the following expression is included in the complex gateway's properties. This is shown in the following code:

```
"bpmn:getDataObject('quoteDO')/ns:Summary/ns:AccountName  =
"FusionNX" and bpmn:getGatewayInstanceAttribute('activationCount')
>= 1"
```

 Activation count is a predefined variable and keeps track of the active tokens at the complex gateway.

Expressions at the complex gateway translate to the fact that if the activation count of tokens at the merge gateway is 1 or greater than 1 and if the account name is FusionNX, the gateway exit expression will evaluate as `true`.

Hence, while testing this process, if the account name supplied with quote request data is FusionNX and the count of active tokens at the complex gateway is equal to or greater than 1, then the synchronization activity in the process instance will be immediately released and the process token will continue ahead.

Testing a process by failing the complex gateway exit expression

Execute the following steps:

1. Test the **PartialJoin** process using the **PartialJoin.xml** test data available in the **testsuites** folder in the project.

2. The **PartialJoin.xml** test data that is provided contains the value for the account name HP. This will never fulfill the condition at the complex gateway.

3. Check the process audit trail to deep drive in the behavior by looking into the **ApprovalsMerge** complex gateway.

4. When the token arrives at the same activity block, the merge gateway will be evaluated. However, the condition (the account name FusionNX) will fail, and the flow will not move forward.

5. Log in to the BPM workspace as a jcooper user and jstein user one after the other to approve the **DealsApproval** and **TermsApproval** tasks.

6. The **TermsApproval** and **DealsApproval** sequence flows will also fail. As no gateway exit expression will get evaluated successfully, the entire token will be suppressed and the process gets completed.

Testing process as success by the complex gateway exit expression

Perform the following steps to test the partial join process for a success gateway condition:

1. Test the process again using the **PartialJoin.xml** test data. However, this time, change the account name and pass Account Name: FusionNX.

2. Check **Audit Trail** for the process in EM.

3. You can find that the process moves ahead of the merge gateway just after receiving the token from the first sequence flow. The gateway exit expression will evaluate as **Success** in the first case itself.

As we passed the account name as FusionNX and the activation count for the **ApprovalsMerge** complex gateway reaches 1, the gateway exit expression will evaluate as `true` and the process token moves ahead, as shown in the following screenshot:

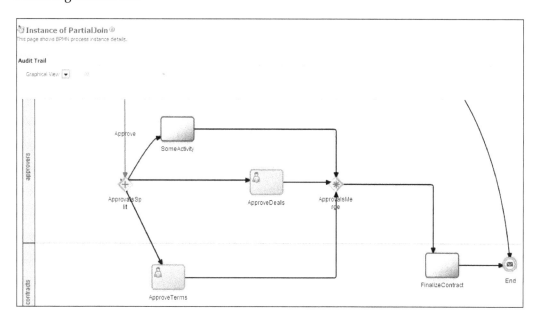

We just tested the "N out of M Join" pattern. You can use the same project and refractor the complex gateway that is merging the parallel split branches and set the activation count as 1. The AND split (parallel gateway) which is the **ApprovalsSplit** gateway, will produce the number of tokens on parallel branches (known as runtime). There are exit conditions defined at the complex gateway, which is the merging point. The process will move ahead to subsequent branches once the gateway exit expressions are evaluated to **Success**. This means that the desired number of activation tokens is reached and all the other logical conditions expressed in the expression are fulfilled.

Complex synchronization pattern

The complex gateway can also be used for complex synchronization. Complex gateway gets activated when the conditional expression is evaluated as `true`. Once the complex gateway gets activated, it would create a token on the output sequence flow.

If **Abort pending flows** is checked on the complex gateway properties, then complex gateway will abort all the pending flows and the remaining tokens will be suppressed. They will not be able to trigger any subsequent branch, as shown in the following screenshot:

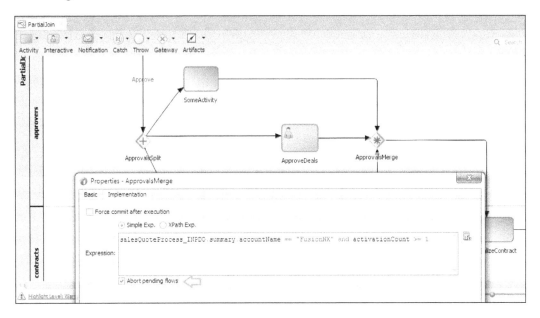

The suppression of tokens is translated to various patterns, which are shown as follows:

- Canceling discriminator pattern
- Canceling partial join pattern

Canceling discriminator pattern

The following table shows the details of the canceling discriminator pattern:

Signature	Canceling Discriminator Pattern
Classification	Advance Flow Control Pattern
Intent	A convergence point in the business process that awaits one of the incoming branches to complete before activating the subsequent activity. It can also cancel the execution of all other remaining branches
Motivation	When the first branch gets completed, the subsequent branch will trigger. However, the remaining incoming branches will not be triggered as they would be cancelled.

Applicability	1-out-of-M joins with a flag being set, is to set to abort the remaining flow pattern.
Implementation	Widely adopted in most of the modeling languages using the complex join. On the complex gateway, **Abort Pending Flows** must be checked, and the completion condition testing for the number of active instances should be equal to 1. When this complex gateway gets triggered, it would cancel the execution of all of the other incoming branches and reset the construct.
Known issues	NA
Known solution	NA

Canceling partial join pattern

The following table shows the details of the Canceling partial join pattern:

Signature	Partial Join Pattern
Classification	Advance Flow Control Pattern
Intent	A convergence point, in the business process of "m" branches into one subsequent branch only when "n" incoming branches are enabled, where "n" will be less than "m". However, once the join is triggered, it would also lead to cancelling the execution of all the remaining incoming paths and reset the convergence point.
Motivation	The convergence point will trigger synchronization and produce a single token for the outgoing edge, only when a defined threshold is reached. In case of N out of M join, N is defined as the trigger for the convergence point (the complex join gateway). Once the trigger is fired and a single token is produced for the outgoing edge, then the remaining incoming paths will be cancelled. The convergence point will reset only when all the active incoming branches will be enabled.
Applicability	N-out-of-M joins and a flag being set to **Abort Remaining Flows**.
Implementation	Widely adopted in most of the modeling languages using the complex join. On the complex gateway, **Abort Pending Flows** must be checked.
Known issues	Determination of cancel region.
Known solution	Structured processes.

Summary

This chapter offered a comprehensive knowledge of the flow control patterns by showcasing the essentials of flow control patterns, which are used in designing and modeling business processes. Recipes can be served as reference to control flow patterns in BPM and are explained with simple sample processes and examples. The next chapter will demonstrate how processes can handle batch jobs and how to simultaneously spawn multiple work item instances in a process. The chapter will also uncover iteration patterns by demonstrating structured loop and unstructured looping mechanisms. Implicit and explicit termination patterns in the end will showcase the termination pattern.

2
Multi-instance and State-based Patterns

The set of patterns included in this chapter will demonstrate how processes can handle batch jobs and how to simultaneously spawn multiple work item instances in a process. This chapter simplifies the usage of loop characteristics while showcasing multi-instance perspectives. This chapter emphasizes on developing solutions for use cases with multi-instance requirement using design-time and runtime knowledge, and it exhibits true dynamism in the process. The focus is simply on the cases where flow paths need to be determined based on the intermediate events converging from external systems and in order to break the usual ordering mechanism of the process flow imposed on tasks. The patterns in this section will offer flexibility in the ordering of process tasks. You will explore how to amalgamate a mechanism to support the conditional execution of tasks and subprocesses when a process instance is in a specific state. This chapter will further cover iteration patterns by demonstrating structured and unstructured looping mechanisms. Implicit and explicit termination patterns at the end will showcase termination patterns. The following are the different patterns that will be discussed in this chapter:

- Multiple instances with prior design-time knowledge pattern
- Multiple instances with prior runtime knowledge pattern
- Multiple instances without prior runtime knowledge pattern
- Static partial join for multiple instances pattern
- Canceling partial join pattern
- Dynamic partial join for multiple instances pattern
- Structured loop pattern
- Arbitrary cycle pattern

- Trigger patterns
    - Transient trigger pattern
    - Persistent trigger pattern

- Implicit termination pattern
- Explicit termination pattern
- Cancellation pattern
    - Cancel multi-instance task pattern

Multiple instances with prior design-time knowledge pattern

This pattern is based on the fact that the number of concurrent threads is known in advance at design time. It's the modeler who will be aware of the fact at design time and will know how many times the activity/task should be performed. The following table summarizes the details around multiple instances with prior design-time knowledge:

Signature	Multiple Instances With Prior Design-time Knowledge Pattern
Classification	Multi-instance Pattern
Intent	The number of concurrent threads is known in advance at design time, and concurrent thread synchronization must be performed.
Motivation	This pattern has a context associated with it, which will determine the number of tasks/activities/subprocess instances; the context will be supplied at design time and will be a static value. Instances can be executed in parallel/sequence and must be synchronized before completion. This pattern behaves as a parallel split of the instances and as parallel merges at the downstream of those instances.
Applicability	This pattern is applicable in a multi-instance subprocess, and split and join.
Implementation	When the BPMN service engine runs a subprocess with a multi-instance loop marker, it creates a set of instances, one for each element on the set of data. You can configure the multi-instance marker to process these instances in parallel or sequence. This pattern allows concurrent tokens to continue independently; however, they get synchronized before they move out of the MI loop segment to execute any subsequent task. Oracle BPM not only offers the parallel mode to create multiple instances, but you can also have the sequential mode, where tasks/activities are performed one by one.
Known issues	NA
Known solution	NA

Executing the multi-instance subprocess with prior design-time knowledge

Scenario: The quote request needs to be approved by the sales representative, who is the user (salesrep) in our process. For each quote line product item, its inventory status will be checked. Download the project (**SalesQuoteProcess**) from the download links of this chapter. It contains the processes used for this chapter. The process (**MIWithPriorDesignTimeKnowledge**) accepts the quote request and assigns tasks to the user (salesrep) to act on **AcceptQuoteTask**. Upon approval from the (salesrep) user, the script task determines the cardinality, which will determine the number of parallel instances to be created. These script tasks will determine a count for the instances. Perform the following steps to learn how the process is configured for this pattern:

1. Expand the **SalesQuoteProcess** project in JDeveloper and open the **MIWithPriorDesignTimeKnowledge** process.

2. **AcceptQuoteTask** is a user task that needs to be approved by the user (salesrep).

3. The process has a process data object, **lineItemNodeCount**, of the number type. The **DetermineCardinality** script task assigns a numeric value (3) to **lineItemNodeCount**. This is the static value supplied to the process to determine the number of parallel multiple instances.

4. Double-click on the subprocess and go to the **Loop Characteristics** tab, as shown in the following screenshot.

5. In the **Loop Characteristics** tab, the loop is set to **MultiInstance** and the mode is set as **Parallel**. The **MultiInstance** markers enable you to run a subprocess for each of the elements on a set of data. When the BPMN service engine runs a subprocess with a multi-instance loop marker, it creates a set of instances, one for each element on the set of data. You can configure the multi-instance marker to process these instances in parallel or sequence.

6. The **Loop Cardinality** expression defines the number of tokens to be created in the subprocess, and this cardinality is set by the **Determine Cardinality** script task, as shown in the following screenshot:

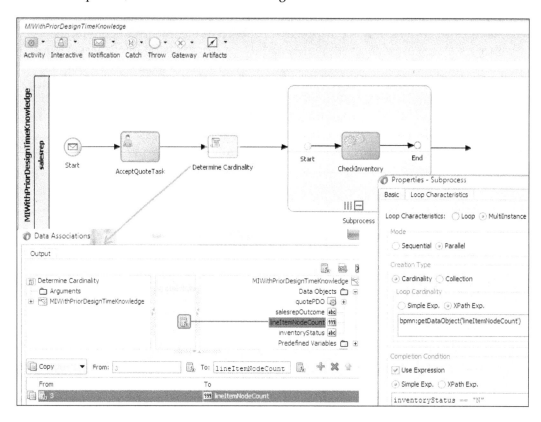

7. **Completion condition** is set using the following expression:

```
inventory Status == "N"
```

Completion Condition determines when the loop will terminate the subprocess and move ahead downstream to execute the subsequent task. The **inventoryStatus** is a process data object. The subprocess invokes the **CheckInventory** process for each token and the status of the inventory for that product item will be assigned to this process data object, as shown in the following screenshot. (You can even assign it to quote the data object and can play around in the process on those checks.)

Before we deploy the process in this chapter, make sure you have performed the steps listed in the *Getting ready for executing use cases* section of *Chapter 1, Flow Control Patterns*. The user (salesrep) should exist in **myrealm** to execute processes in this chapter that contain human tasks. Also, in the message start event of all the processes in this chapter, assign **Organization Unit** (SalesOrg) to the predefined variable (**Organization Unit**) and save the project.

Perform the following steps to test the scenario:

1. Use JDeveloper and deploy the process.
2. Log in to the EM console or use SOAPUI to test the process. We will be using EM to test the process; hence, log in to `http://<server>:<port>:7001/em` as a `weblogic` user.
3. Click on the **MIWithPriorDesignTimeKnowledge** process and supply quote request data using the test data (**MIWithPriorDesignTimeKnowledge.xml**). We can find the data in the project's **testsuites** folder.
4. The test data (**MIWithPriorDesignTimeKnowledge.xml**) contains more than three product items in the quote request, as shown in the following screenshot.
5. Submit the quote request.
6. Log in to Oracle BPM at `http://localhost:7001/bpm/workspace` as the `salesrep` user and approve the **AcceptQuote** task.
7. Log in to the EM console as the `weblogic` user, click on the process instance, and check the audit trail of the process, as shown in the following screenshot.
8. You can see that a thread group is created and three threads are created for processing.

9. The **MultiInstance** option tells the system to create a separate instance of
    the subprocess for each item. As we have checked the **Parallel** mode, all the
    instances are created at once and executed in parallel. This is shown in the
    following screenshot:

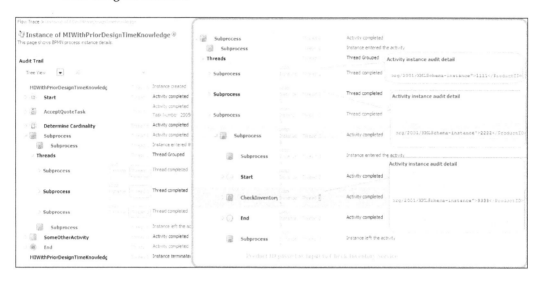

When the process starts, the process token will reach **AcceptQuoteTask** and on
approval, the token will reach the **Determine Cardinality** script task. This will set a
value for the **lineItemNodeCount** variable, which will later determine the number
of instances. When the process token reaches the subprocess, it will create parallel
multiples of three independent instances of the subprocess by creating three tokens
to process each parallel thread. However, the subprocess will wait to synchronize all
the tokens. Once all the tokens are synchronized, then the process moves ahead to
subsequent tasks/activities.

Multiple instances with prior runtime knowledge pattern

Unlike multiple instances with prior design-time knowledge, the number of
multiple instances in this pattern is not known until the process is being performed
and cannot be set ahead of time at design time. However, the number of multiple
instances to be created is determined before the first instance of the multiple
instances gets initiated. In this pattern, the pattern instances can be created
in parallel and sequence.

The following table summarizes the details around multiple instances with runtime knowledge:

Signature	Multiple Instances With Prior Runtime Knowledge Pattern
Classification	Multi-instance Pattern
Intent	The number of concurrent threads is not known in advance at design time and is calculated at runtime. However, it's calculated before the first instance is created. Concurrent thread synchronization must be performed.
Motivation	The determination of the number of instances will be performed at runtime. Instances can be executed in parallel/sequence and must be synchronized before completion. This pattern behaves as a parallel split of the instances and parallel merges at the downstream of these instances.
Applicability	This refers to the multi-instance subprocess and a variable to determine loop cardinality.
Implementation	Creating multiple instances of a subprocess/task within a process instance is provisioned by Oracle BPM's subprocess looping characteristics. The number of multiple instances is determined by cardinality, loop condition, completion condition, or the collection on which it needs to iterate. These instances run independent of each other as well as run concurrently; however, they need to be synchronized before subsequent tasks/activities are triggered.
Known issues	NA
Known solution	NA

Demonstrating MI with prior runtime knowledge

Open the project, **SalesQuoteProcess**, in JDeveloper 12*c* and perform the following steps:

1. Go to **BPM | BPMN Processes** and open the **MIWithPriorDesignTimeKnowledge** process. This is the same process that we used in the previous section.

2. Double-click on **Script task** in the **Properties – Determine Cardinality** tab and then click on the **Implementation** tab.

3. Click on **Data Association**. This will open **XPath expression builder**.

4. Enter the `quoteDO.productItem.length()` string.

The product item is an array, and the cardinality of the subprocess loop will be now be based on the length of the product items' array, that is, how many product items are there in the quote request. This translates to the fact that the cardinality of the subprocess will be determined at runtime by the XPath expression condition (`quoteDO.productItem.length()`), which basically means that the subprocess' cardinality is equal to the number of product items. This is shown in the following screenshot:

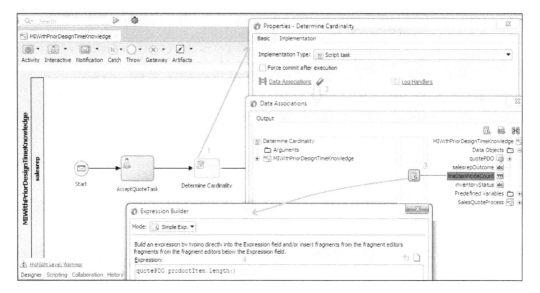

Perform the following steps to execute the project:

1. Save the project and deploy it.
2. Test the project from the EM console using the test data (**MIWithPriorDesignTimeKnowledge.xml**). The test data contains four product line items.

We will see a behavior similar to what you have experienced while testing the process in the *Executing multi-instance subprocesses with prior design-time knowledge* section. However, in the *Multiple instances with prior design-time knowledge* section, cardinality was defined at design time and was fixed as three. Hence, even though the test data contains four line items, we saw only three threads that process the first three line items. However, in this section, cardinality is derived at runtime and is based on the number of product line items.

As the test data contains four product line items, the subprocess cardinality will be four; hence, we will find four threads for four line items.

Understanding how MI with prior runtime knowledge work

A batch of line items, that is, the batch data objects (created by an array/collection); loop cardinality, that is, the number of instances to be created; and predefined variables, such as the loop count (the loop index), instance count, and so on, are supplied to the subprocess. The BPM engine will extract line items from the batch data object at a given index (the loop count value for that token) and will create multiple instances of the subprocess in parallel. A token is associated with each independent instance. The number of multiple instances created will depend on the loop cardinality that you have set in the process, whose value is determined at runtime. When the subprocess ends, the token gets completed and the loop exit condition is evaluated. Here, the number of instances to be created is determined at runtime, and it depends on the number of product items. These multiple instances are then synchronized.

Multiple instances without prior runtime knowledge pattern

The following table summarizes the details around Multiple Instances Without Prior Runtime Knowledge:

Signature	Multiple Instances Without Prior Runtime Knowledge Pattern
Classification	Multi-instance Pattern
Intent	The number of concurrent threads is not known in advance at the design time and is calculated at runtime. However, the number of instances is not known until the last instance is executed. Concurrent thread synchronization must be performed.
Motivation	The determination of the number of instances will be performed at runtime; however, the determination of instances is deferred until the last instance gets executed. Instances can be executed in parallel/sequence and must be synchronized before completion.
Applicability	This refers to the multi-instance subprocess.

Implementation	The BPMN service engine runs a subprocess with a MultiInstance loop marker and will create a set of instances, one for each element in the collection. The number of instances is determined by the collection size, that is, the size of the array. Once each instance gets completed, the instance tokens get synchronized and the process moves to subsequent activities.
Known issues	NA
Known solution	NA

This section will explore how to determine the number of instances of the subprocess based on the collection. We will also learn, through an example, how synchronization works on multi-instance subprocesses.

Working on MI without prior runtime knowledge

Scenario: The **QuoteRequest** task gets submitted to the user (`salesrep`). On **AcceptQuoteTask** approval, the process token reaches the multi-instance subprocess. The number of multiple instances created will be determined by the number of product items in **QuoteRequest**. Business practice approval is for those product items that have `Quantity > 50`. If `Quantity < 50`, then approval is not required for the line items. Perform the following steps to verify the implementation and test the use case:

1. Open the **SalesQuoteProcess** project in JDeveloper.

2. Go to **BPM | BPMN Processes** and click on the **MIWithoutPriorRunTimeKnowledge** process, as shown in the following screenshot:

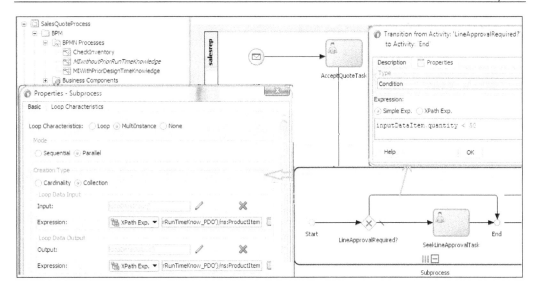

3. The subprocess is configured with the **MultiInstance** marker in Oracle BPM, which enables you to run a subprocess for each of the elements in the product item collection.

4. The process instances will be created in parallel as you can select the **Parallel** mode.

5. **Loop Data Input** is an array data type that is passed as an input to the subprocess, and **Loop Data Output** is the array data type that is produced as a result of the execution of this subprocess.

6. The subprocess will loop on the product item in **SalesQuoteRequest**. Hence, an input data item is created based on the quote process data object (**MIWithoutPriorRunTimeKnow_PDO**), and an expression is created for the product items. This XPath expression is used to assign values to arrays.

7. The number of times that the subprocess is executed is determined by the size of the product item collection/array.

8. Make sure that you use the **Expression** checkbox. The **Completion Condition** remains unchecked, as we are not building any condition to forcefully exit the subprocess.

9. Click on the outgoing conditional flow in the subprocess as shown in the preceding screenshot. This shows that each line will be checked for the condition and only those lines that have `Quantity > 50` will be submitted for approval by the user (`fkafka`).

Testing the use case

Perform the following steps to test the use case:

1. Deploy the **MIWithoutPriorRunTimeKnowledge** process to the Oracle SOA server and test it from the EM console by logging in to `http://localhost:7001/em` as an admin user (`weblogic`).

2. Use the test data (**MIWithoutPriorRunTimeKnowledge.xml**) to enter the **QuoteRequest** information. The test data contains five products items and out of these five product items, two product items (the second and third product items) have more than 50 as the quantity.

3. Submit **QuoteRequest** to execute the process instance.

4. Log in to the Oracle BPM workspace at `http://localhost:7001/bpm/workspace` as the user (`salesrep`) and accept the quote by approving it.

5. Log in to the EM at `http://localhost:7001/em` as a `weblogic` user and check **Audit Trail** for the process.

6. Refer to the next screenshot and we can see that a thread group is created to process five lines.

7. A subprocess instance is created for each product item. As the number of product items you entered in the quote request was five, you can check whether there are five multiple instances of the subprocess being created.

8. Note that the second and third subprocess instances are in the processing state as the entered quantity for the second and third line items is greater than 50. Hence, the second and third line items need business practice approval.

9. All other subprocess multi-instances (the first, fourth, and fifth) are completed; hence, the token for this subprocess gets completed. As the entered quantity for the first, fourth, and fifth line item in less than 50, they don't need business practice approval. This is shown in the following screenshot:

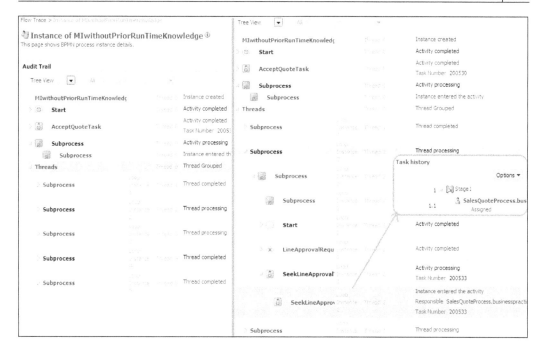

We can see that even though the tokens for the first, fourth, and fifth subprocess instances are completed, the second and third sub processes are in the processing state. Hence, the token does not move out of the subprocess. This is due to the fact that the subprocess needs to synchronize its multiple instances. Once all the tokens are synchronized, the process token can move ahead of the subprocess:

1. Log in to the BPM workspace as the `fkafka` user, and we can see that two tasks (**SeekLineApprovalTask**) are assigned to this user.

2. Approve the two tasks (**SeekLineApprovalTask**) and check the **Audit Trail** for the process in the EM console. All the parallel tokens are now completed, and the process token has moved to subsequent activities.

The BPMN service engine runs a subprocess with a **MultiInstance** loop marker and will create a set of instances, one for each element in the collection. The number of to-be instances is determined by the collection size, that is, by the size of the array. The subprocess will loop on **Product Items** in the **SalesQuote** request. The number of times the subprocess is executed is determined by the size of the collection's product items. Once each instance gets completed, the instance tokens get synchronized and the process moves to subsequent activities.

Static partial join for multiple instances pattern

In multiple instances with a runtime knowledge pattern, the number of multiple instances to be created (say, M) is determined before the first instance of the multiple instances gets initiated. The process moves to the subsequent tasks/activities only when all the tokens of the multiple instances (M) get completed, that is, all the instances of the set of multiple instances (M) get synchronized.

In static partial join patterns, the number of multiple instances to be created (say, M) is determined before the first instance of the multiple instances gets initiated. This is the same as in multiple instances with a prior runtime knowledge pattern; however, the process moves to subsequent tasks/activities only when N instances have been completed, where N is less than M. This pattern allows the process to continue only when a given number of instances have been completed; it's not necessary to wait for all the instances in the **MultiInstance** set to be completed. The remaining m-n instances are clogged from being initiated.

The following table summarizes the details around Static Partial Join:

Signature	Static Partial Join Pattern
Classification	Multi-instance Pattern
Intent	The number of concurrent threads is calculated at runtime when the first instance is created. When n out of m instances are completed, the subsequent task is initiated.
Motivation	The determination of the number of instances is performed before the first instance gets executed. The process instance moves to subsequent activities when a given number of task instances have been completed, rather than requiring all of them to finish.
Applicability	This refers to the multi-instance subprocess with loop completion condition and loop cardinality.
Implementation	The BPMN service engine runs a subprocess with a multi-instance loop marker and will create a set of instances. The number of to-be instances, m, is computed by **Loop Cardinality** before the first instance of the subprocess starts. The given number of instances, n, that can allow the execution of subsequent tasks is determined by **Completion Condition**. Once n instances are completed, the remaining m-n instances are cancelled. However, to reset and subsequently enable the convergence, all instances must be complete.
Known issues	NA
Known solution	NA

The **MIStaticPartialJoin** process is implemented to showcase static partial join pattern. When initiated, this process results in the assignment of the task (**AcceptQuoteTask**) to the user (`salesrep`) for approval. Once approved, the subprocess with the **SalesManagerApproval** task gets initiated. The number of instances of the subprocess is defined based on the cardinality set for the subprocess, and a forceful exit from the subprocess is determined based on **Completion Condition**. Perform the following steps to work on static partial join for the MI process and to test the use case:

1. Open the **SalesQuoteProcess** project in JDeveloper.

2. Go to **BPM | BPMN Processes** and open the **MIStaticPartialJoin** process.

3. Script task (**Determine Cardinality**) sets the number of instances prior to the first instance of the multiple instances subprocess as **Start**.

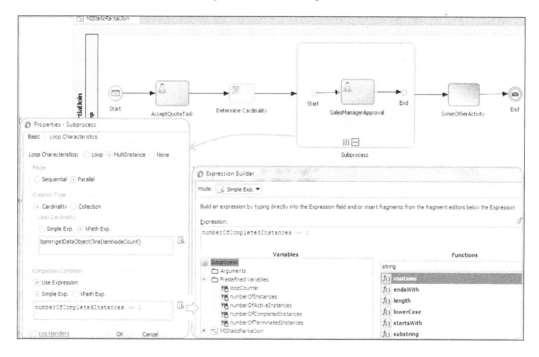

4. Click on **Subprocess** to reach the **Loop Characteristics** tab in the **Subprocess** properties.

5. In the **Completion Condition** section, check the **Use Expression** checkbox and enter the following simple expression:

    ```
    NumberOfCompletedInstances == 2
    ```

6. Save the process and deploy it to the Oracle SOA server.

Testing the use case

Perform the following steps to test the use case, which demonstrates the static partial join pattern:

1. Log in to the EM console at `http://localhost:7001/em` as an admin user (`weblogic`).

2. Test the **MIStaticPartialJoin** process using the **MIStaticPartialJoin.xml** test data. We can find the test data in the **testsuites** folder in the project. The test data (**MIStaticPartialJoin.xml**) contains five product line items.

3. Submit the quote request.

4. Log in to the Oracle BPM workspace as the `salesrep` user and approve **AcceptQuoteTasks**.

5. Click on the refresh button and you will find five tasks (**SalesManagerApproval**) being assigned to the same user (`salesrep`). (For the sake of simplicity, we have used the same user for the **SalesManagerApproval** tasks too).

6. Approve the fourth and fifth tasks.

7. Log in to the EM at `http://localhost:7001/em` as a `weblogic` user and visit **Audit Trail** for the process instance, as shown in the following screenshot:

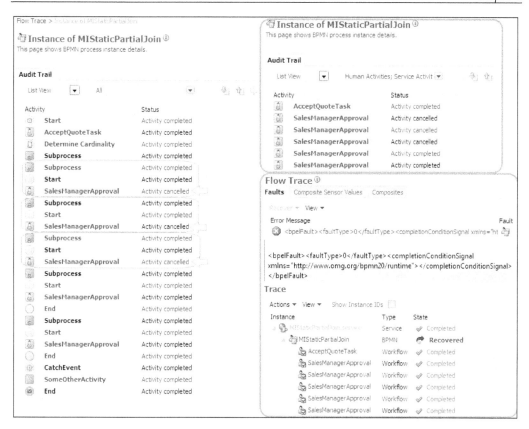

We can see that the fourth and fifth subprocess instance get completed and the activities inside these subprocesses also get completed; however, the first, second, and third subprocess instances are cancelled and so are the activities in this subprocess instance. If we check the audit trail of the process, as shown in the preceding screenshot, we can find that the activities in the first, second, and third subprocess instances are cancelled. If we check the process flow trace, it's evident that a signal is raised by the process when the completion condition results in the cancellation of activities in the rest of the subprocess instances.

Understanding how static partial join for MI works

The BPMN service engine runs a subprocess with the **MultiInstance** loop marker and will create a set of instances. The number of to-be instances (m) is computed by the **Determine Cardinality** task before the first instance of the subprocess is started.

Once each instance gets completed, the instance tokens get synchronized and the process moves to subsequent activities.

As this is in the **Parallel** mode, the subprocess instances get created in parallel. Once each instance gets completed, the **Completion Condition** is evaluated. If this condition returns `true`, the subprocess gets completed and all the active concurrent multiple instances, that is, the remaining (m-n) instances get completed.

There's more

We have set the **Parallel** mode in the multi-instance subprocess properties. However, we can set it to sequential and can test the behavior. In the sequential mode, the **subprocess** instances get created in a sequence one after another. Once one instance gets completed, **Completion Condition** is evaluated. If this condition returns `true`, the subprocess gets completed and no other instances of the subprocess get initiated.

Canceling partial join pattern

The following table summarizes details around the Canceling Partial Join:

Signature	Canceling Partial Join Pattern
Classification	Multi-instance Pattern
Intent	The number of concurrent threads is calculated at runtime when the first instance is created. When "n" out of "m" instances get executed, the subsequent task is initiated and the remaining m-n instances get cancelled.
Motivation	The determination of the number of instances is performed before the first instance gets executed. The process instance moves to subsequent activities when a given number of task instances have completed, rather than requiring all of them to finish; however, the remaining m-n instances get cancelled.
Applicability	The MultiInstance subprocess with the loop completion condition and loop cardinality.

Implementation	The BPMN service engine runs a subprocess with a multi-instance loop marker and will create a set of instances. The number of to-be instances, m, is computed by the loop cardinality before the first instance of the subprocess gets started. The given number of instances n, that can allow the execution of subsequent tasks is determined by **Completion Condition**. Once n instances are completed, the subsequent completion of m-n instances is trivial and m-n instances get cancelled.
Known issues	NA
Known solution	NA

Dynamic partial join for multiple instances pattern

The following table summarizes the details around Dynamic Partial Join:

Signature	Dynamic Partial Join Pattern
Classification	Multi-instance Pattern
Intent	The number of multiple instances to be created is not determined until the final instance of the multiple instances has been completed and all the instances then get synchronized. This pattern is an extension to the multiple instances without prior runtime knowledge pattern; however, in this pattern, a condition is evaluated that clogs further instances from being created.
Motivation	The determination of the number of instances is not performed until the final instance. A completion condition can be specified, which is evaluated each time an instance of the task completes. Once the completion condition evaluates to true, the next task in the process is triggered. Subsequent completions of the remaining task instances are cancelled and no new instances can be created.
Applicability	Multi-instance subprocess with completion condition.
Implementation	Every time a process token gets completed, the completion condition is evaluated. Once the XPath expression condition in the completion condition section of the loop gets evaluated and returns true, further processing of the subprocess's multiple instances gets clogged and they get cancelled.
Known issues	NA
Known solution	NA

Working with dynamic partial join

The **SalesQuoteProcess** project contains the **MIDynamicPartialJoin** process. We will use this process to demonstrate and learn the dynamic partial join pattern. The subprocess (**DynamicPartialJoinSubprocess**) is defined with **Completion Condition**. As soon as the XPath condition in the Completion Condition section of the loop characteristics of the subprocess is evaluated, it will inhibit further instances from being created.

The expression condition will check whether the number of completed instances is greater than the number of active instances; if it is, then the subprocess should get completed and subsequent tasks get executed. This means that if enough lines get approved by the sales manager, then there is no need to get other lines approved. Further processing of the subprocess multiple instances gets clogged and these instances get cancelled. Perform the following steps to check the implementation:

1. Expand the **SalesQuoteProcess** project in JDeveloper and open the **MIDynamicPartialJoin** process.

2. Click on **DynamicPartialJoinSubprocess** to reach the loop characteristics.

3. In the **Completion Condition** section, check **Use Expression** and enter the following simple expression:

   `NumberOfCompletedInstances > numberOfActiveInstances`

4. Save the process and deploy it to the Oracle SOA server.

5. Test the process from the Oracle EM at `http://localhost:7001/em` as a `weblogic` user.

6. When testing, use the test data (**MIDynamicPartialJoin.xml**), which contains five product line items, each with quantity greater than 50. If the quantity is greater than `50`, then we have to check whether the test data is being implemented on the gateway outgoing flow in the subprocess.

7. Submit the quote request.

8. Log in to the Oracle BPM workspace as the `salesrep` user and approve the task (**AcceptQuoteTask**).

9. Log in to the BPM workspace as the `fkafka` user and approve three tasks (`SeekLineApprovalTask`) out of the five takes assigned to this user. Five tasks being assigned to this user as the number of instances will be computed based on the product item collection. The test data contains five line items.

10. Approve the first, second, and third tasks (**SeekLineApprovalTask**).

11. Log in to the EM at `http://localhost:7001/em` as the `weblogic` user to check the **Audit Trail** of the process.

Understanding the functionality behind partial join for MI

We can see from the **Audit Trail** window that we have approved the first, second, and third tasks (**SeekLineApprovalTask**); hence, these subprocess instances get completed. However, the fourth and fifth subprocess instances get cancelled. This cancellation was due to the fact that every time the tokens get completed, the **Completion Condition** is evaluated. As we have approved three instances of the task (**SeekLineApprovalTask**), the **Completion Condition** gets evaluated to `true`. Once the XPath condition in the **Completion Condition** section of the loop gets evaluated and returns `true`, further processing of the remaining subprocess multiple instances get clogged and they are cancelled.

Structured loop pattern

Iteration patterns are the foundation of many complex patterns. Structured loop patterns are an implementation of the `while-do` or `repeat-until` (do-while) loop.

The following table summarizes the details around Structured Loops:

Signature	Structured Loops Pattern
Classification	Iteration Patterns
Intent	The structured loop pattern exhibits the ability to repeat subprocesses. This looping structure comprises of a single entry and exit point where the iteration condition can be determined before a loop execution or after a loop execution.
Motivation	Loops are similar to any traditional programming language loop structure. If a condition is evaluated before an iteration starts, then it's a variant of while-do, and if the condition is evaluated after the first iteration gets completed, then it's a do-while execution.
Applicability	Multi-instance subprocesses with the loop characteristics property set as loop. Loop characteristics (while-do or do-while) are defined by setting the evaluation order of loop characteristics.

Implementation	In a while-do execution, the subprocesses are executed for zero or more times sequentially based on the preiteration condition evaluation. The condition is evaluated even before the first iteration starts, and it gets evaluated every time an instance needs to be initiated. When the evaluation condition fails and returns false, the token moves out of the iterating subprocess to the next subsequent task/activity.
	In a do-while execution, the subprocesses are executed at least once sequentially. The condition is evaluated after the first iteration completes, and it gets evaluated every time an instance is completed. When the evaluation condition fails and returns false, the token moves out of the iterating subprocess to the next subsequent task/activity.
Known issues	NA
Known solution	NA

Working with structured loops

The following section talks about the do-while and while-do looping variants.

Demystifying do-while

In do-while, the loop characteristic is set to check the conditions after iteration. Walk through the following steps to check the loop's configuration:

1. Open the **SalesQuoteProcess** project in JDeveloper.

2. Go to **BPM | BPMN Processes** and open the **StructuredLoop** process.

3. The script task (**Determine Cardinality**) will determine the number of instances to be created sequentially. The number is determined based on the number of product items in the quote request.

4. Double-click on the subprocess (**LoopSubprocess**) to open **Loop Characteristics**.

5. Check the **Loop Condition** checkbox and we can find the entered condition in the loop characteristics. This can be accessed via **LoopCounter | LineItemNodeCount**.

6. **Loop Counter** is a predefined variable and **LineItemNodeCount** is a user-defined variable of the number type. The script task (**Determine Cardinality**) assigns the number of instances to be created of the subprocess (**LoopSubprocess**) to this variable (**LineItemNodeCount**) by counting the number of product line items in the input request.

7. Verify that the evaluation order is **Unchecked**. The evaluation order determines when the loop condition should be evaluated. If it remains unchecked, then the condition will be evaluated post iteration, as shown in the following screenshot:

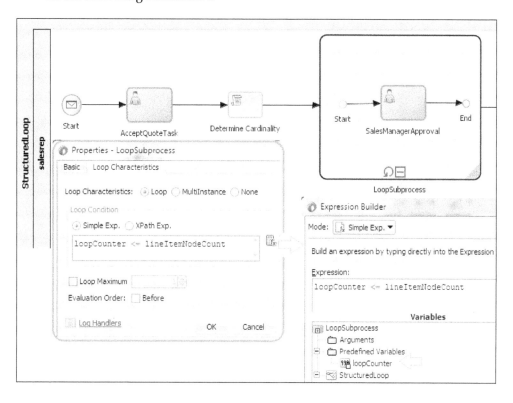

Perform the following steps to test the scenario for do-while:

1. Log in to the EM at `http://localhost:7001/em` and submit a quote request by executing the **StructuredLoop** process with four product items. We can use the test data (**StructuredLoop.xml**) to test the process.

2. Log in to the Oracle BPM workspace as the `salesrep` user and approve the **AcceptQuote** task.

3. Click on refresh and approve the task (**SalesManagerApproval**), assigned to the same user (`salesrep`). For the sake of convenience, we have used the same user for both the tasks.

4. We will find that the second task (**SalesManagerApproval**) is assigned to the `salesrep` user. Go ahead and approve the second **SalesManagerApproval** task, and similarly, do the same for the third instance of the same task.

5. When the loop condition gets evaluated after the third task approval, it returns `true`. The process token will move out of the iterating subprocess to the next subsequent task/activity.

6. Log in to the EM at `http://localhost:7001/em` as a `weblogic` user and then view the **Audit Trail** of the structured loop process.

Understanding the structured loop functionality

Multiple instances are created based on the determination of the number of to-be instances. This number is determined before the first iteration by the script task (**Determine Cardinality**). The token then advances to the subprocess and initiates the first iteration of the subprocess sequentially. After the iteration is completed, the loop condition is evaluated. If it returns `true`, then the token moves out of the iterating subprocess and the process starts executing the subsequent tasks/activities after the subprocess.

Demystifying while-do

In while-do, the loop characteristic is set to check the condition before the iteration.

In the preceding process, *Structured loop pattern*, change the evaluation order in the loop characteristics. Check the **Evaluation Order** checkbox in the loop characteristics. Now, the evaluation of the instance will happen before the iteration. Moreover, as soon as the condition returns `true`, the token moves out of the iterating subprocess to the next subsequent task/activity.

Arbitrary cycle pattern

The following table summarizes the details around Arbitrary Cycle Patterns:

Signature	Arbitrary Cycle Pattern
Classification	Iteration Pattern
Intent	The arbitrary cycle pattern offers a looping construct that allows multiple entry and exit points in and out of the loop.
Motivation	This unstructured loop (iteration/cycle) pattern offers the flexibility to have multiple entry and exit points in the process. The arbitrary cycle pattern provides a mechanism to repeat the process parts in an unstructured way.
Applicability	Exclusive gateways can be used in nonblock structured process models.

Implementation	When a modeler is working on defining an "As-Is" process, there are requirements to shuffle from one activity to another. There are cases in which a task or an activity performed initially in the process needs to be changed/altered after reaching a certain stage in the process. This translates to the fact that one can work on the process in an ad hoc manner. The process should allow you to arbitrarily visit tasks/activities that need to be changed or altered after reaching a certain stage in the process. When a process does this, you can use exclusive gateways to realize arbitrary cycles.
Known issues	NA
Known solution	NA

The use case scenario is based on **SalesQuoteApprovals**. The project contains a process (Arbitrary cycle) that demonstrates the arbitrary cycle pattern. **QuoteRequest** initiates the **SalesQuote** of the "Arbitrary Cycle" process. The following code snippet gives an insight into this:

```
If Quote Status == "Reject" then
Process token moves to "Further Activity" and
Task (Enter Quote) gets reassigned to salesrep.
Else
Some activity is executed and discount check is performed.
```

Now, **Discount Check** is performed on the process flow. This is demonstrated by the following code snippet:

```
If Discount < 10% then
Process performs other activity and process ends.
Else-if Discount > 50%
Accept Quote task is revisited by salesrep user.
Else-if Discount > 10% and Discount < 50%
Sales Manager Approval task is initiated.
```

Exploring arbitrary cycle

Perform the following steps to test Arbitrary cycle use case scenario:

1. Open the **SalesQuoteProcess** project in JDeveloper.

2. Go to **BPM | BPMN Processes** and click on the **Arbitrary cycle** process.

3. Deploy the process to a `weblogic` server.

4. Log in to Oracle EM at `http://localhost:7001/em` as a `weblogic` user and submit a quote request. Make sure that you supply the following values to the quote request:

   ○ The request status: `New`

   ○ Effective discount: `60`

   You can use the test data (**ArbitraryCycle.xml**) as the input data to initiate the BPM process (Arbitrary cycle).

5. Log in to the Oracle BPM workspace at `http://localhost:7001/bpm/workspace` as the `salesrep` user and approve the **EnterQuote** tasks.

 We can create an ADF page (a user interface) for the task. Using the user interface, we can even modify the quote details and change the discount and other details.

6. The quote gets assigned for **AcceptingQuote** to the user (`salesrep`) via the **AcceptQuote** task. (For the sake of convenience, the **AcceptQuote** task is assigned to the `salesrep` user as well).

7. Log in to the BPM workspace as the user (`salesrep`) and approve the **AcceptQuote** task.

8. On approval, the determination of the discount is performed on the **AcceptQuote** task. The following are the conditions:

   ○ If **Discount < 10%**, then the **Discount Check** exclusive gateway will guide the token to another activity and the process ends normally

   ○ If **Discount > 50%**, then the **Discount Check** exclusive gateway will detour the token back to the task (**AcceptQuote**)

   ○ If **Discount > 10%** but **< 50%**, then the **Discount Check** exclusive gateway guides the process flow to the sales manager approval by initiating the task (**SalesManagerApproval**)

9. Log in to the EM console and check the **Audit Trail** process flow, as shown in the following screenshot. As the test data contains a discount greater than 50 percent, the process token is returned back to the task (**Accept Quote**), as we can see on the top of the following screenshot.

10. Log in to the BPM workspace as the user (`salesrep`) and double-click on the task (**AcceptQuote**). This will open the ADF task form.

We can create a task user interface to change values using the interface. To perform this step, please create a task user interface for the **AcceptQuote** task. We can create the task user interface by going to the task editor and navigating to **Forms | Auto Generate Task Form**. Complete the wizard and save the project. Deploy the process project along with the task user interface form project.

11. Using the task user interface, change the effective discount from 60 to 40 and save the quote.

12. After saving the quote, approve the task (**AcceptQuote**).

13. As the quote's effective discount is changed to 40 percent, on reapproval by the user (salesrep) for the **AcceptQuote** task, the process token moves ahead for further processing, and the sales manager approval task is requested.

14. Log in to Oracle BPM and reject the **SalesManagerApproval** task.

15. Log in to the EM at http://localhost:7001/em as the **weblogic** user and check the process flow, as shown at the bottom of the following screenshot.

16. We can see that after rejection from the sales manager, the process token again reaches the **EnterQuote** task.

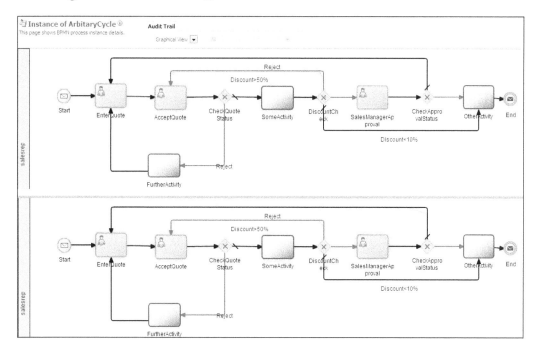

Understanding the functionality of the arbitrary cycle

We have seen two cases previously. First, when the discount was greater than 50 percent, the token reached the **AcceptQuote** task back. Second, when the discount was greater than 10 percent but less than 50 percent, the token reached the **SalesManagerApproval** task. Upon rejection from the sales manager, the token reaches back the **EnterQuote** task.

Thus, we are able to establish multiple entries in the process loop. We are also able to change the quote details based on the outcome of these activities and tasks, which downstream the process. There are various factors, downstream the process, that can govern the process flow, and sometimes it's better to re-perform that task/activity that was performed initially in the process. Hence, mechanisms are required to arbitrarily loop back in the process and the process should allow the arbitrary visiting of tasks/activities to change/alter them after reaching a certain stage in the process.

Trigger patterns

Trigger patterns are a set of patterns that deal with external signals. We will just list the pattern features; however, you will find various occurrences in this book where these patterns are used. There are two variants of trigger patterns: transient trigger and persistent trigger.

Transient trigger pattern

The following table summarizes Transient Trigger Patterns:

Signature	Transient Trigger Patterns
Classification	Trigger Patterns
Intent	The explicit initiation/termination of a task (activity/subprocess) by a signal from the same process or from an external environment.
Motivation	There are cases when an external signal arrives at the process or the process itself raises a signal. However, these signals will be lost if there is no subscriber to act on those signals. These signals are basically events and must be dealt with as soon as they occur, else they will be lost.

Applicability	For example, an activity can be cancelled by a cancel event. However, to cancel the activity, this activity needs to be active. When that activity is active, only the cancellation event meant for the activity will have an effect on the activity. What if cancellation event is raised when the process token has moved out of the activity for which the cancellation event is meant? In this case, the activity will not be cancelled.
Implementation	We can use event subprocesses and boundary catch events. A boundary catch event can be attached to the activity or subprocess, and it can be configured to accept a certain event (signal). When this signal arrives or this event is raised and the activity on which the boundary catch event is configured for this event is active, then the activity/subprocess can act on this event.
Known issues	What if there are duplicate transient triggers, or many signals (events) of the same type are raised?
Known solution	When the first signal/event is raised and the activity that is meant to catch it is active, then the signal/event will be consumed. Hence, there will be no effect when there is a second or duplicate event.

Chapter 6, *Correlation Patterns*, contains the implementation of trigger patterns in the *Cancel activity pattern* section.

Persistent trigger pattern

The following table summarizes the Persistent Trigger Pattern:

Signature	Persistent Trigger Pattern
Classification	Trigger Pattern
Intent	The explicit initiation of a task (activity/subprocess) by a signal from the same process or from an external environment.
Motivation	There are cases when an external signal arrives at the process or the process itself raises signal. However, this signal will not be lost and is dealt with by the process.
Applicability	For example, a process instance can be cancelled by a cancel instance event. The cancel instance event can arrive any time in the life cycle of the process.
Implementation	We can use the event subprocess.
Known issues	NA
Known solution	NA

Implicit termination pattern

The following table summarizes the details around Implicit Termination:

Signature	Implicit Termination Pattern
Classification	Termination Pattern
Intent	To end a process gracefully when no more activities/tasks/ subprocesses need to be performed in the process.
Motivation	The process needs to end successfully, that is, when no remaining objectives are left to achieve in the process.
Applicability	End event.
Implementation	An implicit pattern is similar to an end event, where a process token gets completed for the process and the process instance is completed. This is the point where the last token gets terminated. This is termed as implicit termination, as the process token termination happens implicitly and is taken care of by the BPM process engine.
Known issues	NA (not available in the case of Oracle BPM as it directly supports this pattern).
Known solution	NA

Amalgamating implicit termination in the process flow

To demonstrate implicit termination, we will execute the arbitrary cycle process, which we have worked with in the previous section (the arbitrary cycle):

1. Log in to Oracle EM at `http://localhost:7001/em` as the weblogic user and submit a quote request by executing the process (the arbitrary cycle). Make sure that you supply the following values to the quote request:

    The request status: `New`

    Effective discount: `40`

2. We can use the test data (`ArbitraryCycle.xml`) as the input data to initiate the BPM process (arbitrary cycle). Remember to check the effective discount value and to change it to `40`.

3. Log in to the Oracle BPM workspace at `http://localhost:7001/bpm/ workspace` as the user (`salesrep`) and approve the **EnterQuote** tasks, the **AcceptQuote** task, as well as the **SalesManagerApproval** task.

4. Once the task (**SalesManagerApproval**) is approved, end the process.

You can conclude from the process flow that the process instance gets completed when the process hits the message end event. This is the case when all the tasks and activities in the process are completed and there are no tasks and activities left that need to be performed in future. This is termed as implicit termination.

Explicit termination pattern

There are certain stages in the process when you want to terminate a process instance. For example, if the `salesrep` user rejects the **AcceptQuote** task, you want the quote request to get terminated and all the remaining tasks/activities and subprocesses to end. This is achieved by terminating the end event in the process.

The following table summarizes the details around Explicit Termination:

Signature	Explicit Termination Pattern
Classification	Termination Pattern
Intent	To explicitly end a process when the process has a certain specified flow pattern.
Motivation	The process needs to end explicitly, and this will terminate all the remaining tasks/activities and cause the processes to end.
Applicability	This event terminates the end event and the Error End Event.
Implementation	When the process token reaches this end event node, all the remaining activities in the process need to be cancelled and process instances get completed. However, the state of the process depends on the end event. If the end event is terminated, then the process instance gets terminated. If the end event is an error, then the process instance ends in an error. However, you can catch the error and explicitly complete the process instance successfully.
Known issues	NA
Known solution	NA

Learning how explicit termination works

Scenario: Enter the **QuoteRequest** task when it gets approved by `salesrep`; the **Discount Approval** task gets assigned to the same user. This time, `salesrep` will reject the **Discount Approval** task. All other remaining activities in the process will end, and the process instance gets completed.

1. Open the **SalesQuoteProcess** project in JDeveloper; go to **BPM | BPMN Processes** and click on **ExplicitTermination**.

2. Log in to the EM at `http://localhost:7001/em` as the `weblogic` user and initiate the Explicit Termination process. We can use the test data (**ExplicitTerminate.xml**) to test the process. The test data can be found in the **testsuites** folder in the project.

3. Log in to the Oracle BPM workspace as the `salesrep` user and reject the **AcceptQuote** task.

4. Log in to the EM console and check the process instance's **Audit Trail** and **Process Flow**.

When the process token reaches the **AcceptQuote** task, it gets assigned to the `salesrep` user. When the user (`salesrep`) rejects **QuoteRequest** task, the process gets terminated explicitly. When the process terminates, all the remaining activities in the process are cancelled and the process instance gets aborted.

Cancelation patterns

Cancelation patterns are a set of patterns that deal with the cancellation of case, activity, task, subprocess, and so on. We will just list the pattern features; however, we will find various occurrences in this book where cancelation patterns are used. We will include a reference to those sections where that specific cancelation pattern is implemented or demonstrated. There are various variants of cancelation patterns such as cancel case, cancel task, cancel activity, cancel multi-instance subprocess, complete multi-instance subprocess, and so on. Cancel case pattern is covered in *Chapter 8, Adaptive Case Management*. Cancel task pattern is covered in *Chapter 4, Human Task Patterns*. *Chapter 6, Correlation Patterns*, contains the implementation of trigger patterns in the *Cancel activity pattern* section.

Cancel multi-instance task pattern

The following table summarizes the Cancel Multi-instance Task Pattern:

Signature	Cancel Multi-instance Task Pattern
Classification	Cancelation Pattern
Intent	In this chapter, we have witnessed that multi-instances of the task or subprocess can be known at design time or runtime. We have also seen that these multiple instances are independent of each other and a separate thread is created to process these instances. The intent is to cancel these multi-instances at any time.

Motivation	This includes canceling multi-instances when various instances of the multi-instance task are in process. Cancellation can happen at any time, and the remaining instances of the multi-instances that are not processed should be cancelled.
Applicability	For example, a multi-instance subprocess is executing a subprocess that acts on a product line item collection. The subprocess is meant to request approvals for all the line items in the collection. A cancellation event can result in the withdrawal of the task/activities in the subprocess and can lead to the cancellation of the remaining subprocess instances.
Implementation	We can use multi-instance subprocesses and boundary catch events. Boundary catch events can be attached to the multi-instance subprocess, and they can be configured to accept certain events (signals). These signals/events are meant to cancel the remaining instances of the multi-instance subprocess. When this signal arrives or this event is raised, then the remaining instances of the multi-instance will be cancelled.
Known issues	NA
Known solution	NA

Perform the following steps to test the cancel multi-instance task pattern:

1. Open the **SalesQuoteProcess** project in JDeveloper, go to **BPM | BPMN Processes,** and click on the **CancelMultiInstanceRegion** process.

2. Log in to the EM at `http://localhost:7001/em` as a **weblogic** user and initiate the process (**CancelMultiInstanceRegion**). We can use the test data (**CancelMultiInstanceRegion.xml**) to test the process. The test data can be found in the **testsuites** folder of the project. The test data contains three product line items.

3. Log in to the Oracle BPM workspace as the user (`salesrep`) and approve **AcceptQuoteTask**.

4. As the test data contains three product line items, the subprocess containing the task (**SalesManagerApproval**) will result in the creation of three subprocess multi-instances.

5. Log in to the Oracle BPM workspace as the `salesrep` user, and approve the second instance of the task (**SalesManagerApproval**) out of the three instances of the task (**SalesManagerApproval**).

6. There is a timer event on the multi-instance subprocess. The timer expires in 2 minutes. If the user (`salesrep`) does not act on the task (**SalesManagerApproval**), the timer event gets triggered and the process token reaches the message end event.

7. Log in to the EM console and check the process instance's **Audit Trail** and **Process Flow**, as shown in the following screenshot.

The process is implemented to create a multi-instance of the subprocess containing the task (**SalesManagerApproval**). Each instance of the subprocess results in the task being assigned to the `salesrep` user. Interestingly, there is a catch timer event on the multi-instance subprocess. The timer event is set with 2 minutes of timer cycle. The timer event is an interrupting event. Hence, if a user (`salesrep`) does not act on the remaining tasks in 2 minutes, the timer gets expired and an interrupting event is raised. The event will eventually end the process. However, the remaining instances of the multi-instance subprocess will get cancelled, as shown in the following screenshot:

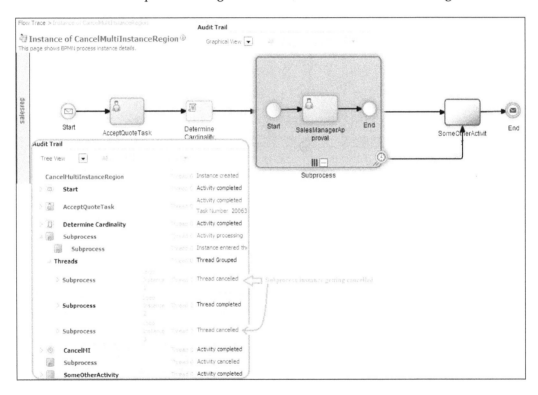

Summary

This chapter demonstrated how processes can handle batch jobs and how to simultaneously spawn multiple work item instances in a process. It also uncovered iteration patterns by demonstrating the structured loop and unstructured looping mechanism. Implicit and explicit termination patterns at the end helped us learn termination patterns.

The next chapter will focus on invocation patterns and will uncover how BPM processes can be invoked by internal and external environments.

3
Invocation Patterns

A BPM process can be invoked or initiated in many different ways. Based on the architectural design and business requirements, a BPM process invocation can be defined. The invocation of a BPM process can be designed by either exposing the BPM process as a web service (Sync/Async), through BPM APIs, or through the **Java Message Service** (**JMS**). In addition, there could be other mechanisms to initiate the BPM process via e-mails/files/batches or by scheduling a BPM process through timers. Also, we can have a human task be the initiator of business processes.

A common integration requirement is to expose the BPMN process as a service. You generally expose BPM processes as Oracle BPM services when you want them to be consumed by BPEL, Mediator, and more specifically by the Oracle Service Bus. Exposing a process as a web service is a built-in capability of the Oracle BPM. A process instance creation or process notification can be exposed as a **Service**. When we are looking for an assured and/or once-only delivery, asynchronous support, publish/subscribe, scalability, reliability, handling high loads, large volumes of messages (EDA), and transaction boundary, the obvious choice is JMS (Queue/ Topics). You can also adopt signals or events to initiate the BPM process if the design guideline is loose coupling.

The following invocation patterns are discussed in this chapter:

- Web service pattern:
    - Asynchronous request callback pattern
    - Synchronous request response pattern
    - One request, one of two possible responses pattern
    - Two request pattern

- One-way invocation pattern:
  - ° Implementing one-way invocation using a timer
  - ° Implementing one-way invocation using e-mail

- Publish/subscribe pattern
- Multievent instantiation
- Human task initiator pattern
- Guaranteed delivery pattern

Web service pattern

The scenario used in this chapter is based on the Loan Origination process. Loan Origination is a core business process in financial services, where a borrower applies and seeks for a loan through a loan application. The bank, which is the lender, will process it and either approve (grant) the loan or reject the loan application. The Loan Origination process is a sequence of steps performed by the lender that start from the point when the customer starts showing interest in a loan product offering to the disbursal or grant or rejection of the funds against the loan application. A fine-tuned Loan Origination process is a requirement for banks (lenders) as they are looking for processes that can overcome many challenges, as follows:

- A customer's need for instant visibility in the origination process, and often, they seek immediate updates
- Customers have the expectation to get the loan processed with the least turnaround time and reduced processing fees
- Customers can initiate Loan Origination via any mechanism/channel such as e-mail/Internet banking (web)/visiting the branch/fax/phone banking/mobile, and so on
- Freedom and agility to switch the lender
- Lenders should be able to have their processes cope with the changing regulations and policies

Processes should be agile to quickly change and remain scalable at the same time. Changing business regulations and policies must be swiftly adopted in the business processes and with a low reaction time. Oracle BPM offers everything that's required for an agile, scalable, and reliable business process. This chapter will focus on initiating a loan origination process from different channels. With the process designed here, banks (lenders) can submit, approve, and track the loan application.

BPM Process as a Service (the web service pattern), where BPM processes are configured as a service interface, can be defined with an asynchronous operation or with a synchronous operation. The use case implemented for this example is based on loan origination over the Web. The enterprise has a loan portal (the loan application) that can be accessed by customers who have applied for loans. These customers (applicants) can initiate loans via the Web using these web applications. These web applications will internally invoke the loan origination BPM process as a web service. As web services are loosely coupled, they allow companies to integrate heterogeneous applications within the enterprise or expose business functions to their customers and partners over the Web (Internet).

Asynchronous request-response (request-callback) pattern

The following table lists the details around the asynchronous request-response pattern:

Signature	Asynchronous Request-Response (Request-Callback) Pattern
Classification	Invocation Pattern
Intent	Exposes an asynchronous operation to allow a client to invoke the process asynchronously. The intent is to generate a service interface that creates request and callback operations for asynchronous processes. Its goal is to serve those scenarios which do not expect a response from the service provider in near real time.
Motivation	The BPM process's service interface, exposed as an asynchronous service, contains a start activity that defines an asynchronous operation to accept the incoming request and an activity that defines a callback operation, which returns the result for the asynchronous operations it has defined.
Applicability	Asynchronous service start operations are defined using the Message Start Event or Catch Event. Callback operations are defined using a Message Throw Event or a Message End Event. Correlation mechanisms should be implemented too. You can also use, Receive and Send Tasks to expose the BPM process operation as the asynchronous operation.

Implementation	The service interface of an asynchronous BPM process shows a Start operation and a Callback operation. A BPM process input is defined using the Message Start Event, Catch Event, or Receive task, and the process output is defined using the Message End Event, Throw Event, or Send task. In the case of an asynchronous interface, there will be two ports: one port is for requests and one is for callbacks. The Message End Event or the Send task has to define a callback operation.
Known issues	Reliability
Known solution	To ensure that a message gets routed to the appropriate requester, message correlation must be implemented to relate inbound and outbound messages.

In this section, we will walk you through the configuration of the service interface of an asynchronous BPM process. Download the **LoanOriginationProcess** application, open **LoanOrigination**, and click on the **LOProcessAsService** process.

Use the following steps to expose the BPM Process as a Service:

1. Right-click on **Start Message Event**, click on the **Implementation** tab, and select the **Define Interface** option in the **Message Exchange** type section. If we have an interface defined and we need to use it to define the service, we can choose the **Use Interface** option to browse for the interface from the business catalog:

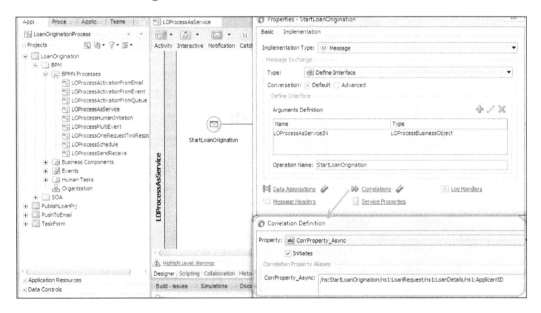

2. In the **Operation Name** section, give a name to the request operation such as `StartLoanOrigination` (this will become the operation name for the service interface).

3. In the **Argument Definition** panel, define the web service request payload. This will be based on a Business Object (**LOProcessBusinessObject**); hence, define a Request Business Object based on the payload schema and use that business object to define the request argument. However, the downloaded process contains the business object that we can use.

4. As we are defining an asynchronous operation for the BPM process, we have to define a callback operation for the BPM process.

5. This process has a defined callback operation that uses a Message End Event. Right-click on the Message End Event (**EndLoanOrigination**) and go to the **Implementation** tab, shown as follows:

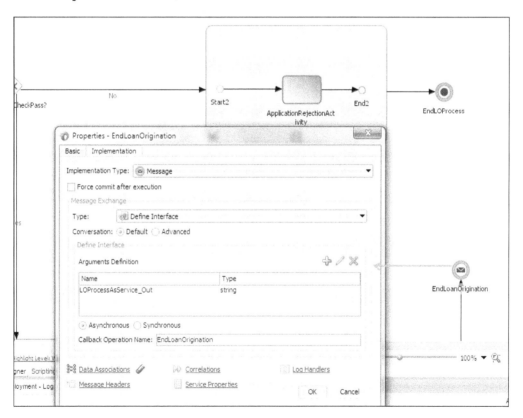

6. Define the interface and select/create the output argument. For this example, we will just return a loan status. The loan status could be either `Success` or `Reject`.

7. Note that the behavior of the BPM Process as a Service is defined here. If we select **Asynchronous**, you need to specify a name for the callback operation.

8. Click on **Data Associations** and complete the data assignment.

9. Deploy the process to a web logic server, and log in to the EM, `http://server:host/em`, as a web logic user.

10. Test the process using either SOAP-UI or EM or any other tool of your choice.

We can check the WSDL file created for the service interface of the process. Go to the project directory and click on **LOProcessAsService.wsdl**, which is the WSDL for the asynchronous service interface. We can witness two different ports being created, one for requests and one for callbacks. We can define a BPEL/OSB or any other client as a service consumer. A service consumer will have a request port and a callback port available for the asynchronous message interaction.

Request-response pattern

The following table lists the details around the synchronous request-response pattern:

Signature	Request-Response Pattern
Classification	Invocation Pattern
Intent	Expose a synchronous operation to allow a client to invoke the process synchronously. The intent is to generate a service interface that creates a request-reply operation for synchronous processes. Its goal is to serve the scenarios that expect responses from the service provider in near real time.
Motivation	The BPM process, exposed as a synchronous service, needs a start activity to accept the incoming request and an activity to return either the requested information or an error message defined in the WSDL.
Applicability	This pattern is applicable to message start event or catch event and a corresponding Message End Event or Throw Event. In case of the Message End Event, an optional fault definition is included in the operation. You can also use the **Receive** and **Send** tasks to expose a BPM process operation as being synchronous.

Implementation	You can configure a message start event, Message Catch Event, or Receive task event to create a service interface. This service interface can be defined with an asynchronous operation or with a synchronous operation. The BPM process input is defined using a Message Start Event, Catch Event, or Receive task, and the process output is defined using a Message End Event, Throw Event, or Send task, respectively. In the case of a synchronous interface, there will be one port for request and response. You can have the fault definition in the operation to return the error message to the service consumer. This can be achieved with the Business Exception implementation type, which would result in the generation of the fault definition in the operation. The Message Start Event can automatically set the conversation to initiate. In the case of the receive task, it should be capable enough to create instances, and a Receive task will always follow the None Start Event.
Known issues	If an immediate response is not received by the service consumer on time, then it will result in a timeout exception.
Known solution	The service should not contain a dehydration point; it should keep the latency at the lowest, and overheads such as marshalling and unmarshalling should be eliminated. The service provider must always be available. The use case for implementing a synchronous interaction must be very well-defined; for example, try not to use the synchronous pattern of interaction when a service needs to interact with multiple backend systems or when a service needs to perform real-time, complex processing. It should be avoided when a service needs to work on multiple requests from child nodes. A better use case and a strategy for lower latency, timeout, complex processing, and so on must be defined while implementing a service as a synchronous service.

Let's change the service message interaction pattern in the process (**LOProcessAsService**) from asynchronous to synchronous by performing the following steps:

1. Click on the Message End Event in the process, navigate to **Properties**, and click on the **Implementation** tab.

2. Change the interface definition to **Synchronous**. You will find that the **Reply To** option gets initiated.

3. From the drop-down list, choose the start event (**Request (StartLOOrigination)**) that this response is meant for.

4. Create the data associations and click on **OK**.

You can check the WSDL file created for the service interface of the process. Go to the project directory and click on **LOProcessAsService.wsdl**, which is the WSDL for the synchronous service interface. You can see only one port for request and response.

With the synchronous variant of the BPM Process as a Service, the client needs to wait for the response. In the case of the BPM processes that are highly human-centric and a situation where the response might take longer, synchronous BPM Process as a Services are rare and not used often.

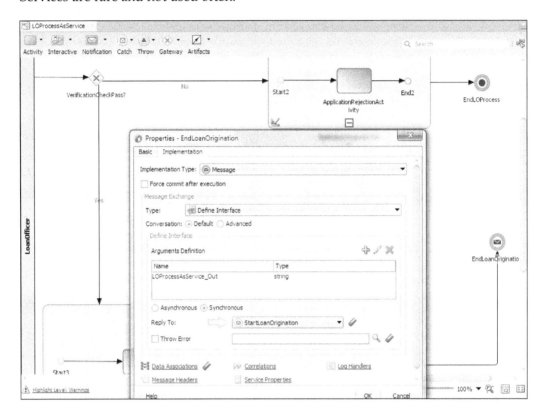

One request, one of the two possible responses pattern

We can create a BPM process that offers multiple operations as the response. This is an asynchronous pattern where the client sends a single request and receives one of two possible responses. For example, the request can be for loan approval and the first response can be either **Approved** (the loan is approved) or **NotApproved** (the loan is not approved).

Perform the following steps to check the configuration of the process that implements this pattern and also check its WSDL file:

1. Open the process (**LOProcessOneRequestTwoResponse**); we can see that it has two Message End Events.

2. Open the WSDL file (**LOProcessOneRequestTwoResponse.wsdl**) for this Process as a service. If we check the WSDL file for this process, we find two operations in the callback port, as shown in the following screenshot:

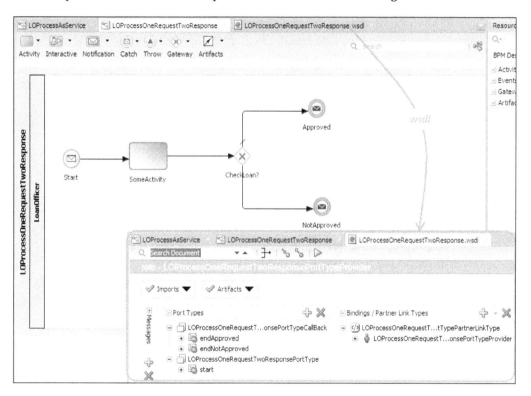

Two request a pattern

We can define a BPM process interface that can have two start events. This can be achieved by a BPM interface that not only exposes the Message Start Event, but also exposes the Message Catch Event. When you try to execute this process interface, the Message Start Event should always be executed first. Also, correlation should be enabled before you plan to expose the service interface of a BPM process with the start event and catch event messages together. Perform the following steps to enable multiple operations for the BPM process exposed as a service:

1. Open the **LOProcessAsService** process in JDeveloper.

2. Drag-and-drop the Message Catch Event between the Message Start Events, verify the web application subprocess, and name it GetAdditionalLoanInfo.

3. Let the other process definition remain the same as it was for the initial process.

4. Right–click on the start message event, **StartLoanOrigination**, and go to the **Implementation** tab.

5. Click on **Correlation** and define the correlation property based on **ApplicantID** from the payload.

6. Remember that you need to define this correlation definition for the start message event as **Initiates** and check the box. We saw the correlation definition in the first diagram of this chapter.

7. Right-click on the catch message event, **GetAdditionalLoanInfo**, and go to its **Implementation** tab to define the correlation.

8. Click on **Correlations** and use the **CorrProperty_Async** correlation property based on **ApplicantID** from the payload.

9. Don't check the **Initiates** box, as the catch event message will participate in the correlation defined and will start with the start message event (**StartLoanOrigination**).

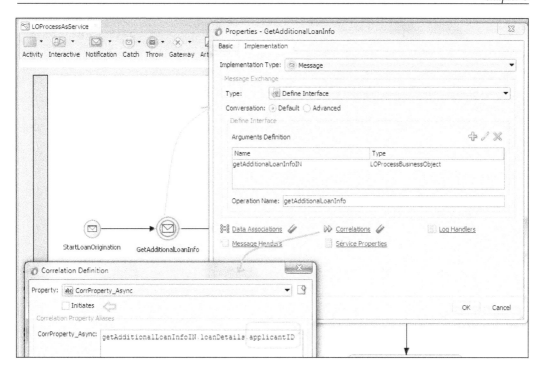

10. Deploy the process and try to test it from the EM, `http://server:host/em`, by logging in as a web logic user.

11. While testing, you will notice that there are two operations: **StartLoanOrigination** (it's a Message Start Event) and **GetAdditionalLoanInfo** (it's a Message Catch Event).

12. Select **StartLoanOrigination** and test the process. Remember that you need to enter an Applicant ID in the payload.

We can browse for the test data that can be found by navigating to **Loan Origination** | **SOA** Content | **testsuites** | **LOProcessAsService. xml**.

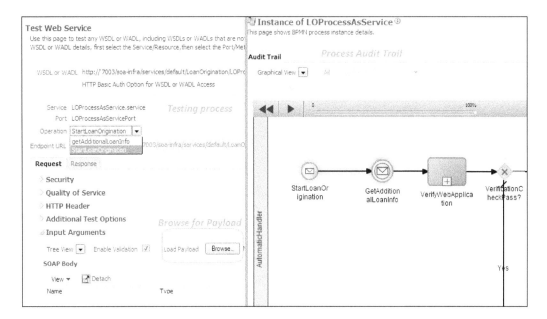

Once the process is executed, we can check the process instance audit trail as shown in the preceding screenshot. The process instance will be in the running state. If we check the flow of the process in the audit trail, we can find the process instance as waiting for the catch event to take place.

13. Go to the Oracle EM console and run the process with the **GetAdditionalLoanInfo** operation using the same test data. Remember that you need to enter the same Applicant ID that you entered while testing the **StartLoanOrigination** operation (as the correlation is based on the Applicant ID payload element).

 Once the **GetAdditionalLoanInfo** catch event is received with the correct correlation ID, the process moves ahead to subsequent flow activities.

Click on the `<ProcessName>.wsdl` file, that is, `LOProcessAsService.wsdl`, which is the WSDL file for the asynchronous service. You can see that two different ports are created, one for requests and one for callbacks. The service request will have two operations, one for **StartLoanOrigination** and one for **GetAdditionalLoanInfo**. While executing the BPM process, the execution process will be stalled until the catch event is received.

Exposing the BPM process using Receive and Send Tasks

The Receive task BPMN component can be used to expose a BPM process as a synchronous/asynchronous service. The Receive task operation must be capable enough to create instances when other processes/services invoke this BPM Process as a Service using the defined Receive task. You can define the input argument using the Receive task and the output argument using the Send Task. The message pattern behavior of the process will be described based on how the Send Task is configured, synchronous/asynchronous. If the message exchange pattern is asynchronous, then the Send Task has to define a callback operation.

Loan Origination over Send and Receive tasks

Download the **LoanOriginationProcess** application to open **LoanOriginationPrj**. Click on the **LOProcessSendReceive** process. To implement Send and Receive Tasks and to demonstrate the instantiation of a process using Send and Receive Tasks, perform the following steps:

1. Open the **LOProcessSendReceive** process in JDeveloper.

2. Verify the start event as **none**.

3. Right-click on the **ReceiveLoanOriginationReq** Receive task and click on the **Implementation** tab to check its properties.

    You will find that the **Create Instance** checkbox is checked. This enables the Receive task to instantiate process instances. The request operation is named **ReceiveLoanOriginationReq**. This operation will be used by the calling process/service to invoke this Process as a service. Click on **Data Associations** to check the association between the Receive task output and the process data object. (Both are based on the Loan Origination business object.)

4. Go to the **Properties** page of the **SendLoanOriginationResp** Send Task to verify its configuration.

5. The message type is used to define an interface for the Send Task. The message exchange pattern is defined as **Asynchronous**; hence, the **Asynchronous** box is checked, and the callback operation name entered is **SendLoanOriginationResp**.

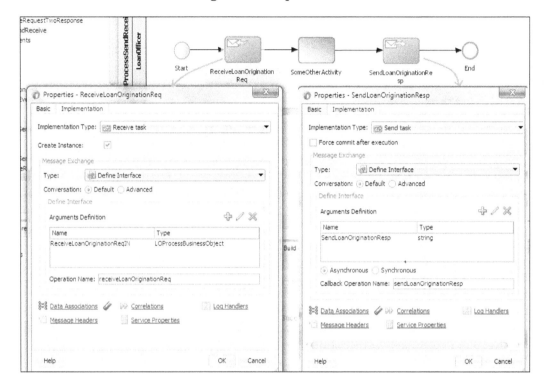

If we check the LOProcessSendReceiveTask.wsdl WSDL file created for this process, we can see that two ports have been created, one for Send and one for Callback.

We can change the message exchange pattern from asynchronous to synchronous in order to make the BPM process service interface synchronous. In this case, you need to define the reply-to (response) operation. Moreover, in the configuration, you need to select the corresponding request operation.

If the service interface is asynchronous, then the service consumer would have the request and callback operations available. We can use the Send Task or a Throw Event to invoke an asynchronous BPM process that has been built using a Receive Task and a Send Task. A BPEL process can invoke this asynchronous process using invoke. If the process service interface is synchronous, then we can use the service task to invoke the process service interface. Interaction patterns are discussed in detail in *Chapter 5, Interaction Patterns*.

One-way invocation pattern

In this section, we will learn about process instantiation using the timer events (the timer start pattern). This pattern enables process instantiation using Timer Events. Timer Events are used extensively in BPM, and Oracle BPM offers rich Timer Event configurations. You can use timers to incorporate a delay before initiating an activity, configure a deadline for an activity/process, trigger activities after a certain amount of time has elapsed, periodically trigger a process, and start a process. This section is dedicated to showcasing how Timer Events can be used to start/initiate BPM processes or to periodically schedule BPM processes.

The following table lists the details around the Timer Start pattern:

Signature	One-way Timer Start Pattern
Classification	Invocation Pattern
Intent	The intent is to configure a process to be triggered based on a time condition.
Motivation	A BPM process can be configured to be triggered based on the time condition by adding a Timer Start Event to your process.
Applicability	It's applicable on the Timer Start Event.
Implementation	A Timer Start Event can raise the BPM process instance either on a specific date (time/date) or periodically (the timer cycle), and you can specify the date or interval using a fixed value or by using an expression through an expression builder. An instance gets created each time the timer condition in the Timer Start Event gets evaluated to true. Similarly, in the start cycle case, the Timer Start Event is configured to use a cycle; hence, the process instance gets created periodically.
Known issues	There is the possibility of having processes with past dates.
Known solution	The solution should be capable of handling immediately created process instances because for any process deployed with a past date, a process instance is immediately created.

Implementing one-way invocation using a timer

A simple BPM process is implemented for the start Timer Event. With the download able files for this chapter (available on the Packt website), we have the **LoanOriginationProcess** application with **LoanOriginationPrj** as the project. Download the application and open the project in JDeveloper.

Click on **LOProcessSchedule**, which is implemented with multiple Timer Start Events. This process will be initiated at the scheduled time, specified in the start Timer Event named StartSchedule, while the other processes will run periodically every 2 minutes and will stop at the time specified under **Run To** in the optional settings of the StartCycle Timer Event.

Walk through the following steps to use the Timer Start Event and the periodic start event to trigger the process on schedule and periodically, respectively:

1. Click on the **LOProcessSchedule** project in JDeveloper.

2. Right-click on the **StartSchedule** Timer Event, and click on the **Implementation** tab in the **Properties** page.

3. The **Timer Definition** type is **Schedule** as it's a scheduled Timer Event.

4. Enter a daily time, say **10:28:00 PM**. You can change this time as per your testing requirements.

   The Timer Event, known as the *process scheduler*, can be configured to act daily, weekly, or monthly. When set as monthly, you can specify the month, day, date, and time; thus, BPM offers rich scheduling options.

5. Right-click on **StartCycle**, click on the **Implementation** tab, and select the type of timer as **Time Cycle** to define the Timer Event as a *periodical cycle*.

6. Enter a time value; say, if the process should get triggered every 2 minutes, then enter the values as shown in the preceding point. The values specified here will cause the timer catch event to run at a defined interval. This is specified in months, days, hours, minutes, and seconds.

7. Deploy the process and check the process instance creation pattern in EM, http://server:host/em.

   You can check, as follows, that some of the instances are created every 2 minutes between the **Run from** and **Run to** timings, and one instance got created at the scheduled time, **10:28:00 PM**.

Here, we have demonstrated that the Timer Start Event and the Periodic Start Event trigger the process on schedule and on a periodic cycle, respectively. We have defined them using fixed values; however, you can use an expression builder and or BPM-offered rich functions to define values for the Timer Event.

An instance gets created each time the timer condition in the Timer Start Event gets evaluated to `true`. In the scheduled Timer Event case, whenever the time is **10:28:00 PM**, the process instance will be created. Similarly, in the start cycle case, the Timer Start Event is configured to use a cycle; hence, the process instance gets created periodically.

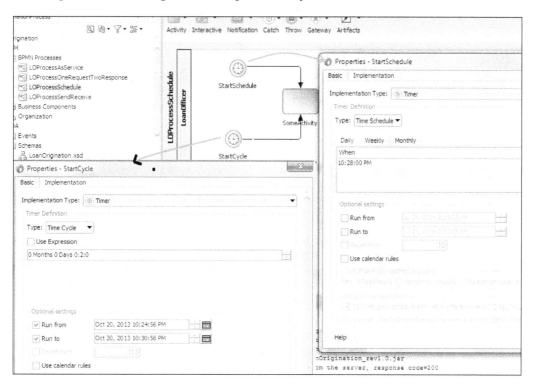

Implementing one-way invocation using an e-mail

In this section, we will learn about process instantiation using e-mail (the one-way pattern). This section demonstrates the invocation of a BPM process by e-mails. The following table lists the details around the Email Start Pattern:

Signature	One-way message – Email Start Pattern
Classification	Invocation Pattern
Intent	The intent is to configure a process to be triggered based on the arrival of an e-mail.
Motivation	The BPM process can be configured to be triggered based on an e-mail.
Applicability	In the message start events and for the UMS configuration in SOA/BPM.
Implementation	The UMS adapter is configured for inbound interaction; hence, the adapter is able to asynchronously receive messages/notifications from UMS. The UMS adapter is configured as a listener and has initiated threads to process it. The UMS adapter will act as a proxy between SOA and the external world. The use-case-adapter will be able to receive messages from the inbox of the loan officer, as the adapter was able to retrieve e-mails from the Gmail IMAP server supporting SSL.
Known issues	Selectively receives messages.
Known solution	The message was received with a subject, body, and one/more attachments. You can configure the adapter to selectively receive incoming messages by defining message filtering, and you also have the option of a Java callout function to execute a certain custom logic before message processing.

Every enterprise has e-mail and various other messaging channels such as SMSs, IMs, voice, and so on for communication and collaboration. A loan request can originate over the phone or e-mail. Let's assume the case where a customer sends an e-mail to the loan origination department to initiate the loan origination process. Oracle BPM has message events that can trigger the BPMN process instance upon the arrival of a message. In this section, we will build a sample BPMN process that is triggered when an e-mail arrives for loan origination. For the sake of our example, we have used the Gmail server to listen to incoming messages.

A client can initiate a loan approval process by filling in a loan form, and they can e-mail the loan form to a loan officer's e-mail address (for example, `weblogic0009@gmail.com`). Once a loan origination request e-mail arrives in the inbox of the loan officer, the loan origination process gets triggered.

Oracle BPM offers **User Messaging Service** (**UMS**), which provides services to send or receive notifications and alerts through various messaging channels such as e-mails, SMSs, IMs, and voice. Oracle BPM also offers the UMS adapter to kick off a BPM process or a BPEL/Mediator process when a new e-mail arrives in the inbox. The UMS adapter enables processes to send e-mail too, along with filtering and transforming/formatting based on business needs. UMS also supports SSL for e-mail channels.

We will configure the Email Driver to enable e-mails as the message delivery channel; hence, the UMS adapter will be able to retrieve e-mails from the IMAP server of Gmail-supporting SSL.

The Loan Origination process over e-mail

To enable the receiving and triggering of a BPMN process via e-mails, UMS server-side configurations need to be accomplished before the actual process is developed and deployed. Use `http://acharyavivek.wordpress.com/2013/10/21/email-driver-properties/` to perform the following activities, which will allow you to send e-mails to the loan officer's inbox in order to initiate the Loan origination request:

- Import SSL certificates to trust the Keystore
- Configure the Email Driver on the web logic server
- Create an SOA/BPEL process to send e-mails to the loan officer's e-mail address

The preceding blog post covers details on importing certificates and configuring the Email Driver on the web logic server. To push a Loan Origination request to the loan officer, the SOA (BPEL) process is available to you when you download the **LoanOriginationProcess** application, available with the downloads for this chapter.

Download the `LoanOriginationProcess` application and open the **LoanOrigination** project. Click on the `LOProcessActivationFromEmail` process. Perform the following steps to witness the UMS adapter configuration:

1. Click on `LoanOrigination` (the Composite file) and click on the UMS adapter (**ReceiveLOEmail**) to check its configuration.
2. Configure the JNDI name as `eis/ums/UMSAdapterInbound` and click on **Next**. You can enter the appropriate JNDI as per your configuration.
3. Choose the operation type as **Inbound Receive Notification**, enter the operation name as `receiveLONotification`, and click on **Next**.
4. The value of **Operation Mode** is set to **Listening** and the listener thread has a value of **1**.

5. Click on **Next** to set the type of notification as **email**.

6. The e-mail endpoint configuration is `weblogic0009@gmail.com`.

    This is the e-mail address of the loan officer to which the e-mail request will be sent in order to initiate the Loan Origination BPM process.

7. In the schema selection, choose `ReceiveEmailEvent.xsd`, which can be found in the `/Schemas` folder of the project, and click on **Next**.

8. Click on **Next** three times and finish the configuration.

9. Click on the **LOProcessActivationFromEmail** process.

10. Right-click on the start message event and check the implementation properties.

11. You can see that the message event is configured with the message exchange type as **Use Interface**. The UMS adapter that we just configured is available as a service that we can refer to.

12. Select the already-existing service that you have defined using the UMS adapter (**ReceiveLOEmail**), as shown in the following screenshot:

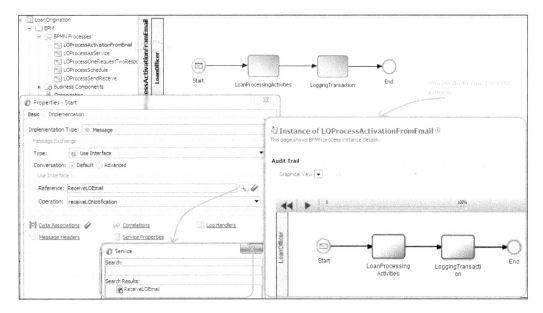

13. Click on **Data Associations** and check the assignment from the UMS adapter to process the data objects that are based on the `ReceiveEmailEvent.xsd` schema.

14. Click on **Save All** and deploy the process.

Testing the flow to instantiate a process over e-mail

With the downloadable file for this chapter, you will receive the
LoanOriginationProcess application. This application contains the **PushToEmail**
project. This project will send an e-mail to weblogic0009@gmail.com, which is the
e-mail address of the loan officer we have configured in the process. Open the project
in JDeveloper and take a look at its configuration. It's being configured with a UMS
adapter to send messages. Use an appropriate JNDI, as we did in the preceding
section. You can enter the JNDI and other properties based on the configuration of
your web logic server. Perform the following steps to test the flow:

1. Open the **PushToEmail** project in JDeveloper and deploy it to the web
   logic instance.

2. Execute the PushToEmail process from the EM, http://server:host/em.

3. Execution of the PushToEmail process will result in an e-mail being sent to
   the e-mail address (weblogic0009@gmail.com).

4. Log in to the EM and check the audit trail for the
   LOProcessActivationFromEmail process.

5. You will find an instance being created for the
   LOProcessActivationFromEmail process.

6. Click on the audit trail of the process to check instance details and the
   payload. We can, of course, use this as an initiating template and can
   extend and build a BPM process that gets initiated from an e-mail.

 We have used PushToEmail to send messages to the e-mail account of
the loan officer (weblogic0009@gmail.com). However, you are not
limited to use the PushToEmail SOA process. You can create or use
your own client to send messages to some-email@some-domain.
com, that is, you can create your own e-mail address and use it.

Publish-subscribe pattern – initiating the business process through an event

Business events comprise of message data published as the result of an occurrence
in a business environment. Other services/processes can subscribe to these events.
Business events are raised when a situation of interest occurs. For example, a
customer visits a lender's/bank's website and browses for a couple of bank products
such as home loans, mortgages, education loans, savings, wealth management, and
so on. During browsing, customers are asked to fill in their details.

Bank sales representatives contact the customer for a follow-up and to check the customer's interest in one/more of the products from the portfolio of products. Once the sales representative gauges a specific product interest of the customer, then they raise a specific product event through an application. For our example, we will assume that a Loan Origination event is raised by the sales representative.

The distinction between business events and direct service invocation based on WSDL is based on the fact that business events separate the consumer from the producer. The design consideration is to use events when the integration is loosely coupled.

Event-driven integration has an edge over the request-response integration pattern. In the request-response pattern, the scalability of the solution is difficult as the change is difficult; this further makes governance difficult. If a service contract changes, then the system needs to be changed. The request-response integration pattern does not result in a loosely coupled integration. The event-driven messaging pattern offers loose coupling, where the scalability and flexibility to add a new application is way easier than the request-response pattern. Events have their own message format (schema), and subscribers need to comply with it and take care of the transformations. Event-driven patterns are asynchronous, one-way message exchange patterns. Subscribers are not durable. They offer a flexible and agile architecture; however, durability remains an issue. The following table summarizes the publish-subscribe pattern:

Signature	Publish-Subscibe Pattern
Classification	Invocation Pattern
Intent	The participating process or application publishes events and messages that are subscribed to by one or more participating processes.
Motivation	The BPM process can be configured as a subscriber to the events that are raised in the **Event Driven Network** (**EDN**). These events trigger the BPM process.
Applicability	In the signal throw, signal end, signal catch, and Signal Start Events. Throw intermediate signal events or signal end events are used to raise and broadcast a signal. The Signal Start Event is used to receive an event in another process. To enable event delivery, you need an eventing platform. Oracle BPM uses Oracle EDN to send and receive signals.

Implementation	On execution, throw intermediate signal event or signal end event will publish an event to the EDN. The EDN will then deliver it to all the subscribers who are configured to listen to that specific event (signal). A subscriber process can trigger only when the signal to which it has subscribed arrives. Oracle BPM leverages Oracle SOA and the EDN runs within every SOA instance. Java/BPEL/Mediator or any component can raise an event to the underlying SOA environment to publish that event to the EDN. Any interested BPMN process as a subscriber to that event will get triggered when the signal to which it has subscribed arrives.
Known issues	Loss of messages, guaranteed message processing, and durability.
Known solution	EDN offers different levels of delivery consistency. You can always configure once and only when the delivery is transactional in nature and is delivered to the subscriber in its own transaction. You can use an effective error handling solution and a retry mechanism to achieve some level of guaranteed message processing. However, this might need every subscriber to make sure that the event gets successfully processed. In spite of that, a durable system cannot be guaranteed. If a system fails, the message may be lost and will not be delivered even when the system is restarted.

Loan origination over an event

As business events are published in the EDN, which runs within every SOA/BPM environment, we will first create a business event. Then, a process (the BPEL process) will be created to raise the sample Loan Origination event. A separate BPM process will subscribe to this event. The raised events are delivered by the EDN to the subscribing business process. Perform the following steps to define an event:

1. Open and expand the **LoanOriginationProcess** application and right-click on the **LoanOrigination** project.

2. Click on **New** to create an event. A gallery will open to create an event definition file and an event.

3. Scroll down in the list and select **Event Definition**. This will open the event creation page.

4. Enter `LoanEvent` as the name of the event definition (EDL) file.

5. Click on the green plus (**+**) sign to define an event and its type.

6. Enter the name as `LoanOriginationEvent` for the event and browse for the event type.

7. Choose the Loan origination schema as **Event Payload** (the event payload).

8. Click on **OK**. This will result in the creation of an event file and an event definition inside the EDL file. This is shown in the following screenshot:

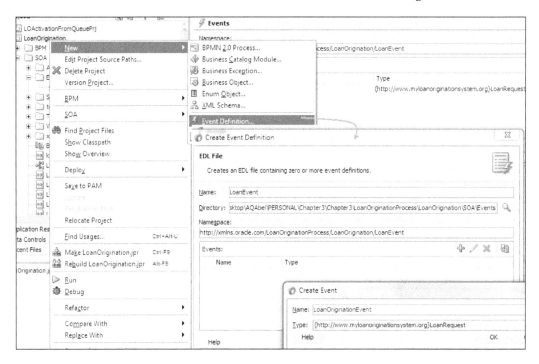

9. Once the event is defined, we can now create a BPEL process to raise an event.

10. Drag-and-drop a BPEL component in the `LoanOrigination` (the composite file) file.

11. Let the BPEL template be one-way and enter the name of the process as `LoanOriginationEventService`.

12. Choose **Loan origination schema** as the input schema of the BPEL process.

13. Click on **OK** in the process creation dialog.

14. Drag-and-drop an invoke activity into the BPEL process.

15. Choose **Interaction Type** as **Event**.

16. Browse for the event and select **LoanOriginationEvent**, and complete the configuration.

17. Drag and assign an activity before the **Invoke** activity, as shown in the following screenshot, and complete the assignment of values from the input receive parameter to the event input variable, **RaiseLoanoriginationEvent_InputVariable**:

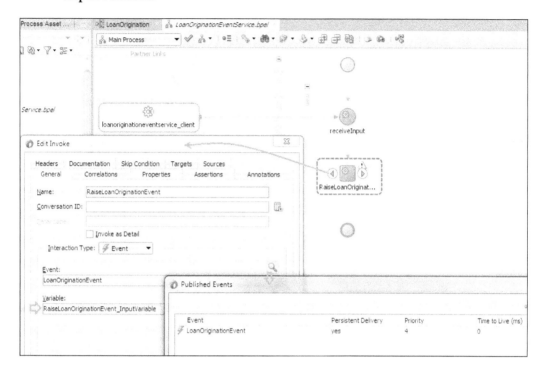

18. When you execute this process, `LoanOriginationEvent` is raised.

19. Your BPEL process should look as per the `LoanOriginationEventService` process defined in the `LoanOrigination` project, which you can download from this chapter's downloadable files.

Now, we will create the BPMN process that gets initiated when the event is raised by executing the BPEL process, `LoanOriginationEventService`, which we just defined in the preceding steps. To do so, perform the following steps:

1. Right-click on the **LoanOrigination** project and select **New** to choose the BPMN 2.0 process. This will open the process creation wizard.

2. Enter the name of the process as `LOProcessActivationFromEvent`.

3. Let the type be asynchronous service and click on **Finish**.

4. Define a process data object (**subscriberProcessIN_PDO**) based on the business object (**LOProcessBusinessObject**). You will find the business object with the project.

5. In the process editor, right-click on the Message Start Event and change the trigger type to **Signal**.

6. Name the Signal Start Event as SubscribeToLoanOrigination.

7. Right-click on the Signal Start Event, **SubscribeToLoanOrigination**, and go to its **Implementation** tab.

8. Browse for the **LoanOriginationEvent** event definition; this will define the subscription of the BPM process to the **LoanOriginationEvent** event.

9. Complete the data associations from the Signal Start Event to process the data object, **subscriberProcessIN_PDO**, as shown in the following screenshot:

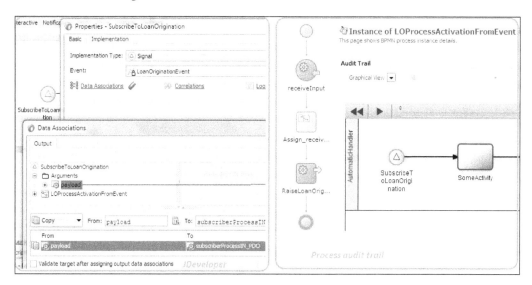

10. Deploy the process.

11. Log in to the EM as the admin user (web logic), http://server:host/em.

12. Execute the LoanOriginationEventService BPEL process, which will raise the **LoanOriginationEvent** event.

13. When the event is raised, the LOProcessActivationFromEvent process gets initiated as it has subscribed to the event.

14. Trace the flow of the **LOProcessActivationFromEvent** process, and we can verify that after the BPEL process raises the event, the BPMN process, **LOProcessActivationFromEvent**, gets initiated.

Business events raised by the **LoanOriginationEventService** BPEL process are published to an EDN that runs within the Oracle SOA/BPM infrastructure. Raised events are delivered by the EDN to the subscribing process, **LOProcessActivationFromEvent**, and the payload exchanged is as per the EDL schema definition.

Multievent instantiation pattern – process instantiation over multiple events

If we have the requirement to branch out our process flow based on external events, then the event-based gateway initiation mechanism is best suited for us. Here, several external events might occur; however, the path is chosen based on the occurrence of an event within your process design. We will use the loan origination use case to demonstrate this pattern. When the process is initiated, it will either be initiated for the new loan and get caught by the `NewLoanApplication` Message Catch Event, or if it gets initiated for an existing loan process instance, it will be caught by the `ReLoanApplication` Message Catch Event.

The Loan Processing event gateway initiates the sequence that has the `NewLoanApplication` message event, and the instance reaches subsequent activities and the downstream flow.

Loan origination over multiple event occurrence

The loan origination process can be instantiated for a new loan application and/or for an existing loan application. We can use an event-based gateway as a mechanism to branch based on the event received and the initiate process instance. There are multiple types of messages or events that can start a Loan Origination business process. Perform the following steps to verify the process configurations that have event-based gateways configured:

1. Download the **LoanOriginationProcess** application from the downloadable files for this chapter (available on the Packt website) and open `LoanOrigination`.

2. Click on the **LOProcessMultipleEvent** process.

3. Right-click on the event-based gateway, **LOProcessing**, and open the **Implementation** tab under its **Properties** page.

4. You can see that the **Instantiate** box is checked. For an event-based gateway to start new instances, it must be checked. However, there could be midprocess event-based gateways, and in such cases, we don't need to check the **Instantiate** box.

5. Right-click on the **NewLoanApplication** Message Catch Event. We can verify that while defining the interface; we can associate data and can enter a name for the operation as `newLoanApplication`, which will be exposed as shown in the following screenshot:

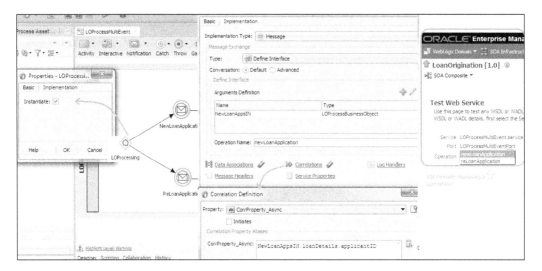

Remember to furnish correlation details. We have set the correlation based on **ApplicantID**. Correlation is a must when using event-based gateways as we will be developing this process to include midprocess events, and in those cases, the process flow needs to be in correlation.

6. Deploy the process and test it through the EM, `http://server:host/em`.

7. While testing the process, you can find two operations being exposed. Any client application or process using this Process as a service will have two operations to choose from.

Event-based gateways can be used midprocess as well as at the start of the process to initiate new process instances. The configuration demonstrated in the preceding steps, using an event-based gateway, is similar to multiple start events in the process. An event-based gateway can initiate a new process instance when it does not have any incoming sequence flow and the initiate property of the event gateway must be enabled. If the new loan application is raised by an external application, then the **NewLoanApplication** Message Catch Event can be initiated, or else the **ReLoanApplication** Message Catch Event can be initiated.

Human task initiator pattern – initiating processes through human tasks

The initiator task is one among the many human task interactive patterns in Oracle BPM. It's used to trigger a BPM process flow from the defined human task user interaction interface. When you are using the initiator task to initiate a BPM process, the process always starts with the none start event. The none start event will not trigger the process; however, the human task initiator will initiate the process. It's the role associated with the swim lane that defines the process participant, and that process participant/assignee is the one the initiator task gets assigned to. The following table summarizes the human initiator pattern:

Signature	Human Task Initiator Pattern
Classification	Invocation Pattern
Intent	The intent is to trigger a BPM process flow from a form initiated by a human activity.
Motivation	The BPM process can be configured to be triggered based on human interaction by submitting a form. The form can be accessed via a workspace application or a work list application.
Applicability	In the initiator human task
Implementation	When you are using the initiator task to initiate a BPM process, the process always starts with a none start event. The none start event will not trigger the process; however, the initiator human task will initiate the process. A user logs in to a workspace application and clicks on the link to kick-start the process. Upon clicking the link, the user is presented with a form where they can enter data as input to the process or the form can be preinitialized too. Once data is entered or edited, the user can click on the **Submit** button to instantiate the process.
Known issues	NA
Known solution	NA

The human task initiator can be used in various business scenarios. For instance, in the insurance claim process, a customer can call the **Customer Service Representative (CSR)** of the insurance organization and the CSR can raise a claim request on behalf of the customer. This claim request is a human task along with a task form available in the CSR's workspace application. The CSR has to fill in the human task form and click on **Submit** to initiate the claim process.

Loan origination via the human task form

In this section, we will build an initiator task and get it assigned to a user, salesrep, defined in myrealm (the embedded LDAP in the web logic server). For this example, we will assume that the user, salesrep, is the loan officer. We have the LoanOrigination project available in JDeveloper from the previous section downloads. We will build a new process for this section as follows:

1. In JDeveloper, navigate to **LoanOrigination** | **Processes** and create a new process by right-clicking on **Processes** and selecting **New**.

2. Enter a name for the process as LOProcessHumanInitiation.

3. Choose the manual process in the **Application Template** panel.

4. Click on **Finish**. This will create the LOProcessHumanInitiation process with an initiator user task.

5. Create the LOProcessHumanInitiationINPDO process data object based on the business object, **LOProcessBusinessObject**, which already exists in the **LoanOrigination** project as we created it in the first section of this chapter.

6. Double–click on the initiator human task and rename the initiator human task to LOProcessHumanInitiationTask.

7. Go to the **Implementation** tab of the **Properties** wizard.

8. Click on the plus (**+**) sign to create a human task.

9. Enter the **Human Task** name as LOProcessHumanInitiationTask and the title as shown in the following screenshot.

10. Add parameters to **Human Task**. This parameter is based on the loan origination schema's business object, **LOProcessBusinessObject**, which is based on the process data object.

11. Click on **OK** and finish the data association.

12. Click on **OK** again.

13. Drag an activity after the human task and name it `SomeOtherActivity`. Check the draft mode for the activity. (This activity is a placeholder or an assumption for further process activities). This is shown in the following screenshot:

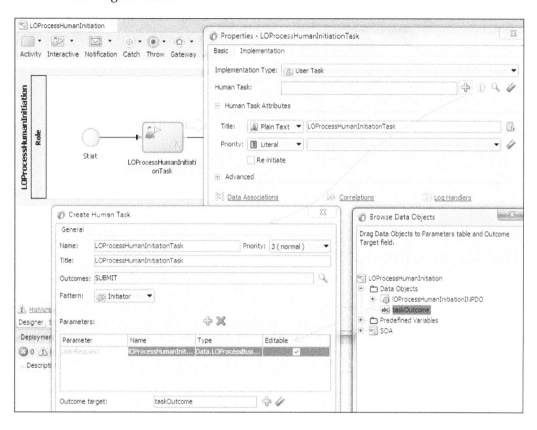

14. In the swim lane, select the **LoanOfficer** role. If it is not available, create the role.

15. Click on **Project (LoanOrigination)** and select **Organization**.

16. In the roles, select **LoanOfficer**, and in the **Members** section, browse for the embedded LDAP (**myrealm**) for the users.

17. Select **salesrep** as the user and click on **OK**.

18. Click on **Save** to save the process.

19. Right-click on the initiator human task in the process and select **Open Human Task**. This will open the `.task` task definition.

20. Confirm whether the application role in the task editor's general section is **LoanOriginationPrj.LoanOfficer**.

21. In the **General** tab of the task editor, click on **Create form** and select **Auto-Generate Task Form** to create a task user interface for the initiator human task.

22. Enter the name for the human task user interface as `Task Form` and click on **OK**.

23. This will launch the UI creation wizard. Complete the wizard and click on **Save ALL**.

24. Deploy the project with the human task UI.

 The LOProcessHumanInitiation process is available when we download the LoanOrigination project for this chapter. You can always create a new process with a new name to implement the scenario we discussed in the preceding steps.

Testing the process

Use the following steps to test the process and learn how you can instantiate process instances using the human task:

1. Log in to `http://localhost:7001/bpm/workspace` BPM workspace as the **salesrep** user.

2. We will find that the **LOProcessHumanInitiation** loan process got assigned to the **salesrep** user.

3. Click on the **LOProcessHumanInitiation** process in the **Applications** section, and this will initiate the user interface.

4. Enter the Loan Origination values and click on **Submit** to submit the loan origination request, as shown in the following screenshot:

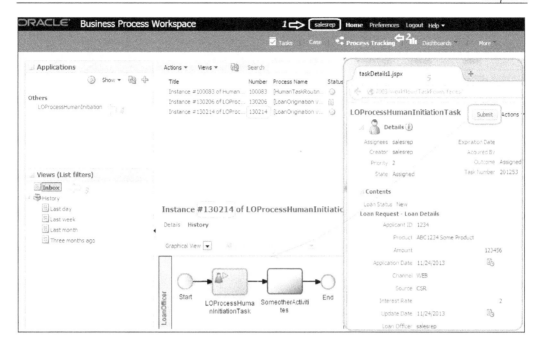

The initiator task followed by the none start event is an effective way to assign an application task with a user interface to the users. Also, users can initiate the BPM process from their inboxes in the BPM workspace application or the work list application.

Guaranteed delivery pattern – process instantiation over JMS – Queue/Topic

The initiation of a BPM process takes place through either exposing the BPM process as a web service, BPM reading a JMS, or through the BPM PAPI APIs, and so on. Other mechanisms may include processes instantiated with e-mails/files/batches (that is, from enterprise information systems) and scheduled mechanisms such as using timers. In this section, we will explore how to initiate a BPM process via a queue. Specifically, we will be using JMS queues, and for the sake of examples, we have limited the discussion around the web logic server and JMS queues. However, this pattern is not limited to web logic and can be used beyond it.

The following table lists the details around the guaranteed delivery pattern:

Signature	Guaranteed Delivery Pattern
Classification	Invocation Pattern
Intent	The participating process gets invoked by reading messages from a queue or a topic.
Motivation	Using queue messaging offers a foundation for the asynchronous and reliable delivery of messages in a distributed heterogeneous system. It also offers a scalable messaging architecture. A queue/topic-based solution offers point-to-point (Queue) and publish/subscribe (Topic) mechanisms, transaction boundaries, guaranteed information delivery, scalability, and interoperability between heterogeneous frameworks.
Applicability	Any web application, process, or service can push the message directly to a queue. The BPM process will pick up the message as soon as the message is dropped in the queue. With this mechanism, the message-producing application can continue to send new messages regardless of whether the BPM process is available or not. A JMS consumer, a BPM process with a JMS adapter, is responsible for dequeuing the messages and initiating the process. It now depends on the transactional boundaries (milestones) to make sure that the message gets removed from the queue only after the successful completion of the task in the BPM process.
Implementation	The source application 'A' pushes messages to Queue#1. The BPM process picks up the messages from the queue and takes care of the business logic. If anything fails, the message should remain in Queue#1. The message gets removed from Queue#1 only after the successful completion of the task in the BPM process.
Known issues	If integrating applications are interacting in an unreliable fashion.

Known solution	A best practice will be the inclusion of logical points (milestones) in the end-to-end integration. This translates to the fact that while implementing guaranteed delivery patterns, transactions should be considered as first-class citizens and must be dealt with effectively.
	For example, the source system pushes the message to the starting queue in one transaction and ensures the guaranteed delivery of the message in its zone. When the message first arrives in the queue— define this point as milestone#1 — the implementation process (service) will pick the message from the primary queue in a new transaction (Trx#1). The implementation process (service) will then enrich the message and routes the message to another milestone (milestone#2). Once the message reaches milestone#2, the services and resources in milestone#1 should be released. Moreover, all the services and components in milestone#1 should be enlisted in one transaction. Another process (service) should pick the message when milestone#2 is initiated and should interact with the target application. Activities in milestone#2, such as picking the message from the queue, transformation, enrichment, and interacting with the target application, should happen in one transaction.
Known issues	Processing overhead and business process performance
Known solution	Adding milestones could lead to processing overhead and performance challenges. Selecting the number of milestones should be given paramount consideration when designing the process. If you minimize the milestones(s), you might end up adding more work in a single transaction. The solution should be designed to allow optimum work between milestones, and transactions must be handled effectively. You should not end up with transactional overhead while ensuring reliable messaging between milestones and applications.

Loan origination over JMS – Queue/Topic

In this section, we will explore how to initiate a BPM process via a queue to demonstrate guaranteed delivery. The scenario is that the lender (bank) offers a portal (web) application that a user can access and request for a loan. That web application is based on the JMS framework, and it pushes messages to a loan queue (the JMS queue). The loan origination BPM process gets initiated when a message arrives in a loan queue.

Creating JMS resources

The JMS queue and topic used during this section are always associated with a number of other enabler resources that need to be defined in the web logic server. A **JMS server** is required to create **JMS modules,** as it is a container for all the resources defined in a JMS module. Your queues, connection factories, topics, bridges, and other resources are defined in the JMS module. **Subdeployment** is an optional resource. However, it is used to group targets. The JMS module and resources within JMS modules, such as queues and topics, are the targets to a JMS server / WSL server instance. We can have a subdeployment created to target the different components of a JMS module to a single/group of targets.

A **Connection Factory** encapsulates the connection configuration information, and enables the clients of JMS applications to create connections to JMS destinations. A Connection Factory supports concurrent use, enabling multiple threads to access the object simultaneously.

JMS supports two messaging models: **point-to-point** (**PTP**) and **publish/subscribe** (**pub/sub**). A **Queue** is used for the PTP messaging model that enables the delivery of a message to exactly one recipient, while **Topic** is used for the pub/sub messaging model to enable the delivery of a message to multiple recipients. Oracle SOA and BPM use the JMS adapter to relate (read/write) to JMS resources. You need connection pools to refer to Connection Factories associated with queues and topics. These JMS adapters are deployed to the web logic server, and the Connection Factories are configured in the JMS adapter.

The following are the steps to create a JMS queue and topic. Activities listed in the following section need to be performed at the web logic console, `http://server:host/console`, by logging in as the admin user (`weblogic`).

Creating a JMS server

Perform the following steps to create a JMS server in the web logic console:

1. In the domain structure, navigate to **Domain** | **Services** | **Messaging** | **JMS Servers**.
2. Click on **New** to create a new JMS server.
3. Enter the name of the JMS server as `LoanOrigJMSServer`; let the persistent store be **None** and click on **Next**.
4. Select the target as **soa_server1** or your available server.
5. Click on **Finish**.
6. The JMS server will be listed with **Health Status = OK**.

Creating a JMS module

Perform the following steps to create a JMS module in the web logic console:

1. Navigate to **Services** | **Messaging** | **JMS Modules** and select **New** to create a new JMS module.

2. Enter the name as `LoanOrigSystemModule` and the description, and click on **Next**.

3. Choose the target as **soa_server1**, or the one you selected while creating the JMS server, and click on **Next**.

4. Don't check the box to add resources and click on **Finish**.

5. You can see that a new JMS module is listed.

Creating a JMS subdeployment

Perform the following steps to create a JMS subdeployment in the web logic console:

1. Click on **LoanOrigSystemModule** and click on the **Sub Deployment** tab.

2. Click on **New** to create a new subdeployment.

3. Enter the name for the subdeployment as `LoanOrigSubDeployment` and click on **Next**.

4. In the targets, select the JMS server, **LoanOrigJMSServer**.

5. Click on **Finish**.

Creating a Connection Factory

Perform the following steps to create a Connection Factory in the web logic console:

1. Navigate to **Services** | **Messaging** | **JMS Modules** and select **New** to add resources.

2. Select **Connection Factory** and click on **Next**.

3. Enter the Connection Factory name as `LoanOrigConnFactory`.

4. Enter the Connection Factory JNDI as `jms/LoanOrigConnFactory`; leave the default as it is and click on **Next**.

5. Click on **Advance Targeting** and select the **LoanOrigSubDeployment** subdeployment, which we created earlier.

6. Click on **Finish**.

Creating a queue

Perform the following steps to create a JMS queue in a JMS module:

1. Navigate to **Services | Messaging | JMS Modules** and select **New** to add resources.

2. Select **Queue** and click on **Next**.

3. Enter the name and JNDI of the queue as `LoanOrigQueue` and `jms/LoanOrigQueue`, respectively.

4. Select the **LoanOrigSubDeployment** subdeployment and click on **Finish**.

5. You can now find the Connection Factory and the queue listed as resources in the JMS module.

Creating a topic

Perform the following steps to create a JMS topic in a JMS module:

1. Navigate to **Services | Messaging | JMS Modules** and select **New** to add resources.

2. Select **Topic** and click on **Next**.

3. Enter the name and JNDI of the topic as `LoanOrigTopic` and `jms/LoanOrigTopic`, respectively.

4. Select the **LoanOrigSubDeployment** subdeployment and click on **Finish**.

Configuring the connection pool

Perform the following steps to create a connection pool in the web logic console:

1. Navigate to WebLogic console | **Domain | Deployments**.

2. Scroll down and click on **JmsAdapter**.

3. Click on the **Configuration** tab, select **Outbound connection pool**, and expand it as `oracle.tip.adapter.jms.IJmsConnectionFactory`. This lists all the connection pools.

4. Click on **New** to create a new connection pool.

5. Select the **oracle.tip.adapter.jms.IJmsConnectionFactory** option and click on **Next**.

6. Enter `eis/wls/LoanOrig` as the connection pool JNDI name.

7. Click on **Finish** and navigate to the outbound connection factory properties.

8. Enter `jms/LoanOrigConnFactory` as the **Connection Factory Location** property value and hit *Enter*.

9. Save the property value configuration.

You will receive a message saying that the changes are activated (if the server is in the development mode). In any case, you will now update the JMS adapter, as follows, for the changes to take effect:

1. Click on the **Configuration** tab, select **Outbound connection pool**, and expand it as `oracle.tip.adapter.jms.IJmsConnectionFactory`. This lists all the connection pools.

2. Click on **New** to create a new connection pool.

3. Select the **oracle.tip.adapter.jms.IJmsConnectionFactory** option and click on **Next**.

4. Enter the connection pool JNDI name as `eis/wls/LoanOrigTopic`.

5. Click on **Finish** and navigate to the outbound connection factory properties.

6. Enter `jms/LoanOrigConnFactory` as the **Connection Factory Location** property value and hit *Enter*.

7. Enter `true` for **IsTopic**.

8. Save the property value configuration.

You will receive a message saying that the changes are activated (if the server is in the development mode). In any case, you now need to update the JMS adapter for the changes to take effect.

Redeploying the JMS adapter

Perform the following steps to deploy the JMS adapter with new configurations by updating the adapter:

1. Navigate to WebLogic console| **Domain**| **Deployments**.

2. Scroll down, click on **JmsAdapter**, and check the box close to **JMS adapter**.

3. Click on the **Update** button.

4. Select the **Update this application in place with new deployment plan changes** option, click on **Next**, and then click on **Finish**.

5. You will receive the following message:

   All changes have been activated. No restarts are necessary.
   Selected Deployments were updated.

Creating the publisher process

In a real-life scenario, as per our use case, a web application would push messages to the loan queue (**LoanOrigQueue**). However, for this demonstration, we will use an SOA process to produce a message to this queue. With the downloadable code for this chapter, we have the **LoanOriginationProcess** application. The **LoanOriginationProcess** application contains the **PublishLoanPrj** project. It's a simple BPEL process that exposes a SOAP interface and pushes messages to the **LoanOrigQueue** queue. Click on the **LoanPublishingProcess** BPEL process and check its configuration. We can visit the .jca file to verify the queue and the Connection Factory JNDI configured in the process in order to publish messages to the **LoanOrigQueue** queue.

Developing the consumer process

We will now create a subscriber process that subscribes to the **LoanOrigQueue** queue as follows, and the process gets initiated when a message of the loan request arrives at the queue:

1. In JDeveloper, go to **Application | LoanOrigination | BPM Processes**.
2. Right-click on **BPM Processes** and create a new process.
3. Select the type of process as **Asynchronous** and enter the name of the process as LOProcessActivationFromQueue.
4. Click on **Finish**.
5. Go to **LoanOrigination** (the composite file) of the **LoanOrigination** project.
6. Drag-and-drop a JMS adapter in the swimlane exposed service. This will open the JMS adapter configuration wizard.
7. Enter the name of the JMS adapter service as ConsumeLoanRequest and click on **Next** in the wizard.
8. Choose **JMS adapter** and click on **Next**.
9. Select the application server connection and click on **Next**.
10. Select the operation type as **Consume_Message** and click on **Next**.
11. Browse for the destination queue (**LoanOrigQueue**), enter the JNDI (eis/wls/LoanOrig), and click on **Next**.
12. Navigate to **Loan origination schema| Loan Request element**, click on **Next**, and then on **Finish**. Click on **Save all**.

This completes the configuration of a JMS subscriber service (the JMS adapter as a service). Now, we will continue with further procedures, as follows:

1. Go back to the **LOProcessActivationFromQueue** BPMN process and create a process input process data object, LOProcessActivationQueueINPDO, based on the business object (**LOProcessBusinessObject**).

2. Double-click on the Message Start Event to open the properties.

3. Enter the name for the Message Start Event as LoanOriginationSubscriber.

4. Click on the **Implementation** tab and select **Use Interface**.

5. Click on **Browse** in the reference interface section.

6. Browse and select the JMS adapter service, ConsumeLoanRequest, which you configured earlier.

7. The operation message (the consumer message) will automatically pop up.

8. Complete the data associations and click on **OK**.

9. Drag-and-drop an embedded subprocess and give it a name. Let the subprocess be in the draft mode. You will place this just as a token to demonstrate that further loan origination process flow activities and tasks will be defined later.

10. Assign a role to swimlane as **LoanOfficer**. It will already exist if you have completed the other sections; if not, create a role with the name LoanOfficer.

11. The process will look as shown in the following screenshot; save and deploy the process to web logic:

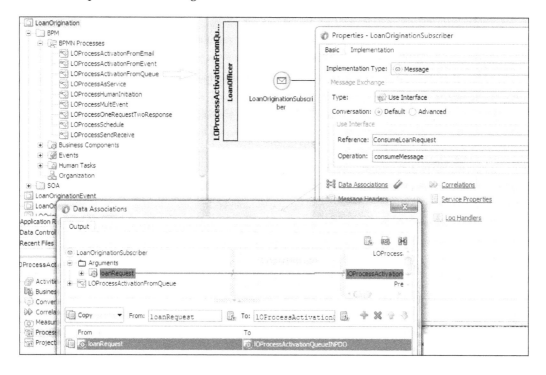

Testing the process

Execute the following steps to push a message to the queue:

1. Go to the EM console, `http://server:host/em`, and initiate the BPEL server loan publishing process. The BPEL service, **LOPublishingProcess**, when executed, will push the message to the queue.

2. Click on the **LoanOrigination** project and you will find an instance created for the **LOProcessActivationFromQueue** process, as follows:

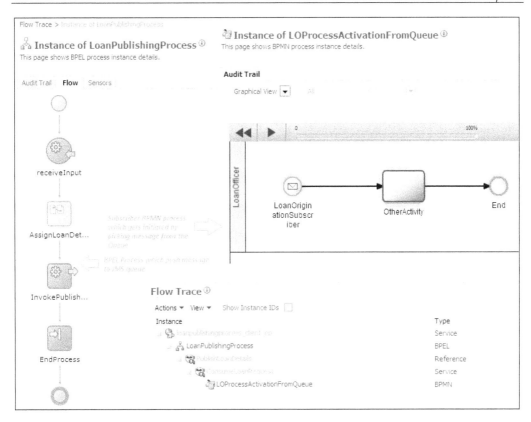

The `LOPublishingProcess` BPEL service pushes the loan request message to the `LoanOrigQueue` queue; the `LOProcessActivationFromQueue` process, which is subscribed to this queue, picks the messages from the same queue and initiates the BPMN process instance.

Publish-subscribe pattern using topics

This section will demonstrate the publish-subscribe pattern using topics. Once the loan origination process is completed — after the underwriting, contracting and legalizing, and loan funding — there might be many other processes interested. For example, when the loan origination process ends, a business might initiate a back office process that would set dates, time, and other follow-up details to check for the initial month's EMI payment of the loan of the customer. There might be a process for when you may be interested to know which applicant's request loans are disbursed, and then these processes can set a follow-up communication with the same customer for other product offerings.

Let's name these processes as `Bank Office Process` and `Advertisement Process`. For enabling this functionality, we will use the JMS topics (which we created in the previous section). We can change the end event for the `LOProcessActivationFromQueue` process. Once the `LOProcessActivationFromQueue` process ends, it will publish a message to the `LoanOrigTopic` topic. We can create two new BPMN processes named `BackOfficeProcess` and `Advertisement Process`, which can be subscribed to the `LoanOrigTopic` topic. As soon as the `LOProcessActivationFromQueue` process ends and loan information is published, these two processes start.

Understanding multiple start events

We can implement processes that can start by multiple methods. In the following screenshot, we can see that there are multiple start activities for the process. The loan process can subscribe to a queue, and at the same time, it can subscribe to a topic. Also, it can be instantiated by a human task or can be scheduled:

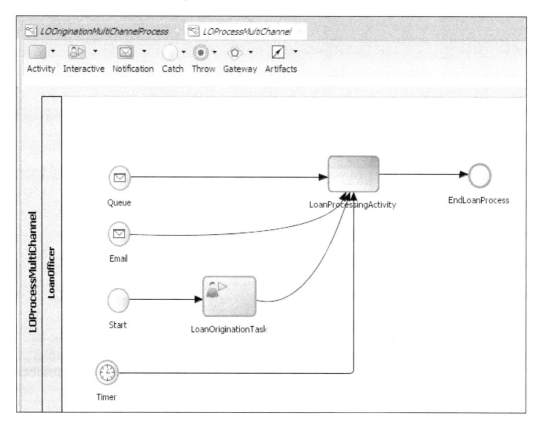

Summary

This chapter demonstrated the different BPM process invocation patterns. BPM processes can be exposed as a service and can be invoked using different message exchange patterns. This chapter showcased the initiation of a BPM process from a human task, e-mail, timers, and so on. You also learned how to engulf loose coupling, scalability, and durability with the publish-subscribe pattern. On the other hand, you have also walked through the details to implement guaranteed delivery and reliability through queues. We also covered the one-request-two-response pattern and two-request-one-response pattern along with the one-way messaging pattern. Different ways to implement patterns are also discussed in this chapter. While learning different patterns, we have also covered various service invocations, tasks, and activities such as Send and Receive tasks, Service tasks, and so on, and have learned various events and activities.

The next chapter is focused on human task patterns. We will learn how to incorporate human intuition in processes and various patterns to support it.

4
Human Task Patterns

Business processes need human interactions for approvals, exception management, interactions with a running process, group collaboration, document reviews or case management, and so on. There are various requirements for enabling human interaction and human intuition within a running BPMN process, which are accomplished using human tasks in the Oracle BPM. This chapter is dedicated to demonstrating human task patterns. In order to bring in the human intuition and human decision mechanism in the process, Oracle BPMN 12c offers you human tasks (user tasks).

Human tasks are implemented by human workflow services that are responsible for the routing of tasks, assignment of tasks to users, and so on. When a token arrives at the user task, the control is passed from the BPM process to Oracle Human Workflow, and the token remains with human tasks until it's completed. As callbacks are defined implicitly once the workflow is completed, the control is returned back to the user task and the token moves ahead to subsequent flow activities. However, if you terminate a BPM process while it is running a user task, the associated human task will keep running as human tasks are independent of the BPM processes. Actions taken on a human task can interact with the process until the process instance has left the user task. Even when the process instance has left the user task, you can still access the user task. However, any actions taken on the task will not bring any interaction with the process and it will not appear even in the audit trail.

This chapter covers a rich set of patterns, from milestone patterns to routing patterns. Oracle BPM offers several human task patterns such as the initiate task, user task, management task, group-voting task, For Your Information (FYI), and complex task patterns, which are covered in this chapter through a detailed description on routing patterns. The chapter also covers patterns that allow you to explore various participant list-building patterns. Task assignment patterns, ad hoc assignment patterns, delegation patterns, and escalation patterns are discussed in depth in the chapter.

Various advanced features such as exclusion, notification, ECM integration, and access policy are covered in detail along with routing patterns, delegation patterns, and so on. These set of patterns and features offer formalized best practices that allow process analysts, developers, and designers to build solutions for the commonly occurring issues and challenges, seamlessly bringing in human intuition in the BPMN process.

In this chapter, we will focus on the following patterns and features:

- Milestone pattern
- Routing pattern
- Assignment patterns
- List builder patterns
- Parallel routing pattern
- Serial routing pattern
- Single routing pattern
- FYI pattern
- Task aggregation pattern
- Dispatching pattern
- Escalation pattern
- Rule-based reassignment and delegation pattern
- Ad hoc routing pattern
- Request info feature
- Reassignment and delegation pattern
- Force completion pattern
- Routing rule pattern
- Error assignees and reviewers
- Deadline
- Escalation, expiry, and renewal
- Exclusion
- Error assignee and reviewer
- Notification
- Content access policy and task actions
- Enterprise content management for task documents

Learning about human tasks

In this section, we will create a simple BPM process and configure the human task for each pattern. However, before we start talking about human task patterns, let's understand some of the definitions that we will follow throughout this chapter.

We will discuss building a list of participants, routing to participants, task assignments, escalations, and so on in this chapter. Participants will remain the core of the discussion. Participants are users who act on the tasks. They are defined in the assignment and routing policy definition. In the first screenshot of this chapter, each participant block with the icon that represents people is a participant. We are talking about human tasks and user tasks, and it's the user (participant) who needs to act on them. The following are the types of participants:

- **Users**: This refers to the individual users who act on a task. Users are defined in an embedded LDAP (`myrealm`) in Oracle SOA, or they can be in the Oracle Internet directory or an external/third-party LDAP directory.

- **Groups**: A task can be assigned to a group. A group contains individual users who can claim and act on the task. For example, `Christine` and `Richa` could be from **SalesAgentGroup** and the task could be assigned to a **SalesAgentGroup** group. A group can be defined in the LDAP, such as `myrealm`, or a group can be generated dynamically.

- **Roles**: They are created as application roles under the `OracleBPMProcessRolesApp`. `OracleBPMProcessRolesApp` application, which is a `weblogic` application that contains application roles and swimlane roles. There are two types:
  - **Application roles**: Users and other roles can be grouped logically using application roles. They represent any roles in the organization. They are created in addition to the swimlane roles defined during design time. These roles are specific to applications and are not stored in the identity store. An application role can be used as a task assignee or as a grantee of another application role. As they are application-specific, they are defined in the application policy store and are used by the application directly. These roles basically define a policy. Roles that can be defined at design time can also be defined at runtime using the EM console. They can be created by using either the Oracle BPM Studio or the process workspace.

- ° **Swimlane roles**: These roles are created at design time in the BPM studio. Once defined, they are mapped to an application role that was created during deployment. This mapping cannot be changed after the deployment. Participants are assigned swimlane roles while defining organizations in the BPM studio or from the workspace application. Members of the roles can perform actions on the task at runtime. Swimlane roles are application roles that are also contained in `OracleBPMProcessRolesApp`.

- ° **Approval Groups**: This is used to define and manage a group of participants/users. Approval groups are defined in the BPM workspace. They can be static or dynamic approval groups. To learn more about dynamic approval groups, refer to `http://acharyavivek.wordpress.com/2012/02/27/dynamic-approval-group-bpm-workspace/`.

- **Organizational roles (parametric roles):** These are logical roles. Members of parametric roles are evaluated dynamically at runtime. Parametric roles are based on the process roles that are created when you deploy a BPM process, or you can also create them in the administration section of the Oracle BPM workspace. They basically use the application roles to build a query on `OracleBPMProcessRolesApp`. These roles have defined parameters and based on these parameters, assignees of a task are derived. This is a dynamic way to assign participants. For example, if the industry is IT, then the `ITSalesrepApproverRole` application role must be selected. If the industry is MFG, then the `MFGSalesrepApproverRole` application role must be selected. Here, the industry can be defined as a parameter (the plain text or Xpath expression) and can be passed from the task to the parametric role. The parametric role will have the condition to evaluate the parameters based on the parameter industry.

In this section, we will perform the following exercise in order to understand the human task configuration offered in the project delivered with this chapter. This project will remain the baseline for the demos that we will execute while learning various patterns:

1. Download `HumanTaskApps` from the download link for this chapter.

2. Open `HumanTaskPrj` and click on the **SalesQuoteProcess** BPM process.

You will find all the user task patterns being configured in the process. Click on each task and analyze its task metadata:

- **Initiator user task**: This is used to initiate the process from worklist applications. Assignees are calculated from the roles associated with the swimlane. Click on the `.task` file for the initiator task to analyze the task configuration in the task metadata. Click on the **Assignment** tab in the task metadata. You will find that you can neither add more stages nor participants. A user who has the swimlane role will find a link in the workspace, and the user can initiate the process from that link.

- **User task**: This is the default pattern with the participant type as single. This pattern is useful when a single user action is required, such as confirmation, decision, and so on. Participants are defined by the swimlane for this pattern.

- **FYI task**: This is similar to the user task pattern; however, it's meant only to send notifications and participants are not supposed to act on the task. The participant type is FYI. When a token arrives at the FYI task, the control is not passed from the BPM process to Oracle Human Workflow, and the process does not wait for the task completion and executes subsequent activities. Default assignees are the role associated with the swimlane to which a task belongs, and a notification is sent to all the participants that belong to the role.

- **Group task**: This pattern is useful when the tasks need to be performed in parallel.

- **Management task**: This pattern is useful when users are defined based on levels in the management hierarchy.

- **Complex task**: This pattern allows you to define a complex routing slip.

When analyzing each human task in the project, it's evident that it comprises of various features such as assignments, routing, participant lists, assignment patterns, and so on. Oracle BPM offers these patterns as a template for developers, which can be extended. We will be using complex approval patterns to look into all the building components in subsequent sections of this chapter.

Participants are logically grouped using stages that define the assignment within the routing slip. Assignments can be grouped based on assignment modeling patterns. Based on assignment modeling patterns, these can be sequential, parallel, or hybrid. The participant configuration and routing of the human task is enabled in the routing slip. The routing of the tasks to participants is governed by the routing pattern, which is a behavioral pattern. This defines whether one participant needs to act on a task, many participants need to act in sequence, all participants need to act in parallel, or participants need not act at all (covered in the routing pattern). Participants of the task are built using participant list-building patterns, such as approval groups, management chains, and so on.

The assignment of the participant is performed by task assignment mechanisms such as static, dynamic, and rule-based. Tasks can be manually claimed by the user, or they can be automatically assigned by automatic task dispatching through dynamic assignment patterns (covered in the *Dispatching pattern* section).

Milestone pattern

The following pattern table highlights facts around Milestone Pattern:

Signature	Milestone Pattern
Classification	Human Task Pattern
Intent	The logical indicative of the key milestones within the approval sequence.
Motivation	The motive is to define the task routing. Modeling task routing and assignments are termed as milestone patterns. A stage(s) defines the milestone and is the core task sequence modeling pattern. Stages are used to model task routing, which allows you to identify the key milestones within the approval sequence. They are a logical grouping of participant blocks.
Applicability	Stages can be in sequence or in parallel, and while modeling a routing slip, you can have one or more stages. Each stage has a participant block that has a participant type, which in turn consists of a list builder that determines the list of approvers. The stages are for the following reasons: • Dividing the complex task into smaller scopes • Grouping participant types in blocks • Modeling, and hence, defining the execution sequence of the approval process for the task • Defining a set of approvals for a collection • Defining the state model that can be simple, complex, and can be sequential, parallel, or hybrid
Implementation	When collections are defined, JDeveloper will determine whether they can be repeating elements or not. This definition of collections is helpful when collections are associated with stages. Associate a nonrepeating collection with a singular stage. However, associate a repeating collection with the stage that needs to get repeated in parallel for each element in the collection. The repetition of stage on collection elements, as explained previously, is the runtime behavioral pattern.
Known issues	NA
Known solution	NA

A stage can be repeating or nonrepeating. You can associate a nonrepeating collection with a nonrepeatable stage. However, if you want to repeat a stage in parallel for each element in the collection, then a repeating collection needs to be associated with the stage. For example, if a sales quote has 10 lines, the stage is repeated 10 times in parallel. Download `HumanTaskApps` and open **HumanTaskPrj**. Perform these steps if you have not already downloaded `HumanTaskApps`. Open the `ComplexTasks.task` files. We will develop the complex task for this scenario with the following steps:

1. Click on the **ComplexTasks.task** file; this will open the human task metadata editor. Go to the **Data** section and analyze the data element. This is based on the quote request element in `Quote.xsd`.

 Navigate to `HumanTaskPrj` |SOA |XSD/Schemas |Quote.xsd to open and analyze the quote schema.

2. Double-click on **Stage 1 (ProductLineItemApproval)** to open the stage editor.

You can verify that a collection is being defined on product items. Product items are repeating data elements in the quote schema. The Xpath expression for it is / `task:task/task:payload/ns0:QuoteRequest/ns0:ProductItem`.

We would repeat a stage in parallel for each item in the product collection, and hence, a collection is defined here. This can also be based on the entity or SDO. The following steps show you the nature of each stage in the sequence task flow:

- **Stage 1 (ProductLineItemApproval)** is for the line items, and it is based on collections as will be repeated.
- **Stage 2 (ProductHeaderApproval)** is nonrepeating and is based on header values.
- **Stage 3 (LegalApproval)** and **Stage 4 (ContractApproval)** are also nonrepeating.
- **Stage 1** and **Stage 2** are in sequence, while **stage 3** and **stage 4** are in parallel. However, **stage 2** is in sequence with **stage 3** and **stage 4**.

Walk through the following steps to model the sequence flow:

1. Open the **Assignment** section of the task metadata. The assignment and routing section helps you define the sequence flow of the task. For a new complex task, this would be empty. This is an Oracle-BPM-offered task with no seeded template and can be modeled and build as per business requirements.

2. Click on the stage and name it `ProductLineItemApproval`.

3. Enable the radio button repeat stage in parallel for each item in a collection. This will open the collection item that is based on a voting pattern. If 50 percent of the items (elements) in the collection are approved, then the task is approved, or if 30 percent of the items (elements) are rejected, then the task is rejected. Choose either to trigger the outcome immediately or wait until all the votes are in before triggering the outcome.

4. Click on the green plus sign on top of the screen and select **Sequential Stage**.

5. A new stage in sequence with the **ProductLineItemApproval** stage will be created. Name it `ProductHeaderApproval`.

6. Enable the radio button – nonrepeating – as we don't want it to be based on collections and it needs to be performed only once for the header level information.

7. Click on the green plus sign on top of the screen and select **Sequential Stage**. You will create a third stage. Name it **LegalApproval** and let it be nonrepeating too.

8. While you are in the third stage, which is **LegalApproval**, click on the green plus sign to create a parallel stage. This will create a stage in parallel with the third stage. Name the newly created stage **ContractApproval** and let it be nonrepeating as well.

The stage will be a sequence flow that defines task routing, as shown in the following screenshot:

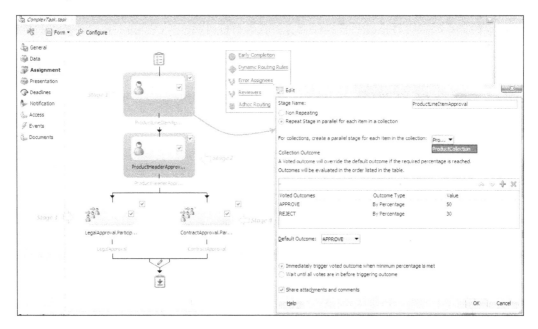

Now, you might be thinking that we can perform such task modeling in a BPM process too. Why model in a human task? The following section answers this question.

Modeling in a human task versus a BPMN process

The routing of tasks can be modeled in a human task, as well as in a BPMN process. This purely depends on the business requirement and various modeling considerations. For instance, if you are looking for greater business visibility and if there is a requirement to use exceptional handling, then it's good to model the task in the BPMN process itself. However, if you are looking for dynamism, abstraction, dynamic assignment, dynamic routing, and rules-driven routing, then modeling task routing in the human task assignment and routing is an enhanced modeling mechanism.

Routing pattern

The following pattern table highlights facts around Routing Pattern:

Signature	Routing Pattern
Classification	Human Task Pattern
Intent	Assignment of task participants. At each stage, you can define participant blocks that have participant types that participants are associated with. Behaviors of participants are defined by the routing patterns.
Motivation	Tasks can be routed to participants based on the routing pattern that governs the behavioral pattern of the participants.
Applicability	A participant type is grouped in a participant block under a stage. You can create a parallel or sequential participant block that contains participant types. Each participant type can have its own routing pattern and its own way to build the list of participants. However, it's the routing pattern defined for the participant type that defines the behavior of the participant.
	Whether all the participants need to act in parallel or in sequence or whether they don't need to act at all is defined by the routing pattern defined in the participant type. Hence, the routing pattern defines the behavioral patterns of the participants. The list of participants is derived based on list-building patterns such as management chain, approval group, and so on.

Implementation	This chapter demonstrates various types of routing patterns in detail.
Known issues	NA
Known solution	NA

The following are the different routing patterns that are required to route a task:

- **Single approver**: The task is assigned to a single user, group, or role. For example, a vacation approval request is assigned to a manager. If the manager approves or rejects the request, the employee is notified of the decision. If the task is assigned to a group, then one of the managers acts on it and the task is completed. If the list of participants is built using an approval group, then the task is assigned to the group; however, once one of the users in the group acts on the task, it's considered complete.

- **Parallel**: This is like voting. The task is assigned to a set of people who must work in parallel. For example, a task gets approved once 50 percent of the participants approve it. You can also set it up to be a unanimous vote. For example, a loan request is considered approved when 50 percent of the participants approve it, it's considered rejected when 40 percent of the participants reject it, and so on.

- **Serial**: Participants must work in sequence. The most common scenario for this is the management chain escalation. For example, a list of participants is built using a dynamic approval group, and the participants are assigned tasks in a sequence. If one participant completes the task, then the next participant is assigned the task, and so on. Participants have to act in a serial fashion.

- **FYI**: The task is assigned to participants who can view it, add comments and attachments, but cannot modify or complete the task. It's just like a notification, and no one is supposed to act on it. The process token remains with the BPM process and the control is not passed on to the human workflow, and the main process executes subsequent activities.

Task assignment pattern

The following pattern table highlights facts around Task Assignment Pattern:

Signature	Task Assignment Pattern
Classification	Human Task Pattern
Intent	The assignment of user(s), group(s), and roles to human tasks.
Motivation	Assigning participants to tasks either statically, dynamically, or derived based on business rules.

Applicability	There are different methods to assign user(s), group(s), and roles to tasks, which are covered in this section.
Implementation	The user(s), group(s), and roles can be assigned to tasks at design time or can be derived at runtime. Runtime derivation can also be based on rules.
Known issues	NA
Known solution	NA

After going through the types of participants, it would be interesting to know how participants (users, groups, and application roles) are assigned to the tasks. The following are the methods for assigning users, groups, and application roles to tasks:

- **Static assignment**: Static users, groups, or application roles can be assigned to a task at design time. You can statically assign a user(s), group(s), and roles to a task where the decision of an assignment is taken at design time.

- **Dynamic assignment**: Users, groups, and application roles can be assigned to a task dynamically at runtime when the task assignment pattern is getting executed. The following are the ways to perform the dynamic task assignment:

  - **Task assignment patterns**: We will go into more detail on this subject in subsequent sections. This chapter has covered various routing patterns, and varied task assignment patterns have been covered in these patterns.

  - **Using the XPath expression builder**: With the XPath expression builder, you can derive users. You can use XPath expression builders to define queries that will result in assigning users to tasks during the process execution.

  - Business rules.

  - The organizational role (parametric roles).

  - External routing.

 Dynamic task assignment is covered in detail in the article published on the Packt Publishing website (http://www.packtpub.com/article-network).

- **Nonfunction-based derivation**: Queries that result in assigning a user(s), group(s), and roles to the task during the process execution can be based on the XPath expression that derives values from the task payload itself. For example, if payload contains data that has approvers, then you can build an XPath expression to determine a user from there just like the `/task:task/task:payload/ns0:QuoteRequest/ns0:LicenseTerm/ns0:Approval/ns0:Approver` field in the `SalesQuote` schema offers the approver.

- **Function-based derivation**: You can use functions in XPath expressions to derive the users, groups, and so on. This is shown in the following bullet list:

    - `ids:getManager` (`richa`, `jazn.com`): This returns the manager of `richa`

    - `ids:getReportees` (`christine`, `2`, `jazn.com`): This returns all reportees of Christine up to two levels

    - `ids:getUsersInGroup` (`SalesOfficerGroup`, `false`, `jazn.com`): This returns all direct and indirect users in the `SalesOfficerGroup` group

- **Rule-based assignment**: You can use business rules to build the list of participants by using complex expressions.

List builder pattern

The following pattern table highlights facts around List Builder Pattern:

Signature	List Builder Pattern
Classification	Human Task Pattern
Intent	Deriving the actual list of participants to act on the task.
Motivation	Stages have participant blocks, which have participant types. Each participant type has a routing pattern that defines the participant's behavioral pattern. In a specific routing pattern, the list of participants is derived based on list-building patterns such as the management chain, approval group, and so on.
Applicability	This specifies the collection of participants. The list builder pattern can be hierarchical, nonhierarchical, or it can be rule-driven.
Implementation	This is implemented inside the routing pattern. Each routing pattern section in this chapter covers the associated list builder pattern in detail.
Known issues	NA
Known solution	NA

The following are the different categories and functions of the list builder pattern.

Absolute or nonhierarchical list builders

These list builders create participant lists based on the static assignment of a user(s), group(s), and roles, deriving statically/dynamically from approval groups or dynamically from application roles. However, the list is not based on an organizational or role hierarchy. The following is the list of nonhierarchical list builder patterns:

Pattern	Description
Name and expression	These lists enable you to statically or dynamically select users, groups, or application roles as task assignees. This pattern enables you to construct a list using static names or names that come from XPath expressions. If the identification type is the name or group, it would allow you to browse and build the list from the LDAP. If the identification type is the application role, you are allowed to browse **OracleBPMProcessRolesApp**. Here, the group is a group defined in the LDAP and is different from the approval group defined in the workspace application.
Approval groups	This is a pattern that defines and manages the group of participants/users. Approval groups are defined in the BPM workspace. They can be static or dynamic approval groups. You can use worklist applications to configure approval groups. The static approval group is a static and predefined list of approvers. Approvers are derived at runtime in the case of dynamic approval groups. Use dynamic approval groups when you need to calculate the approval group dynamically, based on the task payload. For example, for each sales quote line, we can have a different set of approvers based on the quantity defined in the line. If the quantity is greater than 100, you might need to derive a different group, or if the quantity is less than 100, then derive a different set of users based on an approval group. You can use business rules and model this flow in the BPM process; however, it becomes more efficient to model such scenarios in rule-based dynamic/static approval groups. An approval group can be defined as a value in the approval group pattern, or it can be based on rules.
Lane participant	Participants are derived based on the swimlane in which the user task is positioned in the BPM process. This could be the current swimlane participant or the previous swimlane participant.

Pattern	Description
Parametric Role	These are logical roles. Members of parametric roles are evaluated dynamically at runtime. Parametric roles are based on the process roles that are created when you deploy a BPM process, or you can also create them in the administration section in the Oracle BPM workspace. They basically use the application roles to build a query on OracleBPMProcessRolesApp. These roles have defined parameters and based on these parameters, assignees of a task are derived. This is a dynamic way to assign participants. For example, if the industry is IT, then the ITSalesrepApproverRole application role must be selected. If the industry is MFG, then the MFGSalesrepApproverRole application role must be selected. Here, the industry can be defined as a parameter (plain text or the Xpath expression) and can be passed from the task to the parametric role. The parametric role will have the condition to evaluate the task based on the industry parameter.

You can read more about the parametric role by reading the dynamic task assignment article published on the Packt Publishing website (http://www.packtpub.com/article-network). For more information on dynamic approval groups, please visit http://acharyavivek.wordpress.com/2012/02/27/dynamic-approval-group-bpm-workspace/.

Hierarchical list builders

These patterns are mostly used for serial routing patterns. The participant list is built using the organization or role hierarchy. The following is the list of hierarchical list builder patterns:

Pattern	Description
Management chain	The management chain list builder pattern is used for serial approvals through multiple users in a management chain hierarchy. To configure a management chain list-building pattern, you have to specify a starting participant (user/group/role), a top participant title, and/or the number of levels. The computation of the number of level is absolute and starts from the starting participant. For example, if you want the task to be approved by the starting participant and his/her manager, then specify the starting participant and number of level as 1. The management chain hierarchy is always computed based on users defined in the embedded LDAP, active directory, or third-party-configured LDAP.

Pattern	Description
Supervisory	Starting from a given approver, the list of participants climb up the approvers list and generates a chain that has a fixed number of approvers in it. While configuring the supervisory list builder pattern, you have to supply starting participants, top participants, and the supervisory level. The starting participant is the default to the initiator's manager. Hence, if no value is specified, then the initiator's manager is considered as the starting participant and the task gets assigned to it. Here, the top participant is not a title. While in the job level hierarchy, you can use a title as the top participant. This pattern traverses the supervisory hierarchy.
Job level	Starting from a given approver, the list of participants climbs up the supervisory hierarchy until an approver with a specified job level is found. This can be value-based or rule-based. This pattern traverses the job level hierarchy. This pattern allows you to specify the starting participant and top participant. Levels that are defined are relative to the starting participant or task creator. This allows you the flexibility to include all managers at the last level. It also allows you to define the utilization of the participants. You can define whether you want to utilize all the participants from the list, or the first and the last person from the list, or only the last person from the list. It stops when the top participant is reached or the top job level criteria are met.
Position	List building starts at the requester or a given approver's position and goes up until a specific number of level or a position is met.

Rule-based list builders

Business rules can be used to create a list of participants. However, business rules can also be part of a different type of list builder. For example, **Name and expression** is the main list builder mechanism; however, attributes are specified using rules and not values. When using rule-based attributes inside a different list builder, the action of the rule is in accordance with the type of the main list builder.

It's always effective to use the rule-based list builder in comparison to using rules in some other list builder, because the action of the rule is based on its definition and is not in accordance with the other list builder type in which it is included.

Rules are defined using Oracle business rules. The moment you configure the rule-based list-building pattern, a decision service is created. You will get the rule dictionary created at `<Task Name>Rules.Rules` and `<Task name>RulesBase.rule`.

The first one is referred to as the runtime rule dictionary (the custom dictionary) and the other is referred to as the base design time rule dictionary. Always use the first rule dictionary to engulf any runtime changes. Different rule dictionaries have advantages for customization scenarios. For example, you create and ship Version 1 of an application to a customer. The customer then customizes the rule sets in the application with the Oracle SOA composer. These customizations are now stored in a different rule dictionary and not the base rule dictionary.

The rule dictionary that stores the customized rule sets links with the rules in the base dictionary. When you ship Version 2 of the application later, the base rule dictionary might contain additional changes introduced in the product. The rule set customization changes that were previously performed by the customer are preserved and available with the new changes in the base dictionary.

We can use one of the following functions in the business rule's action to derive the list of participants:

- **CreateResourceList**: This function matches the **Names and Expressions** list builder
- **CreateApprovalGroupList:** This function matches the approval groups list builder
- **CreateManagementChainList:** This function matches the management chain list builder
- **CreateSupervisoryList**: This function matches the supervisory list builder
- **CreateJobLevelList:** This function matches the job level list builder
- **CreatePositionList**: This function matches the position list builder

With the specified rule set, two other rule sets are created: the substitution rule set and the modification rule set. The substitution rule uses the seeded substitution function that allows you to substitute users, groups, and roles in the created lists with different users, groups, and roles. Modification rules use seeded functions — extend and truncate — that allow you to extend or truncate the participant lists. However, the modification rule is applicable to the job level and position-based list builders. The example that demonstrates the list substation is covered in the *Serial routing pattern with list builder* section.

Parallel routing pattern

The following pattern table highlights facts around Parallel Routing Pattern:

Signature	Parallel Routing Pattern
Classification	Human Task Pattern
Intent	A set of the people (participants) must work in parallel.
Motivation	This is like a voting process where multiple users have to provide their opinion or vote.
Applicability	This pattern is useful in scenarios where multiple users have to provide their opinion or vote. You have to specify a voted-upon outcome that will override the default outcome selected in the default outcome list. The voted-upon outcome takes effect when the required percentage is reached. Voted-upon outcomes are evaluated in the order in which they are listed in the table.
Known issues	NA
Known solution	NA

A task is assigned to a set of people who must work in parallel. For example, a task gets approved once 50 percent of the participants approve it. You can also set it up to be a unanimous vote. For example, a loan request is considered approved when 50 percent of the participants approve it, and it's considered rejected when 40 percent of the participants reject it, and so on. In this section, we will enlist the working of a parallel routing pattern for different list builders.

Getting ready to test sample use cases

To test the samples demonstrated for this pattern, we need to perform the following activities:

- Log in to the `weblogic` console and create users (`Christine`, `Jim`, `Kim`, `Lata`, `salesrep`, and so on) in `myreal` (the embedded LDAP). Other users will be available to you if you have installed the demo community by following the installation steps enlisted in *Appendix, Installing Oracle BPM Suite 12c*.

- Log in to the BPM workspace as an admin user and navigate to the following path to create an organization unit (SalesOrg) and assign users (Christine, achrist, cdyole, lata, jcooper, jstein, Kim, Jim, fkafka, wfaulk, and cdickens) to the organization. The path is BPM Workspace | Administration | Organization | Organization Units.

- Log in to the BPM workspace and navigate to the mentioned path to create a static approval group (MFGSalesAdmin) and associate user (Christine, salesrep, Jim, and Kim) to the static approval group. The path is BPM Workspace | Administration | Task Administration | Approval Group. Static approval groups are predetermined lists of approvers, while dynamic approval groups generate approver lists at run time. The outcome will be decided based on the voting pattern.

- Log in to the WebLogic console and navigate to **myrealm** to create a group (ITSalesrepAdmin) and to assign users (achrist, jcooper, jstein, and fkafka) to this group.

Parallel routing pattern with name and expression list builders

If you want to configure the parallel routing pattern with the name and expression list builder pattern using the participant identification type (users/groups/roles), then you can browse the LDAP to identify the user/group. If the identification type is the application role, we are allowed to browse OracleBPMProcessRolesApp. Download and open the project in order to open the task and check its configuration. The stage is configured over a collection to implement the product items. Create the participant type with the parallel routing pattern using the following steps:

1. Download HumanTaskApps and open the HumanTaskRouting project in JDeveloper 12c.

2. Open the ParallelRoutingTask task, and navigate to the assignment section in the task metadata editor.

3. Enter a label for the routing pattern as ProductItem. ParallelParticipantBasedOnNameExpression.

4. Configure the voting pattern. The voting outcome is defined in the percentage. Hence, if 75 percent of the participants approve the task, then the task outcome will be **APPROVE**. If 25 percent of the participants reject the task, then the task outcome will be **REJECT**, and the task will get completed.

5. Select **Names and expressions** to build the participant list. Let the list building be based on values. Browse the embedded LDAP and select the users, as shown in the following screenshot:

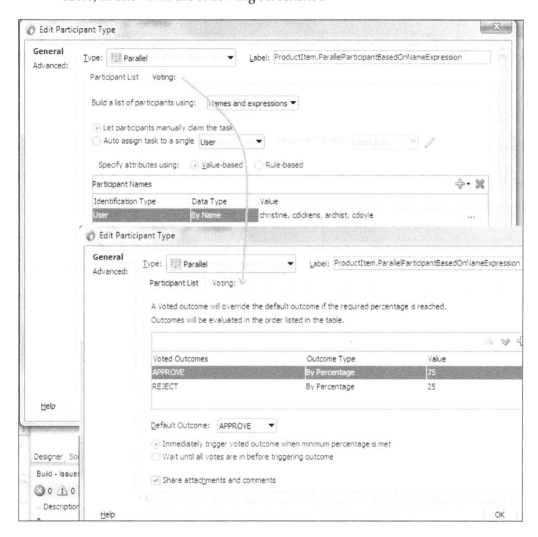

6. Click on the stage and check its configuration. The stage is based on the collection, and the voting pattern is defined as follows:

    ○ This is configured with the fact that if 50 percent of the line items in the collection are approved, then the stage is considered as **APPROVE**.

    ○ If 30 percent of the line items in the collection are rejected, then the stage is considered as **REJECT**, as shown in the following screenshot:

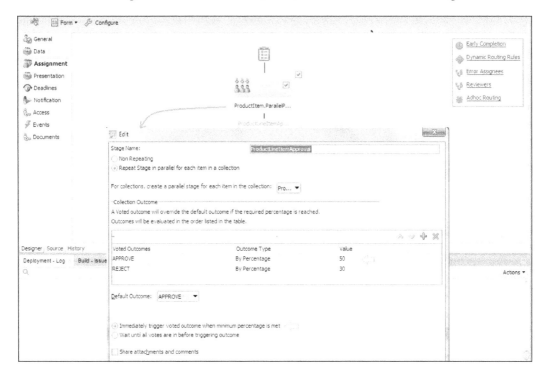

We can check the **Wait until all votes are in before triggering outcome** option if we want the task to wait for all the participants in the list in order to act on it. We can check **Immediately trigger voted outcome when minimum percentage is met** if we want to trigger the outcome as soon as minimum percentage for **APPROVE** or **REJECT** is met.

Deploy the project (HumanTaskRouting) to weblogic 12*c* and test the service (HumanTaskRouting) using the test data that is available by navigating to **Project (HumanTaskRouting) | SOA | testsuites**.

The test data contains three line items for the element that is used to frame the collection for the stage. Testing results reveals the following:

- The task gets repeated for three items as the test data has three product items, hence three tasks will be assigned to each user.

- For each stage, the task gets assigned to `Christine`, `cdickens`, `archist`, and `cdoyle` in parallel.

- As we have set 75 percent for **APPROVE** and 25 percent for **REJECT**, if one participant out of the four rejects it, the task will get completed with **REJECT** as the outcome. However, if three of the four participants approve it, then the task will get completed with **APPROVE** as the outcome.

- So, when you test the process with three product items, all the users get the task at the same time. There will be three tasks assigned to each user, one for each line item.

Log in as `Christine`, `cdickens`, and `archist` and approve the first task (the first task out of the three tasks), and you can see that the first task gets completed with **APPROVE** as the outcome. When three users approve it, the task gets withdrawn from the fourth user (`cdoyle`).

All the users will still have two more tasks in the task list for the other two line items. Log in again as `archist`, `Christine`, and `cdickens` and approve the second task. This time, we will have an interesting observation:

- The second task gets withdrawn from the user (`cdoyle`) after it gets approved by three users (`Christine`, `cdickens`, and `archist`).

- The process gets completed as two line items out of the three line items in the collection are approved.

This underlines the fact that the voting pattern gets applied at two levels, one at the participant level and the other at the stage level. You can see this in the following screenshot that showcases the stage level voting pattern. It's configured with the fact that if 50 percent of the line items in the collection are approved, then the stage is considered as **APPROVE**. You can check this in the preceding screenshot in this section, which demonstrates the participant-level voting pattern. Hence, when 75 percent of the participants approve the task, that task is considered as **APPROVE**.

Parallel routing pattern with approval group list builder

Approval groups are defined in the BPM workspace. They can be static or dynamic approval groups. Browse `http://acharyavivek.wordpress.com/2012/02/27/dynamic-approval-group-bpm-workspace/` to know more about dynamic approval groups.

To configure the parallel routing pattern with the approval group list builder, we will start with the following:

- Log in to the Oracle BPM workspace and create a static approval group, which is **MFGSalesAdmin**. Associate the user (`Christine`, `salesrep`, `Jim`, and `Kim`) with the static approval group. This will create a static approval group. The task will get assigned to all the users in the static list at the same time, as the routing pattern is parallel.

- As you have already configured a parallel routing pattern in the *Parallel routing pattern with Names and expressions list builder* section, use the same user task and change the list builder pattern from **Names and expressions** to **Approval Groups**.

- Browse **Approval Groups** in the weblogic application server and select the **MFGSalesAdmin** static approval group.

- Deploy the process and test the user task.

Testing results will reveal that for each stage, the task will get assigned to `Christine`, `salesrep`, `jim`, and `kim` in parallel. As we have set 75 percent for **APPROVE** and 25 percent for **REJECT**, and if one participant out of the four rejects it, then the task will get completed with **REJECT** as the outcome. However if three of the four participants approve it, then the task will get completed with **APPROVE** as the outcome. Hence, when you test the process with three product items, all the users get the task at the same time. Let `jim` reject the task, and you can see that the task gets completed with **REJECT** as the outcome.

As the participant type is defined in the stage that is a repeating stage, all the four participants will receive three tasks each. This is because the input payload has three lines and the stage is configured to repeat for each line. Hence, when `jim` rejects one task, only the first stage is considered as **REJECT**. All other users still have two other tasks each. At the stage level, it's the voting pattern defined at the stage level that is considered. Click on **Stage configuration** in the task metadata editor's assignment section. The stage will be repeated on the product item collection. The task will be considered complete when 50 percent of the stages are completed. Walk through the following steps to browse the task status:

1. Log in as `kim` and reject the second user task.

2. Log in to the Oracle BPM workspace as an admin user — `weblogic` — and go to the **Administrative task** tab. You can browse the completed task, select the user task, and check its flow diagrams in the history of the task.

You can see that the second stage shows **REJECT**. As half of the total stages show **REJECT**, the task is completed with the **REJECT** outcome.

Parallel routing pattern with lane participant list builder

In the lane participant list builder, the participant is derived based on the swimlane in which the user task is positioned in the BPM process. It could be the current swimlane participant or the previous swimlane participant. Perform the following steps to enable the lane participant list builder pattern or the parallel routing task that we used in the preceding section:

1. Open the `HumanTaskRouting` process in JDeveloper 12c and check the swimlane role (`salesrep`).

2. Navigate to **BPM studio (JDeveloper)** | **Task Metadata editor** | **Assignment** and click on the **ProductItem** participant type.

3. Change the list builder pattern from **Approval Group** to **Lane Participant**.

4. Select the **Current Lane** participants, save, and deploy the project.

5. Log in to the Oracle BPM workspace as an admin user and click on **Roles** in the administration task.

6. Select the `HumanTaskRouting.Salesrep` role and associate `Christine`, `jstein`, `salesrep`, and `fkafka` with the application role.

The task gets assigned to all swimlane roles. They are assigned to the sales representative, and hence, to all the users which belong to the application role, `HumanTaskRouting Salesrep`.

However, as soon as one user in the role approves the task, that task is considered approved, and it gets withdrawn from the other users' lists. If you check in the preceding section, you will see that there are three stages, as there are three items in the lines and the stage gets repeated three times. However, for each stage, the task gets assigned to the `HumanTaskPrj.Salesrep` swimlane role. Once a user in the role approves the task, the task gets approved.

Parallel routing pattern with rule-based list builder

Rules are defined using Oracle business rules. The moment you configure the rule-based list-building pattern, a decision service is created. You will create the rule dictionaries—`<Task Name>Rules.Rules` and `<Task name>RulesBase.rule`. The first one is referred to as a runtime rule dictionary, and the other is referred to as a base design-time rule dictionary. Always use the first rule dictionary to engulf any runtime changes. Use the following steps to build a list using the rules:

1. Use the same task metadata that you created while working in the preceding section.

2. Go to the **Assignment** section in the task metadata and click on the participant type. Let the stage remain the same as the repeating stage on the product item.

3. Let the routing pattern or the participant type be the same as the preceding one (parallel).

4. Change the list builder pattern to a rule-based pattern.

5. Enter the name of the rule as `ComplexTypeListbuildingRule`.

6. A decision service will be created, and the `ComplexTaskRules.rule` and `ComplexTaskBaseRules.rule` rule dictionaries will be created.

This is shown in the following screenshot:

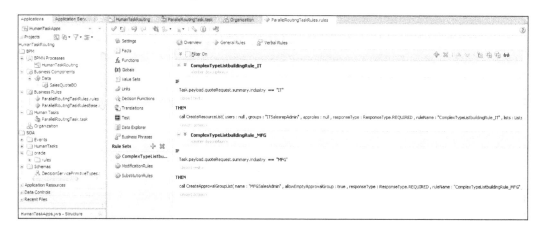

Configure the rule as shown in the preceding screenshot. If the industry is IT, then the list should be based on the `ITSalesrepAdmin` user group (the group is defined in myrealm, which is an embedded LDAP). However, if the industry is MFG, then the list should be based on the approval group, which is defined in the workspace application. Save the rule configuration, deploy the project, and test the project using `TestData12c.xml`.

The task was executed with a payload that has three line items, and the industry is IT. This will lead to building the list from the `ITSalesrepAdmin` group defined in the LDAP. Four users (`achrist`, `jcooper`, `jstein`, and `fkafka`) are members of this group in the LDAP. As this is a parallel routing pattern, all the users have received the task. As there are three product lines in the input payload, the stage will be repeated three times. Each user will receive three tasks for each line.

Log in as `fkafka`, `achrist`, `jstein`, and `jcooper` to verify that they have the three tasks assigned. All the users receive the tasks in their task list. However, they have to claim and approve it. As soon as one user from the group claims the task, the task is considered as **COMPLETE**. It's withdrawn from the list of other users. It does not follow the voting pattern.

In the case of **approval group** and **Dynamic/Static approval group**, the list of users is built using the group, and tasks are assigned to all four users. However, it follows the voting pattern, and when 75 percent of the users approve it, the task gets approved. Or, if 25 percent of the users reject it, the task is considered as **REJECT**.

There are many functions available in rule dictionaries that facilitate list building. In the rule, you have to specify the condition, and in the action of the rule, you can call one of the following functions to build the list of participants:

- `CreateResourceList`
- `CreateSupervisoryList`
- `CreateManagementChainList`
- `CreateApprovalGroupList`
- `CreateJobLevelList`
- `CreatePositionList`

Parallel routing pattern with management chain

While specifying the management chain, you have to specify a starting participant (the user/group/role), the top participant title, and/or the number of levels. The number of level computation is absolute and starts from the starting participant. The management chain hierarchy is always computed based on users defined in the embedded LDAP, active directory, or the third-party configured LDAP. Perform the following steps to build a list using the management chain:

1. Use the same task metadata that you created while working in the preceding section.

2. Go to the **Assignment** section in the task metadata and click on **participant type**. Let the stage remain the same as the repeating stage on the product item.

3. Let the routing pattern or participant type be the same as the one in the previous case, that is, parallel.

4. Change the voting outcome pattern value of **APPROVE** to 50 percent and **REJECT** to 50 percent.

5. Change the list builder pattern to the management chain.

6. Configure the management chain list builder pattern with the following details:

    The starting participant user: `jcooper`

    The top participant: `TitleVice President`

    Number of value levels: `4`

The management chain list builder stops when the top participant is reached or the number of levels is met. Hence, the management chain list builder will stop when four levels are met or the top participant (Vice President) is reached. `Jcooper` is the starting participant. His manager is `jstein`, and jstein's manager is `wfaulk`. `Wfaulk` is also titled the Vice President.

Deploy and test the user task. Perform the following steps to analyze the pattern:

1. Log in to the Oracle BPM workspace as a user (`jstein`), and we can find three tasks that have been assigned (as the stage is getting repeated and the input payload contains three items). Approve the first task and log out.

2. Log in as `jcooper` and approve the first task. At this stage, the first task is approved by two users (`jstein` and `jcooper`), and as we have modified the voting pattern to 50 percent, the task will be withdrawn from the user (`jstein`) task list.

3. Log in again as `wfaulk` and approve the second task. We would expect that as `wfaulk` is the Vice President and the stage is being met, the second task should be approved and get removed from other users' lists. However, this does not happen.

4. Log in to the BPM workspace as an admin user (`weblogic`) and navigate to the administration tasks in the inbox. Browse this task in the task list and check its history.

When you click on the user task in the history, it will open **Task history**, as shown in the following screenshot:

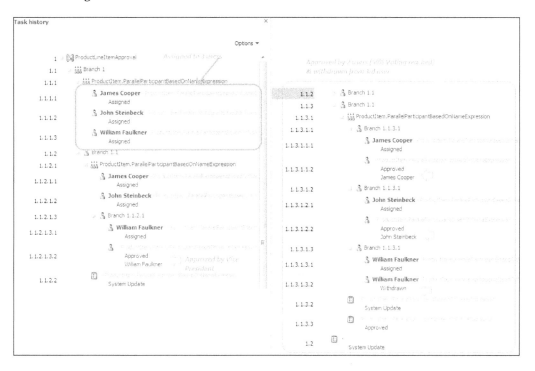

We can see that the hierarchy gets resolved in one go and all the participants are assigned the task. Participants are derived based on the list builder configuration.

In this case, although the level was entered, the list has been built up to three levels, starting from `jcooper` and stretching till the Vice President (`wfaulk`). We can act on tasks irrespective of their level, and based on the voting pattern defined for the parallel participant type, the outcome will be decided.

Serial routing pattern

The following pattern table highlights facts around the Serial Routing Pattern:

Signature	Serial Routing Pattern
Classification	Human Task Pattern
Intent	A set of people (participants) must work in sequence.
Motivation	The participants have to act in a serial fashion, one after another.
Applicability	This pattern is useful in scenarios where multiple users have to provide their opinion in a serial fashion.
Implementation	This is implemented using serial routing in participant blocks. Though this pattern intends to allow participants to work in a sequence, the assignment of tasks to participants also depends on the list-building pattern. For example, if the list-building pattern is the name and expression, then the task gets assigned to participants in a sequence; however, if the list builder pattern is a group, then the task gets assigned to all the users at the same time. However, one of the participants has to claim it and then act on it.
Known issues	NA
Known solution	N/A

Serial routing enables participants to work in a sequence. The most common scenario for this is the management chain escalation. For example, a list of participants is built using a dynamic approval group, and the participants are assigned tasks in a sequence; if one task is completed, then the next task is assigned, and so on. Participants have to act in a serial fashion. This participant type enables you to create a list of sequential participants for a workflow. The following are the serial behavioral patterns in conjunction with different list builders.

Serial routing pattern with list builder – name and expression

Name and expression can be used for users, groups, and application roles.

Participant identification type – users

The task gets assigned to participants in a serial fashion, for example, if the name and expression and the value-based list contains users such as `jstein`, `jcooper`, and `Christine`. Use the following steps to configure the participant type for users:

1. Use the same task metadata that you have been using so far. Modify the stage and make it nonrepeating.

2. Click on the participant type and edit it.

3. Make the participant type serial.

4. Choose the list builder pattern as name and expressions.

5. Enter values for the participants as jstein, jcooper, and Christine.

6. Deploy and test the process.

A task gets assigned to the first user in the list. Once the participant acts on the task, it gets assigned to another user in the list, and so on.

Participant identification type – groups

The task is assigned to the ITSalesrepAdmin group. A couple of users are members of this ITSalesrepAdmin group (the myrealm LDAP group). Users (achrist, jcooper, jstein, and fkafka) are members of this group in the LDAP. When the task is initiated, it gets assigned to all the users, as there is no sequence defined for the users in the group. One of the participants has to claim the task and act on it. Once claimed, the task gets withdrawn from other users' lists.

Participant identification type – application role

The task is assigned to the HumanTaskRouting. Salesrep application role. Users (salesrep, Christine, jcooper, and fkafka) are members of the HumanTaskRouting. Salesrep application role. When the task is initiated, the task gets assigned to all the users, as there is no sequence defined for the users in the group. One of the participants has to act (approve or reject or some other defined action) on the task. Once it is acted upon, the task gets withdrawn from other users' lists.

Serial routing pattern with list builder – approval group

Configure the serial participant type with the approval group list builder pattern. The MFGSalesAdmin approval group is a static approval group with users (Christine, salesrep, Jim, and Kim) defined in a sequence. Save, deploy, and test the process. Tasks get assigned to the users in a sequence. As it's a static list, Christine gets the task first. Once the assigned participant acts on the task, it gets assigned to the subsequent participant.

Serial routing pattern with list builder – management chain

The management chain list builder stops when the top participant is reached or the number of levels is met. Configure the management chain participant list builder with Jcooper as the starting participant. Let the top participant title be Vice President. The number of levels is four. The hierarchy for Jcooper is defined with Jstein as its manager and wfaulk as the manager of jstein. Wfaulk is also titled the Vice President. Perform the following steps to test the scenario:

1. Deploy and test the user task.

2. Log in to the Oracle BPM workspace as a user (jcooper), and approve the task.

3. Log back in to the BPM workspace as an admin user (weblogic) and navigate to the administration tab and browse the task in the assigned task list.

4. Go to the task's history section, and you can view the task flow. You can see that the list is created in one go with three participants— jcooper, jstein, and wfaulk—and the task gets assigned to users in a sequence.

Serial routing pattern with list builder – job level

Starting from a given approver, the list of participants climbs up the supervisory hierarchy until an approver with a specified job level is found. This can be value-based or rule-based. This pattern traverses the job level hierarchy. It allows you to specify the starting participant and the top participant. The level defined is relative to the starting participant or the task creator. It allows you the flexibility to include all managers in the last level. This also allows you to define the utilization of the participant. You can define whether you want to utilize all the participants from the list, the first and the last person from the list, or only the last person from the list. This stops when the top participant is reached or the top job level criteria are met.

Use the same task metadata that you used in the preceding scenario. Change the assignment configuration. Let the stage be a nonrepeating stage. In the participant type, select the **Serial** routing pattern. Build the list using **Job Level**. Enter the following details for the list builder configuration, as shown in the following screenshot:

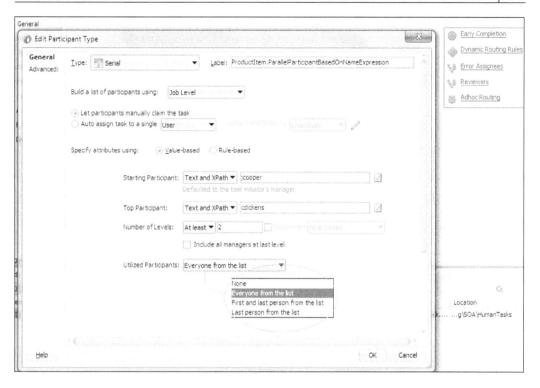

- **Starting Participant**: This is the first participant in the list. If you don't enter a value, then the task initiator's manager will be considered the first participant. The task initiator in this case is jcooper. You can define the task initiator in the user task's implementation properties in the advanced section.

- **Top Participant**: The user cdickens is the last participant in the hierarchy chain, and the task approval request will not go beyond this participant in the chain.

- **Number of Levels**: Two levels will be traversed in this case. However, the number of levels specifies the levels to be traversed for the job level. In this case, the number is relative to **Starting Participant**. However, you can specify the number relative to **Task Creator**. Also, you can create a number that can be an absolute value.

- **Include all managers at last level**: If the job level equals that of the previously calculated last participant in the list, then it includes the next manager in the list.

- **Utilized Participants**: Select a value from the calculated list of participants. If you specify the first and last person from the list, then the task will get assigned to only the first and last person from the calculated participant list. If you select everyone from the list, then everyone from the list will receive the task.

When you test the preceding configuration, you will find that starting from `jstein` (`jstein` is the manager of the task initiator), the task gets assigned to `cdickens`, as the level specified is 2. Remember, the user `cdickens` is two levels senior to `jstein`.

Job Level can be built using a rule-based attribute. However, with **Job Level** and the position list builder, you can use the substitution and modification rules. These rules are offered as seeded rules when you create a rule-based list builder. Users, groups, and application roles appearing in a list can be substituted using list substitution. Similarly, you can extend or truncate job levels and positions from the rules. List modification is applied after the list is created.

Modifying participant lists using list modification

After the list creation, you can modify the list using a list-modification rule. You can extend and/or truncate **Job Level** and position list builders from rules using list modification. The rule dictionary will always contain a pre-seeded rule set named `ModificationRules` by default. This rule is available for use only when **Job Level** and position list builders are asserted in the list that created the rule sets. The following are the functions that are available to enable and facilitate list modifications:

- Extend
- Truncate

Substituting participants using list substitution

You can substitute users, groups, or application roles. With each rule dictionary, you have access to a pre-seeded rule named **SubstitutionRule** with a **Substituterule** function, which facilitates list substitution. The substitute function carries four parameters.

As shown in the following screenshot, **Job Level** is built using a **rule-based** attribute. The starting participant will be derived as the manager of the task initiator. In this case, the task initiator is the user `jcooper`. Hence, the starting participant of the user task will be the manager of `jcooper`, who is `jstein`. However, if you check the substitute rule, `jstein` will be substituted with `wfaulk`. Hence, when the task is executed, it will derive the starting participant as `jstein`. However, it will be substituted with `wfaulk`.

The user `wfaulk` becomes the starting participant and the task gets assigned to `wfaulk`. It then moves the supervisory chain till the at-most/at-least level is reached or till the participant is met:

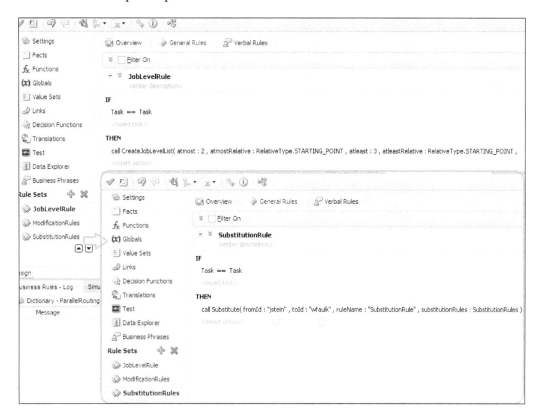

Serial routing pattern with list builder – position

List building starts at the requester or a given approver's position and goes up until a specific number of levels or a position is met. Use the same task metadata that you used for the previous section and modify the list builder. Let the routing pattern be serial and change the list builder to the position. It will ask you to enter a rule name, as it's always based on rules. Enter the rule name as `PositionRule`.

When you configure the position list builder, you encounter almost the same properties as we defined in the preceding section, such as utilized participants, and so on.

Serial routing pattern with list builder – supervisory

Starting from a given approver, the list of participants climbs up the approver list and generates a chain that has a fixed number of approvers in it. While configuring the supervisory list builder pattern, you have to supply **Starting participant**, **Top participant**, and **Level**. If no value is passed, then **Starting participant** defaults to the initiator's manager. Here, the top participant is not a title. While in the **Job level** hierarchy, you can use a title as the top participant. This pattern traverses the supervisory hierarchy. In this section, you will create a supervisory list builder based on a rule. You can configure a supervisory list builder based on values. However, we will choose to create a supervisory list based on rules. The following is the configuration of the rule for the supervisory list builder:

```
IF Industry = "IT" THEN
call CreateSupervisoryListcall CreateSupervisoryListcall
CreateSupervisoryListcall CreateSupervisoryListcall
CreateSupervisoryListcallCreateSupervisoryList( levels:3,
startingPoint:HierarchyBuilder.getManager("supervisory",Task.
creator,-1,"",""), uptoApprover:HierarchyBuilder.getPrinicipal("wfau
lk",-1,"",""),
AutoActionEnabled: false, autoAction: null, responseType:
ResponseType.REQUIRED, ruleName:"SupervisoryListRule", lists: Lists)
```

The preceding rule configuration makes it clear that the number of levels is three, starting from the manager of the user who is the task creator. In this case, configure the user task property with the task initiator as jcooper. As the user jstein is the manager of jcooper; the task will first get assigned to jstein and will move in the chain until the user wfaulk is reached or the number of levels is met. A response is required from the participant as it's not an FYI. The following are the parameters that you need to set while invoking the createsupervisoryList() function:

- StartingPoint and topApprover: **Starting point** and **top approver** are specified as users, but you can also build a hierarchy principal as the starting point and the top approver. To build a hierarchy principal, you have the following functions available:
  - getManager
  - getPrinciple
  - getManagerofHierarchyPrinciple

- AutoActionEnabled and autoAction: Configuring these properties enables the users resulting from a particular list builder to act automatically on the task.

- **The response type:** The assignee has to act on the task if the response type selected is required. If it's not required, then the task will be converted to an FYI assignment.

Serial routing pattern with list builder – rules

Rules build the list of participants. Oracle BPM offers many built-in seeded functions that can be used to create the list of participants. The following are the functions that are available:

- `CreateResourceList`
- `CreateSupervisoryList`
- `CreateManagementChainList`
- `CreateApprovalGroupList`
- `CreateJobLevelList`
- `CreatePositionList`

When you enter the name of the rule, a decision service is created, and two rule dictionaries are created — `<Task Name>Rules. Rules` and `<Task name>RulesBase. rule`. In the rule designer, model your conditions, and in the action part, call one of the functions mentioned previously to complete building your lists.

When the rule conditions are met, the function gets executed. The function will return the list of participants. However, it's the routing pattern that will define how the task will be assigned. Let the approval group be `MFGSalesAdmin`. This is a static approval group defined in the BPM workspace with users (`Christine`, `salesrep`, `Jim`, and `Kim`) defined in a sequence. The task gets assigned to the users in a sequence. As it's a static list, `Christine` gets the task first. Once the assigned participant acts on the task, it gets assigned to the subsequent participant.

Single routing pattern

The task is assigned to a single user, group, or role. For example, a vacation approval request is assigned to a manager. If the manager approves or rejects the request, the employee is notified of the decision. If the task is assigned to a group, then once one of the managers acts on it, the task is completed. If the list of participants is built using an approval group, then the task is assigned to the group; however, once one of them acts on the task, it's considered complete.

Single approver pattern with list builder – name and expression

Configure the task metadata with the list builder pattern—name and expression. Let the participants be users (Christine, jstein, or jcooper). Upon execution, the task gets assigned to all three participants—Christine, jstein, and jcooper. However, once one of them acts on the task, it's considered complete.

Single approver pattern with list builder – approval group

Configure a single participant type with the approval group list builder pattern. The MFGSalesAdmin approval group is a static approval group with users (Christine, salesrep, Jim, and Kim) defined in a sequence. Save, deploy, and test the process. The task gets assigned to all the users in one go. Once any one of the assigned participants acts on the task, the task is considered complete and is withdrawn from other users' lists.

Single approver pattern with list builder – management chain

The management chain list builder is best utilized with the serial routing pattern. However, if you use it with the single routing pattern, then all the users in the management chain will receive the task. However, once a participant acts on the task, the task is considered complete, and it gets withdrawn from other users' lists. All other list-building patterns work as they should; however, their behavior is governed by the routing pattern. In the case of a single routing pattern, once a participant acts on the task, the task is considered complete and gets withdrawn from other users' list.

Notify/FYI pattern

The task is assigned to participants who can view it, add comments and attachments, but cannot modify or complete the task. It's just like a notification and no one is supposed to act on it. We will cover two list builder patterns for the FYI routing patterns. The remaining patterns are quite similar, as their behavior is to just notify participants. The process token remains with the BPM process, the control is not assigned to the human workflow, and the main process executes subsequent activities.

FYI approver pattern with list builder – job level

The task will be assigned from the starting participant to the top participant/level. The flow of the assigned task will show you the task assigned from the starting to the top level/participant. All participants will receive the task. The control will not get assigned to the task, and the token remains with the BPM process. The BPM process will move ahead to subsequent activities.

FYI approver pattern with list builder – name and expression

Create a simple user task with the stage as nonrepeating and the routing pattern as FYI. Let the list builder pattern be names and expressions. Enter values for users as `Christine`, `jstein`, `jcooper`, and `fkafka`. The task will be sent to all the participants in one go, which means in parallel. The control will not get assigned to the task and the token remains with the BPM process. The BPM process will move ahead with subsequent activities. Now, let's modify the stage and make it a parallel stage. Let the stage be repeating on the `Product Item` collection. This is the same collection that you created in earlier sections. Let the rest of the configuration remain the same. Deploy and test the process. As there are three product lines, each user will get the task information three times. An FYI task will be offered to them three times. We will try to solve and simplify this problem using task aggregation.

Task aggregation pattern

As you have seen in the *FYI approver pattern with list builder – name and expression* section, the task gets assigned to the same user multiple times. This holds true for other patterns too. However, Oracle BPM offers the task aggregation mechanism that will enable you to configure how often a user can see the task.

For the same task metadata that you created in the *FYI approver pattern with list builder – name and expression* section, as it's a repeating stage, click on the stage and then on the **Task will go from starting to final participant** link on the aggregate section in the task metadata. This will open the **Assignment and Routing Policy** dialog box. Click on the **Assignment** tab.

In the task aggregation drop-down list, select **STAGE**. Save and execute the process. This time, the task will get assigned to the user once. This means that the user will see the task only one time in the stage.

The task aggregation, when defined as none, indicates that there is no approval aggregation, which means that the user sees the task as many times as it is assigned to him or her. If the task aggregation is selected as **TASK**, then the user sees the task only one time in the life cycle of the task. The following table highlights the facts:

Routing pattern	Stage	Aggregation	Action	Assignment
FYI	Nonrepeating	None, stage, task	N/A	The task gets assigned to all the users once.
FYI	Repeating	None, stage, task	N/A	The task is in the recoverable error.
Single	Nonrepeating	None, stage, task	N/A	The task gets assigned to all the users once, and then, the single routing pattern gets applied.
Single	Repeating	None	The stage is repeating and the input data contains three line items. Hence, all the users will receive three tasks (one for each line item). Users can claim and act on the task. Once it is claimed by a user, the other user will see the task in their list but cannot act on an already-claimed task by some other user.	All the users will receive three tasks (one for each line item).
Single	Repeating	Stage, task	Once the user can claim and act on the task, the task gets completed.	The input contains three line items; however, the aggregation happens at the stage level, and each user will receive the task just once.

Routing pattern	Stage	Aggregation	Action	Assignment
Serial	NonRepeating	None, stage, task	N/A	Tasks get assigned to users in a serial fashion, and there will be just one task.
Serial	Repeating	None	As it's repeating, and if the input contains three line items, then three tasks get assigned to the first user in the list.	Three tasks get assigned to the first user in the list.
Serial	Repeating	Stage, task	Even if it's repeating, and if the input contains three line items, only one task gets assigned to the first user in the list, and the rest of the behavior is based on the serial routing pattern.	Tasks get assigned to users in a serial fashion and there will be just one task.
Parallel	Nonrepeating	None, stage, task	N/A	All the users receive one task.
Parallel	Repeating	None	The stage is repeating and the input data contains three line items. Hence, all the users will receive three tasks (one for each line item).	All the users will receive three tasks (one for each line item).
Parallel	Repeating	Stage, task	Although the stage is repeating and the input data contains three line items, the aggregation happens and all the users will receive just one task.	All the users will receive just one task.

You might be wondering whether the stage and task aggregation behave in a similar manner. However, this is not true. As we have just used one stage and one participant type and constructed the preceding table, we have not witnessed the stage aggregation. Let's refractor the assignment routing slip and add another participant block in the same stage, which is parallel to the first participant block. We can use the `ParallelRoutingTask.task` human task. Let the routing pattern for both the participant blocks be parallel routing.

Let's use the name and expression list builder pattern for both the parallel routing participant blocks. Let the first participant block have the users jstein, jcooper, Christine, and fkafka and the second participant block have the users jstein, jcooper, rivi, and lata. The following are the observations when the task aggregation is staged:

- The task gets assigned to all the users in both the participant blocks just once.

- Users jstein and jcooper are common in both the participant blocks; still, they will receive the task just once, as aggregation is set at the stage level.

Dispatching pattern

We learned about the task assignment patterns in the *Task assignment patterns* section. In this section, we will cover the dispatching pattern. Dispatching patterns select a particular user or group from either a group or a list of users or groups. There are many patterns offered by Oracle BPM for escalating and dispatching; interestingly, we can create our own patterns too. Usually, a user needs to manually claim the task. However, using dispatching patterns, we can configure the task to dispatch messages based on one of the following patterns:

- LEAST_BUSY: The tasks will be dispatched to the user who has the least number of tasks currently assigned. This will pick the least busy user, group, or application role with the least number of assigned tasks. In the case of users, tasks that are assigned to the user and the task that the user has claimed are counted. In the case of groups and roles, all the tasks assigned to the group and role are counted, irrespective of the fact that they were assigned or claimed.

- MOST_PRODUCTIVE: The task is dispatched to the user who completes the most tasks over a time frame. For groups and application roles, the total number of tasks completed by all the users who are direct members of that group or role is counted. The time period to be used can be specified using the time period parameter. If no time period is specified, then the default value specified in the dynamic assignment configuration for the instance is used.

- ROUND_ROBIN: The task is dispatched to each user or group in turn. Every time the Round_Robin functions are executed, a new participant is picked from the list of potential participants. When all the participants are picked, the patterns iterate again from the start of the list.

Dynamic assignment patterns can also be called using an `Xpath` function in any Xpath expression in the task definition. The signature of the function is given by the following:

```
hwf:dynamicTaskAssign(patternName, participants,
inputParticipantType, targetAssigneeType, isGlobal,
invocationContext, parameter1, parameter2, ..., parameterN).
```

Escalation pattern

Escalation is a common requirement while implementing Oracle BPM's processes with human interactions. Processes don't do the work, it's the people who do it. This concept leads to those processes that have heavy human interactions. There are scenarios where a participant does not act on an assigned human task, and such scenarios contribute to the candidate being escalated.

Custom escalation empowers the BPM system with the capability to introduce a check on the task's outcome. A participant is assigned a task, and if he/she doesn't act on the task in a specified time frame, then nonavailability should be accounted, published, and notified. If a participant does not act in the duration provided, the task is escalated to the manager or another user, as deemed appropriate.

Escalation makes sure that **service level agreements (SLAs)** are met and the processes are performed as per the exceptions within the time frame in which they are supposed to be performed. For example, if a task is assigned to a participant and the participant was supposed to respond in two days and it's overdue by four days, it basically hampers the fabric of the process and might lead to loss of business. Let's assume a loan approval process. If the loan document request is awaiting a loan officer's approval and it's overdue in its queue by four days, then the best practice is to escalate the overdue information and the task to another participant.

The `https://blogs.oracle.com/acharyavivek/` blog post is meant to showcase the process of custom escalation and how the participant list can be built dynamically. The duration deadline section in the human task metadata can be used to create a human task definition.

By default, escalation is based on the management chain hierarchy and the task gets escalated up in the hierarchy from the user to his/her manager, and so on. You can control the level to which a task can be escalated and can also use a title to which the task gets escalated. The level and title assignment can be configured while configuring the human task definition's duration deadline.

Oracle BPM offers you various ways to escalate:

- Role-based escalation
- Level-and-title-based escalation
- Custom escalation

To know more about escalation and download the escalation project, visit my blog post at `https://blogs.oracle.com/acharyavivek/`.

Rule-based reassignment and delegation pattern

Task reassignment and delegation can be performed automatically, based on rules. Reassignment rules are defined within the preferences page in the BPM workspace application. The following pattern table highlights facts around the Rule-based Reassignment And Delegation Pattern:

Signature	Rule-based Reassignment And Delegation Pattern
Classification	Human Task Pattern
Intent	Automatic reassignment and delegation of tasks based on rules.
Motivation	Defining personal or group rules that can perform rule-based auto reassignment, delegation, and automatic actions on the tasks.
Applicability	The rule-based reassignment and delegation pattern offers you the flexibility to reassign, delegate, and auto-act on tasks by applying the participant's personal rules or group rules.
Implementation	Personal rules are implemented in the BPM workspace. A participant can log in to the BPM workspace and define his/her personal rules. Group rules are defined by administrators who can reassign tasks to users/groups/roles.
Known issues	NA
Known solution	NA

To walk through the use case and sample project, visit the article associated with this book available on the Packt Publishing website at `http://www.packtpub.com/article-network`. There, we defined a rule for the user **buny**, which demonstrates the implementation of the rule-based reassignment and delegation pattern.

Ad hoc routing pattern

The following pattern table highlights facts around Ad Hoc Pattern:

Signature	Ad Hoc Routing Pattern
Classification	Human Task Pattern
Intent	Dynamically adds task participants at runtime.
Motivation	Allows task participants to invite other participants to act on the task.
Applicability	We need ad hoc routing to cater to the business requirements, where participants want to add other participants in an ad hoc fashion at runtime.
Implementation	The routing pattern in 12*c* offers you the flexibility to allow each participant to invite other participants as the next assignees to the task when approving the task. Before routing to the next assignees in the workflow, we can allow the initiator to invite other participants too. Using **Allow participant to edit new participant**, we can edit other ad hoc participants that were added to the routing slip.
Known issues	Privileges need to be assigned to participants to perform ad hoc routing, and the task should have at least one participant.
Known solution	By default, task owners and assignees have the grants to the ad hoc routing action in the **Access** tab of the task editor. The ad hoc assignee should not be added for FYI participants.

We'll continue with `DynamicTaskAssignment`, which you created in the dynamic task assignment section in the article associated with this book, which is available on the Packt Publishing website at `http://www.packtpub.com/article-network`. In this section, we will explore the ad hoc routing pattern:

1. Open the `DynamicTaskAssignment` project in JDeveloper 12*c*.

2. Click on **ValidationTask.task** to open the task metadata editor and go to the assignment section.

3. Click on the **ad hoc routing** tab in the **Assignment** section.

4. Check all or one of the options as per your requirements. These options are discussed in the implementation box in the ad hoc routing pattern table, as shown previously. For this sample, we have selected all three options.

5. Save all and deploy the project.

6. Test the service using the test data (`TestData12c.xml`) from the `DynamicTaskAssignment` project's **testsuites** folder.

7. The validation task gets assigned to different participants based on the organization unit you have passed. Log in to the BPM workspace as the participant `anju`.

8. Click on the task to open up the task user interface.

9. Expand **Actions** and click on **Ad hoc Route**. This will open the **Route Task** dialog box.

10. We can route the task to **Single Approver**, **Group Vote**, or **Chain of Single Approvers**. However, for this sample, check **Single Approver**.

11. Enter the comment that you want to pass into the **Comments** section of **Single Approver**.

12. Browse/search for the user (**Single Approver**), and select the new participant.

13. Click on **OK**.

Once you click on **OK** in the route task dialog box, the task gets approved by the participant `anju` and gets assigned to the newly invited participant `jstein`. This is shown in the following screenshot:

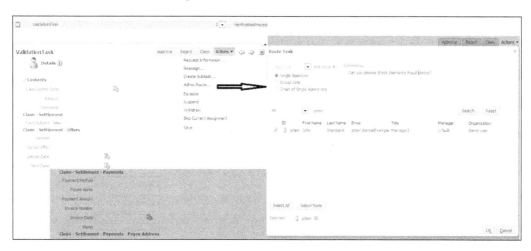

As we can see in the preceding screenshot, the task gets routed to other participants once the task is acted upon by the user. This option works at any current point in the task's routing. However, if we want to add participants at a future point in the task's routing, then check the **Allow participants to edit new participants** option in the ad hoc routing dialog box.

With this option checked, the user can use the history region in the task form to add additional participants at the desired point in the task's routing. To do so, perform the following steps:

1. Click on the task to open the task form.
2. Scroll down to the history section and expand it.
3. Click on **+** to add the assignee.
4. You can also edit and delete assignees.

Request information feature

In the preceding section, we learned about various human task patterns; however, in the following sections, we will explore and implement various features that greatly enhance BPMN. The following table highlights facts around the Request Information Feature:

Feature	Request Info Feature
Classification	Human Task Pattern
Intent	Requests information from other participants.
Motivation	Allows task participants to request for information from other participants.
Applicability	The request information pattern offers you the flexibility to request for additional information from participants or other users. All those participants who have acted on the task will be listed in the participant list, while we can also browse for other users. The task state will be **Info Requested** when the task is routed to the participant from whom the information is requested.
Implementation	The task participant who is requesting for information will click on **Request Information...** in the action, as shown in the following screenshot. However, the user who has requested for the information will be assigned the task. The requested participant can enter the information in the **Comments** section of the task and can hit **Submit Information** to provide the information being requested. Based on the return option configured by the request initiating participant, the task will either come back to the requesting participant after information is submitted, or it can be rerouted through all intermediate participants, as defined in the routing slip.
Known issues	NA
Known solution	NA

As we can see in the following screenshot, the participants who have **Validation Task** assigned can request for information from other participants. The participant `rivi` will receive the task and submit the information. The task is then rerouted through all intermediate participants as per the routing slip as shown in the following screenshot:

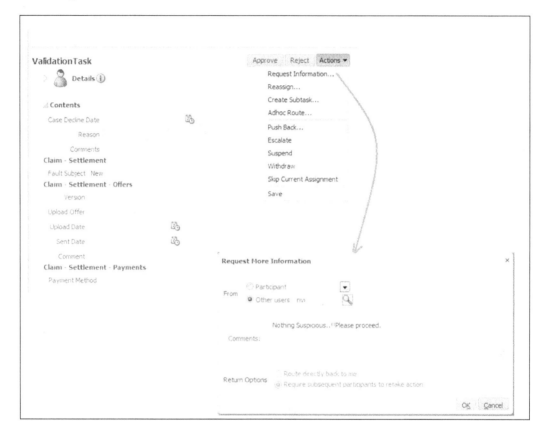

Reassignment and delegation pattern

The following pattern table highlights facts around the reassignment and delegation pattern:

Signature	Reassignment And Delegation Pattern
Classification	Human Task Pattern
Intent	The participant can reassign and delegate the task to other users/groups/roles.
Motivation	To change the task assignment or allow someone else to perform on behalf of the original assignee.
Applicability	The Reassignment And Delegation pattern offers you the flexibility to reassign a task to another assignee who can work on the task as if the task was assigned to her or him. However, in the case of task delegation, the assignee to whom the task is delegated will work on behalf of the original assignee.
Implementation	The task participant who wants to reassign the task to another assignee can click on **Reassign...** in the **Actions** tab. The **Reassign Task** dialog box will allow the original assignee to reassign the task to another user or delegate the task to another user.
Known issues	NA
Known solution	NA

As you can see in the following screenshot, the original assignee can click on **Reassign...** in the **Actions** tab to perform the task reassignment or delegation.

Reassign... will allow the transfer of the task to another user or group, and the delegate will allow the new assignee to act on behalf of the original assignee. This is shown in the following screenshot:

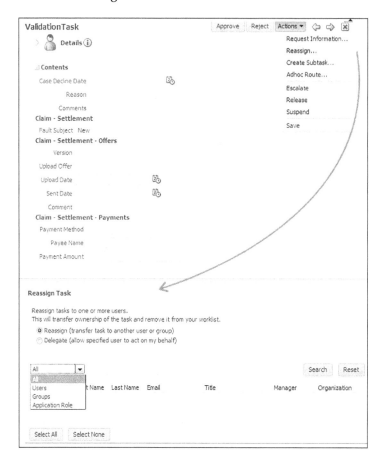

Force completion pattern

The following pattern table highlights facts around the force completion/early completion pattern:

Signature	Force Completion/Early Completion Pattern
Classification	Human Task Pattern
Intent	Forcefully or abruptly completing a task.
Motivation	To cater to those business requirements that require early completion of the task regardless of other participants in the workflow.

Applicability	The early completion pattern offers you the flexibility to abruptly complete a task. For example, an insurance claim goes to an insurance agent and then to the claim manager. If the first participant (the insurance agent) rejects it, we can end the workflow without sending it to the next participant (the claim manager). Such cases can be modeled in the BPMN flow; however, this makes the model complex. Hence, modeling them in the routing slip makes things efficient.
Implementation	To perform the abrupt completion of the task, there are two methods: • Outcome • XPath expression-based routing condition If outcomes are defined in the early completion pattern, then any time the specified task outcome occurs, the task gets completed. If the routing condition is defined, then any time the specified routing condition occurs, the task gets completed. However, if both the outcome and routing conditions are defined, the workflow service performs a logical operation of the two conditions.
Known issues	Evaluation of the routing condition defined using the XPath expression is not performed until at least one user has acted upon the task.
Known solution	Effective modeling.

We can define early completion in the verification task, which is defined in the `DynamicTaskAssignment` tab.

The following are the steps:

1. Click on the **VerificationTask** task to open the task editor and navigate to the assignment section.

2. Click on **Early Completion**, as shown in the upcoming screenshot.

3. Check **Complete task when participant chooses**; this will open the **Completion details** dialog box.

4. Select **REJECT** to complete the task if any of the participants rejects the task.

5. We can also enter a routing condition. The entered routing condition says that if the claim is not validated, then the task can be completed.

If both the situations happen, then a logical `OR` is performed. You can test the scenario by executing `DynamicTaskAssignment` with the supplied `TestData12c. xml`; however, change the `claimValidated` value from **YES** to **NO**.

Enabling early completion in parallel subtasks

When we have a multistage configuration and each stage (group) has multiple participant blocks, stages are parallel to each other. Check **Enabling Early Completion in Parallel Subtasks** if you want to model in such a way that if any participant rejects/approves the task, then all the tasks in that stage get abruptly completed.

Check **Completing Parent Subtasks of Early Completing Subtasks** if you want to model in such a way that if any participant rejects/approves the task, then all the tasks in that stage get abruptly completed and the parallel stage also gets completed.

Routing rule pattern

The following pattern table highlights facts around the Routing Rule Pattern:

Signature	Routing Rule Pattern
Classification	Human Task Pattern
Intent	To solve complex rules based on routing scenarios. This offers you the flexibility to complete the task or route it based on rules.
Motivation	Rules can be routing rules or participant rules. Routing rules will provide solutions to back and forth and complex task routings.
Applicability	We can define stages and participant blocks to route tasks between participants; however, this offers you a linear flow from one set of participants to another. We can use early completion, reassignment, delegation, skipping, and other features to cater nonlinear requirements. However, if we need to perform complex routing that includes back and forth routing between participants, then we need a rule-based routing solution. For example, if certain conditions are met, we want to give back the task to the previous participant. Else, if the amount is less than a certain threshold, we want to complete the task or maybe allow the task to go to some other participant, and so on.
Implementation	When we define a dynamic rule, a routing rule set is created in base and custom rule dictionaries. Whenever a task is completed by a participant and/or when the task gets assigned to a participant, the task service will assert the facts into the decision service and will execute the routing rule set.
Known issues	NA
Known solution	NA

There are some facts that are available for only the routing rule and not participant rules. Facts such as **Previous Outcome** and **Task Action** are available to only routing rules.

The task service routes the tasks based on **Task Actions** defined in the routing rule set. The following is the list of **Task Actions** that you can call from the routing rule to guide the task service routing:

Action	Comment
GO_FORWARD	This is the default behavior that guides the task flow to the next participant in the list.
PUSHBACK	This guides the task flow to the last participant who just set the task outcome.
GOTO	Use this if you want to assign the task to a specific participant.
COMPLETE	The task will be marked as complete, and it will not be routed further.
ESCALATE	Based on the escalation policy that is defined, the task will be escalated and reassigned.

As you can see in the following screenshot, we can click on **Dynamic Routing Rules** in JDeveloper. This will open the **Use Advance Rules** dialog box. Enter a name of the rule, say, **ValidationTaskRule**. A **RoutingRules** set will be created. We can create an if-then-else rule or a decision table to build the logic. As we can see in the following screenshot, an if-then-else rule is created, which calls for **Task Action complete ()** to complete the task when the specified condition is met:

Deadlines

While performing task modeling, we have to deal with situations such as deadlines, reminders, escalation, expiration, and renewal. A BPMN offering should have features such as deadline, warning, reminders, escalation, renewal, and so on. The following table highlights facts around the Deadline Feature:

Feature	Deadline Feature
Classification	Human Task Pattern
Intent	To offer a preventive solution to task participants to ensure deadlines are met by ensuring reminders and warnings. In case deadlines are missed, escalations can be performed.
Motivation	While performing task modeling, we have to deal with situations such as deadlines, reminders, escalation, expiration, and renewal. A BPMN offering should have features such as deadline, warning, reminders, escalation, renewal, and so on. In this section, we will define a deadline feature and escalation feature. All other features will be included with it. These features essentially answer questions such as the following: • What to do when the allocated task's time expires • What to do if the task needs to be escalated • What to do if the participant/user needs to be informed/reminded before the task expiration
Applicability	To ensure that corrective measures are taken when participants don't act on assigned tasks in a timely manner, Oracle BPMN offers you the deadline feature at the task level and participant level. Oracle BPMN offers deadlines at different levels: • Task level • Participant level
Implementation	The task level deadline is defined in the **Deadline** section in the task routing slip. The participant level deadline can be defined in the **Advance** tab of the **Participant** dialog box.
Known issues	The what-if task deadline and the participant deadline are both specified in the routing slip and participant block, respectively.
Known solution	The deadline specified in the participant block takes precedence over the deadlines specified in the task routing slip.

The following are the task level deadlines:

- **Duration deadline**: The duration deadline at the task level is like a global policy and is applicable to all participants associated with the task. The length of the idle time for the task is defined by the duration deadline, and once the idle policy expires, the following actions can be performed:
    - ○ The task can be expired
    - ○ The task can be renewed
    - ○ Escalation can be performed

- **Warning:** Before deadlines are approached, it is always preventive to send the participants a warning to make them aware of an overdue task. Specify a value in the **Action Requested Before** section in the **Deadlines** tab of the routing slip. Remember to set a value for **Action Requested Before**, which should be less than the value for **Task Duration Settings**.

    Warning is essentially a due date. It's the date by which the task should be completed; else, it's considered overdue. A task is considered overdue after it's past the due date that we have specified in the global task deadline policy. If enabled, we can list overdue tasks in the worklist applications, or we can filter tasks based on overdue tasks in the task list in worklist/workspace applications.

- **Reminder**: Reminder offers you the flexibility to model task routing with a reminder to the task user/participant before the task is expired or before the due date or after assignment. We can set the reminder once, twice, or multiple times.

Perform the following steps to experience a task deadline. The use case is a `DynamicTaskAssignment` project that contains a deadline and escalation process (`Deadline&EscalationProcess`). This process, when executed, assigns human tasks (`DeadlineEscalationTask`) in a serial routing pattern to the `jstein` and `achrist` users. If the user `jstein` does not approve it in 5 minutes, the task expires:

- If you have not downloaded the project (**DynamicTaskAssignment**) from the downloads for *Chapter 4, Human Task Patterns*, then download the project and open it in JDeveloper 12*c*.

- Open **DeadlineEscalationTask.task** and check the **Deadlines** tab in the routing slip, as shown in the following screenshot.

- We can set the duration deadline for the task (enforcing it for all participants) by setting **Task Duration Settings**. For this use case, we have set the task to expire if the user does not act on it in 5 minutes as shown in the following screenshot:

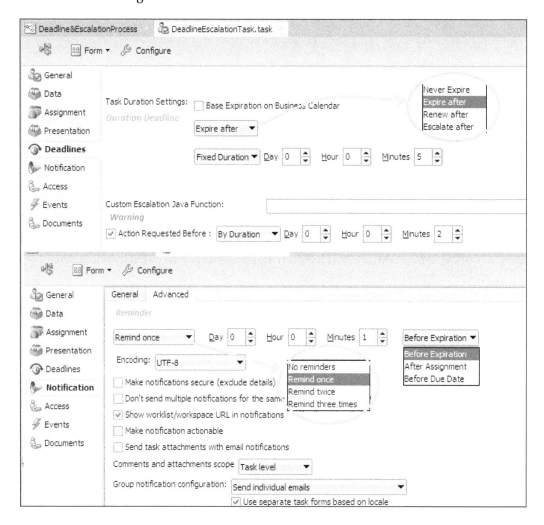

- We can check **Action Requested Before**; it has a value of 2 minutes to send a warning.

- Click on the **Notification** tab and check the **Reminder** setting. The task is set to **Remind once**, 1 minute before the task expires. Notification settings of the task will take care of sending the reminders.

- Click on the **Assignment** tab and open the **Participant** block; we can find that it's a serial routing pattern that builds the participants' list using **Names and expressions**. The task, when executed, first gets assigned to `jstein` and then to `achrist`.

- Deploy the process and test it using the test data (`TestData12c.xml`) that we can find by navigating to **HumanTaskAssignment | SOA | testsuites**.

Upon execution, we can see that the task gets assigned to the user `jstein`. If we check the process flow trace, we can find the **Created Date** and time and **Expiration Date** and time specified for the task. As shown in the following screenshot, they show you a difference of 5 minutes, which is the task expiration limit:

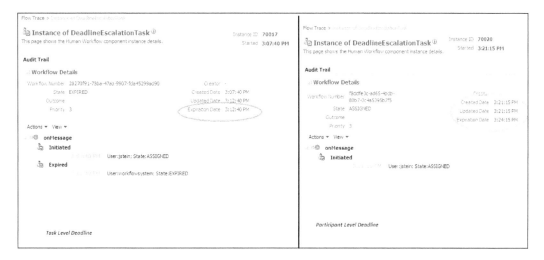

Participant Level Deadline can be set by navigating to **Participant Block | Participant Type Editor**. If we have **Task Level Deadline** and **Participant Level Deadline** defined for the task, then **Participant Level Deadline** takes precedence over **Task Level Deadline**. So, we will extend the **Task Level Deadline** use case, which we discussed previously. We will define **Participant Level Deadline** too. For this, perform the following steps:

1. Click on the **Assignment** tab in the task routing slip, and click on the participant block to open the **Edit Participant Type** window.

2. Go to the **Advanced** tab of the **Edit Participant Type** window, and check the **Limit allocated duration to** set a limit on the task allocation for that specific participant. Let's set this to 3 minutes for this use case, as shown in the following screenshot:

   ° Save and deploy the project. Remember that we have not changed the **Task Level Deadline** setting that we performed earlier.

   ° Execute the project, and you can see **Created Date** and the time and **Expiration Date** and the time specified for the task. As shown in the preceding screenshot, these show a difference of 3 minutes, which is the participant limit's allocated duration.

   ° Check the process trace, and you can see that if the user does not act on it, then the task expires after 3 minutes of being created.

Escalation, expiry, and renewal feature

To implement escalation for human tasks, you can implement it from the **Duration Deadline** section in the human task definition. By default, escalation is based on the management chain hierarchy, and the task gets escalated up in the hierarchy from the user to his/her manager, and so on. You can control the level to which the task can be escalated and also use a title to which the task gets escalated. The level and title assignment can be configured while configuring the human task definition's **Duration Deadline**. Oracle BPM offers you varied ways to escalate:

- Role-based escalation
- Level-and-title-based escalation
- Custom escalation

The following table highlights facts around the Escalation, Expiry, And Renewal Features:

Feature	Escalation, Expiry, And Renewal Feature
Classification	Human Task Pattern
Intent	To offer a preventive solution to escalate a task if it's not being acted on in the allocated time or if the deadline duration has expired.
Motivation	While performing task modeling, we have to deal with situations such as escalation, expiration, and renewal. A BPMN offering should have features such as expiry, escalation, renewal, and so on. In this section, we will define the escalation feature.
Applicability	To ensure that corrective measures are taken when participants don't act on assigned tasks in a timely manner, Oracle BPMN offers you various mechanisms to escalate the nonaction on the task, and while the escalation is performed, the task can be renewed or expired.
Implementation	The expiration policy is defined at the task and participant level where the participant level definition takes precedence over the task level specifications. In a serial routing pattern, each task assignment (basically each participant) gets the same time as the time specified in the expiration duration. So, if we have three users going to work on the task in a serial fashion and the expiration policy is 5 minutes, then each participant will have 5 minutes to act on the task (collectively, 15 minutes); otherwise, the escalation and renewal policy will be applied. However, if the routing pattern is the parallel routing pattern, then a routing slip is created for each participant, and each participant will have the same time. However, as it's being assigned in parallel and the expiration duration is decremented by the time that is elapsed in the task, if none of the users act on the parallel task in the specified duration, then the escalation and renewal policy will be applied.
Known issues	In the parallel routing pattern, if the parent task has subtasks, what would happen with the subtasks?
Known solution	In case the parent task has subtasks and the parent task has expired, then the subtasks are withdrawn if they have not been completed.

As we can see in the following screenshot, we can specify **Expire after** (pointer 1), **Renew after** (pointer 2), **Escalate after** (pointer 3), and **Never Expire** (pointer 4):

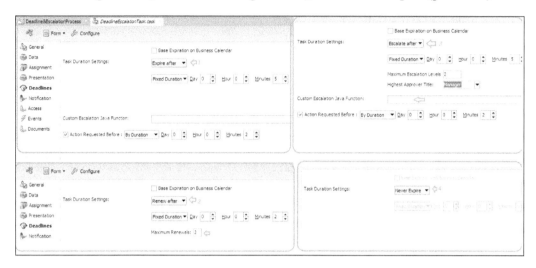

Never Expire allows a task to never get expired even if the allocated time has elapsed. With **Expire after action**, we can expire the task by specifying the time duration. (We have seen the demonstration of this in the **Deadline** section that we discussed previously). **Escalate after** allows you to escalate the task. The escalation can be role/position-based, or there can be customer escalation. To implement renewal, let's use the same use case that we used in the **Deadlines** features section and perform the following steps:

1. Expand the **DynamicTaskAssignment** project, and click on **DeadlineEscalationTask.task**.

2. Navigate to the **Deadlines** tab, and change the **Task Duration Settings** by selecting the **Renew after** action.

3. Specify a time list, say, 2 minutes, for this case.

4. Enter a value of **Maximum Renewals** (say, 2 times). This value specifies the maximum number of times the task will be renewed after expiring. When the maximum renewal number is reached, the task expires.

5. Open the **Participant** block and verify that the time limit of the allocated duration is 3 minutes.

6. This is the time that is allocated to the participant for him/her to act on the task; otherwise, the global escalation and expiry policy will be executed.

7. Save and deploy the project.

8. Test `Deadline&EscalationProcess` using the test data (`TestData12c.xml`).

9. Click on **Process Trace** and keep noting the changing process trace after every 3 minutes. Remember that 3 minutes is the time that you have allocated for each participant to act on the task.

As we can see in the following screenshot, for the first time the task gets created, the expiration time is the time specified in the duration of the allocated limit (**Participant Level Settings**), which is 3 minutes after the task creation. When the task expires after 3 minutes, it gets renewed for 2 minutes again (this is the time we have specified in the renewals). The maximum number of times the task gets renewed is 2, as this is the limit that we have set in **Maximum Renewal** in the global renewal policy. This is shown in the following screenshot:

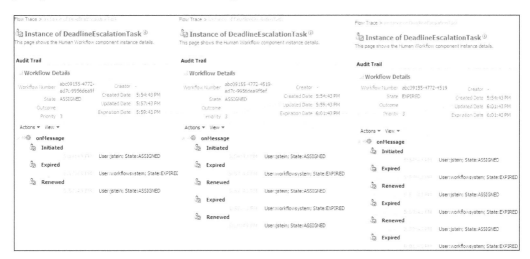

 To learn more about custom escalation and other details related to escalation, please visit my blog at `https://blogs.oracle.com/acharyavivek/`.

Exclusion feature

When performing task modeling, we have to deal with situations such as deadlines, reminders, escalation, expiration, and renewal. A BPMN offering should have features such as deadline, warning, reminders, escalation, renewal, and so on. The following table highlights facts around Exclusion Feature:

Feature	Exclusion Feature/Skipping Assignee/Participants
Classification	Human Task Pattern
Intent	To offer a mechanism to allow the exclusion of the participants.
Motivation	While perform task modeling, if we have specific conditions that result in bypassing the participants, then you need an exclusion mechanism.
Applicability	The exclusion feature finds applicability by ensuring that scenarios such as self approval or skipping a participant who has already acted on the task or bypassing a participant if some specific conditions are met.
Implementation	Navigate to the **Assignment** tab in the routing slip, and open the Participant block that opens up the **Participant Type** dialog box. Go to the **Advance** tab, and you will find the **Specify Skip Rule** checkbox. If you need to enable the skipping condition, then check the box and specify a skipping condition. When the skipping condition is evaluated and it results in true, then the participant is skipped (bypassed).
Known issues	NA
Known solution	NA

Error assignee and reviewers

When an error occurs, we need a mechanism to assign participants who can act or review errors. The following table highlights facts around Error Assignees And The Reviewer Feature:

Feature	Error Assignees And The Reviewer
Classification	Human Task Pattern
Intent	To offer a mechanism that performs a corrective mechanism when errors occur.
Motivation	While performing task modeling, we should be able to specify a user/group/role whose task gets assigned in case of an error and can be assigned to a user/group/role to review the task.

Applicability	Tasks get assigned to error assignees if they are specified. However, if there are no error assignees being specified, then the error task gets assigned to error assignees. Error assignees can perform ad hoc routing, task reassignment, or mark errors in the task as an indication that the task cannot be rectified further.
Implementation	Errors are of two types, recoverable and nonrecoverable. Recoverable errors include invalid users/groups, invalid Xpath expressions that evaluate assignees, invalid Xpath expressions that evaluate the deadline duration, escalation on expiration errors, evaluating escalation policy, and so on. Nonrecoverable errors include invalid task metadata, custom escalation functions, evaluation errors, and so on. The error assignee is implemented in the assignment and the routing section in the task metadata.
Known issues	What if there is an error in the evaluation of an error assignee?
Known solution	A task will be marked as an error.

To implement the scenario, we can extend the use case that we have implemented in the sections of this chapter that discuss escalation, expiry, and renewal:

1. Open `DeadlineEscalationTask.task`, and go to the **Assignment** tab.

2. Click on **Error Assignees**, and assign a user/group/application role that will receive the task in case there's an error (for the use case, we can assign it to any user, say, user `lata`).

3. Click on **Reviewers** and assign a user/group/role as a reviewer who can review the task and add comments in the **Comments** section. However, reviewers cannot perform any other action on the task.

4. Open the **Participant** block to change the spelling of the assigned user `jstein`. (Bring a change in the name so that the user cannot be identified in the LDAP/**myrealm**.)

5. Save and deploy the project.

6. Execute the project by running `Deadline&EscalationProcess` by passing the test data (`TestData12c.xml`).

We can see that the human task engine tries to look for the user `jstein`. However, as its spelling is changed (`jstin`), the user will not be found in **myrealm** (LDAP). This will result in a recoverable error, and the error task gets assigned to the error assignee (`lata`), as we can check in the instance history in the following screenshot:

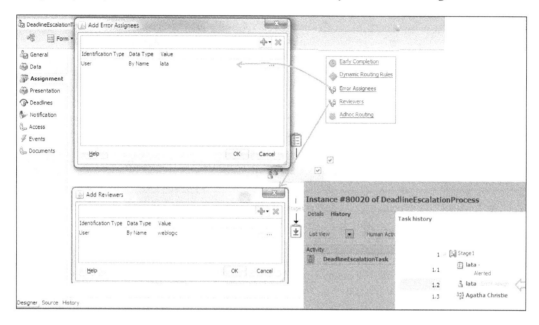

Notifications

When an error occurs, we need a mechanism that notifies participants (assignees, approvers, owners, and so on) via e-mails, SMSes, IMs, and so on. The following table highlights facts around Notification Feature:

Feature	Notification Feature
Classification	Human Task Pattern
Intent	To notify assignees, initiators, approvers, owners, and reviewers in case the task attains a status such as error, completed, update, and so on.
Motivation	This feature ensures that specified recipients are notified when the task reaches a defined status. This feature will also allow you to configure notification messages and set their behavior.
Applicability	Along with the feature that notifies interested users, when a task reaches a certain status, this feature is applicable in case we need to set reminders, defining Unicodes, make notifications secure, make notification emails actionable, send attachments, and so on.

Implementation	Notifications are implemented in the **Notification** tab in the task metadata definition, and notification leverages the UMS driver and workflow properties defined in the EM console.
Known issues	NA
Known solution	NA

Implementing notifications is a multiple-step process. For instance, we want to notify participants with e-mail as the channel. To enable notification, we have to first configure the e-mail driver. Then, we have to set the workflow properties. Along with this, the e-mail address should be associated with the user (the LDAP user/ **myrealm**) as its e-mail attribute. Finally, we need to configure the **Notification** tab in the task metadata.

Configuring driver properties and attributes

The notification feature leverages **User Messaging Service** (**UMS**). For the notification mechanism, we will first configure the e-mail driver:

1. Log in to the **Enterprise Manager** console, and navigate to **User Messaging Service**

2. Right-click on **User Messaging Service**, and select **Email Driver Properties**.

3. Furnish details to configure the e-mail driver by supplying SMTP and other details as per the e-mail server configuration. Click on **OK** to persist the driver configuration as shown in the following screenshot:

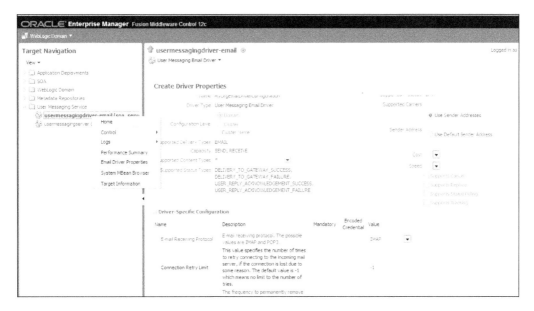

4. Configure workflow properties to enable e-mailing. Expand **SOA | SOA-Infra**.

5. Navigate to **SOA-INFRA | SOA Administration** and right-click on **Workflow properties**.

6. Select the notification mode as e-mail, furnish the notification service details, and apply the changes.

7. Log in to the WebLogic console, and navigate to **Domain | myrealm | Users And Groups | Attributes**.

8. Enter the e-mail address for the user in the mail attribute.

Configuring the notification definition

Once the driver is configured and the attributes and properties are set, it is now time to configure the notification definition in the task editor. Specify the task status, recipient, and notification header details:

- The **Task Status** column specifies when the notification will be initiated and on what status of the task that specific notification will be initiated. Various task statuses are shown in following screenshot. For example, if the **Task Status** is completed, then the task initiator will be notified.

- The **Recipient** column enlists the possible recipient of the notification:
    - **Assignees**: This is the group/user to whom the task is being assigned currently.
    - **Initiator**: This refers to the creator of the task.
    - **Approvers**: This includes the list of all the users who have acted on the task till this point.
    - **Owner**: This refers to the owner of the task.
    - **Reviewer**: This refers to the reviewer of the task who can add comments and attachment to the task; however, he/she cannot act on the task This is shown in the following screenshot:

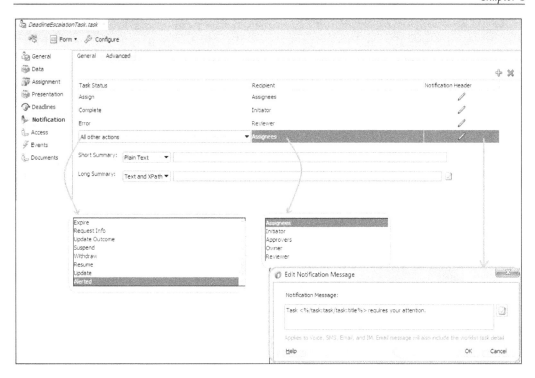

The **Notification Header** column shows you the message that will be sent to the recipient when the task reaches the specified status. We can edit the notification message, and the message will be applicable to all the supporting channels, that is, e-mail, voice, IM, SMS, and so on.

The **Advance** tab allows you to configure reminders, Unicode, secure notifications, and various other features, as enlisted:

- The reminder subsection in the notification's **Advance** tab allows you to send a reminder before a task expires or after the task assignment.

- Unicode allows you to store information in a single character set by proving a unique code value for each character irrespective of its language or platform. Select UTF-8 (default), or you can use a Java class to specify the character set.

- **Make notification secure**: Checking this box will allow you to make the task secure; however, if you do so, you will not be able to make notifications actionable and will not be able to send task attachments with e-mail notifications.

- **Show worklist URL in notifications**: Checking this box allows you to display the BPM worklist application URL in the e-mail notification sent to the recipient.

- **Make notification actionable**: Check this box if you want to allow the notification recipient to perform the task action through e-mail.

- **Send task attachments with e-mail notifications**: Checking this box will allow you to send task attachments via e-mail notifications. You can send notifications to individual e-mails. Checking this option will result in an individual receipt of the e-mail by each user in the group/role.

- **Use separate task forms based on locale**: This is enabled by default, with notifications to individual e-mails. When checked, this option will result in the receipt of individual e-mails by the users based on the language locale; otherwise, the task form will be reused and shared.

- Send one email containing all the user addresses; this will result in the receipt of an e-mail by all users in the group/role.

E-mail address are picked from the LDAP for the users; hence, we just set the e-mail address for the user in the embedded LDAP.

Content access policy and task actions

Tasks have contents such as attachments, comments, payload, history, and so on. BPMN offers you a mechanism that controls access to the contents and performs actions selectively. The following table highlights facts around the Content Access Policy And Task Actions Feature:

Feature	Content Access Policy And Task Actions Feature
Classification	Human Task Pattern
Intent	To specify access rules on the contents and define actions that are to be performed on these contents.
Motivation	To define which part of the task can be viewed and updated by participants and what actions can be performed on the contents.
Applicability	Access rules are basically rules that are enforced by the workflow service during the task update and retrieval.

Implementation	In the task metadata editor, navigate to **Access	Content**.
	Here, we can grant privileges to users (owner, approvers, and so on) so that they can act on specific task content such as payload, header, flex field, and so on.
	In the task metadata editor, navigate to **Access	Actions**.
	Actions allow you to define the actions (access or no access) for the defined users so that they can act on the task contents that we have configured in the **Contents** tab.
Known issues	What if access rules and action rules conflict with each other?
Known solution	In Oracle BPMN, access rules exist independent of one another.

Enterprise content management for task documents

The following table highlights facts around Enterprise Content Management For The Task Documents Feature:

Feature	Enterprise Content Management For Task Documents
Classification	Human Task Pattern
Intent	To offer a BPMN task solution that integrates with the enterprise content management solution.
Motivation	Human tasks can be configured to use attachments from contents and documents stored in the enterprise content management store.
Applicability	Applies to the feature of querying and fetching documents and attaching them with the task where the documents are stored in the enterprise content management store. Also, it offers you the flexibility to provide query properties at design time and at runtime in the task form.
Implementation	Enables document packaging in order to connect ECM and queries based on properties that can be implemented in the **Documents** tab in the task editor.
Known issues	NA
Known solution	NA

The document will be stored in ECM; however, documents have metadata properties, consuming services, applications, or task configuration, which can be used to retrieve that specific document from the ECM store. Make sure that the underlying SOA infrastructure is configured to integrate with the ECM solution of the enterprise. We can manage documents, document folder, version, and so on in the ECM solution application. However, to enable the human task to retrieve documents from ECM, perform the following steps:

1. Navigate to the `.task` file and visit the **Documents** tab.

2. Check the **Use Document Package** checkbox in order to enable using ECM.

3. Once **Use Document Package** is checked, the task properties are enlisted.

4. Select specific properties such as **Document Folder**, **Content Id**, **Version Label**, and so on along with the default specified properties (the security group and document type). This is shown in the following screenshot:

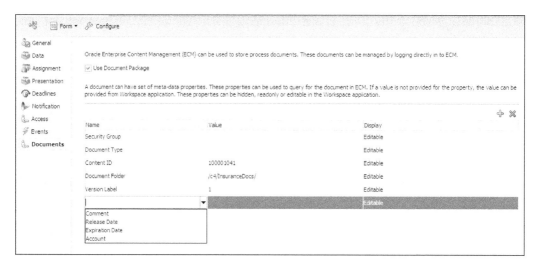

5. Set the display property as **Editable**, **Hidden,** and **Read Only**.

The value provided in the display mode that defines the behavior on the task means that we can enter the value at design time in the **Documents** tab, as shown in the preceding screenshot, or we can define value of the properties in the **Task** form, if that property is **editable**. If the display mode is editable, then in the task form, a value can provided for the properties while attaching the document. If the display mode is hidden, then the value will not be displayed at runtime in the task form. If it's **Read Only**, then the value of the property will not be visible, and it cannot be edited.

Summary

This chapter concentrated on human task patterns and during this journey, we covered various patterns that facilitate human task patterns. We now know that a stage defines the milestone of the approval sequence. Stages contain participant types, which defines the behavior of the routing pattern. A task can be assigned to participants through different means. There are different derivation patterns, and there are different assignment patterns as well. During the course of this chapter, we explored various Oracle BPMN features, which enhances human task patterns such as the request info feature, reassignment and delegation pattern, force completion pattern, routing rule pattern, error assignees and reviewers, deadline, escalation, expiry and renewal, exclusion, error assignee and reviewer, notification, content access policy and task actions, and enterprise content management for task documents.

The next chapter elaborates on the interaction patterns.

5
Interaction Patterns

Processes are not always isolated. They interact and integrate with other systems, processes, and services. These interactions are facilitated by various interaction patterns. This chapter covers various patterns that offer best practice around communications with other processes, systems, and services. It showcases various patterns of interactions of a BPM process with other BPM processes and services. Interaction patterns are more commonly known as **Inter Process Communication (IPC)**, which facilitates collaboration of a process with other processes, services, and events. There are many reasons that lead to collaborative communications:

- Your process needs to invoke other services, for example, the Loan Origination process needs to invoke a credit check service or your process might need to invoke another process; for example, the Loan Origination process may need to invoke the BackgroundCheck process.

- You might need to implement reusability, develop modular processes, and collaborate with them.

- You might need to iterate over a collection/set of data and hence, need subprocesses and multi-instance features in a separate process or subprocess.

- You might need to widely broadcast an information enterprise and let other interested processes/services interact via subscription to these events. There might be cases where you might have to deal with human interactions and patterns such as escalation, reminders, and so on.

This chapter is focused on events, interaction tasks, and activities. The following interaction patterns are a part of this chapter:

- Conversation pattern
- Asynchronous interaction pattern
- Synchronous interaction pattern

- Subprocess interaction pattern
  - ° Reusable processes interaction pattern
  - ° Embedded subprocess interaction pattern

- Event-driven interaction pattern

 Visit the following link to learn more about BPM events:
`http://acharyavivek.wordpress.com/2013/11/20/`
`understanding-bpm-event/`.

Defining use cases to demonstrate interaction patterns

Download the Loan Origination application from the downloadable files of *Chapter 5, Interaction Patterns*. The downloaded project contains the processes and components described in the upcoming sections. This section will help you understand the different processes that we will be covering in this chapter.

The BackOffice process

The BackOffice process invokes the loan origination process using the Message Throw Event (**RequestLoanOrigination**). Upon receiving the response from the Loan Origination process on the Message Catch Event (**RespLoanOrigination**), the BackOffice process initiates a feedback process. When the feedback process is completed, the feedback process raises an event. The BackOffice process resumes when it gets a message on the subscribed queue on which it's waiting for the feedback to complete. The following screenshot showcases the BackOffice process model:

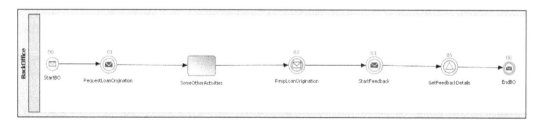

The Loan origination process

The Loan Origination process checks for application verification. If the application is verified, then the loan origination process checks for the applicant's credit, and does a background and fraud check. The Loan Origination process is modeled as shown in the following diagram:

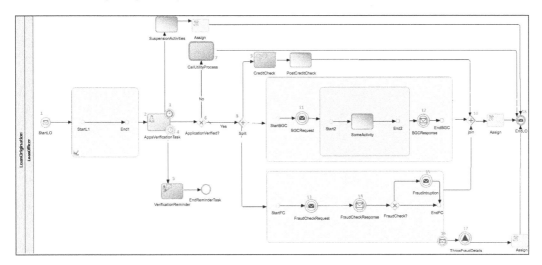

The CatchFraudDetails and Feedback processes

The Feedback process is demonstrated in the *Event-driven interaction pattern* section of this chapter. It handles customer feedback based on signals (events). It starts with a message; however, it ends by raising a feedback event using the Signal End Event (**EndFeedback**). The CatchFraudDetails process starts with an event and ends with a None End Event.

The following diagram illustrates the **CatchFraudDetails** and **Feedback** processes:

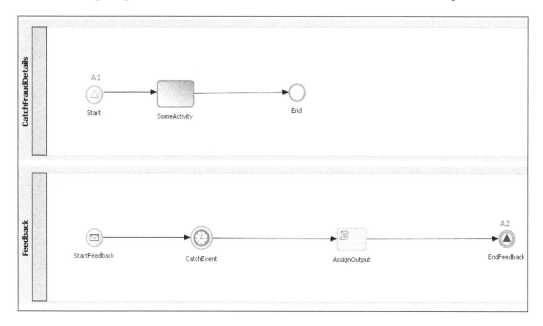

The following points illustrate the entire use case that we will cover in this chapter. The purpose of listing these bullet points is to make you aware of how different processes are woven. However, each process is demonstrated in its respective section. For example, the feedback process is invoked by the BackOffice process. When the feedback process completes the application's customer feedback, it will raise a feedback event. The following list shows the relation of different processes; however, the implementation of the individual process (for example, the feedback process) and description of the pattern is described in that respective section. Walk through the following steps to understand the relation between different processes:

1. The BackOffice process invokes the Loan Origination process.

2. Upon receiving a response from the Loan Origination process, the BackOffice process initiates a feedback process.

3. The feedback process raises an event when the feedback gets completed.

4. The BackOffice process resumes when it gets a message on the subscribed queue on which it's waiting for the feedback to complete.

5. The Loan Origination process performs the application verification using a human task.

6. The application verification's human task has a timer, which ensures:

   If the task assignee doesn't act on the task in a day's time, a reminder e-mail is sent to the task assignee's e-mail address.

   If the task assignee doesn't act on the task in 3 days' time, the suspension activities are performed and the process ends.

7. Upon approval of the application verification task, the process is split into the following three activities:

   ° Checking customer credit using the credit check service invocation

   ° Background check by invoking the `BackgroundCheck` process

   ° Fraud check by interacting with the fraud check service

     If the fraud check process is positive, then a fraud interruption message is raised. The boundary catch event gets the interruption message, and the process throws a **FraudDetails** signal and ends. The fraud details signal is caught by a subscribed **CatchFraudDetails** process.

     If the fraud check is negative, then the process moves normally, and all paths merge at the join gateway.

8. Upon rejection of the application verification task, the Loan Origination process calls a `LOUtility` service to perform escalation and other activities, and the process ends.

Oracle BPM offers various components that interact with a process and enable its collaboration with other events/signals, services, processes, and so on. The following table includes BPMN 2.0 components and their demonstration in the use case. A number is defined in the diagrams for back office, Loan Origination, and other processes for a specific component, as shown in the following screenshot. This number is included adjacent to the component. All these details and discussions around them are part of this chapter. This is shown in the following screenshot:

Component	Number in Diagram
Message Start Event	00 (Back Office process) and 1 (Loan Origination process)
Message End Event	06 and 18
Message Throw Event	01 (Back Office Process) , 11 and 13 (Loan Origination Process)
Message Catch Event	02, 12 and 14
Signal Start Event	A1 (Catch Fraud Details Process)
Signal End Event	A2 (Feedback Process)
Signal Throw Event	17 (Loan Origination Process)
Signal Catch Event	05 (Back office process)
None Start	Background Check process and All Sub process
None End	Background Check process and All Sub process
None Throw	
None Catch	
Terminate	Catch Fraud Details Process
Timer Start	Chapter 3
Timer Catch	3,4 (Loan Origination Process)
Error Catch	Chapter Error handling
Error End	Chapter Error handling
Timer Start	Chapter 3
Timer	3 and 4 Loan Origination Process
Message	16 Loan Origination Process
Signal	Error Handling Chapter
None	Error Handling Chapter
Error	Error Handling Chapter

Other than the components, you have certain activities that are a must to enable collaboration with other processes and services. These activities are demonstrated in the following screenshot:

Activity	Number in Diagram
Send Task	Background Check Process
Receive Task	Background Check Process
Service Task	9 Loan Origination Process
Call	7 Loan Origination Process
Embedded Sub process	Loan Origination Process
Reusable Sub Process	LOUtilityProcess
Multi-Instance Sub process	Demonstrated in Chapter 1 and Chapter 2
Peer process	
Event Sub process	Included as part of Error Handling Chapter

Conversation pattern

Conversation pattern allows a BPM process instance to collaborate with another process or service instance. Conversation patterns find usage when you have multi-instance scenarios where a master process needs to establish multiple parallel conversations with a child process/subprocess, or those scenarios where a process instance collaborates with other process/service instances.

The following pattern table highlights the facts around the conversation pattern:

Signature	Conversation Pattern
Classification	Interaction Pattern
Intent	Conversation allows a BPM process instance to collaborate with another process or service instance.
Motivation	Grouping of message exchange (collaboration) between processes is performed using conversations. Collaboration can be synchronous or asynchronous. Collaborating participants could be BPM processes, BPEL/mediator processes, human tasks, business rules, external services, references, and so on.
Applicability	In BPM, a conversation can be defined for a Send/Throw/End message and Receive/Catch/Start message, using the conversation property. The BPM engine uses the WS-addressing correlation or message-based correlation, and default/advance-defined WS-conversation ID for each conversation.

Implementation	The BPM process starts an outbound conversation when it participates in a conversation that has already been started by a participant process or service. The conversation can be a scoped conversation, default conversation, or advance conversation:
	• **Scoped conversation**: This refers to the conversations that are defined in scope, which is inside the subprocess. When you define a scoped conversation, make sure that you define it in the structure panel; otherwise, it would inherit a process scope.
	• **Advance conversation**: This refers to an explicitly defined conversation. A default conversation is available by default in a BPM project; however, you can define an advance conversation in some cases, such as those cases that involve multi-instance collaboration and so on.
	• **Default conversation**: Other than defining an advance conversation, you can also use the default conversation. The default conversation is available with a BPMN process by default, and you don't have to explicitly define a conversation.
Known issues	These include message correlation.
Known solution	If the message exchange pattern is a synchronous request and response, then the BPM engine uses the WS-addressing correlation and default/advance-defined WS-conversation ID for each conversation.
	However, if the message exchange pattern is an asynchronous (one-way) request-callback, then you need to define the message-based correlation along with the conversation ID (default/advance defined).

 If you define a conversation, then you can visualize the collaborative conversation in collaboration diagrams.

In this section, we will witness the implementation of an advance conversation. An advance conversation is defined between a BackOffice process and the Loan Origination process. We will notice the usage of the advance conversation in the BackOffice process in this section. However, for the rest of the sections in this chapter, we will find the implementation of the default conversation. The following is the screenshot of the BackOffice process that will be discussed in this chapter. The back office process interacts with the Loan Origination process and has conversations being defined.

Use the following steps to check how conversations are defined and witness them in action while checking the collaboration diagram:

1. Download the Loan Origination application from *Chapter 5, Interaction Patterns*.

2. Start JDeveloper and open `LoanOriginationApps.jws` to open the Loan Origination process.

3. Navigate to **LoanOriginationApps | LoanOriginationProject | BackOffice process**.

4. Go to the **BackOffice – Structure** window in the bottom-left corner of the screen, as shown in the following screenshot:

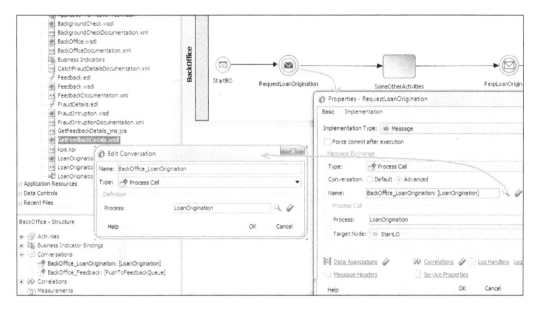

5. Check the conversation defined in the structure window shown in the preceding screenshot. There are two conversations defined: one between the `BackOffice` process and Loan Origination process, and another between the `BackOffice` process and feedback process.

6. Right-click on the **BackOffice_LoanOrigination** conversation defined in the structure window. You can verify that it's being defined for the process call.

7. Right-click on the **RequestLoanOrigination** Message Throw Event in the `BackOffice` process and check its properties. You can find that the defined conversation is selected there as an **Advanced** conversation.

8. Click on the **Collaboration** tab, as shown in the upcoming screenshot.

The process flow is shown through the collaboration diagram, which also shows a process's interactions and collaboration with other processes and services. You can check the following facts from the collaboration diagram:

- The `BackOffice` process interacts with the Loan Origination process by sending a message through the **RequestLoanOrigination** throw message event and receiving a response message through the **RespLoanOrigination** Message Catch Event.

- The `BackOffice` process interacts with an external service through the **StartFeedback** throw message event. This is shown in the following screenshot:

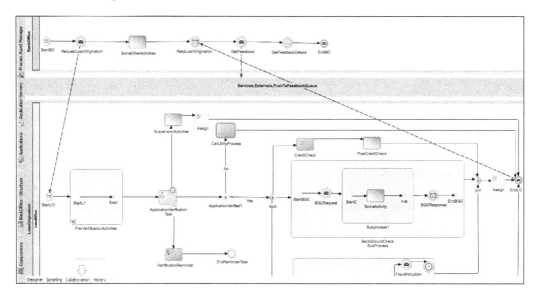

We can define different types of conversation. For example, you can define a conversation in which a BPMN process can be exposed as a service or a process; then, you can define the interaction operations using the **Define Interface** conversation type. If our process needs to interact with another BPMN process or service, then define the conversation type as process call and service call, respectively. Also, you can define the conversation using an interaction interface (which already exists) from the business catalog, using the **Use Interface** conversation type.

While walking though this chapter, we will notice that while interacting with a BPM process, the conversation type is used heavily. For some interactions, we will witness the usage of the service call conversation type. The service call conversation type is used to invoke a service. The process call conversation type is used to invoke a BPM process. Essentially, a conversation type defines different types of interactions that our process can establish with other processes or services. The following list describes the different types of conversations:

- **Define interface**: This conversation type is used when you want to define operations for your BPMN process with which other services and processes can interact.

- **Use interface**: This conversation type is used when you want to use an interface that is already defined and is available in the business catalog.

- **Process call**: This conversation type is used to invoke another BPMN process.

- **Service call**: This conversation is mostly used to invoke a service defined in your BPM project.

 Before you execute any process in this chapter, make sure that you create **LOFeedbackQueue** in the weblogic service with the **jms/LOFeedbackQueue** JNDI, using the steps mentioned in the *Guaranteed delivery pattern* section of *Chapter 3, Invocation Patterns*.

Asynchronous interaction pattern

The BPM process can invoke an asynchronous process or service using the Message Throw Event or Send Task. The process can use either the Message Catch Event or Receive Task to receive a response from the invoked process/service. When we invoke an asynchronous process or a service, the invoked process or service becomes a child of the calling (invoking) process. This section will uncover how to invoke an asynchronous process or service using the Message Throw and Catch Event. This section also has a subsection on invoking an asynchronous process or service using the Send and Receive Tasks. The following pattern table illustrates the pattern signature for an asynchronous request response (request callback) pattern:

Signature	Asynchronous Request-Response (request-callback) Pattern
Classification	Interaction Pattern
Intent	Invoke an asynchronous operation on an asynchronous service or process.

Motivation	When an asynchronous process or service is invoked, the BPMN engine will not wait for the response and will start executing subsequent activities that follow the Message Throw or Send Task. The calling process will invoke the called process's callback operation using the Message Catch Event or Receive Task to get the response.
Applicability	The BPM process can invoke an asynchronous process or service using the Message Throw Event or Send Task. It can use either the Message Catch Event or Receive Task to get the response. When you invoke an asynchronous process or service, the invoked process or service becomes a child of the calling (invoking) process.
Implementation	The Message Throw Event or Send Task, when used to invoke a BPM process/service, essentially initiates a conversation. While executing a Throw Event or Send Task, the BPM engine creates the following features: • An XML message based on the asynchronous operation • Input required by the asynchronous operation • Data association defined in the intermediate Message Throw Event This XML message is sent to the asynchronous BPM process or service. The calling (invoking) process does not wait for the response, and it will continue the subsequent process flow. The called (invoked) asynchronous service or process will execute the asynchronous operation. The calling process will invoke the callback operation to get a response from the called (invoked) process using the Message Catch Event or Receive Task. In the calling process, when the process token arrives at the Message Catch Event or Receive Task, the process waits for the asynchronously called (invoked) process to respond. If the called process has already responded, then the calling process will receive the response at the Message Catch Event or Receive Task. If not, then the process token will wait at the Message Catch Event or Receive Task until a response is received.
Known issues	These include reliability.
Known solution	To ensure that the message gets routed to the appropriate requester, the message correlation must be implemented to relate inbound and outbound messages.

Interacting with an asynchronous process using the Message Throw and Catch events

The message events (Throw Event and Catch Event) enable interaction with asynchronous services and asynchronous processes. In this section, we will learn how to interact with asynchronous processes using the Message Throw and Catch Events while walking through the `BackOffice` process scenario. We will use Message Throw and Catch Events to invoke the Loan Origination process, which is an asynchronous process. To enable this invocation, the advance conversation is used and the **Process Call** conversation type is defined. The Loan Origination process is an asynchronous BPMN process, which starts with a Message Start Event and ends with a Message End Event. The `BackOffice` process invokes the Loan Origination process using a Message Throw Event. The process receives a response from the Loan Origination process by configuring a Message Catch Event. It will then implement the **Process Call** conversation type to interact with the Loan Origination process.

Perform the following steps to understand the conversation configuration in the `BackOffice` process, which enables collaboration with the Loan Origination process:

1. Start JDeveloper and open the **LoanOriginationApps** application.

2. Navigate to **LoanOriginationProject | BackOffice Process**.

3. Open the **BackOffice** process.

4. Open the properties of the **RequestLoanOrigination** Message Throw Event and go to the **Implementation** tab.

5. While implementing the Message Throw Event, the message exchange type, that is, the conversation type, is **Process Call**. This is because the Loan Origination process is an asynchronous BPM process. Remember to use the **Process Call** conversation type to invoke another BPMN process.

6. **Advance Conversation** is defined because you have already defined a conversation for the `BackOffice` and Loan Origination processes.

7. Select the **BackOffice_LoanOrigination** conversation. You will find details of the Loan Origination process populating in the process name and target node. The target node is the Message Start Event of the Loan Origination process.

8. Click on **Data Associations** to view the data assignment.

9. We can check the correlation configuration. However, the details around correlation will be discussed in *Chapter 6, Correlation Patterns*.

10. Verify the properties of the **RespLoanOrigination** Message Catch Event. The Message Catch Event in the `BackOffice` process receives a response from the Loan Origination process.

11. We can witness the conversation type as **Process Call**. The same **BackOffice_LoanOrigination** conversation that we used while configuring the Message Throw Event, is used.

12. The process name will be **LoanOrigination**. However, this time, the target node is **EndLO**, which is the Message End Event of the asynchronous Loan Origination process, as shown in the following screenshot:

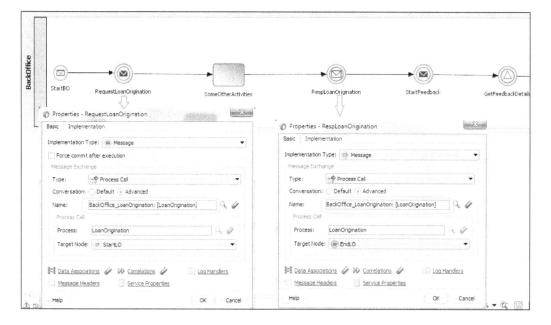

13. Check the data association; we can find the data assignment from the Loan Origination process output to output the process data object of the `BackOffice` process.

14. Open the Loan Origination process and check the properties of its Message Start Event.

15. You can find that an asynchronous operation, **startLO**, is defined to accept any asynchronous requests based on the Loan Origination data object (Loan Origination schema).

16. Check the Message End Event, **endLO**, which ends the Loan Origination process, as shown in the following screenshot.

17. You can verify that the message exchange interface pattern is defined as asynchronous. This configuration makes the Loan Origination process an asynchronous process.

18. You can check whether the **endLO** operation is exposed as the callback operation. This is demonstrated in the following screenshot:

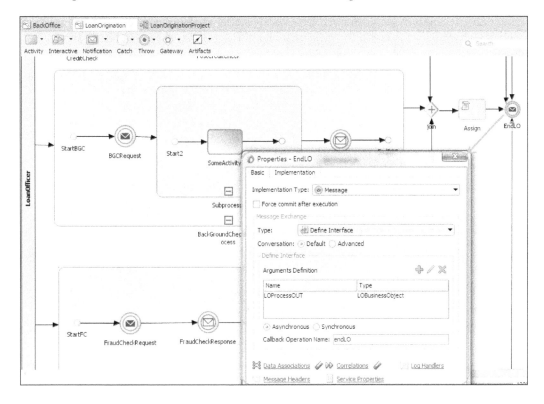

The BackOffice process will obtain the response from the Loan Origination process by invoking the **endLO** service callback operation using the Message Catch Event. Even if the Loan Origination process ends much before the BackOffice process reaches the Message Catch Event, the BackOffice process will not receive the response message. The BackOffice process will receive the response only when the Loan Origination process completes and the BackOffice process has reached the **RespLoanOrigination** Message Catch Event.

Interacting with an asynchronous service using the Message Throw and Catch Events

In this section, we will learn to interact and invoke an asynchronous service using the Message Throw and Catch Events. Let's consider an example scenario:

The Loan Origination process performs various checks such as application verification and some parallel verification such as credit card check, background check, and fraud check. Fraud check is implemented as a subprocess, which has a Message Throw and Message Catch Event being configured to interact with the **FraudCheck** service. This fraud check service is implemented using Oracle SOA's BPEL as an asynchronous service. In this section, we will learn to invoke an asynchronous service using the Message Throw and Catch Events. The **Service Call** conversation type is defined to enable this interaction.

Perform the following steps to witness how the Message Throw Event in **FraudCheckSubProcess** invokes the **FraudCheck** asynchronous service by interacting with the operations exposed by the fraud check service:

1. Open the Loan Origination process and go to **FraudCheckSubProcess**.

2. Right-click on the **FraudCheckRequest** Message Throw Event and go to the **Implementation** tab in the properties dialog.

3. We can verify that the conversation type is **Service Call**. This is because the **FraudCheck** service is implemented as a web service.

4. We can find the **FraudCheck** service operation being populated in the operation dropdown. This operation is the request operation of the **FraudCheck** process.

5. Check the data association to learn the data assignment.

6. For the **FraudCheckResponse** Message Catch Event, the response operation gets populated as the callback operation. This is shown in the following screenshot:

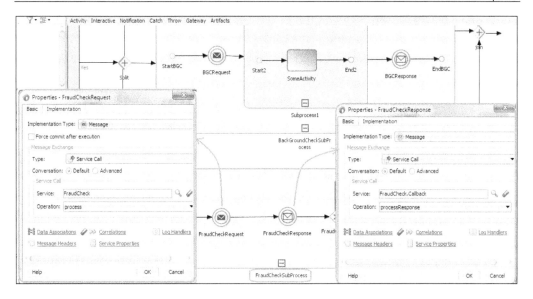

Enabling external services interaction

In this section, we will uncover how we can enable the external web service interactions in BPM. As you saw earlier, the Loan Origination process is able to invoke the **FraudCheck** service, which is an asynchronous service, even though the **FraudCheck** service is not a part of the **LoanOriginationProject**. To enable communication with the external service, we need to configure a service adapter. For example, say we need to interact with queues, and then, we have to define a JMS adapter that exposes queues as services and helps the BPM processes interact with them.

As we are going to implement this project in our environment, we will perform the following steps:

1. Download **LoanOriginationApps** and open it in JDeveloper 12*c*.

2. Along with **LoanOriginationProject**, we can also find the **FraudCheck** and **CreditCheckPrj** projects.

3. Deploy the **FraudCheck** project to your web logic service and go to the EM console at `http://service:port/em`.

4. Click on the **FraudCheck** service and copy its WSDL.

To enable a conversation between the Loan Origination process and the **FraudCheck** service, we need to define a web service adapter as a reference service in project's (**LoanOriginationProject**) `composite.xml`. Perform the following steps to verify the web service adapter configuration:

1. Go to the composite file of **LoanOriginationProject** and open it.

2. Click on the **FraudCheck** service reference properties. It is configured using the web service adapter.

3. Open the web service adapter configuration of the **FraudCheck** service in the composite file of **LoanOriginationProject** as seen in the following screenshot.

4. Enter the copied WSDL of the **FraudCheck** service and hit the **Tab** button. This will populate the request and callback operations. This is shown in the following screenshot:

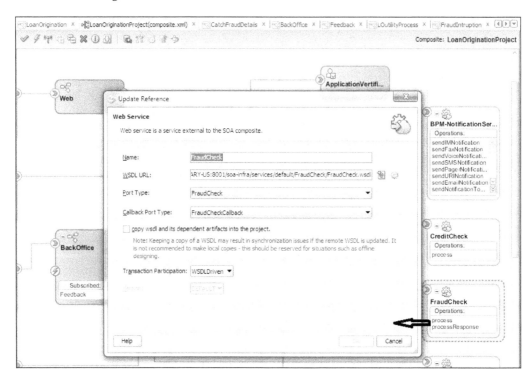

Interacting with an asynchronous process and service using Send and Receive Tasks

Communication with other BPM processes and services in the project can be implemented using the Send and Receive Tasks. Send and Receive Tasks are similar to throw and catch events. However, we can define a boundary event on the Send and Receive Tasks. Boundary events can be used in various business scenarios such as enabling an SLA on a particular task or defining an escalation, and so on. Send and Receive Tasks can be used to communicate with other processes and services. They can be used to expose a process, which can be initiated with a Receive Task. Such a process can be invoked by a Message Throw Event and also by a Send Task.

For the scenario in this section, the BackOffice process initiates a Loan Origination process. It's based on the fact that a loan customer is interacting with a bank's back office, and it's the back office that initiates the loan on behalf of the customer. However, there might be other channels too. Lets' create a web process, keeping the fact that this process will be the process that gets kicked off when a user interacts with a user interface, such as a web application, and fills in the loan details. The Loan Origination process gets initiated when the web process gets started from the user interface.

A Send Task will invoke the asynchronous Loan Origination process's **startLO** operation and will receive the task to invoke the callback operation paired with the asynchronous service/process.

Perform the following steps to create a web process that invokes the Loan Origination process through the Send and Receive Tasks.

1. Navigate to **LoanOriginationProject | BPMN | BPMN Processes** and right-click on the processes to create a new process.

2. Enter the name of the process as Web and let it be an asynchronous process.

3. Create the **WebProcessIN** and **WebProcessOUT** process arguments as web process input and output arguments, respectively, based on **LOBusinessObject**. This business object is used throughout the project, and it's based on the Loan Origination schema.

4. Click on **Finish** to end the process wizard.

5. Create the **webINPDO** and **webOUTPDO** process data objects based on **LOBusinessObject**. We can create **process data objects** (PDOs) from the structure window.

6. Click on the Message Start Event and open its properties.

7. Click on data association on the Message Start Event and assign the **WebProcessIN** web process's input argument to the PDO of the **webINPDO** web process input.

8. Drag-and-drop a Send Task in the process and name it **SendLoanRequest**.

9. Go to **SendLoanRequest** Send Task's implementation properties.

10. Choose the conversation type as **Process Call** and set the conversation to default.

11. Click on **Browse** to select the **Loan Origination** process from the process list.

12. Select the **Loan Origination** process and click on **OK**.

13. You will find **startLO** as the target node, which gets automatically populated.

14. Use data association to assign the PDO of the **webINPDO** web process input to the **LOProcessIN** input argument of the Loan Origination process.

15. Click on **OK** in the properties of the **SendLoanRequest** Send Task and save the changes.

16. Drag-and-drop the Receive Task and name it **ReceiveLoanResponse**. Then, go to its **Implementation** tab.

17. Select the conversation type as **Process Call** and let the default conversation be checked.

18. Browse to select the **Loan Origination** process.

19. The target node will get populated with the **endLO** end node of the Loan Origination process.

20. Use data association to assign the **LOProcessOUT** output of the Loan Origination process to **webOUTPDO**, which is the PDO of the web process output, and click on **OK**.

21. Click on **Message End Event** in the web process and configure the data association from **WebOUTPDO** to the **webProcessOUT** output argument of the web process.

22. Save all the changes and deploy the project.

Test the scenario by initiating the web process. When the Loan Origination process is invoked by the web process's Send Task, the web process will not wait for a response from the Loan Origination process and will continue with the subsequent flow. However, the web process will receive a response from the Loan Origination process by invoking the **endLO** callback operation of Loan Origination using a Receive Task. If the Loan Origination process finishes before the web process reaches the Receive Task, the web process will not receive a response. It would only receive a response when the web process reaches the Receive Task and invokes the **endLO** callback operation of Loan Origination.

However, if the web process is quick and the process token for the web process reaches the Receive Task much before the Loan Origination process gets completed, the BPM service engine will wait at the receive task for the Loan Origination process to complete.

Attaching boundary events on Send and Receive Tasks

The boundary events, when triggered, can either interrupt the normal process flow, or they can be mutually exclusive with the normal flow. They can also start an exception flow parallel to the normal flow. This behavior depends on the boundary event's configuration.

We will be visiting the boundary events in detail later in this chapter. In this section, we will define a **Service Level Agreement** (**SLA**) for the loan process. Let's consider a use case where, if the Loan Origination process is not completed in 7 days, then the loan process initiator (the web process) will end the flow. This means the boundary event will be a timer, and it will be of the interrupting type as it's going to stop the normal flow of the process. Execute the following steps to enable a boundary event on the Receive Task:

1. Open the web process that you implemented earlier in JDeveloper.

2. Drag-and-drop a catch timer event on the **ReceiveLoanResponse** Receive Task and name it SLA.

3. Check the interrupting event check box and configure the implementation properties, as defined in the preceding screenshot.

4. Set the time cycle as 7 days. (For a quick test, we can set it to 5 minutes).

5. Save the process and deploy it.

Enabling the timer with 7 days as the time cycle will trigger the timer 7 days after the process initiation. If the web process doesn't receive a response from the Loan Origination process in 7 days, then the timer gets triggered and the web process will interrupt the normal Loan Origination process flow. The loan details will be saved, and the process will end.

Interacting with a process defined with Receive Task as a start activity

In this section, we will implement an asynchronous process with a Receive Task as the start activity. The Loan Origination process is an asynchronous process with a Message Start Event. However, we can also define an asynchronous process with a Receive Task as the start activity. The **BackgroundCheck** process is implemented as an asynchronous process that starts with a receive activity. A BPM process that starts with a Receive Task enables an asynchronous conversation. While creating a BPM process, the Receive Task should be followed by a **None** event (None Start Event).

The None Start Event does not have any special properties, and it is also not associated with any trigger mechanism. However, to enable a conversation with processes that have the None Start Event, remember to use an Initiator Task event or Receive Task event, with the **Create Instance** property being checked.

Walk through the following steps to check the **BackgroundCheck** process's implementation:

1. Navigate to **JDeveloper | LoanOriginationProject | BackgroundCheck** and open the **BackgroundCheck** process.

2. You will find a **ReceiveBackgroundCheckReq** receive activity after a None Start Event.

3. Right-click to open the properties and go to the **Implementation** tab.

4. We can verify that the conversation type is **Define Interface**.

5. We have used the default conversation; however, an advance conversation can be defined.

6. We can check whether an operation is exposed with the name **ReceiveBackgroundCheckReq**. This is the operation that any other process can use to communicate with the background check process.

7. Click on the **sendBackgroundCheckResp** Send Task and check its properties; you can witness that a callback operation is defined with the name **sendBackgroundCheckResp**.

8. The message exchange pattern is selected as **Asynchronous**. This makes the process an asynchronous process. This is shown in the following screenshot:

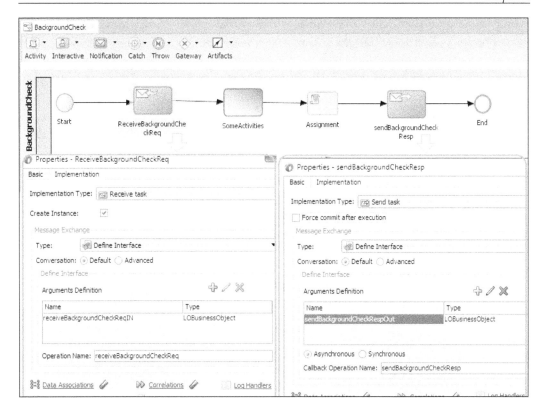

Open the Loan Origination process and expand **BackGroundCheckSubProcess**. You can find that a Message Throw Event and Message Catch Event are configured to interact with the **BackgroundCheck** process. Click on **BGCRequest** in **BackGroundCheckSubProcess** and check its properties.

As you can see in the following screenshot, the **Conversation** type defined to interact with the **BackgroundCheck** process is **Process Call** because it is a process. You can verify that the target node exposed has the same name as the operation, **ReceiveBackgroundCheckReq**, defined in the Receive Task activity in the **BackgroundCheck** process.

In the Message Catch Event, you can find the callback operation selected as the target node. This is shown in the following screenshot:

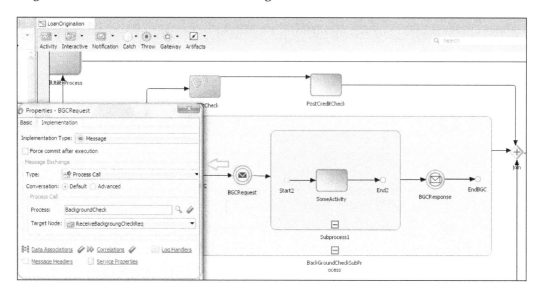

The Loan Origination process will obtain the response of the **BackgroundCheck** process by invoking the **sendBackgroundCheckResp** callback operation using the **BGCResponse** Message Catch Event.

Synchronous request-response pattern

When we need to interact with a process or service and when an immediate response is required, use the synchronous interaction pattern. The following table lists the details of the synchronous request-response pattern:

Signature	Request Response Pattern
Classification	Interaction Pattern
Intent	The intent is to invoke a service interface that is defined with the request-reply operation. The goal is to serve those scenarios that expect a response from the service provider in near real time.
Motivation	To invoke synchronous operations in services and BPMN processes. Essentially, a BPM process should be able to invoke a BPEL process, SOA mediator, SOA adapters, external service, and so on, which expose synchronous operations.
Applicability	These include the service task.

Implementation	When you need to design a synchronous interaction, use a service task. Service task invokes processes and services, synchronously. When a service tasks invoke a process or service, the token waits at the service task until a response is returned. After the response is received, the token continues to the next sequence flow in the process. You use process data objects to assign input data to an invoked service's input, and the service output is assigned back to PDOs.
Known issues	If an immediate response is not received by a service consumer on time, it results in a timeout exception. Also, the service consumer might receive faults.
Known solution	The solution for service providers were discussed in *Chapter 3, Invocation Patterns*. The service consumer should build logic to handle the errors and also have logic to handle timeout exceptions. A meticulous exception-handling mechanism is required.

To demonstrate this pattern, we will interact with a synchronous web service using a service task in a BPM process. The Loan Origination process interacts with the credit check service to check the credit details of the loan applicant. A credit check service is a synchronous web service that we would invoke from the Loan Origination BPM process. Perform the following steps to deploy a credit check service and enable it in your project:

1. Download **LoanOriginationApps** and open it in JDeveloper.

2. Along with **LoanOriginationProject**, you will also find **CreditCheckPrj** as a separate project.

3. Deploy the **CreditCheckPrj** project to your web logic service, and go to the EM console at `http://service:port/em`.

4. Click on the **CreditCheck** service and copy the WSDL of the **CreditCheck** service.

5. Open the web service adapter configuration of the **CreditCheck** service in `composite.xml`.

6. Enter the copied WSDL of the **CreditCheck** service and hit the **Tab** button. This will populate the request reply operations. Only one port is enabled as it's a synchronous service.

Walk through the following steps to check the synchronous interaction pattern:

1. Go to the Loan Origination process and open the process in JDeveloper.

2. Double-click on the **CreditCheck** service task and go to the **Implementation** tab.

3. Examine whether the conversation type is **Service Call** and the conversation defined is the default one.

4. Browse for the **CreditCheck** service and click on **OK**.

5. Verify that the operation is in process for request-reply interaction of the **CreditCheck** service.

6. Check the data association. The data from the process data objects is assigned to the service's input argument, which is passed to the service when it's invoked. The service output argument is assigned back to the process data objects when the response is received.

The business catalog

The service task interaction pattern enables conversation and collaboration with only those services that are available in the BPM process business catalog. Hence, if you want some other external services to be invoked by your BPM process, remember to make them available in the business catalog. To interact with JMS queues or with any RESTful service, you need to configure a specific adapter in the project's `LoanO riginationProject(composite.xml)` file. For example, to push messages from a BPM process to a queue using the JMS adapter, configure the JMS adapter. The JMS adapter will expose itself as a service, and it will be available in the business catalog. Once available in the catalog, we can use this service in the BPM process. Along with the entire adapter in the component pallet, we can have a BPEL process, mediator, restful services, and so on being implemented and available in the business catalog to be used by the BPM process.

Along with this, you can always use MDS to share common artifacts such as XSD and WSDL.

When the **CreditCheck** service task in the Loan Origination process invokes the **CreditCheck** service, the token waits at the service task until a response is returned. After the response is received, the token continues to the next sequence flow in the process. Until the response is received, the process token waits at the service task. Upon response from the **CreditCheck** service, the data is mapped to the data objects in the project using the data association of the **CreditCheck** service task.

Subprocess interaction patterns

There are varied ways available to interact with subprocesses in Oracle BPM. The following bullet points classify the various subprocesses:

- The embedded subprocesses are in-line with the parent process.

- The multi-instance subprocess is a process over which a parent process can iterate. It is basically an embedded subprocess; however, you can define multi-instance and looping behavior for this kind of an embedded subprocess.

- The reusable subprocesses are defined outside the parent process model, and they execute within the parent process flow.

- The event subprocess is similar to the embedded subprocess; however, it is useful in handling errors and will be discussed in *Chapter 7*, *Exception Handling Patterns*.

- The peer subprocesses are those processes that can be invoked by a Send and Receive Task, via a throw and catch event, or even via a service task.

The following table categorizes the subprocess, its scope, and exception-handling behavior:

Subprocess type	Scope	Definition	Execution	Exception handling behavior
Embedded subprocess	Inline	Defined inside the main process in which it is embedded.	Executed as part of main process in which it is embedded.	Exceptions get propagated to the next level's subprocess, if not caught and handled in the embedded subprocess.
Multi-instance subprocess	Inline	Defined inside the main process in which it is embedded.	Executed as part of main process in which it is embedded.	Exceptions get propagated to the next level's subprocess, if not caught and handled in the embedded subprocess.

Subprocess type	Scope	Definition	Execution	Exception handling behavior
Reusable subprocess	Outside	Defined outside the parent process.	Executes within the parent process.	Exceptions will be propagated to the calling parent process.
Peer subprocess	Outside	Defined outside the calling process.	Executes as an independent process.	Exception behavior for the peer subprocess. When the called process is invoked via the Message Throw Event, you can handle the fault in the invoked peer process and then propagate it to the invoking process or let the invoking process handle the fault. When the called process is invoked via the Send and Receive Tasks, the exceptions are propagated to the calling process. When it is invoked via the service task, exceptions are propagated to the calling process.

Subprocess type	Scope	Definition	Execution	Exception handling behavior
Event subprocess	Enclosing a process or subprocess	Defined inside a subprocess or process.	It remains active till the time the process/ subprocess in which it is in-line is active. If in that active time frame, the specified event gets triggered, then the event subprocess will be executed.	

When peer processes are invoked, the calling process behavior depends on the called process's conversation message exchange pattern. If the called process is asynchronous, then the calling process will not wait for the callback. If the calling process is synchronous, then the called process waits for the response.

 The multi-instance subprocess is discussed in *Chapter 2, Multi-instance and State-based Patterns*. The error-handling patterns will be discussed in *Chapter 7, Exception Handling Patterns*. This section will concentrate on peer subprocess, reusable subprocess, and embedded subprocess.

Reusable process interaction pattern

When we create a new BPM process, we have four process templates available to choose from: asynchronous process, synchronous process, manual process, and reusable process. When we have the business requirement to create processes that can be invoked by many parent processes, we use the reusable template. Using the reusable template, we can create a reusable subprocess, for example, utility processes, such as **LOUtilityProcess**, in the **LoanOriginationProject** project.

The following table lists the details of the reusable process' interaction pattern:

Signature	Reusable Process Interaction Pattern
Classification	Interaction Pattern
Intent	To establish a separate scope for processes; this also encourages reusability in the process design.
Motivation	When you have the business requirement to create processes that would be invoked by many parent processes, use the reusable template to create reusable subprocesses. For example, the utility process in this section will be reused by many processes and is an ideal candidate for being a reusable process.
Applicability	A reusable subprocess is defined outside of its parent processes. It is also stored outside its parent process model. You can invoke a reusable process with the CALL task. At runtime, the reusable subprocess executes in-line within the process that called it.
Implementation	The CALL tasks invoke other BPMN processes to enable process chaining. The BPM offers the CALL task to invoke a reusable process. When a token reaches the CALL task, it gets inhibited, and a new instance of the reusable subprocess is created.
	The main process waits until the control is returned by the called reusable subprocess. When the reusable process completes, the control is returned to the CALL task, and the process token moves ahead to the subsequent process flow. The BPM processes with a None Start Event and None End Event are considered reusable processes; however, if you change the trigger type of the None Start and End Events, then a process no longer remains a reusable process.
Known issues	No access to the parent process data.
Known solution	You can use data association to assign data from a parent process to a reusable process.

The following are the characteristics of the reusable process:

- It is independent of the parent process.
- It can have many parent processes.
- It should be included in the same project as the parent processes.
- It has a separate process model; however, the audit logs show it executing in-line within the calling process.
- It cannot be transactional.
- It has an atomic independent process definition.

- It cannot be invoked as a service/process from outside of the project.

- As the name suggests, it encourages reusability in the process design.

- It does not have access to the parent process data; however, you can use data association to assign data from the parent process to the reusable process.

- Check the properties of the CALL task, and you will not find the conversation options as they cannot fall into the conversation initiated from the parent processes.

- As you can define swimlanes in a parent process, you can define swimlanes for reusable processes too.

- It can be looped; however, there is no direct mechanism to do so. Hence, it needs to be wrapped in an embedded subprocess to enable iteration over a reusable process.

- At runtime, the reusable subprocess executes in-line within the process that called it.

Use a reusable subprocess when you have the requirement to establish a separate scope for those processes that encourage reusability in the process design, such as the **LOUtilityProcess** utility process.

Use case scenario for reusable process interaction pattern

The Loan Origination process checks and validates the loan application. A human task is used to assign an approval task to a loan officer for the verification of the loan application. The loan officer checks the application and verifies it by either approving or rejecting the application. The application's verification status is checked at the exclusive **Application Verified** gateway in the process.

If the application is verified and approved, the process moves ahead for other verifications. However, if the **ApplicationVerified** gateway is rejected, then the Loan Origination process calls a **LOUtilityProcess**. This utility process will perform various activities such as saving the applicant's details, notifying sales and other concerned departments, and taking other proactive steps. Once the called utility process gets completed, the Loan Origination process ends.

The following steps will enable you to analyze the implementation of the CALL task:

1. Open JDeveloper and click to open **LOUtilityProcess**. This is a reusable process, which is created with the reusable process template.

2. You can witness that the process has no access to the parent process data. However, we defined the process data objects' input and output arguments for the **LOUtilityProcess**.

3. Check the data association and verify that the data is assigned from the **LOUtilityProcess** input argument to the data object of the **LOUtilityProcess** input process. Also, check whether a similar association between the output process data object and the output argument is implemented in the None End Event.

4. Open the Loan Origination process in JDeveloper and go to the properties of the **CallUtilityProcess** call task. This is a call task defined to interact with the **LOUtilityProcess** reusable process.

5. Click on data association to verify the input data assignment from the data object of the Loan Origination process to the input argument of the utility process. Similarly, the utility process output arguments are assigned to the Loan Origination process data object.

You can check whether any conversation type can be defined for a reusable process. The implementation type is **Call Activity** as it's a CALL task. The data association shows how data can be interfaced between the parent process and the reusable called process.

When the Loan Origination process token reaches the **CallUtilityProcess** call task, the tokens gets inhibited, and a new instance of the **LOUtilityProcess** reusable process is created. The Loan Origination process gets hold until the **LOUtilityProcess** utility process gets completed. The utility process will execute its activities, and when it completes, control is returned back to the Loan Origination process, and the process moves ahead.

Embedded subprocess interaction pattern

A subprocess is a process in itself that handles a part of the main process's functionality. It's a set of activities that have a sequence and a defined purpose. One of the many types of subprocesses is the embedded subprocess, which is a part of our discussion in this section.

The following table summarizes the details of the interaction pattern of the embedded subprocess:

Signature	Embedded Subprocess Interaction Pattern
Classification	Interaction Pattern
Intent	To establish subprocesses that are in-line within the main process.
Motivation	When you have the business requirement to create subprocesses that are embedded within the parent processes, are not reusable, and loops can be created on the subprocess, then the obvious choice is the embedded subprocess.
Applicability	The embedded subprocess is not independent of the parent process and hence, is in-line within the process and is often termed an in-line subprocess.
Implementation	An embedded subprocess will always start with a None Start Event, and it cannot be changed for the embedded subprocess. Also, the None Start Event does not have data association capability because the embedded subprocess is in-line within the main parent process and hence, has access to all data and information of the main parent process. You can change the End Event trigger type for an embedded subprocess to signal, message, error, and terminate. When the End Event is changed, then the events thrown by these subprocesses should be handled by the subprocess or the main parent process, whichever is up in the hierarchy of the subprocess.
Known issues	Cannot have a separate swim lane.
Known solution	The embedded subprocess is in-line with the main process and hence, it is within one of the swimlanes of the main process. The modeling should be performed meticulously.

The following are the main characteristics of an embedded subprocess:

- It shares the same data and information with the parent process in which it is embedded.

- It has a defined business objective and hence, has a None Start Event and a None End Event to clearly define its start and end.

- It is not reusable, and it can be expanded and contracted to hide and show details.

- It can be nested while each subprocess can have its own set of data objects and other objects.

- The boundary events can be associated with an embedded subprocess.

For **BackGroundCheckSubProcess** and other embedded subprocesses too, you can create data objects, activities, conversations, correlations, and measurements.

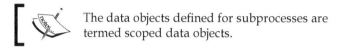 The data objects defined for subprocesses are termed scoped data objects.

It's a good design practice to use a scoped data object when you are aware of a data object's life cycle. The subprocess can be nested. Check **BackGroundCheckSubProcess**, which also has another subprocess inside it, as BPM allows subprocesses to be nested.

Interrupting a boundary event

The boundary events are defined as the catch events that can be associated with a subprocess or an activity. The catch events can be configured as a boundary event on various activities and subprocesses. These boundary catch events can be of interrupting or non interrupting type, depending on the way they deal with the normal process flow. You can implement the timer as a boundary event to introduce a delay, SLA, or a wait on an activity or an embedded subprocess. The catch intermediate events are also used as boundary events to a subprocess or activities of a certain type. When any associated boundary event is executed, the process flows to an exception path. A boundary event can be of interrupting or non-interrupting type. In a non-interrupting boundary event, the process flow moves to a normal process flow and exception flow, as both are mutually exclusive; however, in an interrupting boundary event, the process flow moves only to exception flow.

Boundary event on an activity

Check the Loan Origination process. There, we have a human task defined to perform the application's verification. There are two timer boundary events associated with the human task:

- **Non-interrupting event**: Click on the lower timer event and check its properties. This timer event is named **VerificationReminder**. It's a non-interrupting boundary event. The time cycle set for this timer is 1 day. You can change it to 1 minute for the sake of testing it.

- **Interrupting event**: The upper boundary event is an interrupting boundary event named **LOSuspended**. The time cycle set for this timer is 3 days.

These timer events serve as a reminder and can be used to implement SLA for the Loan Origination process.

For the loan verification process, an application verification task is assigned to a loan officer. If the task in not acted upon by the loan officer (`salesrep`) in 1 day, then a notification e-mail will be sent. This is the reminder policy of the Loan Origination process. However, if the loan officer does not act on the task in 3 days, then the Loan Origination process will end after performing some suspension activities.

The following steps demonstrate an interrupting timer boundary event configuration:

1. Click on the **LOSuspended** boundary timer event and open its **Implementation** properties.

2. You can witness that the **Interrupting Event** checkbox is checked and the time is set to 3 days. This is shown in the following screenshot:

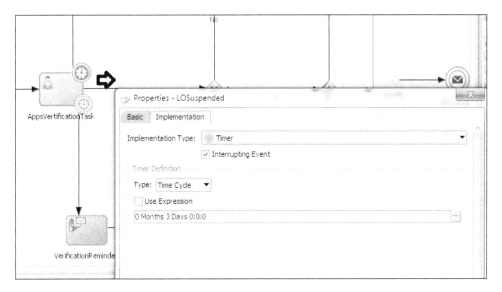

3. Check the **Non-interrupting** boundary timer event, **VerificationReminder**, and verify the time as 1 day. However, the **Interrupting Event** checkbox is not checked in this case, and this makes the **VerificationReminder** boundary timer event non-interrupting.

When the process token arrives at the embedded subprocess, the token (initial token) gets inhibited, and a new token is started for the embedded subprocess. When the subprocess reaches its End Event and if there are no available tokens in the subprocess (which also includes tokens for all non-interrupting event handlers), then the subprocess ends. The token that initially started the subprocess (initial token) gets resumed, and it gets propagated to the outgoing sequence flow from the embedded subprocess.

Non-interrupting event: In the case of a non-interrupting event associated with a subprocess, all the tokens associated with non-interrupting event handlers must get completed before the original token is propagated to the outgoing sequence flow from the subprocess. Hence, when the loan officer does not act on the application's verification task in 1 day, the non-interrupting boundary timer event triggers the non-interrupting event handler, which sends a notification to the loan officer.

Interrupting event: In the case of an interrupting event associated with the subprocess, if the interrupting event executes, then all the available tokens in the subprocess are consumed, and the original token that started the subprocess gets propagated to the outgoing sequence flow. Hence, when the loan officer does not act on the application verification task in 3 days, the interrupting boundary timer event triggers the interrupting event handler, which consumes all the Loan Origination process tokens, and the original process token moves to suspension activities.

Event-driven interaction pattern

By definition, an event is an occurrence that has happened. It can be a change in a state, a condition that triggers a notification, and so on. An event can be a notification, alert, business event, or a complex event. The events are always named in the past tense such as OrderShipped, OrderCancelled, and so on, and notification events are named as inventoryLow, CartCleared, and so on.

The Oracle SOA/BPM platform offers the **Event Delivery Network** (**EDN**), which deals with the publishing and subscription of events. The EDN also performs various activities such as pattern matching, event publishing, event subscription, and so on. In Oracle BPM, the events are defined using the **Event Definition Language** (**EDL**) editor. The EDL can be based on the XML schema and can leverage Oracle BPM/SOA MDS (metadata service) to be distributed as a shared artifact. When you deploy an event to the MDS repository along with its artifacts (XSDs), it is known as publishing the EDL (or event definition). Events are published to an EDN. Once an event (EDL) is published, it can be subscribed to by other applications. EDLs cannot be unpublished; the definition always exists. The raised events are delivered by EDN to the subscribing service components. The Oracle mediator service components and BPEL process service components can subscribe to and publish events.

The event system has following components:

- Event producer
- Event consumer (listener/subscriber)
- Event processor
- Messaging infrastructure

The event producer is the process that publishes the event to EDN. The subscriber is a process that has shown interest in the occurrence of the event. In the case of Oracle BPM, the EDN is the event processor, and the messaging infrastructure can be a database or JMS. You can use the database or JMS as a back-end store.

The following table lists the details around the event-driven interaction pattern:

Signature	Event-driven Interaction Pattern
Classification	Invocation Pattern
Intent	To design a system that's geared for extension, interoperability, and unanticipated use. The participating process or application publishes events and messages, which are subscribed to one or more consumers/subscribers.
Motivation	When you are looking for loosely coupled, asynchronous, and stateless interaction. When you want to tell the downstream component what happened and what not to do. When the potential of reuse is low.
Applicability	The Signal Throw, Signal End, Signal Catch, and Signal Start Event. The intermediate Throw Signal Event or Signal End Event are used to raise and broadcast a signal. The Signal Start Event is used to receive an event in another process. To enable event delivery, you need an eventing platform. Oracle BPM uses the Oracle EDN to send and receive signals. The events are defined using the EDL editor, and these defined events are available in the business catalog. The Signal Throw Event is used to broadcast a signal, or a signal can be broadcast through a Signal End Event. However, you can use a Signal Catch Event to receive a signal in the BPM process.
Implementation	Upon execution, the throw intermediate Signal Event or Signal End Event will publish an event to EDN. The EDN will then deliver it to all the subscribers that are configured to listen to that specific event (signal). A subscriber process can trigger only when the signal arrives to the event it has been subscribed to. Oracle BPM leverages Oracle SOA, and an EDN runs within every SOA instance. The Java/BPEL/Mediator or any component can raise an event to the underlying SOA environment to publish that event to the EDN. Any interested BPMN process, as a subscriber to that event, will get triggered when the signal arrives to the event it has subscribed to.
Known issues	These include the loss of message, guaranteed message processing, and durability.

Known solution	The signal-based collaboration pattern doesn't offer guaranteed delivery. There are chances that a signal might be lost in the event of failures, as you cannot create durable subscribers. You can use various interaction mechanisms between applications and processes. If you are looking for a guaranteed delivery, then the solution is using queues such as the JMS queue. The queues offer guaranteed delivery of messages. When you need a real-time low-volume integration and interaction, the solution is a web service.

There could be various scenarios for event-driven messaging, such as tracing and tracking (FedEx, UPS, and so on), government systems (taxes), service level agreements, and so on. For example, the order-processing system could have events such as inventory low, stock cancelled, order cancelled, and so on. Other use cases can be broadcasting telecom number changes or address change, triggering a signal when a quote gets approved to trigger all the processes that depend on the approval of a quote, and so on.

In a signal-based interaction pattern, neither the sender knows about the receiver nor the receiver knows about the sender, and this offers a loosely coupled interaction pattern, where processes can be added and removed without affecting any other process or service. Other than the BPM process, BPEL and mediator processes and services can also deal with BPM events. The events have a payload associated with them based on the schema associated with the event definition.

While sending an event through a Signal End Event or Signal Throw Event, use data association to add data to the event payload. This is how data is communicated from a sender process/service to a receiver process/service.

Defining an event-based interaction pattern scenario

A BackOffice process will invoke a feedback process after the Loan Origination process gets completed. This feedback process is a BPM process. When the feedback process completes the application's customer feedback, it will raise a feedback event. The BackOffice process has a **GetFeedbackDetails** Signal Catch Event configured as a subscriber to an event (feedback). The BackOffice process will wait at the **GetFeedbackDetails** Signal Catch Event for the feedback event to occur. The following steps will help you understand the Signal Catch Event configuration:

1. Open the feedback process and check the Signal End Event for the process.
2. You can find the **Feedback** event configured for the End Event.

3. Data association assigns data from the feedback's process data object to the feedback's event argument.

4. Open the `BackOffice` process and right-click on the **GetFeedbackDetails** Signal Catch Event to check its **Implementation** properties. This is shown in the following screenshot:

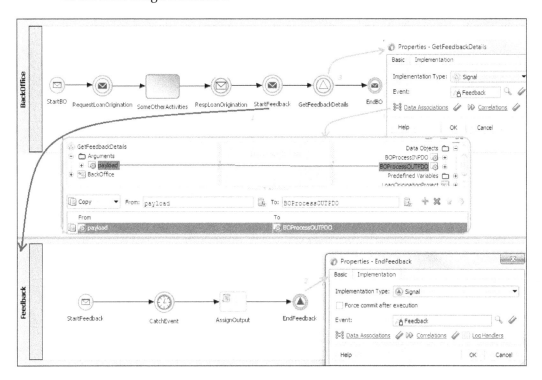

5. The event configured is **Feedback**, and the data assignment is from an event argument to the `BackOffice` PDO.

The `BackOffice` process initiates the feedback process by invoking the Feedback process using the **Start Feedback** Message Throw Event. When the process token in the feedback process reaches the **End Feedback** Signal End Event, the feedback event is raised to the EDN. The EDN will perform data association and raise the event. It will deliver this event to the `BackOffice` process and all other subscribers configured to listen to that specific signal. The `BackOffice` process is subscribed to catch the feedback event using the **GetFeedbackDetails** signal catch event. When the signal arrives at the `BackOffice` process, the process gets triggered by this signal.

Summary

This chapter demonstrated how the BPM process interacts with other processes, services, and events. While walking through the various recipes in this chapter, you analyzed advance and default conversation, and their implementation in the BPM process collaborations. You also witnessed the interaction patterns of synchronous and asynchronous processes and services using events and tasks. The embedded inline and reusable subprocess interaction patterns are also housed in this chapter. The next chapter is focused on correlation patterns.

6
Correlation Patterns

In the previous chapter, we witnessed many conversations between processes and services. There were conversations and collaborations to not only create new instances of the process but also conversations and interactions with the in-flight process. Imagine when there are many instances of the Loan Origination process and each instance is handling a different applicant, how will the BPM engine make sure that an interaction is meant for a specific process instance of a Loan Origination application? The previous chapter contains a BackOffice process, Loan Origination process, and many other processes. The BackOffice process interacts with the Loan Origination process; however, there might be cases where a loan originates from some other source such as a web application or by an applicant visiting the branch and so on. How does a system make sure that if the feedback process has started it should deal with that particular applicant's details for which it was initiated? Or, when the feedback process ends, should it respond to the correct instance of the BackOffice process? Similarly, we have a background check process and other verification processes. There might be many Loan Origination processes in the system. How does the background process make sure that once it gets completed it responds to the instance of Loan Origination that it is supposed to respond to?

For example, we have four instances of the Loan Origination process, LO1, LO2, LO3, and LO4. All these four instances have created four instances of background checks as BG1, BG2, BG3, and BG4 for four different applications, applicant 1 to 4.

LO1 started BG1 for applicant number 1, LO2 started BG2 for applicant number 2, and so on. While all these instances are in the BPM system, BG2 and BG3 instances get completed before BG1 and BG4. The question is how will the system make sure that BG2 responds to LO2 and not to LO1, LO3, or LO4, and that too for applicant number 2 and not for any other applicant? Similarly, when the Loan Origination process is completed how will the system make sure that it interacts with the correct instances of the BackOffice process?

This chapter will deal with all the questions related to correlating the conversation and collaboration between different processes and services. The following patterns around correlation are included in this chapter:

- Message-based correlation pattern
- Cancel instance pattern
- Update task pattern
- Query pattern
- Suspend process pattern
- Suspend activity pattern
- Cancel activity pattern

Correlation mechanism

In the last chapter, we learned about conversations. However, we now need to associate a message with the instance to which it belongs. This message association with the conversation is performed using the correlation mechanism. The correlation mechanism enables the identification of a correct instance in another process through an instance, and it enables us to send a message to that specific instance.

We can use correlation to communicate between the BackOffice process, web process, and Loan Origination process. When the Loan Origination process completes a loan process for an applicant, it sends a message to the BackOffice process or web process, whichever has initiated the Loan Origination process, using the **Applicant ID** to locate the instance in both processes. The correlation is done using the **Applicant ID**.

Types of correlations

The different types of correlations are as follows:

- **Automatic correlation**: Let's say we have a process interacting with services, which understands WS-addressing, processes/services with JMS message IDs, or conversation with synchronous services. In all these cases, correlation is handled automatically; this type of correlation is termed as automatic correlation. With WS-addressing, a unique correlation ID is infused in the message header, which is then used by the BPM engine to correlate a conversation.

- **Payload/message-based correlation**: This refers to the customary way of correlation based on your business logic and design, wherein you can identify keys/values to use for the correlation. These keys/values are identified from the message payload that belongs to your process design and hence, it's termed as custom correlation. However, it's based on the message and more appropriately termed as message-based correlation. For example, we will use **Applicant ID** to correlate instances in this chapter. However, you can also create a correlation based on multiple keys such as **Applicant ID** and **Tax ID**.

When we create multiple correlations, we would need the values of all those correlations to identify an instance, which is sort of a primary key in a database relationship. For example, if we have used **Applicant ID**, **SSN#**, and **Tax ID** as three different correlations, then we need all these correlation values to identify the same instance.

When two processes start exchanging messages, they establish a conversation between them. As one process starts a new instance of another process, they know whom to route messages to, because the first-time interaction between them has established a conversation between them. This means that the invoked process would know whom to send the response to, and they can continue to collaborate and interact using WS-addressing, which is the default, automatic correlation mechanism of Oracle BPM. However, this correlation mechanism will not work when the interaction needs to happen between two already running instances of the collaborating processes. Then, we need to know whom to route messages to so that the messages land and correlate with the correct process instance. Also, we need a mechanism to establish a conversation with the in-flight processes. This is performed by a payload-based correlation mechanism, also known as message-based correlation. We may also need correlation when any of the application/process/service in the conversation does not support WS-addressing, such as any legacy application, non-SOA based applications, and so on during collaboration.

Components of correlation

The correlation mechanism has the following components:

- **Correlation property**: In a message-based custom correlation, you will identify a common identifier such as **Applicant ID**, **SSN ID**, and so on. They are identified based on the name and data type assigned to them.

- **Correlation keys**: These keys are identified with a name; the correlation key defines the properties to be used in correlation. You can use a correlation key in any process/BPEL service in your project as its scope is within the project. Even the correlation defined in the BPEL process in the projects can be used in BPM processes. A correlation key can contain one/more correlation properties. It has two modes: **Uses** and **Initiates**. The correlation key can be defined as simple and advance.

- **Correlation property alias**: We have defined a correlation property and assigned a name to it. However, it's the correlation property alias that actually maps the element(s) of the message to the property. We can use the expression builder to define the mapping of the message element(s) to the property that helps you to use either an argument or any predefined variables.

- **Correlation set**: This refers to a set of correlation keys. It's also known as the correlation definition as it defines and configures the set of correlation keys.

Configuring the environment

In this section, we will perform some of the elementary steps that will allow us to run the samples in this chapter.

The downloads available for *Chapter 6, Correlation Patterns,* have two application files. One file is in the `Correlation` directory, and the other file is in the `NonCorrelation` directory. Both the applications are the same. You can use the application from the `NonCorrelation` directory if you want to create correlation and run the samples. However, if you just want to verify the correlation and deploy the project, you can use the application from the `Correlation` directory. The only difference is that the applications in the `Correlation` directory have the correlation defined, while applications in the `NonCorrelation` directory do not have correlation defined in the processes.

To enable the sample application, we need the `salesrep` user in the `myrealm` weblogic. We also need to have a JMS queue (`LOFeedbackQueue`). The following are the mandatory steps you need to perform in order to enable the sample application to work for you:

1. Log in to the WebLogic console and navigate to `myrealm`.
2. Click on **Users And Groups** and create a user (`salesrep`).
3. Apply the changes.

4. Go to **JMS module | SOAJMSModule**.

5. Click on **New** to create a JMS queue with the name `LOFeedbackQueue`.

6. Let the JNDI mechanism be `jms/LOFeedbackQueue`.

7. Update the JMS adapter from deployments.

8. Along with the application, you will get the **CreditCheckPrj** and **FraudCheckPrj** projects. Deploy **CreditCheckPrj** and **FraudCheckPrj** to the server.

9. Navigate to the EM console to get the WSDL URL (`webservice.wsdl`) for the **CreditCheck** service and the **FraudCheck** service.

10. Open the **LoanOrigination** project's `composite.xml` and change the WSDL URL for the **CreditCheck** and **FraudCheck** references, as shown in the following screenshot:

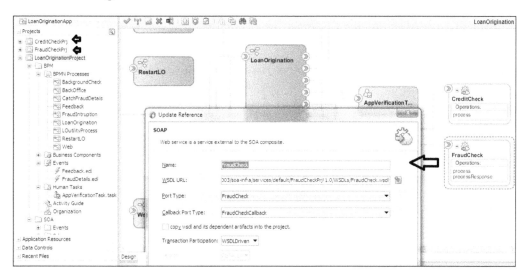

 The data files to perform the test can be found by navigating to **LoanOriginationApp | LoanOriginationProject | SOA | testsuites**.

Defining correlation properties

In the calling process, we will define correlation on the flow object that will send messages to the called process. The correlation mechanism defined on the calling process's flow object should initiate the property aliases. In the called process, we will define correlation on the flow object that will receive the message. The correlation mechanism defined in the called process's flow object should have the property aliases defined as join.

Correlation can be defined in two modes: simple and advanced. Use the simple mode when you are defining just one property. For example, using only **Applicant ID** for the correlation in the Loan Origination process, we define a simple correlation. However, if you are defining multiple properties, using multiple correlation keys, and assigning those multiple properties to one or more keys, then use the advanced mode.

Download LoanOriginationApps which is a part of the *Chapter 6, Correlation Patterns*, downloads available on the Packt Publishing website. Open it in JDeveloper. Go to **LoanOriginationProject** and select **LoanOrigination** process.

Perform the following steps to check the correlation definition on the message start event of the process:

1. Click on the **startLOEvent** message start event to check its implementation properties.

2. Click on **Correlation** in the implementation properties.

3. In the **Properties** tab, we can choose a correlation property if it's already defined, else use the **+** icon adjacent to **Property** in order to create a new simple correlation property.

4. Enter a name and data type, as shown in the following screenshot, and click on **OK**.

5. Check the **Initiate** box if you want the mode to be **Initiates**. As the startLOEvent message starts event is the start point for the Loan Origination process, the **LOCorrProp** correlation property is defined as **Initiates**.

6. Click on **Expression Filter**, adjacent to the correlation property alias to define a map between the message element and the correlation property. Select **Applicant ID** as we will be mapping the **Applicant ID** message element with the **LOCorrProp** correlation property.

7. We can switch to the **Advance** mode, if we have advanced definition requirements.

Defining correlation keys and configuring the correlation definition

We can define correlation at the project level using the structure window, or we can use an **Activities Correlation** tab to define and configure the correlation keys.

If you have a simple requirement of one key with one/more properties, then perform the following steps:

1. Go to the structure window for this particular process.

2. Expand **Correlations**.

3. Right-click on **Correlation Key** and select **New**; this will open the **Create Correlation Key** wizard.

4. Enter the name of the correlation key and select one/more correlation properties that we need to assign to this correlation key.

5. We can also use the same wizard to create a correlation property by clicking on the **+** sign adjacent to the correlation properties.

To define a correlation key in the advance mode and to configure a correlation definition, perform the following steps:

1. Click on an activity or the event in the process flow.

2. Go to **Implementation** in the **Properties** tab.

3. Click on **Correlations**.

4. Select **Switch to Simple Mode**. This will open the **Correlation Definition** dialog box.

5. Click on the **+** sign to create a new correlation key.

6. Select the **Correlation Key** if it's already defined, else click on the **+** sign to create a new correlation key.

7. Enter the name of the correlation key.

8. Click on the **+** sign to create a correlation property, else select one/more correlation properties to be assigned to the correlation key from the property list.

9. Select the mode, **Uses/Initiates** as per the design. The entire process is shown in the following screenshot:

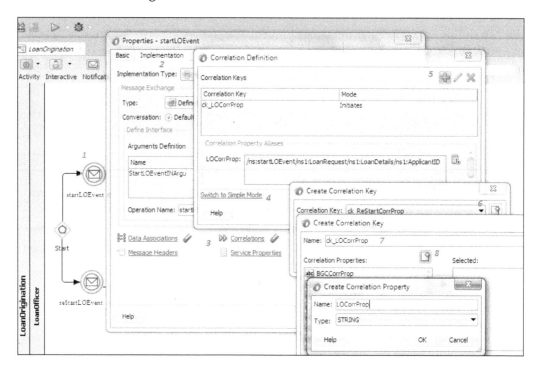

In *Chapter 5, Interaction Patterns*, we witnessed the correlation definition as we have seen the usage of correlation properties. In the Loan Origination process, you will find that for the **LOCorrProp** correlation property, we have selected the **Applicant ID** using a simple expression builder. We can use an advanced expression builder and functions offered by the expression builder if we have complex requirements. This is shown in the following screenshot:

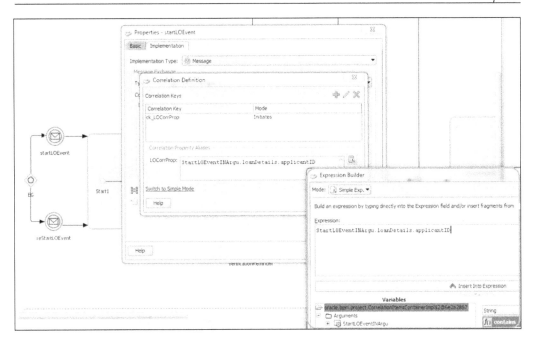

We can check the **startLOEvent** message event to check the correlation property, which is shown in the preceding screenshot. We can verify that for the **startLOEvent** message event, the correlation key mode is set to **Initiate**.

Understanding the correlation behavior

The **startLOEvent** message start event will initialize the value of the correlation property defined in the correlation key from the value of the correlation properties in the message, as its mode is **Initiate**. For all the nodes that have their mode set to **Uses**, the value of the correlation property is compared with the incoming message element when a message arrives. This message element is defined in the correlation key for correlation properties, which is mapped using the correlation alias, with all the active instances in the system.

As in the Loan Origination system, we are invoking a background check process. When you invoke it with a message throw event, you have used the same correlation property with an alias, that maps a property with its **Applicant ID**. To get a response from the background check process, you have to define a message catch event with the same **LOCorrProp**, that maps with the **Applicant ID** message element.

So, when the message arrives from the background check process to the catch event in Loan Origination process, the value of the correlation property is compared with the value of the correlation property for all the existing active Loan Origination process instances. If one of the Loan Origination process instance's correlation property matches with the incoming message's correlation property, then the message is passed to this catch/receive activity. Else, if no instance matches or more than one instance matches, then this would lead to an exception.

When we have a correlation key with multiple properties, then the value of each correlation property is compared with the incoming message element. This is used in the correlation property alias as a map to the correlation property with all the active instances of that process. If only one instance matches, then the message is passed to that instance's receive/catch event or else an exception is raised. In case of multiple instances for a subprocess, each subprocess instance will have its own copy of a correlation key. However, when the subprocess is to be executed in parallel, then the best practice is to define a scoped conversation rather than defining a correlation.

Message-based correlation pattern

The following pattern table explains the features of the message-based correlation pattern:

Signature	Message-based Correlation Pattern
Classification	Correlation Pattern
Intent	This is the customary way to establish correlation based on your business logic.
Motivation	This provides the flexibility to identify and define custom keys and values for correlation based on business requirements.

Applicability	Managing message context across the process and the different partner services/processes that are collaborating.
	We need the message-based correlation pattern for the following reasons:
	• Establishing a conversation between already running instances.
	• Any of the collaborating process/service cannot maintain a conversation message exchange.
	• There is a need to converse with an in-flight process/service.
	• The collaborating system does not support WS-addressing.
	• Interaction with the third-party system takes place using an interaction mechanism such as a file, database push/pull, and so on.
	• A multihop interaction and response may come from any process in the hop. For example, process A interacts with process B that interacts with process C, which in turn interacts with process D. Process D might respond to process B, which in turn responds to process A, or process C responds to process A, and so on.
Implementation	• Flow objects such as throw events and Send Task can be used to initialize a correlation. However, flow objects such as `Receive` and `Catch` join a correlation by setting the correlation to **Uses**.
	• A service task flow object can initialize and use correlation at the same time as it defines two types of correlations, input and output.
	• Correlation cannot be defined on a call activity that is used to invoke a reusable process.
	• If the embedded subprocess is single-flow inside the process, that is, subprocess characteristics are none, then you can use correlation.
	• If the embedded subprocess is multi-instance, that is, subprocess characteristics are multi-instance or loop, then using scoped conversation is the best practice. Scoped conversations have been covered in *Chapter 5, Interaction Patterns*.
Known issues	NA
Known solution	NA

Enlisted here are some of the main characteristics of message-based correlation pattern:

- Once initialized, a correlation value cannot be changed as it's the value of the correlation that the Oracle BPM service engine will use to identify the instance
- We cannot assign a new value to the correlation
- We can create one or many correlations
- We can create a correlation property with many values
- We can create a correlation key with many correlation properties.
- We can create many correlation keys with one/more correlation properties
- The scope of the correlation is the process instance or the subprocess instance in which they are defined
- The correlation key can be defined in either of the two modes, **Initiate** or **Uses**
- The correlation can be defined as simple or advanced
- The correlation keys can be scoped similar to the way data objects and conversations can be scoped

The download section of *Chapter 6, Correlation Patterns*, contains the `LoanOriginationApps` application. The `loan origination apps` contains the loan origination project and other supporting services such as the `FraudCheckPrj` and `CheditCheckPrj` projects. The Loan Origination project constrains the processes that we will be discussing in this chapter. If you have not deployed the `Deploy Credit Check` and `Fraud Check` services while performing labs of the previous chapter, deploy these supporting services and change the web service references in the Loan Origination processes as per the steps you have performed in the previous chapter, in the *Interaction pattern with asynchronous service using message throw and catch events* section.

Carry out the following steps to create a correlation for all the processes and perform tests to uncover how the correlation will work:

1. Open the Loan Origination project and click on the **BackOffice process**.
2. Go to the structure window and expand **Correlation | Correlation properties**.
3. Right-click on **Correlation properties** and select **New**. This will open the **Create Correlation Property** dialog box.

4. Enter a name for the correlation property as `BOCorrProp`, a short name for the BackOffice correlation property, and select the type as `string`. This correlation property will be mapped to the **Application ID** in the message that has a type of string; hence, the string type is selected.

5. Click on **OK**, and you can find `BOCorrProp` being created in the structure window.

6. Right-click on **Correlation Keys** in the structure window and select **New**. This will open the **Create Correlation Key** dialog box.

7. Enter a name for the correlation key as `ck_BOCorrProp`. We will use a similar structure throughout this chapter as a naming convention to the correlation key, which is `ck_<correlation property name>`.

8. Select **BOCorrProp** from the list of properties, select the arrow to move the property from the available list to the select list, and click on **OK**. If you have a business requirement to define a correlation key with multiple properties, then you can select multiple properties in this dialog.

    We have just defined the correlation property and the correlation key. Now, we will define the correlation definition and configure it as **Initiates** or **Uses** for the different process flow objects.

9. Right-click on the **StartBO** message start event of the BackOffice process and go to implementation properties.

10. Click on **Correlation.**

11. Select **BOCorrProp** from the correlation properties dropdown.

12. Select the mode as **Initiates** by checking it.

13. Use an expression to map the message element with the correlation property.

    As shown in the following screenshot, **Applicant ID** will be mapped to the BOCorrProp correlation property, where **Applicant ID** is a message element in BackOffice process's input argument. This is shown in the following screenshot:

14. Click on **OK** thrice and when you are done, click on **Save All**.

15. Click on the **RequestLoanOrigination** message throw event and configure the correlation definition similar to the BOCorrProp correlation property. However, don't check the **Initiates** box as we want it to be on the **Uses** mode, as this flow object will use the already existing and initiated correlation.

16. Use the expression builder and map BOCorrProp with **Applicant ID**. Click on **OK**.

17. Repeat steps 15 and 16 for the RespLoanOrigination catch message event, the CatchCancelLoan catch message event, StartFeedback, GetFeedbackDetails, and the endBO message end event.

18. Click on **Save All**.

This completes the correlation definition of all the objects in the BackOffice process. The BackOffice process will be invoking the Loan Origination process. However, the BackOffice process also needs to correlate the feedback process response, which itself will be invoked by other applications. Hence, we have created a correlation definition with **Initiates** as the mode for BackOffice process's message start event.

Open the Loan Origination process and perform the preceding steps to create the following:

- The correlation property: `LOCorrProp`
- The correlation key: `ck_LOCorrProp`

For the `startLOEvent` message start event, define correlation with the **Initiates** mode and for all other events, define correlation as **Uses**. Remember to select `LOCorrProp` as the correlation property throughout the Loan Origination process. Also, remember to map `LOCorrProp` with the **Applicant ID** message element.

The loan origination process invokes the background check process. Perform the following steps to create the correlation key, properties, and definition with the following details:

- The correlation property: `BGCCorrProp`
- The correlation key: `ck_BGCCorrProp`

Remember to select `BGCCorrProp` as a correlation property throughout the background check process. Also, remember to map `BGCCorrProp` with the **Applicant ID** message element.

The Loan Origination process also invokes the `FraudCheck` asynchronous service. It's a BPEL service. Open the `FraudCheck` BPEL service and you can see that a correlation is created in this too. Moreover, the correlation property is mapped with the **Applicant ID** message element in the **FraudCheck** BPEL service too.

In the Loan Origination process, open `FraudCheckSubProcess` and for `FraudCheckRequest` and `FraudCheckResponse`, throw and catch message events, respectively. Select the correlation property as `LOCorrProp` and mode as **Uses** for both the events. This is because when `FraudCheckSubProcess` invokes the **FraudCheck** asynchronous service, **Applicant ID** will be used to correlate its response so that the **FraudCheck** asynchronous service responds to the correct instance of the process.

The Loan Origination process includes the query and cancel patterns offered by the `QuerySubprocess` and `CancelLoanSubprocess` event subprocesses. For both the event subprocesses, use `LOCorrProp` as a correlation property and map this with the **Applicant ID** message element in the `CancelLoan`, `EndCancelLoan`, and `RestartLO` events in the `CancelLoanSubprocess` event subprocess, and the `CheckLoanStatus` and `EndCheckLoanStatus` events in `QuerySubprocess`.

The event subprocesses are correlated as we want to make sure that the query subprocess responds to the loan status for the requested Loan Origination instance, and not for any running instance. Similarly, cancel loan subprocess should cancel the Loan Origination process instance for which the request is meant and not just any running instance. Message-based correlation ensures that request and response are correlated and the fabric of conversation remains perfect. Similarly, click on **FeedBack** process and **Create Correlation Property** and map `FeedCorrProp` with the **Applicant ID** message element throughout the feedback process. However, ensure that for the `startFeedback` message start event, you select the mode as **Initiates** and for all the others, select the **Uses** mode. Save all your efforts and deploy it to the weblogic instance.

Testing the message-based correlation pattern

The web process and the BackOffice process will invoke the Loan Origination process. Navigate to **LoanOriginationProject | SOA | testsuites**.

Use the following test data files to test start the web process and the BackOffice process:

- `Web.xml` to test the web process
- `BackOffice.xml` to test the BackOffice process

Using `BackOffice.xml`, initiate the first BackOffice process instance with the applicant ID as `1111` and the second BackOffice process instance with the applicant ID as `2222`. Similarly, use the `Web.xml` file and initiate the first web process instance with the applicant ID as `3333` and the second instance with the applicant ID as `4444`.

Check the test results by carrying out the following steps:

1. Log in to the EM (`http://server:host/em`) as an admin user, `weblogic`.

2. You will find that four instances have been created: two for the web process and two instances for the BackOffice process.

3. Log in to the BPM workspace (`http://server:host/bpm/workspace`) as the `salesrep` user and approve the instance application verification task for applicant ID `2222` and applicant ID `3333`.

4. Re-login to the EM as an admin user and check the audit trail for the BackOffice process for which the request was sent with the applicant ID `2222`.

5. In the instance trace for the BackOffice process, click on the `LoanOrigination` process. This will open the audit trail of the process. Click on **startLOEvent** and expand it. Click on the **Instance left the activity** link to check the payload that entered the Loan Origination process and to verify that the applicant ID is `2222`, which you have passed while creating the second instance for the BackOffice process.

6. Now, click on the BackOffice process in the instance trace, which will open the audit trail of the process.

7. Click on the **RespLoanOrigination** message catch event, and then click on **Instance entered the activity** to check the payload that was returned from the Loan Origination process. This is shown in the following screenshot:

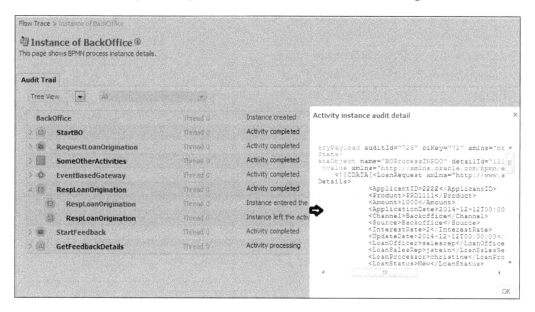

8. You can verify that the returned data from the Loan Origination process is for the applicant ID `2222`. This correlates the BackOffice instance with the correct response from the Loan Origination process. Now, let's verify for the web process. Click on the completed process of the web process instance. This completed instance will be for the web process instance that has the applicant ID `3333`.

9. Click on the Loan Origination process component in the web process trace. This will open the instance of loan origination. Click on **Instance left the activity** by expanding **startLOEvent**. Verify that the instance of loan origination created by the web process for the applicant ID is `3333`.

10. Click on the web process trace and open the audit trail of the web process. Expand **ReceiveLoanResponse**, then click on **Instance left the activity**, and verify that the response contains the applicant ID 3333.

Re-login to Oracle BPM at http://server:host/bpm/workspace as the salesrep user and approve the other two application verification tasks, one for the web process and the other for the BackOffice process. You can verify the data request and response pattern for these two instances; they remain correlated for the request and response based pattern on the applicant IDs.

Cancel instance pattern

The following pattern table explains the features of the cancel instance pattern:

Signature	Cancel Instance Pattern
Classification	Cancellation Pattern
Intent	Canceling the BPM process instance.
Motivation	There are business requirements to cancel the already running process instances. BPMN processes should be developed with the flexibility to provide process consumers with the option to cancel the running instances.
Applicability	The cancellation of a process instance should be correlated. A request to cancel instances cannot just cancel any process instance. A cancellation request must be correlated with the correct instance to be cancelled. It's the correlation which makes sure that the cancellation process results in the cancellation of the correct instance of a process that it is meant for and does not affect any other instances.
Implementation	The cancel instance pattern can be implemented using event subprocess, event gateways, and correlation properties. The following section demonstrates the implementation and testing of Cancellation pattern.
Known issues	NA
Known solution	NA

 The cancel instance pattern is included in correlation because defining a correlation is a must for establishing the cancel instance pattern. However, this pattern is a part of the cancellation and completion patterns.

The Loan Origination process takes care of an applicant's loan request and fulfills that request. However, there might be cases when a customer wants to cancel a loan application. Cancellation might happen at any stage of the loan application. To fulfill the requirement to implement Cancelation pattern in the Loan Origination process, we will use event subprocesses. The **CancelLoanSubProcess** event subprocess defined in the Loan Origination process takes care of loan cancellation. The following code snippet checks for the application verification task's status:

```
If
Application task is already executed i.e. Loan officer has taken
appropriate action on the task then
    Process moves ahead.
Else
Application task is suspended.
```

In both cases, the process checks for the stage in which it is present.

If the process has passed all the verification steps and is in the underwriting stage and then a cancel request arrives, the customer will be contacted. The customer will be asked if he/she is interested to restart the loan process. If the customer wants to restart the loan process, then the `RestartLO` message throw event will be raised; else, the loan process will be ended.

Understanding the components

In this section, we have used event gateways and event subprocesses. Let's invest some time to understand the concept of event subprocesses and event gateways.

An **event subprocess** is a kind of inline subprocess. Its scope is the process/subprocess in which it is defined. The event subprocess is active as long as the process/subprocess in which it's enclosed is active. An event subprocess can either be of the interrupting type or the non-interrupting type.

If the event subprocess is of the interrupting type and the event occurs, then the original process/subprocess in which it's enclosed will be stopped and the event handler will be executed. The event handler could be a boundary event, and in this case, the token moves to the boundary handler path (you can learn more about boundary events in *Chapter 7, Exception Handling Patterns*). If the event handler is an event subprocess, then the event subprocess will be executed. The event subprocess has access to the data and conversations of the process or subprocesses in which it is defined and enclosed.

If the event subprocess is of the non-interrupting type, then the normal process flow will not be hampered. The process/subprocess in which the event handler is enclosed will run in parallel to the event subprocess; however, a new token will be created for the event subprocess. In *Chapter 5, Interaction Patterns*, we learned the working of the boundary event. Event subprocesses are similar to boundary events. However, use cases for event subprocesses are different in many ways from those scenarios that need boundary events.

Event subprocesses can also handle complex business requirements. For example, we can throw events from inside the event subprocess, and these events can be caught by another subprocess/process, which is not the case if we are using boundary event handlers.

An **event gateway** has been defined in *Chapter 1, Flow Control Patterns*, and *Chapter 2, Multi-instance and State-based Patterns*, in detail. We can associate multiple catch events or receive tasks or timers with an event gateway. An event gateway can be defined with the `Instantiate` property. When defined in the `Instantiate` mode, it will pick the first event that occurs among the events associated with the event gateway. It works on an event's occurrence. Flexibility with event gateways is that we can use them to initiate process instances based on one of the many event occurrences, or they can be used as a midprocess to wait for any of the many event occurrences. We can check for the noninstantiate type of event gateway in the BackOffice process. The BackOffice process has event gateways being defined which wait to catch the response of the Loan Origination process. If the Loan Origination process ends smoothly at the `endLO` message end event, then its response is caught at the `RespLoanOrigination` message catch event. However, if a cancel loan request is raised for a Loan Origination process and the cancel loan process does not lead to re-application, then it would end at the `EndCancelLO` message end event. Also, to catch `EndCancelLO`, the BackOffice process has a `CatchCancelLoan` message catch event being defined in the noninstantiate event gateway.

In the Loan Origination process, we have used the event gateway. Click on the **Tart Event** gateway and check its properties. We can verify that its mode is **Instantiate**. It will either wait for a new loan process to get started from either the web process or the BackOffice process or for a re-application of the loan.

A re-application of the loan process will get triggered from the event subprocess that is handling the **Cancel Loan** request.

Perform the following actions to check the correlation definition:

- Open the Loan Origination process and go to the `CancelLoanSubProcess` event subprocess.

- Click on the `CancelLoan` message start event and verify that the correlation is defined with `LOCorrProp` as a correlation property, which is mapped with the **Applicant ID** message element. Verify the same for the `EndCancelLoan` and `RestartLO` events in the `CancelLoanSubprocess` event subprocess.

Testing cancelation pattern

Process cancelation patterns can be tested as follows:

1. Log in to the EM at `http://server:host/em` as an admin user, `weblogic`.

2. Instantiate the BackOffice process instance with the applicant IDs `1101`, `1102`, and `1103`.

3. You will find that three instances have been created for the BackOffice process.

4. Log in to the BPM workspace at **http://server:port/bpm/workspace**, and you will find three application verification tasks being assigned to the `salesrep` user.

5. Go back to the EM and instantiate Loan Origination process by selecting the **CancelLoan** operation.

6. Execute the `CancelLoan` operation for the application ID `1102`.

We have run a similar test when correlation was not defined. However, this time we have defined a correlation; let's check the audit trail for the BackOffice process to verify that the result is as per the expectation. We would expect only the instance with applicant ID `1102` to be cancelled and the process token to reach the **EndCancelLO** message end event.

The process instance will be completed and the human task application verification will be withdrawn from the `salesrep` user task list for that process instance which was cancelled. This is shown in the following screenshot:

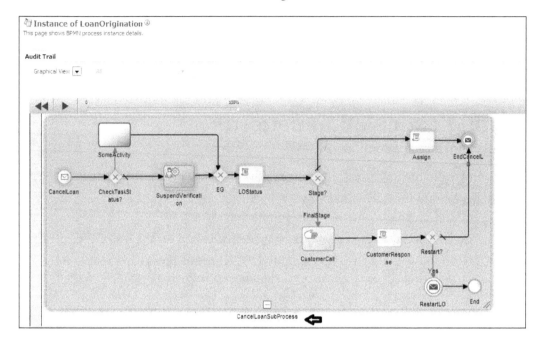

Click on the BackOffice process instance trail. You can check whether a new instance gets created for the Loan Origination process when a cancel loan request is raised; however, we have enabled correlation this time. Also, because of the correlation, the BPM engine was able to identify the correct instance of the Loan Origination process that needs to be cancelled. The cancel event handler subprocess will take the appropriate action, and this will lead to process instance completion for the Loan Origination process, which you can verify in the following diagram. We have just learned how correlation makes sure that the cancellation process results in the cancellation of the correct instance of a process that it is meant for and does not affect any other instances.

Restart instance pattern

Let's make another test to check correlation and its importance:

1. Go to **Cancel Event Subprocess** (`CancelLoanSubProcess`) click on the **CustomerResponse** script task, and then click on the **Implementation** tab.

2. Change data association from **No CustomerResp** to **Yes CustomerResp**.

   We need to change the customer response from **No** to **Yes** as we explicitly want a restart. Check the event gateway to flow towards the **Yes** path. This will lead to restarting the loan process.

3. In the Loan Origination process, go to the **reStartLOEvent** message catch event after the **Start** event.

4. Clear the correlation. Let there be no correlation defined for this node.

Testing the Loan Origination process to restart a loan

Walk through the following steps to test the restart scenario:

1. Log in to the EM as an admin weblogic user.

2. Click on **LoanOriginationProject** and instantiate an instance of the BackOffice process for the applicant ID 7799.

3. Create another instance of the Loan Origination process with the cancelLoan operation and applicant ID 7799.

4. Check the BackOffice process's audit trail.

You can verify that a new instance of the Loan Origination process is created for the cancelLoan event; however, this lands into a error as no correlation was being defined on the reStartLOEvent message catch event, which is defined after the start event gateway.

Redefine the correlation on the reStartLOEvent message catch event using LOCorrProp with the mode set to **Initiate**.

1. In the Loan Origination process, go to the reStartLOEvent message catch event after the start event.

2. Choose LOCorrProp as the correlation property and **Initiates** as the mode.

3. Map LOCorrProp with its **Applicant ID**.

4. Save and deploy the process.

You would have an obvious question as to what happened with the already running instance of the BackOffice process that initiated the Loan Origination process. This behavior is determined by how the event subprocess is configured. An event subprocess can be configured to be of the interrupting type or non-interrupting type. The following are the steps for configuring an event subprocess:

1. Click on the **CancelLoanSubProcess** event subprocess.

2. Open the **CancelLoan** message start event.

3. Check its implementation properties.

4. You can see that the implementation type is **Interrupting Event**.

Testing the restart scenario

Perform the following steps to instantiate the BackOffice process:

1. Log in to the BPM workspace as the salesrep user and approve the application verification human task. Post human task approval, the script task will set **CustomerResp** to **Yes**; we can see that **reStartLOEvent** will get invoked with the same applicant ID.

2. Go to the EM at http://server:host/em and select instances of the BackOffice process and check its audit trace.

If the event subprocess is of the interrupting type and if this event occurs, then the original process/subprocess in which it's enclosed will be stopped and the event handler will be executed. The token for the cancel loan event subprocess will reach the RestartLO message throw event, and this will lead to a restart of the Loan Origination process because the RestartLO throw event would be caught at the reStartLOEvent message catch event. As we can check in the audit screenshot, there is a separate instance that got created for the Loan Origination process.

Log in to the BPM workspace and approve the application verification human task; let the restarted Loan Origination process instance complete.

Now, you might be expecting that once the restarted Loan Origination process instance gets completed, the process token will reach the BackOffice process back; however, in the case of the restarted Loan Origination process, this would not happen. Even if the restarted Loan Origination process ends, the token never reaches the BackOffice process or even if we implement a correlation or conversation between the BackOffice process and Loan Origination process.

Check the audit trail trace for the BackOffice process which is shown in the following screenshot.

We can verify that when we execute the cancel loan operation on the Loan Origination process, this particular old instance of Loan Origination gets completed and a new instance is started for the Loan Origination process. This new instance is correlated with the original instance using the correlation definition based on the **Applicant ID** message element. This is shown in the following screenshot:

However, the BackOffice process will be in the running state even if new instances of the Loan Origination process get completed. Hence, implement the **CancelEvent** subprocess with a mechanism to restart a process instance, only when it's the main process and not when it is a "called" process being invoked by another other process "calling" process. Hence, if we invoke just the Loan Origination process and then execute cancel loan, cancellation would work as expected, which can be seen in the following screenshot:

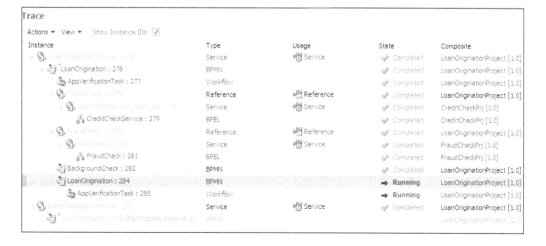

If the event subprocess is of the non-interrupting type, then the normal process flow will not be hampered. The process/subprocess in which the event handler is enclosed will run in parallel with the event subprocess; however, a new token will be created for the event subprocess. We will explore a non-interrupting event subprocess while walking through the query pattern in this chapter.

Update task pattern

The following pattern table explains the features of the update task pattern:

Signature	Update Task Pattern
Classification	Human Task Pattern
Intent	To update the human task properties.
Motivation	Based on the process status or business logic, there are requirements to update user tasks. Using update task, we can define a updating sequence in our business process, which makes the process flow easier.
Applicability	We can update specific user tasks in our BPMN process using update tasks. We can selectively update users' tasks, or we can even update all the user tasks. We can only update the active user tasks. If the user task is completed or has not started yet, then we cannot update it using an update task.
Implementation	Update tasks have been added from 11*g*, and they offer a rich set of operations to be performed on human tasks. Using these operations, we can update the properties of the human tasks in our process. We can update a human task or a set of human tasks, and it does not need a task ID or task context to be dealt explicitly.
Known issues	NA
Known solution	NA

 Though this pattern should be demonstrated in human task patterns, I have included it in this section as we are working on a Loan Origination process that has a use case to demonstrate it here.

To demonstrate an update task, we will use the Loan Origination process's use case. The Loan Origination process has the `CancelLoanSubProcess` event task. This event subprocess first checks the application verification human task's status based on its outcome. The following code snippet checks the application verification human task's outcome:

```
If
ApplicationVerificationOutcom == "REJECT" or
ApplicationVerificationOutcom == "APPROVE" Then
    Bypass Update task "SuspendVerification" and directly move to Merge
exclusive gateway.
Else
Execute "SuspendVerification" update task.
```

This means if the application verification is performed by an assignee loan officer, then the subprocess can directly move ahead, as the update task cannot be performed on the `AppVerificationTask` human task because it would no longer be active. An update task can be applied on a human task only when the task that needs to be updated is active, that is, as long as the human task is active. If `AppVerificationTask` is active, then the task will be updated using the `SuspendVerification` update task. Use the following steps to check the update task configuration:

1. Open the Loan Origination process.

2. Go to the **CancelLoanSubProcess** event task.

3. Go to the `SuspendVerification` update task and check its implementation properties.

4. The target selected for the update task is **User task**. However, select **All User Tasks** if you want to update all user tasks in the process, or you can also use the task ID to work around using the task identifier.

    As we have just one human task, `AppVerificationTask`, we have selected **User task** as the **Target** and selected `AppVerificationTask` in the **User Task** dropdown.

5. The selected operation is **Suspend**; however, there are many other operations that we can perform based on our business requirements. This is shown in the following screenshot:

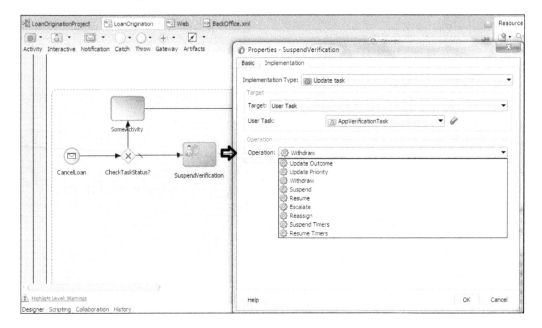

Demonstrating the update task functionality

The **SuspendVerification** update task gets instantiated when the process token reaches the cancel loan event subprocess. This happens on the event when the cancel loan is initiated. If the Loan Origination process is at a stage where the AppVerificationTask human task is active, the **SuspendVerification** update task will suspend the AppVerificationTask human task.

Query pattern

The following pattern table explains the features of the query pattern:

Signature	Query Pattern/Query Instance Pattern
Classification	Correlation Pattern
Intent	To query an already executing process instance.
Motivation	Based on the process status or business logic, there are requirements to query an already running process for varied information.

Applicability	When a query event occurs, the regular flow of the process will be interrupted and the query event subprocess will execute in parallel with the main BPMN process.
Implementation	We can use the event subprocess to query an existing process without even interrupting the main process, and both the main process and the query event subprocess will run in parallel. A new token is created for the query event subprocess.
Known issues	Making certain that the request to query a process instance must result from the process instance that it is meant for.
Known solution	Correlation.

Event subprocesses are powerful mechanisms as they can be used for varied use cases and scenarios in real time BPM process implementation. As we have seen previously, the event subprocess was used to implement cases when executing cancelation patterns in the BPM process. The cancelation pattern, in turn, can be used to implement the update task pattern. With the event subprocess, we always have the option to go back to the main process, which we have witnessed using the `reStartLoanEvent` message catch event and the `RestartLO` message throw event combination.

Another major use case of an event subprocess is the query pattern. We can use an event subprocess to query an existing process without even interrupting the main process and both the main process and the query event subprocess will run in parallel.

The Loan Origination process contains the `QuerySubprocess` event subprocess, which is a noninterrupting subprocess to query the loan status while the Loan Origination process is running. Perform the following steps to check the configuration of `QuerySubprocess`:

1. Open the loan origination process to find the `QuerySubprocess` event subprocess.

2. Click on the `CheckLoanStatus` message start event to define its properties in the **Implementation** tab.

3. Don't check **Interrupting event** or **Suspending event**, as we are defining this event subprocess as a noninterrupting subprocess.

4. We can verify this noninterrupting event subprocess offers the `checkLoanStatus` operation.

5. Click on correlation and select **LOCorrProp** as the correlation property.

6. Map to the **Applicant ID** message element by entering the following code using expression builder:

    ```
    /ns:checkLoanStatus/ns1:LoanRequest/ns1:LoanDetails/
    ns1:ApplicantID
    ```

7. Click on **OK** twice; save and deploy the process to the BPM 12*c* server.

8. At various nodes in the Loan Origination process, we have set the loan status. To verify this, perform the following steps:

    1. Click on the **startLOEvent** message catch event and open its data association. We can check whether the **StartStage** value is assigned to the loan status message element.

    2. Similarly, check the **reStartLOEvent** data association and you can witness that the **ReStartStage** value is assigned to the loan status message element.

    3. Click on the **FinalAssign** script activity, which we can locate before the **Underwriting** subprocess. The data association for the final assign script task shows the **FinalStage** value assigned to the loan status message element.

Depending on where the process instance is, we will receive different results to query the instance. So if we query a new instance of the Loan Origination process before the process token reaches the underwriting subprocess, we will get `StartStage` as the loan status; however, if the query restarted the instance of a Loan Origination process, we will receive `ReStartStage` as the loan status. Moreover, if we query after the underwriting subprocess or when the underwriting subprocess is executing, we will receive `FinalStage` as the loan status in response.

Testing the query pattern

This query pattern can be tested as follows:

1. Log in to the EM at `http://server:host/em` and instantiate a new instance of the Loan Origination process by executing the `startLOEvent` operation.

2. Log in to the BPM workspace as the `salesrep` user and approve the application verification human task.

3. Check the process flow in the EM and you will find the process token at the underwriting subprocess.

4. Instantiate two instances of the Loan Origination process from the EM by selecting the **checkLoanStatus** operation.

Remember to pass the applicant ID when executing the Loan Origination process for the `startLOEvent` operation and then for the `checkLoanStatus` operation. As we have queried twice, we will find that two new instances have been created for the Loan Origination process started for the `checkLoanStatus` operation. They are in the running state, and they keep running till the original instance with which they are correlated gets completed. The original instance means the instance that got created when instantiating the Loan Origination process via the `startLOEvent` operation. The Loan Origination process flow trace is shown in the following screenshot:

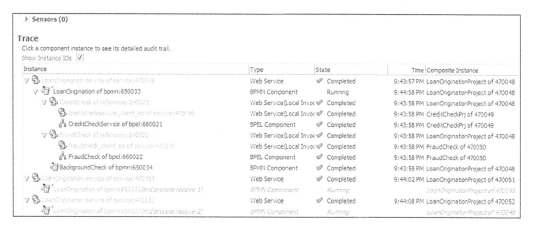

If you check the Loan Origination process's audit trail and check the payload associated with the assigned activity, you can find the current status of the process. Check the process's audit trail as shown in the following screenshot:

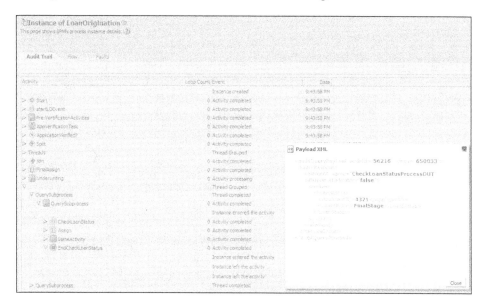

We can see that two threads are created for the `QuerySubprocess` event subprocess. Expand any one of the query subprocess threads and click on the **Instance left the activity** link, as shown in the preceding screenshot. We can see that the output contains the current loan status.

Threads are created to execute the event subprocess after the `Underwriting` subprocess, as the process was queried when the process token was at the underwriting subprocess.

When the query event occurred, the regular flow of the Loan Origination process was not interrupted, the query event subprocess was executed in parallel with the Loan Origination process, and a new token was assigned to it. As we have queried twice, we will find that the two instances of the query event subprocess are running in parallel to the Loan Origination process.

However, as we can check in the previous screenshot, even though the threads associated with the query subprocess got completed, the event subprocess will not complete and the instances created for the subprocess remains in the running state till the main process and all other noninterrupting event handlers get completed. Hence, when the Loan Origination process gets completed, the other two instances of the Loan Origination that were created while executing the query subprocess will also get completed.

Suspend process pattern

The following pattern table explains the features of the suspend process pattern:

Signature	Suspend Process Pattern
Classification	Correlation Pattern
Intent	To suspend an already executing process instance.
Motivation	Based on the process status or business logic, there are requirements to suspend an already running process instance and then to resume it from the point it was suspended or maybe to start from the next activity from the point it was suspended.
Applicability	When a suspend process occurs, the regular flow of the process will be suspended and the BPM engine will run the process flow in the event subprocess.
Implementation	We can use the event subprocess to suspend an existing process. We can resume the process flow by assigning **Resume** to a predefined variable, **Action**. **Resume** will resume the suspended process flow. However, if we want to advance the process flow to the next activity in the process flow that caught the suspension, then assign **Send** to the predefined variable.

Known issues	NA
Known solution	NA

The Loan Origination process in `LoanOriginationProject` contains an event subprocess named **SuspendProcess**. This event subprocess is configured as a **Suspending Event**, as we can see in the following screenshot:

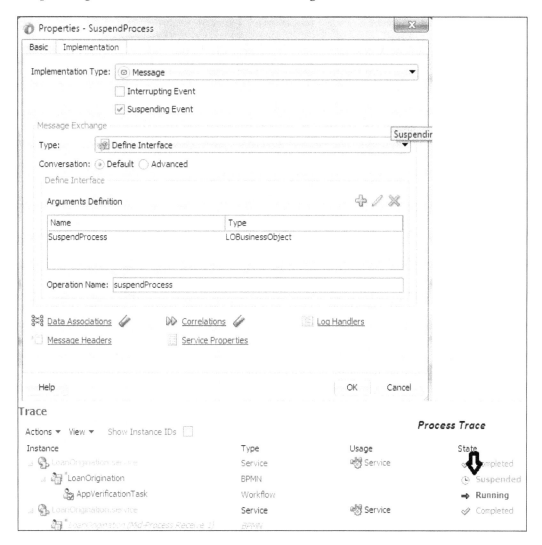

Remember to check the correlation defined for the **SuspendProcess** message start event. It's also based on the applicant ID and is using `LOCorrProp` as the correlation property. This also demonstrates another use case for correlation.

Execute the Loan Origination process with the `StartLOEvent` operation. Then, execute the Loan Origination process with the **SuspendProcess** operation. Remember to use the same application ID as you have passed in `StartLOEvent`. Check the process flow trace; you can find the Loan Origination process in the **Suspended** state.

Suspend activity pattern

The following pattern table explains the features of the suspend activity pattern:

Signature	Suspend Activity Pattern
Classification	Correlation Pattern
Intent	To suspend an already executing process activity or subprocess.
Motivation	Based on the process status or business logic, there are requirements to suspend an already running process activity or subprocess, and then to resume it from the point it was suspended or maybe to start from the next activity from the point it was suspended.
Applicability	When suspended process happens, the regular flow of the process will be suspended and the BPM engine will run the alternative sequence flow.
	After running a task in an alternative sequence flow, the BPM runtime checks the value of the predefined variable action. If the value of the predefined variable action is **Resume** or **Send**, it resumes the main process flow and cancels the event handler sequence flow.
Implementation	To suspend an activity or subprocess, we can use a boundary event. A message event, timer event, or signal event can be configured as the boundary event.
Known issues	NA
Known solution	NA

When the process token reaches the boundary event, the process instance gets suspended and an alternative sequence flow will be executed. After executing a task/activity in the alternate flow, the BPMN engine will check for the value of the predefined variable action. If the value of the predefined variable action is **Resume**, then the main process flow is resumed and the alternative flow is cancelled. If the value of the predefined variable is **Send**, then the main process flow is resumed from the next activity.

Cancel activity pattern

The following pattern table explains the features of the cancel activity pattern:

Signature	Cancel Activity Pattern
Classification	Cancellation Pattern
Intent	To cancel process activities.
Motivation	Based on the process status or business logic, there are requirements to cancel certain activities of the process.
Applicability	The cancel activity pattern is a useful cancelation pattern as it will allow you to initiate the cancellation of activities based on business requirements. An activity can only be cancelled when it's active; hence, when we initiate the cancellation for an activity, make sure that the activity is running in the instance.
Implementation	We can use event subprocesses and boundary catch events. The following section includes a implementation sample for this pattern.
Known issues	Makes it certain that the request to cancel an activity must result in the cancellation of the activity in the process instance for which it is initiated.
Known solution	Correlation.

To implement this pattern, we will create an interrupting boundary event on an activity. When the event is raised, the process token will follow the path guided by the interrupting boundary event.

Until this point, we are working on the Loan Origination process. We will extend the process to implement this scenario. Perform the following steps:

1. Expand the **Pre-VerificationActivities** subprocess and drag-and-drop a timer between the start and end of the subprocess.

2. Set a wait time of 1 minute in the timer.

3. Go to the **Pre-VerificationActivities** subprocess to define the boundary catch event on an activity.

4. Drag-and-drop the message catch event as a boundary event on the **Pre-VerificationActivities** subprocess and name it as **CatchConditionalCancel**.

5. Go to the **Implementation** tab and define an interface with the operation name **CatchConditionalCancel**.

6. Define the **conditionalCancelIN** argument of the LOBusinessObject type and click on **OK**.

7. Define data association and click on **OK**.

8. Define the event subprocess as an interrupting event subprocess by checking the **Interrupting** event.

9. Define a sequence flow from the **CatchConditionalCancel** boundary event to the message end event of the main process.

10. Save and deploy the project. This is demonstrated in the following screenshot:

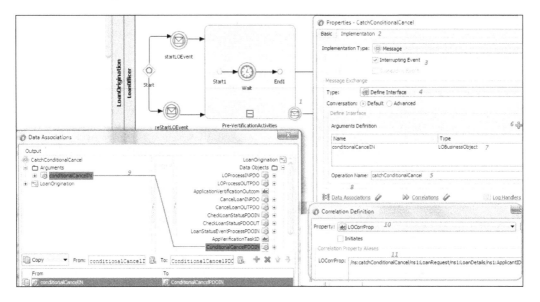

When the **Pre-VerificationActivities** activity gets cancelled, the process gets completed. We can also define other ways to deal with cancellation of an activity.

How a boundary event based activity correlation works

Execute the Loan Origination process using the `startLOEvent` operation. When the process token reaches the **Pre-VerificationActivities** subprocess, execute the Loan Origination process again using the `CatchConditionalCancel` operation.

The CatchConditionalCancel operation will result in execution of the ConditionalCancelSubprocess interrupting event. As this is an interrupting boundary catch event, it will interrupt the Loan Origination process. This would hold the main process token, and the token will follow the path defined for the boundary catch event.

We can also use other mechanisms to implement a conditional cancel on an activity/subprocess. With this implementation of conditional cancel, we have witnessed the usage of a noninterrupting subprocess and interrupting boundary event to cancel an activity.

Remember that for activity cancellation to work, the process token should be on the activity. This means that the activity/subprocess must be active, else conditional cancel being invoked in either of the previously mentioned methods will not work.

Testing the cancelation pattern on an activity

Perform the following steps to test the cancelation pattern on an activity:

1. Go to the EM at http://server:host/em and select **Loan Origination Project**. From the test dropdown, choose **Loan Origination Service**.

2. In the operation dropdown, select the startLOEvent operation to instantiate loan origination.

3. The process token will now be waiting at the **Pre-VerificationActivities** subprocess. It will wait here for 1 minute as this is the time set in the timer inside the subprocess.

4. Execute another instance of the Loan Origination process; however, select the CatchConditionalCancel operation this time.

   Remember to use the same applicant ID that you used while executing the StartLOevent operation, because the **Applicant ID** is the correlation key.

5. Go to the EM and check the Loan Origination process's audit flow. This is shown in the following screenshot:

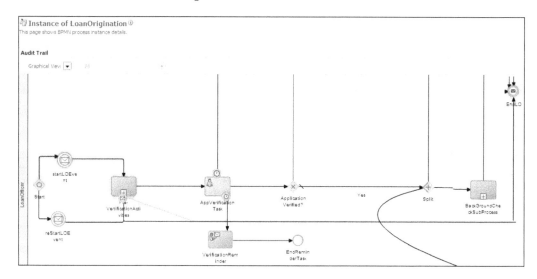

You can verify that when the subprocess gets interrupted by the `CatchConditionalCancel` operation, it will end the Loan Origination process.

Summary

The chapter started with defining correlation as well as the correlation mechanism and its components, along with its types. We learned to define correlation and various patterns to implement it. It offered us an opportunity to test all the patterns with a sample application. We uncovered how correlation caters to scenarios such as cancel instance/activity/subprocess or query process instances. We also witnessed suspending processes and suspending activities. The sample application offered with this chapter helps us to learn subprocesses, event subprocesses (interrupting, noninterrupting and suspending events) boundary events (interrupting, noninterrupting and suspending events) event gateways, and so on. The update task pattern, which is a human task pattern, was also covered here.

The next chapter focuses on exception-handling patterns.

7
Exception Handling Patterns

Anything that hampers the normal flow of execution of a BPMN process is termed as an **exception**. Exceptions happen due to undesirable situations such as the system may be down, a business condition is not satisfied, a deadline has expired, and so on. These undesirable situations result in an exception. To lay down the foundation for an effective exception-handling mechanism, we need to classify exceptions. Along with the classification of exceptions, it's equally important to know how exceptions propagate. Once an exception propagation mechanism is defined, we can implement exception handling based on Exception Handling Patterns discussed in this chapter. A distinct approach is used in this chapter to define Exception Handling Patterns. This chapter deals with Exception Handling Patterns only for the Oracle BPM suite and hence the terms and terminologies will revolve around this product suite.

It's always a good process-modeling practice to analyze, define, and implement exceptions for BPM processes from the beginning. We can use the underlying technology to implement generic solutions to handle exceptions. Generic solutions could be at process level, project level, or enterprise level. At whatever level the solution is implemented, the pattern remains the same. Normal process execution flow and exception sequence flow are mutually exclusive. Hence, when an exception is caught by a boundary catch error event, the normal process execution flow is interrupted and the token flows to the exception sequence flow.

The following patterns are covered in this chapter:

- Reassigned Exception Handling Pattern
- Allocated Exception Handling Pattern
- Force-Terminate Exception Handling Pattern
- Force-Error Exception Handling Pattern
- Force-Complete Exception Handling Pattern
- Invoked Exception Handling Pattern

- Invoked State Exception Handling Pattern
- Continue Execution Exception Handling Pattern
- Force-Terminate Execution Exception Handling Pattern
- Force-Error Execution Exception Handling Pattern
  - ° External Exception Handling Pattern
  - ° Internal Exception Handling Pattern
    - Internal Complete Exception Handling Pattern
    - Internal Terminate Exception Handling Pattern
    - Internal Error Exception Handling Pattern
  - ° Reallocated Exception Handling Pattern
- External Exception Handling Pattern
- Process Level Exception Handling Pattern
- System Level Exception Handling Pattern
- External Triggers

Classifying exceptions

Unexpected issues can result in process failure. The problems that arise in the BPMN ecosystem are software or hardware failure, and sometimes system error occurs. System errors are connectivity issues, remote faults, timeouts, and so on. To handle system errors, we use system exceptions. Issues in the regular process development such as a credit card not authorized, an out-of-stock inventory, and so on are business-related issues that result in business error. They are handled using business exceptions. Exceptions can be classified as system exceptions, business exceptions, timeout/deadline exceptions, external triggers/process exceptions. These exceptions are further described as follows:

- **System exceptions**: Exceptions that occur due to system errors such as database failure, infrastructure failure, connectivity issues, web service not available, and so on come under this category. These exceptions are meant to handle system errors. System errors are highly unpredictable. A fault-handling management system is needed to handle system errors.

- **Business exceptions**: Errors due to problems in the process behavior are called business exceptions. They are caused due to the interference of problems in your regular process flow. For example, a process is designed in such a way that if the inventory doesn't have the stock available, then the quotation cannot be processed normally. This would lead to a business exception. Predictable/unpredictable circumstances that arise in the business logic or in the business process result in business errors. With an effective process analysis and modeling, most of the business errors can be identified and you can term them as predictable business errors. You can define the exception-handling mechanism for predictable as well as nonpredictable business errors too.

- **Timeout/Deadline exceptions**: These exceptions arise whenever an activity/task does not happen in a defined time interval or at a specified time. For example, application verification in the Loan Origination process has to be completed in 3 days. If this does not happen, then an exception should be raised. SLA violation and such time-based scenarios are subject to deadline exceptions. You need to have a defined approach as to what needs to be done when a deadline is met; the timeout/deadline exception deals with those scenarios.

- **External triggers/process exceptions**: External systems or process interaction with external systems can lead to cases that affect normal process execution, for example, when the Loan Origination process has to be either cancelled or queried. These external events are raised by external systems, and your process needs to be equipped to deal with such scenarios. External triggers can be of interrupting or noninterrupting type, for example, cancelling the Loan Origination process will stop the normal process flow and end the process based on the process exception flow. `QueryLoanOrigination` is a noninterrupting type process and it would be mutually inclusive with the main process execution flow; however, it might affect the normal execution flow of main process too.

Business process state

An exception might occur in a process component. Oracle BPM process components are: human tasks, send and receive activities, call tasks, service tasks, subprocesses, and reusable processes. Together, they are termed as **Activities**. There are various patterns to handle exceptions. However, before we talk about exception handling patterns, it is wise to understand and analyze different states through which a process component travels in the process instance. The following activity state diagram explains an activity's state as well as exception handling pattern paths. We will be walking through all the paths in this chapter.

Remember, we have defined the states for the activities, just for the sake of learning Exception Handling Patterns.

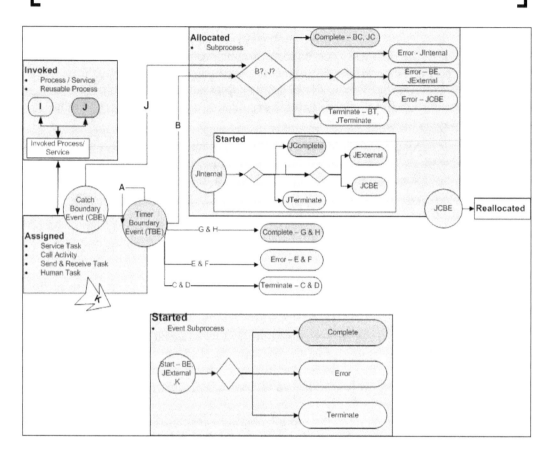

A BPM process belongs to a BPM system and runs on the BPM engine in the Oracle BPM suite. Hence, the system is mentioned as an environment in which a process instance executes. The following are the states shown in the activity state diagram:

- **Assigned**: This is the first state of a process activity. When the process instance starts, it could start through various means such as JMS, an event, and so on. However, here we are going to refer to only the BPM activities as we are discussing exception handling on them. While the process instance is executing, a token is assigned to an activity. This activity could be a human task, service task, and so on.

- **Allocated**: This is the state where a process token reaches from an activity. It could be the case that a deadline exception or an error catch event allocates the token from the activity to the subprocess, as shown in the preceding state diagram. When the **Timer Boundary Event** (**TBE**) timer expires, as pointed by arrow **B**, the token gets allocated to a subprocess.

- **Started**: An event subprocess can start due to various reasons. An event subprocess can start due to an external event as shown in the state diagram. It can also start by an Error Start Event, which basically catches an exception and handles it. In these cases, the token gets assigned to the event subprocess and gets started.

- **Reallocated**: This means that the token from an allocated state is passed to a subprocess/activity.

- **Invoked**: A BPM process can invoke processes or services. For example, a service task might invoke a synchronous service or a call activity might invoke a reusable process. Hence, the state is termed as invoked state. The following are the components that we will talk about while walking through the invoked state:

  - **Service task**: In case of the service task, the token remains with the service task until the response is received from the process/service that is invoked synchronously. Once the response is received, the token moves ahead to subsequent activities.

  - **Send and Receive Tasks**: When send and receive tasks are used to invoke an asynchronous process, calling (invoking) the process token will keep executing subsequent activities after the Send Task until it reaches a receive activity, which is paired with the called process's Send Task. The token then waits at the receive activity until a response is received from the invoked process. When a called process is initiated by a receive activity, which has a create instance property set to `true`, a new token gets created in the called (invoked) process and this token has its own lifecycle. In the case of an invoked process, a new token is created.

  - **Message Throw and Catch Events**: Message Throw Events are used to invoke an asynchronous process or service. When a Message Throw Event sends a message and invokes a process or service, a token immediately moves to subsequent process activities. However, when it reaches the Message Catch Event, it waits for the response from the invoked process/service. When the token reaches the Message Catch Event, the process will invoke the callback operation of the invoked process/service, using the Message Catch Event.

○ **Call activity**: This is used to invoke a reusable process. When a reusable process is invoked, new tokens are not created for the invoked process. Instead, the same token is passed from the main process to the invoked, reusable process. The reusable process becomes the child process. When the token completes the child process, it returns to the parent process to continue running subsequent activities that follow the call activity.

We have defined exception types and process states. Now, it's time to define the Exception Handling Patterns and to analyze the state transitions from exception handling perspectives. After listing the various Exception Handling Patterns, we will categorize the exception pattern based on exception types.

Reassigned Exception Handling Pattern

The following table highlights some important facts about the Reassigned Exception Handling Pattern:

Signature	Reassigned Exception Handling Pattern
Classification	Exception Pattern
Intent	The intention is to reassign the process token to the same activity on which the exception has occurred.
Motivation	When exception occurs, there would not be any change in the state of the process.
Applicability	A token is assigned to an activity. When the exception occurs, the token gets reassigned to the same activity. Hence, when the exception occurs, there would not be any change in the state of the process.
Implementation	Implementation is discussed as follows.
Known issues	NA
Known solution	NA

When we check the preceding process state diagram, we can notice that TBE is a timer event and a sequence line flows from the TBE back to the activity. Perform the following steps to realize the scenario and test it:

1. Download the `ExceptionHandlingApps` folder from the downloadable files for *Chapter 7, Exception Handling Patterns* from the Packt Publishing website.

2. Expand the `ExceptionHandlingPrj` project and click on the `ExceptionDemoProcess` process.

3. Notice the `ApplicationVerification` human task. Click on the boundary catch timer **A**. It's a noninterrupting timer. Verify that time is set to 1 minute. In real-life scenarios, we can set the SLA on the task/activity using timers.

4. Deploy the process and create an instance of the Reusable process by passing the value `AppsVerify-BC`. (As input is a single string argument, no test data file is provided with this chapter.)

When the process starts, the token gets assigned to the `ApplicationVerification` human task. If the user does not act on the task in 1 minute, the timer expires. As it's a noninterrupting timer and the end activity is the `none` event, the token gets reassigned to the same activity. We can implement the same scenario on any other activity as well by using timers. In the exception path, we can build a notification mechanism to let others know that the task is overdue.

Allocated Exception Handling Pattern

The following table highlights some important facts about the Allocated Exception Handling Pattern:

Signature	Allocated Exception Handling Pattern
Classification	Exception Pattern
Intent	The intention is to handle the timeout exception in subprocesses.
Motivation	To handle timeout exception in subprocesses.
Applicability	The token is assigned to an activity. When the exception occurs, the token gets allocated to the subprocess. The state of the process instance now depends on the state of the allocated subprocess. The following are different scenarios for that: • **Allocated-Complete**: The token gets allocated to a subprocess and the subprocess gets completed • **Allocated-Error**: The Token gets allocated to a subprocess and the subprocess gets an error • **Allocated-Terminate**: The token gets allocated to a subprocess and the subprocess gets terminated

Implementation	Check the process state diagram. This has a sequence flowing from TBE (timer **B**) timer to the subprocess (Allocated). This sequence is to demonstrate the process flow when timeout happens at point B (timer B). Timer B is an interrupting timer and when the timer expires, the process token will reach the subprocess (Allocated). Based on the input data we pass, the subprocess might lead to three different scenarios: the subprocess will complete (marked as **Complete-BC**), the subprocess will itself lead into error (marked as **Error-BE**), or the subprocess will terminate (marked as **Terminate-BT**). In this section, you will learn how the interrupting Boundary Catch Event can be used to handle timeout exceptions. You will also learn about the different patterns that arise when the token gets assigned to a subprocess.
Known issues	NA
Known solution	NA

Check the preceding process activity state diagram. We can notice that TBE is a timer event, and a sequence line flow exists from TBE to a subprocess (Allocated). Perform the following steps to realize the scenario and to test it:

1. Open the `ExceptionDemoProcess` process in JDeveloper and click on the timer B. We can notice that timer B is an interrupting timer and the time for it is set to 2 minutes. When the timer B expires, the token gets allocated to the subprocess (**Allocated-B**).

2. Deploy the process if not deployed already.

3. Test the process through the SOAPUI or EM or any tool of choice. Pass the following values to test each of the following patterns:

    ○ **Allocated-Complete**: To test the Allocated-Complete Exception Handling Pattern, pass `AppsVerify-BC` as the input parameter.

    A human task gets assigned to a user. If the user does not act in 2 minutes, the token gets assigned to the subprocess (Allocated-B). As timer A is also connected with the human task, it would get activated in 1 minute as it is set to 1 minute, but the token will be assigned back to the human task. However, when 2 minutes gets completed, timer B expires and the following are some interesting observations:

    After the expiration of timer B, the token gets assigned to the subprocess (Allocated-B). There is a wait activity in the subprocess (Allocated-B) that allows readers to dig into the instance and verify that the token was with the subprocess (Allocated-B), as it's an interrupting timer event. The input passed is `AppsVerify-BC`, where BC means the state will transition to the None End Event which will complete the subprocess (Allocated-B).

The subprocess (Allocated-B) gets completed; however, the task gets reassigned. As you can check in the following screenshot, a new instance of the `ApplicationVerification` human task is created and the older instance of the task gets withdrawn:

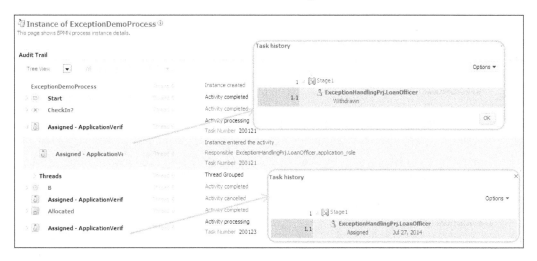

- ○ **Allocated-Error**: To test the Allocated-Error Exception Handling Pattern, pass `AppsVerify-BE` as the input parameter, where `BE` translates to the subprocess (Allocated-B) in Error. This pattern states that the token is assigned to an activity. On exception (deadline or timer exception), the token is withdrawn from the activity and is allocated to a subprocess. The process instance state will depend on the allocated subprocess behavior. If the allocated subprocess ends with an error, the error gets reported and the fate of the instance will depend on whether the error was caught or not. We have built the scenario where a catch-all exception handler will catch the exception. However, if there is no exception handler then the exception propagates to the system where it's handled and reported by the BPM service engine.

  Now, test the process by passing `AppsVerify-BE` as the input parameter and click on the process instance in EM to check the process flow and trace.

You can notice that the subprocess (Allocated-B) will raise an error when you pass `AppsVerify-BE`. The error raised by the Allocated–B subprocess is caught by an exception handler at the process level.

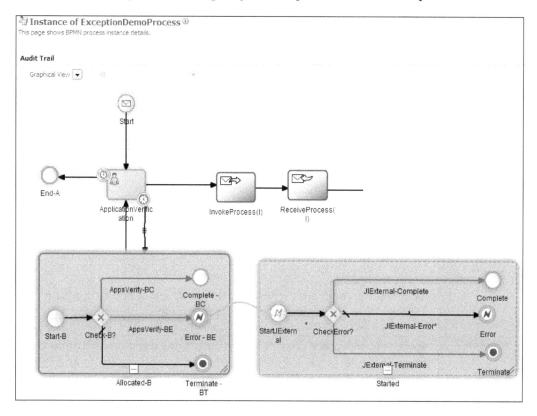

This pattern highlights certain facts related to the exception. When being raised in the subprocess (Allocated-B), it can lead to the following scenarios:

○ If the allocated subprocess gives errors, then that exception should be caught either at a Boundary Catch event associated to the allocated subprocess, by an event subprocess inside the subprocess itself, or by a process-level event subprocess.

○ In the preceding test case, when we pass `AppsVerify-BE`, the process instance gets recovered from the business exception and it gets completed; however, it reports errors raised by the subprocess (Allocated-B). Recovered from the exception means that the process got an exception which was handled by the event subprocess.

5. Create a sequence flow from the subprocess (Allocated-B) to a None End Event as pointed by an arrow in the following screenshot:

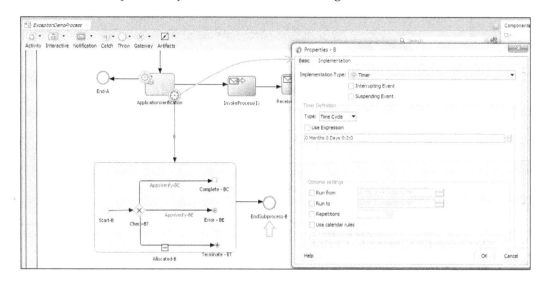

6. Test the process by passing the appropriate input parameter. The following table shows the input parameters along with their results:

Input parameter	Results
AppsVerify-BC	We can check that when timer B expires, the subprocess (Allocated-B) gets initiated. Also, as we have passed input as AppsVerify-BC, the token will reach to the None End Event named Complete-BC in the subprocess. The subprocess (Allocated-B) will end and the sequence flow moves to EndSubprocess-B, the None End Event.
	Again, the token reaches the ApplicationVerification human task. However, this time, the task is not reassigned to the user and hence you don't find multiple instances of human task. Remember you have witnessed multiple assignments of tasks in the *Allocated Exception Handling Pattern* section.
	As the timer exception is not handled, it would lead to infinite assignment. Hence, you need to implement logic to end the reassignment of the token to the same activity and to handle timer exception.

Input parameter	Results
AppsVerify-BE	This input parameter will eventually enable the subprocess (Allocated-B) to raise an error. This error would be handled by an exception handler at the process level. The ExternalErrorHandlingEventSubprocess event subprocess is a process-level event subprocess to handle all exceptions. Exceptions thrown by the subprocess (Allocated-B) are handled at the process level by the event subprocess and defined at the process level. Once the error is handled by the exception handler event subprocess, the process instance gets completed normally. If there was no process-level exception handler, then the exception will reach the Oracle Enterprise Manager fault recovery system.
AppsVerify-BT	Timer expiration will terminate the process instance.

7. Click on the process instance in EM to check the process flow and trace.

Force-Terminate Exception Handling Pattern

The following table highlights some important facts about the Force-Terminate Exception Handling pattern:

Signature	Force-Terminate Exception Handling Pattern
Classification	Exception Pattern
Intent	The intention is to terminate the process instance if a deadline/timer exception occurs.
Motivation	Handle timeout exception.
Applicability	The token is assigned to an activity. When the timeout exception occurs, the process flow from the Boundary Catch Timer Event to the Terminate End Event.
Implementation	Check the process state diagram. It has a sequence flowing from the TBE to terminate **C & D** (Terminate End Events). This sequence is to demonstrate the process flows when a timeout happens at the TBE. If the TBE is a noninterrupting timer, the process instance gets terminated when the timer expires. This holds true even if the TBE is an interrupting timer.
Known issues	NA
Known solution	NA

Expand the exception-handling project, `ExceptionHandlingPrj`, in JDeveloper and click to open the `ExceptionDemoProcess` process. Click on the Boundary Catch Timer Event A and verify its implementation. Let it be set to 1 minute and its implementation type should be noninterrupting. Change the associated end event, End-A, from the None End Event to Terminate End Event. Save and deploy the project.

The timer A is a noninterrupting timer set to 1 minute. Hence, when the token gets assigned to the `ApplicationVerification` human task and if the user does not act in 1 minute, timer A expires and it raises an exception. The sequence flow that connects to timer A, moves the token to the Terminate End Event. Test the process from EM by passing `AppsVerify` as the input parameter. As expected, the entire instance will get terminated. The same holds true for the interrupting timer too. To test the interrupting scenario, we can change the timer from noninterrupting to interrupting and test the process by passing `AppsVerify` as input parameter. As this pattern forcefully terminates the process instance, it is termed as Force-Terminate Exception Handling Pattern.

Force-Error Exception Handling Pattern

The following table highlights some important facts about the Force-Error Exception Handling Pattern:

Signature	Force-Error Exception Handling Pattern
Classification	Exception Pattern
Intent	The intention is to raise an error when the timer expires.
Motivation	Implement an Exception Handling Pattern that would raise an error when the deadline/timer expires.
Applicability	The token is assigned to an activity. When the timeout exception occurs, the process flows from the Boundary Catch Timer Event to the Error End Event.
Implementation	Check the process state diagram. It has a sequence flowing from TBE to error **E & F** (Error End Events). This sequence demonstrates the process flow when timeout happens at the TBE. If the TBE is a noninterrupting timer, the process instance throws a business exception when the timer expires. The business exception is caught by the event subprocess defined at process level. The process instance is recovered from the error as the exception is handled and the process instance is completed. A human task assigned to the participant gets withdrawn. The same holds true if the TBE is an interrupting timer.
Known issues	NA
Known solution	NA

Expand the **ExceptionHandlingPrj** project in JDeveloper and click to open **ExceptionDemoProcess**. Right-click on **Business Components** and navigate to **New | Business Exception** to define a business exception named `Deadline Exception`. Click on the **Create Business Exception** dialog and save all. Click on the Boundary Catch Timer Event **A** and verify its implementation. Let it be set to 1 minute and its implementation type should be noninterrupting. Change the associated end event, **End-A**, from None End Event to Error End Event. Browse for the business exception and select **Deadline Exception**. Perform data association as required and save all. Now, we will change the properties of the **ExternalErrorHandlingEventSubprocess** event subprocess.

Click on the catch error event in the event subprocess and implement it for the business exception, **Deadline Exception**, as shown in the following screenshot. Then, save and deploy the project:

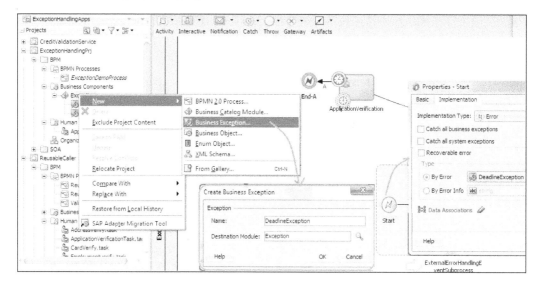

Test the process from EM by passing `AppsVerify` as the process input. A token gets assigned to a human task activity. If the user does not act in 1 minute, timer A expires and raises a deadline exception. When the timer expires, the following events happen:

- If the timer A is a noninterrupting timer and the timer expires, the process instance throws the **Deadline Exception** business exception.

- This exception is caught by the `ExternalErrorHandlingEventSubprocess` event subprocess defined at the process level.

- The process instance gets recovered from the error as the exception is handled and the process instance gets completed. The human task assigned to the participant gets withdrawn. The same holds true if the timer A is an interrupting timer.

Exceptions are caught at process level by the **ExternalErrorHandlingEventSubprocess** event subprocess. Remember, the fate of the process instance will depend on how the event subprocess ends. For this particular case on Deadline Exception, the event process gets started and it would end with the None End Event. This would complete the process instance. We will visit more complex scenarios with a different ending mechanism for an event subprocess later in this chapter.

Force-Complete Exception Handling Pattern

The following table highlights some important facts about the Force-Complete Exception Handling Pattern:

Signature	Force-Complete Exception Handling Pattern
Classification	Exception Pattern
Intent	The intention is to complete the process, when the timer expires.
Motivation	To implement an Exception Handling Pattern that will forcefully end the process when the deadline/timer expires.
Applicability	The token is assigned to an activity. When the timeout exception occurs, the process flow from the Boundary Catch Timer Event to the Message End Event of the process.
Implementation	Check the process state diagram. It has a sequence flowing from TBE to message **G & H** (Message End Events). This sequence shows the process flows when timeout happens at the TBE. If the TBE is a noninterrupting timer, the process instance reaches a Message End Event when the timer expires. The token again reaches the activity (human task); however, the task is neither withdrawn nor reassigned, which is different from the behavior in the Allocated and Complete Exception Handling Pattern. If the TBE is interrupting and when process reaches the Message End Event, the activity (human task) gets cancelled and the process instance gets completed. If the TBE is a suspending event, then the activity (human task) gets cancelled and the process instance gets completed.
Known issues	NA
Known solution	NA

In **ExceptionDemoProcess**, click on **End-A**, the Error End Event that we used earlier, and change the trigger type from the Error End Event to the Message End Event. Rename the Message End Event to **TBE-End-Process**. Click on timer A and change its trigger type to noninterrupting. Test the process by passing `AppsVerify` as the input parameter to the process. After 1 minute, check the process flow. We can find that the process instance is still running. The human task remains with the participant (user) and timer keeps evaluating as long as the user does not act on the task.

If you change the trigger type of timer A from noninterrupting event to interrupting event, we can find that the activity (human task) gets cancelled and the process instance completes. The scenario will be same if we make the timer A suspending event. The following screenshot shows the process instance details of **ExceptionDemoProcess**:

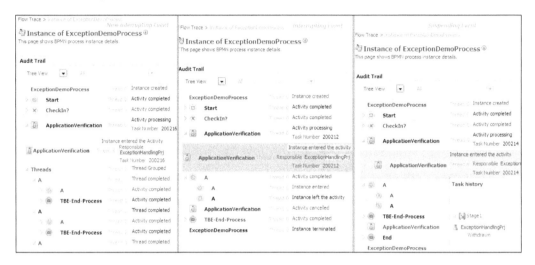

Invoked Exception Handling Pattern

A BPM process needs to interact and collaborate with other processes and services. We have read a lot about invocation patterns in *Chapter 5, Interaction Patterns*. However, when we invoke a process/service, those invoked processes/services might end in error and raise an exception. This section will help you to learn about exception handling patterns in scenarios where an invoked process raises an error. This section will also include exception propagation pertaining to each pattern.

As per the process state diagram, an activity state transits from ASSIGNED to INVOKED when that assigned activity invokes a process or a service. The following are the activities used to invoke a process or a service:

- Call activity invokes a reusable process.

- An activity such as service task is used to invoke synchronous services and processes.

- Send and receive tasks and throw and catch message events are used to invoke asynchronous services and processes.

Whatever the invocation mechanism, the following are the broad categories of exception handling:

- Handling exceptions in the invoked process/service itself, that is, exception handling at the INVOKED state

- Catching exceptions using a catch boundary event on the activity that has invoked the process/service

- Catching exceptions by an event subprocess at a level outside the activity

- Catching exceptions at process level by event subprocess (process-level event subprocess) or using the Fault Management Framework

- Using the BPM service engine to catch the exception

To understand the exception handling mechanism, we need to walk through the exception propagation pattern in Oracle BPM.

Invoked State Exception Handling Pattern

The following table highlights some important facts about the Invoked State Exception Handling pattern:

Signature	Invoked State Exception Handling Pattern
Classification	Exception Pattern
Intent	The intention is to handle exceptions in the invoked (called) process itself.
Motivation	Implement an Exception Handling Pattern that results in exception handling in the invoked process itself. The invoked process that has experienced the error will not propagate the exception to the called process.
Applicability	This pattern considers the fact that an assigned activity has invoked a process/service and the process/service has the capability to handle the exception itself. This means that when an exception rises in the invoked process/service, it gets handled there and the invoking process (assigned activity) will never know about it.

Implementation	To implement the scenario, we will consider an asynchronous process. This asynchronous process will be invoked by the Send Task and to get a response from the invoked process, a receive task will be used to invoke the callback operation. When send and receive tasks are used to invoke an asynchronous process, the process token will keep executing subsequent activities after the Send Task until it reaches a receive activity that is paired with the called process's Send Task. The token then waits at the receive activity until a response is received from the invoked process. The invoked process will encounter an error and will handle the exception by itself. The invoking process (calling process) will receive a normal response from the invoked process.
Known issues	The invoking process (calling process) will never know about the exception.
Known solution	It's a subject of architectural design and is based on how the business wants to consider this modeling pattern. If the invoking process needs to be made aware of the exception, then the exception should be propagated to the calling process. In this case, the calling process should handle the exception.

The BPMN project, `ExceptionHandlingPrj`, contains the `ExceptionDemoProcess` process, which has the `Invoke Process (I)` Send Task that invokes an asynchronous process (`Validation Process`). The `ExceptionDemoProcess` process also has `Receive Process (I)`, which is a receive task. It's the receive task where the token awaits until the invoking process, `ExceptionDemoProcess`, gets a response from the invoked process, `ValidationProcess`.

Open the **Properties** dialog box of **ExceptionDemoProcess** and uncheck the **Is Draft** checkbox for send and receive tasks, respectively (by default, `ExceptionDemoProcess` provides all activities in the draft mode). In JDeveloper, open the validation process and check its configuration. The Validation process is designed in such a form that on receiving any input, it will raise a `Validation_BizException` exception. The Validation process has an exception handler in it which will handle the raised exception, `Validation_BizException`. Perform the following steps to test the scenario:

1. Use any tool of choice or login to EM to test the reusable process.

2. Pass the input as `AppsVerify`. You can notice that a token gets assigned to the Send Task, **InvokeProcess (I)**. This assigned activity will invoke the validation process.

As we can see in the following image, on the right-hand side an instance of
ValidationProcess is displayed. It gets completed normally and returns a response
based on the business requirement. However, the exception raised in the validation
process is handled by the process itself and it's not propagated to the assigned
activity, that is, **Invoke Process (I)** (invoked the validation process).

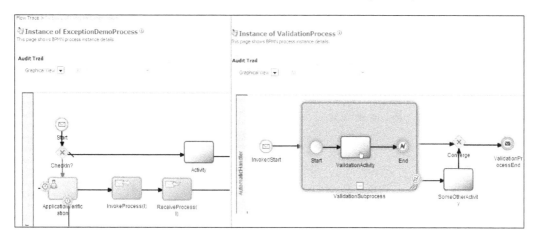

Also, you can see on the left-hand side of the screenshot, the process flow of
ExceptionDemoProcess moves ahead of the **Receive Process (I)** receive task
as the validation process has not returned an exception and in fact handled the
exception itself.

The major challenge with this approach is that the invoking process (calling process)
will never know about the exception.

Continue Execution Exception Handling Pattern

The following table highlights some important facts about the Continue Execution
Exception Handling pattern:

Signature	Continue Execution Exception Handling Pattern
Classification	Exception Pattern
Intent	The intention is to handle exceptions raised by the invoked (called) process/service in the invoking (calling) process / service.
Motivation	Handle exception in invoking activity using boundary event.

Applicability	This pattern showcases those scenarios of exception handling where an exception is not handled by the invoked process/service. That exception will propagate outside the invoked process/service. An assigned activity has invoked a process/service that experiences an error. That exception propagates to the assigned activity and it's then caught by an error catch boundary event.
Implementation	If you check the process state diagram and look into the INVOKED state, the sequence "J" points to the scenario where the invoked process/service has raised an exception. The assigned activity catches that exception using a Boundary Catch Event shown as **CBE**. The CBE (boundary event) will catch the exception and the process token moves to the ALLOCATED state, that is, the token moves to the subprocess. Now, there could be various scenarios:
	• Allocated state completes (the allocated subprocess ends with the None End Event)
	• Allocated state terminates (the allocated subprocess ends with the Terminate End Event)
	• Allocated state errors (the allocated subprocess ends with the Error End Event)
	Continue Execution Exception Handling Pattern is about the scenario where the allocated state completes, that is, the allocated subprocess ends with a None End Event.
Known issues	NA
Known solution	NA

To implement this scenario, we developed a reusable process, ReusableProcess, in the **ExceptionHandlingPrj** project. Inside **ExceptionDemoProcess**, a call activity will invoke ReusableProcess using a CALL task, shown as **CallReusableProcess (J)**. When invoked, ReusableProcess raises an exception; it is caught by the Boundary Catch Event associated with the **CallReusableProcess (J)** call task. The process token will move from the Boundary Catch Event to the subprocess (**Allocated**). The Allocated subprocess can reach to various states (complete, error, or terminate) based on the input values being passed. This is modeled to demonstrate process behaviors in various exception handling scenarios where an exception is propagated from a Boundary Catch Event to a subprocess.

We have downloaded the `ExceptionHandlingPrj` project from the downloadable code files of *Chapter 7, Exception Handling Patterns*. Deploy the project to 12*c* WebLogic server. Perform the following steps to test the process for continuous execution exception handling:

1. Open `ExceptionHandlingPrj` project in JDeveloper

2. Go to **ExceptionDemoProcess** and click on **InvokeProcess (I)** and **Receive Process (I)**, the send and receive tasks, respectively.

3. Change their implementation type to `draft`, as we want the token to be passed directly to the **CallReusableProcess (J)** call activity.

4. Test the reusable caller process by passing input, **JComplete**.

5. Log in to the EM console and check the process flow of **ExceptionDemoProcess**, as shown in the following screenshot:

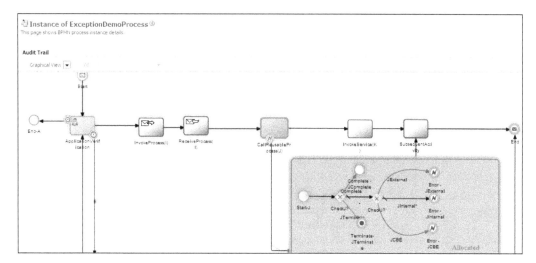

As we can witness from the process flow, when the token gets assigned to a call task, **CallReusableProcess (J)**, it invokes a reusable process, `ReusableProcess`. The token gets assigned to the reusable process as the reusable process acts as a child to the main process. The reusable process will raise an exception and it will not be handled by **ExceptionDemoProcess**. Hence, the exception gets propagated to the assigned activity, **CallReusableProcess (J)**.

When the exception is raised by the reusable process, the catch boundary event configured on the assigned activity (**CallReusableProcess (J)**) will handle the exception. The sequence flow attached to the catch boundary event will detour the process execution flow to the subprocess (Allocated).

As the input passed is **JComplete**, the token flow will detour to the None End Event **JComplete** in the subprocess (Allocated). You can include any exception handling logic as per business requirement such as logging, notification, and so on. When the Allocated subprocess completes, the process starts executing subsequent activities as guided by the outgoing flow from the allocated subprocess (Allocated). Hence, this pattern is termed as continue execution pattern.

Force-Terminate Execution Exception Handling Pattern

The following table highlights some important facts about the Force-Terminate Execution Exception Handling Pattern:

Signature	Force-Terminate Execution Exception Handling Pattern
Classification	Exception Pattern
Intent	The intention is to handle exceptions raised by the invoked (called) process/service in the invoking (calling) process/service.
Motivation	Handle exception in invoking activity using the boundary event.
Applicability	This pattern showcases those scenarios of exception handling where an exception is not handled by the invoked process/service. That exception will propagate outside the invoked process/service. An assigned activity has invoked a process/service that experiences an error. That exception propagates to the assigned activity and it's then caught by an error catch boundary event.
Implementation	If you check the process state diagram and look into the INVOKED state, The sequence "J" points to the scenario where the invoked process/service has raised an exception. An assigned activity catches that exception using the Boundary Catch Event shown as CBE. The CBE will catch the exception and the process token moves to the ALLOCATED state, that is, the token moves to the subprocess. Now, there could be various scenarios and one of them is when the ALLOCATED state terminates (the allocated subprocess ends with the Terminate End Event).
	The Force-Terminate Execution Exception Handling Pattern is about the scenario where the Allocated state terminates, that is, the allocated subprocess ends with a Terminate End Event
Known issues	NA
Known solution	NA

Test the `ExceptionHandlingPrj` process by passing `JTerminate` as the input. The process token flows from the `ASSIGNED` state to the `INVOKED` state. The invoked process (reusable process) will not handle the raised exception and the exception will be caught at the CBE placed on the `CallReusableProcess (J)` assigned activity. The flow will detour to the allocated state from the catch boundary event and will hit the Terminate End Event, `JTerminate`.

Go to the EM console and check the process flow. When the exception is raised by the reusable process, the catch boundary event configured on `CallReusableProcess (J)`, the assigned activity, will handle the exception. The sequence flow attached to the catch boundary event will detour the process execution flow to the subprocess (Allocated).

As the input passed is `JTerminate`, the flow of the token will detour to the Terminate End Event, `JTerminate`, in the subprocess (Allocated). When the allocated subprocess terminates, the process instance gets terminated and no subsequent activities will be executed. Hence, this pattern is termed as the terminate execution pattern.

Force-Error Execution Exception Handling Pattern

The following table highlights some important facts about the Force-Error Execution Exception Handling Pattern:

Signature	Force Error Execution Exception Handling Pattern
Classification	Exception Pattern
Intent	The intention is to handle the exception raised by the invoked (called) process/service in the invoking (calling) process/service.
Motivation	Handle exception in the invoking activity using a boundary event.
Applicability	This pattern is used to showcase those scenarios of exception handling where the exception is not handled by the invoked process/service by itself. That exception will propagate outside the invoked process/service and is caught by the attached Boundary Catch Event. From there, the process token is allocated to a subprocess which lands into error.

Implementation	If you check the process state diagram and look into the INVOKED state, the sequence "J" points to the scenario where the invoked process/service has raised an exception. The assigned activity catches that exception using the Boundary Catch Event shown as CBE. The CBE will catch the exception and the process token moves to the ALLOCATED state, that is, the token moves to the subprocess. Now, there could be various scenarios that can happen in the allocated subprocess and one of them is **Allocated state error** (this allocated subprocess ends with the Error End Event).
	Error Execution Exception Handling Pattern is about the scenario where there is Allocated state error, that is, the allocated subprocess ends with an Error End Event.
Known issues	Handling exceptions raised in the ALLOCATED state.
Known solution	The following are the patterns to handle exceptions raised at the ALLOCATED state:
	• Allocated state-External Exception Handling Pattern
	• Allocated state-Internal Exception Handling Pattern
	• Reallocated exception handling pattern

The invoked process/service has raised an exception and the exception is handled by the assigned activity, which has invoked that process/service. The exception is caught by a catch boundary event and the process state will change to the ASSIGNED state. The Allocated subprocess will raise an exception by itself. There could be multiple scenarios to handle the exception raised by the Allocated subprocess. The following are the patterns to handle exceptions raised at the ALLOCATE state:

- Allocated state-External Exception Handling Pattern
- Allocated state-Internal Exception Handling Pattern
- Reallocated Exception Handling Pattern

These patterns are useful in the scenario where the allocated subprocess itself throws a business exception.

Allocated state – External Exception Handling Pattern

When the process is in the ALLOCATED state and it raises an exception, the following case can be identified:

If the exception is not handled in the allocated subprocess itself, the exception will then get propagated outside the subprocess and can either be caught at the process level or caught by a fault-handling framework or a BPM engine.

We can verify the same from the process activity state diagram (as shown in the following screenshot). We can relate what we have discussed based on the arrow coming out of the subprocess (Allocated) to the event subprocess (Started). This shows how exceptions raised by the subprocess (Allocated) are caught at the process level by the event subprocess (Started). So, when an exception arises in the subprocess (Allocated), it is neither caught by an event subprocess inside the subprocess (Allocated), nor it is handled by a Boundary Catch Event; hence, it gets propagated outside the subprocess. So for the exception raised by the subprocess (Allocated), there is an event subprocess configured to catch it and hence the exception is handled by the external event subprocess at process level.

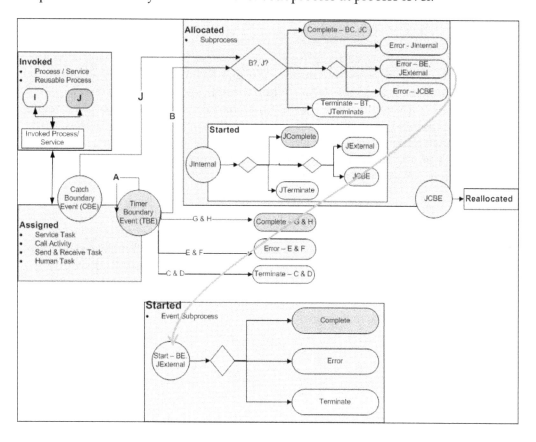

Implementing Allocated state – External Exception Handling Pattern

Open `ExceptionDemoProcess` in JDeveloper. Navigate to the Allocated subprocess and click on the Error End Event, **Error - JExternal**. Remember there are two Error End Events with the same name in the Allocated subprocess and **Event subprocess**, that is, `InternalExceptionHandler` (which is inside the Allocated subprocess). To demonstrate this pattern, click on **Error - JExternal** inside the Allocated subprocess, and not the one which is inside **Event subprocess**, `InternalExceptionHandler`. This Error End Event is configured to raise the business exception, **JExternal_ BizException**.

Log in to the EM console and test `ExceptionDemoProcess`. If you pass the input as `JExternal-Complete/JExternal-Terminate/JExternal-Error`, the process token gets allocated to the subprocess (Allocated). The Allocated subprocess will raise the exception, `JExternal_BizException`. When the subprocess (Allocated) raises an exception, the BPMN engine then tries to find a handler for it. This exception neither has an exception handler in the subprocess (Allocated) nor does the subprocess (Allocated) have a Boundary Catch Event to catch the exception. Hence, the exception gets propagated outside the subprocess (Allocated) and it results in the `STARTED` state for an event subprocess (Started).

The External event subprocess (Started) can also land in one of the following three cases:

- External event subprocess (Started) can complete normally: If we pass input as **JExternal-Complete**, the subprocess will raise **JExternal_BizException**, which is caught at the process level by event subprocess (Started) and the process token will detour to the sequence flow, **JExternal-Complete**. Finally, the process gets completed.

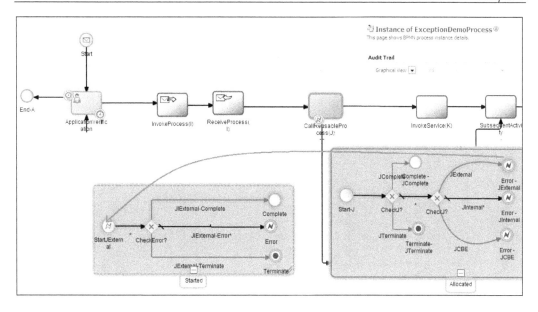

- External event subprocess (Started) can be aborted. If we pass the input as **JExternal-Terminate**, the subprocess will raise an exception, **JExternal_ BizException**, which is caught at the process level by the event subprocess (Started) and the process token will detour to the sequence flow, **JExternal-Terminate**, and the process gets aborted (reaches the TERMINATE state).

- External event subprocess (Started) can output an error. If we pass the input as **JExternal-Error**, the subprocess (Allocated) will raise an exception, **JExternal_BizException**, which is caught at the process level by the event subprocess (Started) and the process token will detour to the sequence flow, **JExternal-Error**, and the process gets an error (ERRORED).

Check the process audit trail as shown in the following screenshot. We can see that the process needs a recovery (**Recovery required**). This happens because an exception was raised by the event subprocess (Started) at the process level.

There is neither an event subprocess nor any fault policy to handle the exception raised by the event subprocess. Hence, the exception gets propagated to the environment and the exception is logged to the **Enterprise Manager Fault** recovery system. We can log in to the EM console and can abort or recover from the exception.

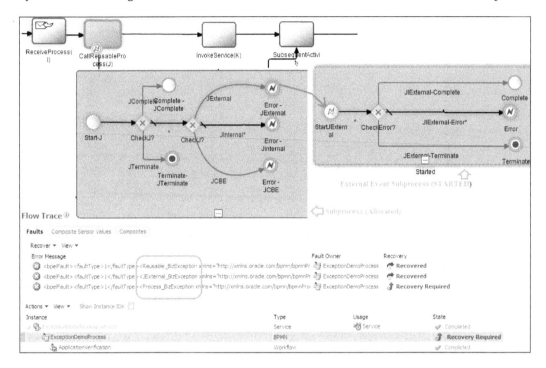

There are three end states when the token is at the STARTED state and the input passed is in one of the following:

- **JExternal-Complete**: When the ALLOCATED state raises an exception, it STARTS an event subprocess to handle it. The STARTED state ends with COMPLETE, which results in the process instance to complete.

- **JExternal-Error**: When the ALLOCATED state raises an exception, it starts (reaches the STARTS state) an event subprocess to handle it. The STARTED state also raises an exception. As there is no fault-handling framework to handle the exception, the exception is handled by the BPMN engine and the process instance ends in the FAULTED state with the RECOVERY status.

- **JExternal-Terminate**: When the ALLOCATED state raises an exception, it STARTS an event subprocess to handle it. The STARTED state will end with TERMINATE, which will eventually terminate (abort) the process instance too.

Allocated state – Internal Exception Handling Pattern

When the process is at the ALLOCATED state and it raises an exception, it can either be caught (handled) at the ALLOCATED state itself or a boundary event on the allocated subprocess or it will get propagated outside the allocated subprocess. This pattern focuses on the scenario where the exception raised at the ALLOCATED state gets caught in the allocated subprocess itself.

Visit the process activity state diagram to check the ALLOCATED state. It shows a block for the STARTED state too. When the subprocess (Allocated) raises an exception, JInternal, this exception is caught at the event subprocess (Started), which is defined inside the subprocess. As the exception is handled internally at the allocated subprocess, this pattern is named as Internal Exception handling Pattern. The internal event subprocess (Started), defined inside the subprocess (Allocated), starts with the JInternal error catch and has three end cases:

- **Complete**: The internal event subprocess catches and handles the JInternal exception and gets completed

- **Terminate**: The internal event subprocess catches and handles the JInternal exception and gets aborted

- **Error**: The internal event Subprocess catches and handles the JInternal exception and it raises an exception

Allocated State Internal Exception Handling Pattern has the following three broad categories of patterns:

- Internal Complete Exception Handling Pattern

- Internal Terminate Exception Handling Pattern

- Internal Error Exception Handling Pattern

Implementing Allocated state – Internal Exception Handling Pattern

Open ExceptionDemoProcess in JDeveloper. Navigate to the Allocated subprocess and click on the Error End Event, **Error-JInternal**. This Error End Event is configured to raise a business exception, **JInternal_BizException**. Log in to the EM console and test ExceptionDemoProcess.

If you pass the input as **JInternal-Complete** / **JInternal-Terminate** / **JInternal-Error**, the process token gets allocated to the subprocess (Allocated). The Allocated subprocess will raise an exception, `JInternal_BizException`. When the Allocated subprocess raises the exception, `JInternal_BizException`, then the BPMN engine tries to find a handler for it. For the exception, `JInternal_BizException`, the subprocess (Allocated) has an exception handler (event subprocess) defined in the subprocess (Allocated) itself. Hence the exception gets caught inside the subprocess (Allocated) and it results in the STARTED state for an internal event subprocess (Started).

There are three end states when a token is at the STARTED state in internal event subprocess (Started):

- Internal Complete Exception Handling Pattern
- Internal Terminate Exception Handling Pattern
- Internal Error Exception Handling Pattern

Internal Complete Exception Handling Pattern

Test `ExceptionDemoProcess` and pass the input as `JInternal-Complete`. We can check below, when the subprocess (Allocated) state raises an exception, it starts an event subprocess to handle it (reaches the STARTS state). The internal event subprocess (Started) ends with a COMPLETE state, which will result in the completion of the process instance state.

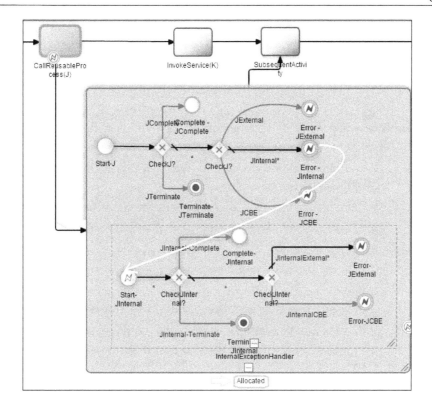

Internal Terminate Exception Handling Pattern

Test ExceptionDemoProcess and pass the input as JInternal-Terminate. When the ALLOCATED state raises an exception, it STARTS an internal event subprocess (Started) to handle it. The STARTED event subprocess will end in the TERMINATE state, which will eventually terminate the process instance (reach the ABORT state).

Internal Error Exception Handling Pattern

Test ExceptionDemoProcess and pass the input as JInternal-Error. When the ALLOCATED state raises an exception, it STARTS an internal event subprocess (Started) to handle it. The STARTED event subprocess will end in the ERROR state, which means that the process instance will eventually cause an error.

If the internal event subprocess (Started) raises an exception, there could be various possibilities, some of which are given as follows:

- The internal exception raised by the event subprocess gets caught by a catch boundary event associated with the event subprocess.
- If no boundary catch is defined for the event subprocess (Started), then the exception gets propagated to the subprocess (Allocated) into which this event subprocess is defined. The possibilities are as follows:
  - If another event subprocess to handle it exists, then the exception is caught there
  - If there is a Boundary Catch Event defined on the subprocess (Allocated), then the exception will be caught there
- If not handled in the subprocess (Allocated), then the exception gets propagated to the process level. Then there are following possibilities:
  - If there is an event subprocess defined at process level to catch that exception, then the exception is caught by the event subprocess.
  - If there is no event subprocess at process level, the exception gets propagated to the parent process exception handler. If no fault policy is defined, then the exception gets propagated to BPMN engine.
- If the exception is not handled anywhere, it gets logged by BPMN engine in the EM fault recovery system.

For the sake of demonstration, we have modeled an internal event subprocess (Started) and defined it inside a subprocess (Allocated), with two exceptions:

- **Reallocated**: An exception raised at the internal STARTED state is caught by the catch boundary event, which reallocates the token to a subprocess.
- **Restarted**: An exception raised at the internal STARTED state is propagated outside the ALLOCATED state, which will restart (reach the RESTART state) the external event subprocess (Started) to handle the exception at the process level.

Testing the Restarted scenario

The following screenshot shows the BPMN process instance details:

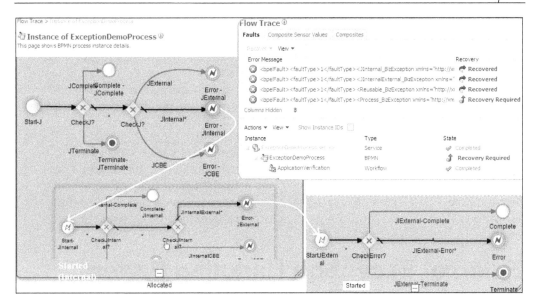

If you pass the input as **JInternal-Error**, the process token gets allocated to the subprocess (Allocated). The subprocess will raise an exception, `JInternal_BizException`. When this exception is raised, the BPMN engine tries to find a handler for it. For this exception, the subprocess (Allocated) has an exception handler (event subprocess) defined in the subprocess (Allocated) itself. Hence, the exception gets caught inside the subprocess (Allocated) and it results in the `STARTED` state for an internal event subprocess (Started). However, the internal event subprocess, `InternalExceptionHandler`, will raise an exception `JExternal_BizException`. However, neither the exception handler in the subprocess (Allocated) nor does the subprocess (Allocated) has a Boundary Catch Event to catch the exception. Hence, the exception gets propagated outside the subprocess (Allocated) and it results in the `STARTED` state for an external event subprocess (Started).

Reallocated Exception Handling Pattern

Test `ExceptionDemoProcess` and pass the input as `JInternal-Error`. When the `ALLOCATED` state raises an exception, it starts (the `STARTS` state) an internal event subprocess (Started) to handle it. The `STARTED` event subprocess will end in the `ERROR` state. If the internal event subprocess (Started) raises an exception, there could be various possibilities that we have enlisted in the Internal Error Exception Handling Pattern section. One of the many possibilities is the exception raised at the internal event subprocess (Started) is caught by the catch boundary event, which reallocates the token to a subprocess.

Visit the process activity state diagram to check the reallocated scenario. When the subprocess (Allocated) raises an exception, `JInternal`, this exception is caught at the internal event subprocess (Started), which is defined inside the subprocess. The internal event subprocess (Started) defined inside the subprocess (Allocated) starts with the `JInternal` error catch and raises the `JCBE` exception. The `JCBE` exception is caught by a catch error boundary event that detours the process token from the subprocess to the subprocess (Reallocated).

To test the scenario, execute `ExceptionDemoProcess` and pass the input as `JInternalCBE`. This will result in the business exception, `JCBE_BizException`. This business exception is caught at the catch error boundary event defined on the subprocess (Allocated). When caught, the process token is detoured to the subprocess (Reallocated) and the process moves ahead to subsequent activities.

External Exception Handling Pattern

When a process/service is invoked and it raises an exception, there are various exception-handling mechanisms to deal with these exceptions. This section is dedicated to the third scenario where an exception raised by an invoked process/service is handled by an external exception handler. Check the process state diagram and you can relate this scenario with the pointer **K**. An assigned activity invokes a process/service. The invoked process/service raises an exception. The exception is not handled inside the process/service nor does the assigned activity (invoking activity) has a Boundary Catch Event. Hence, the exception gets propagated outside the assigned activity and it's caught by an external event subprocess (Started) in the process diagram. Therefore, we can find the symbol **K** in the start event for the external event subprocess. You learned about the external exception handling pattern in previous sections when we tried to catch the fault in the external event subprocess. This is just to demonstrate the fact that even an exception raised by an invoked process/service is handled by an external exception handler.

Process-Level Exception Handling Pattern

If the fault is not handled in the subprocess or by a Boundary Catch Event, or if there is no event subprocess to handle an exception, then the exception gets propagated at process level. If there is a fault policy defined to handle such an exception, then the fault policy will catch that exception. This section is dedicated to those scenarios where the fault policy will catch the exception.

If you check the process state diagram, we will be walking through the **L-Fault Policy** scenario in this section. You can use the Fault Handling Framework to handle faults. The Fault policy can be used to handle runtime faults and business faults. The Fault policy file along with the fault binding file allows you to define and implement the fault-handling framework. It's the fault policy binding file that associates the policies defined in the fault policies file with one of the following:

- Composite with a BPMN process
- Oracle BPMN process service component
- Reference binding component (for example, another BPMN process or a JCA adapter)

The following fault recovery actions are supported in the fault policies file for Oracle BPM Suite:

- Retry
- Human intervention
- Terminate
- Java code

For more information, you can also refer to *Oracle BPM 11g Developer's Cookbook, Vivek Acharya, Packt Publishing*.

Implementing Process-Level Exception Handling Pattern

To implement the fault-handling pattern, the fault policy and fault binding files need to be defined. When we define the fault-handling framework, we define fault policy and fault binding. These are XML files, where the fault-binding file will associate the policies defined in the policy file with the composite application and the components defined in the composite.xml file. The fault policy bindings are identified in the following order in the composite.xml file:

- Reference binding component
- Service component
- BPM/SOA composite application

The **InvokeService (K)** service task invokes the credit validation service. If the Credit validation service is down, then a runtime exception will be raised. There is no fault handling defined at the service task nor is the process-level event subprocess configured to handle system faults. Hence, the fault gets propagated at process (composite) level. The fault policy is defined at the process level to handle such system faults (runtime faults). The following screenshot is the configuration of the `fault-policy.xml` file:

```xml
<?xml version="1.0" encoding="UTF-8"?>
<faultPolicies xmlns="http://schemas.oracle.com/bpel/faultpolicy"
               xmlns:xsi="http://www.w3.org/2001/XMLSchema-instance">
  <faultPolicy version="0.0.1" id="MyFaultPolicy"
               xmlns:env="http://schemas.xmlsoap.org/soap/envelope/"
               xmlns:xs="http://www.w3.org/2001/XMLSchema"
               xmlns="http://schemas.oracle.com/bpel/faultpolicy"
               xmlns:xsi="http://www.w3.org/2001/XMLSchema-instance">
    <Conditions>
      <faultName xmlns:bpelx="http://schemas.oracle.com/bpel/extension" name="bpelx:remoteFault">
        <condition>
          <action ref="Action-Retry"/>
        </condition>
      </faultName>
      <faultName xmlns:bpelx="http://schemas.oracle.com/bpel/extension" name="bpelx:bindingFault">
        <condition>
          <action ref="Action-Retry"/>
        </condition>
      </faultName>
      <faultName xmlns:bpelx="http://schemas.oracle.com/bpel/extension" name="bpelx:runtimeFault">
        <condition>
          <action ref="Action-Retry"/>
        </condition>
      </faultName>
    </Conditions>
    <Actions>
      <Action id="Action-Abort">
        <abort/>
      </Action>
      <Action id="Action-Retry">
        <retry>
          <retryCount>3</retryCount>          <==
          <retryInterval>10</retryInterval>
          <exponentialBackoff/>
        </retry>
      </Action>
    </faultPolicy>
</faultPolicies>
```

The following is the configuration of the `fault-bindings.xml` file that associates the fault policies defined in `fault-policies.xml` with the reference.

As you can check, when a process is called using a service reference, the reference used is not the BPMN process reference, but rather the reference created to call the `CreditValidationService` BPMN process named `Services.Externals.CreditValidationService.reference`.

The reference name is created as follows:

- The term `Services.Externals.` is prefixed to the reference name of `CreditValidationService`

- The term `.reference` is appended to the reference name of `CreditValidationService`

We can obtain the reference name to specify in the `fault-bindings.xml` file either from the reference section of the `process_name.componentType` file or from the *From the wire* section of the `composite.xml` file.

The fault policy is configured with a retry option. There are different ways to treat a fault. One way is to retry a fault. For example, if an invoked service is down, the fault-handling framework can be configured to retry three times and once the retries are exceeded, the instance will be marked as `open.faulted` (in-flight state). This would keep the instance active. If you keep the instance as active, you can perform the following different actions on the instance which has faulted:

- You can manually perform instance recovery from the EM console if you configure `ora-human-intervention` as another action to be performed after retries exceed
- You can terminate the instance to mark the instance as closed

Testing Process-Level Exception Handling Pattern

Perform the following steps to instantiate a process instance:

1. Open JDeveloper and navigate to ExceptionDemoProcess.
2. Check the **IsDraft** box for the **ApplicationVerification** human task, **InvokeProcess(I)**, **ReceiveProcess(I)**, and **CallReusableProcess(J)**. We are bringing these activities in the draft mode as we directly want to execute the **InvokeService(K)** service task.
3. Save and deploy the project.
4. Open the EM console and shut down Credit Validation Service.

The process token will get assigned to the `InvokeService (K)` service task. The Credit Validation Service will be invoked. As we have shut down the Credit Validation Service, a runtime fault is raised. As there is no Boundary Catch Event configured at the `InvokeService (K)` service task to catch the runtime fault, hence, the fault gets propagated outside the `ASSIGNED` state of the service task. As there is no fault handling outside the `ASSIGNED` state too; hence, the fault gets propagated to the level outside. At the process level, a fault policy is configured, which will handle the runtime exception as per the configuration in the fault policy file. As the fault policy is configured with a retry option, the system will retry three times. If the number of specified instance retries is exceeded, the instance is marked as Recovery Required.

As we can check in the following screenshot, retry was attempted three times and then the instance is marked as **Recovery Required**:

System-Level exception handling pattern

Consider a scenario where a fault is not even handled at the process level. It would get propagated to the runtime system BPMN engine. In this case, the fault gets propagated to the BPMN engine and then the exception is logged to the Enterprise Manager Fault recovery system.

External Triggers

Querying a BPM process or a BPM process cancel event are termed as external events. You learned in the *Cancel message pattern* section of *Chapter 6, Correlation Patterns*, how an external event can trigger a process instance cancellation. Similarly, you have also learned in the *Query Pattern* section of *Chapter 6, Correlation Patterns*, how a noninterrupting external trigger can impact a process instance. External triggers such as cancelling messages are interrupting triggers and you can find them marked as **External Trigger-O** in the process state diagram. Noninterrupting external triggers are marked as **External Trigger-N** and you can use the *Query Pattern* section of *Chapter 6, Correlation Patterns* to learn about the behavior. As these patterns are described in the previous chapter, details are not included in this section and you can refer to it to understand these patterns.

Summary

The content of this chapter was more focused on Exception Handling Patterns and not on the mechanism to handle the exception. While walking through the chapter, you learned various exception handling mechanisms and their implementation and usage in Oracle BPM. It gradually covered almost all the exception propagation mechanism in Oracle BPM. This chapter covered event subprocess, inline subprocess, and boundary events as mechanisms to handle exceptions, and their implementations too are a part of the content. The chapter also included the fault-handling framework while covering other mechanism to handle faults. While demystifying various exception handling patterns, you learned exception propagation mechanisms too. This chapter started with defining states of activities in the process and exception handling is centered on those states. However, states are just used for the sake of demonstration and better categorization of exception handling patterns. This chapter will surely lead you to a footprint in your mind to model exceptions, way before they occur. The next chapter is focused on some advance BPM patterns and case management patterns.

8

Adaptive Case Management

The landscape of enterprise processes has changed drastically. A process can be predictable or unpredictable, data-intensive or process-intensive, and structured or unstructured. The business process vista has changed from predetermined steps to unknown events; today, businesses demand a higher degree of agility, which needs to coexist with the unknowns and unpredictable factors. Business processes now need to include knowledge workers, customers, and various sets of case participants to collaborate in the decision-making. Often, an ad hoc inclusion of knowledge workers is required as the processes experience unknown contents and events. Hence, a solution is required to model the patterns of work which are complex, unpredictable, unstructured, unknown, and those which require a higher degree of collaboration, complex decision-making, dynamism, and so on.

Case management is a framework that enables you to build case management applications. Case management applications comprise of business processes, human interaction, decision-making, data, collaboration, events, documents, rules, policies, reporting, and history. This chapter elaborates on Oracle's **Adaptive Case Management (ACM)** solution, and over the course of learning about ACM, we will explore various patterns and features that enable designers, developers, and analysts to model case management solutions. For example, the milestone pattern showcases how the logical indicatives of a case's progress are included in the ACM solution and how these logical indicatives help in case modeling. A topic such as event patterns elaborates on how an unknown's case should be handled. A holistic view pattern brings depth to the ACM solution by offering a 360 degree view of the case.

The following table lists the terms that we will refer to in this chapter:

Case	A case is the focal point for all the information required for the work.
Case management	Case management is a way of organizing and framing work around the case.
Process versus case	Process is a path to accomplish tasks/activities, and case is the work that needs to be performed from opening to closure.
ACM	ACM is a novel mechanism of managing work. For me, ACM is about defining a milestone-oriented, state-based, rule-governed, content-outbid, and event-driven case.
What is ACM about?	It is about defining case and work. It is about working on ad hoc, dynamic, unstructured, and unpredictable processes/cases. It is also about design at execution, milestones, content management, and process and social collaboration as well as about the incorporation of Business Intelligence, valuing human intuition, empowerment, and optimizing real-time known and unknown events.
Who works on cases?	Practically everyone — case and knowledge workers, participants, and so on.

This chapter covers the following patterns:

- Case stage
- Event pattern
- Milestone pattern
- Case interaction pattern
- Localization feature
- Holistic view pattern
- Ad hoc feature

Defining adaptive case management

This section will walk you through the definitions and try to give you the essence of what adaptive case management (ACM) is all about.

Case

A case is a unit of work. It's a package in itself. There are goals and milestones in the case's life cycle, which are achieved when some work is performed on the case. A case is a superset of work, processes, transactions, and services which traverse from being open to closed over a time frame in order to reach a collaborative solution of an investigation, incident, service request, or a long running process. Essentially, it's a coordination of works. Examples of cases are an insurance claim, contract management, managed health care, and so on.

Case management

Case management is a way of organizing and framing work around the case. We have used the term *framing work* in the definition as it's evident that work cannot be defined for a case in one shot or in one go. It's an ongoing process, and as the work keeps deriving, the case keeps evolving.

It's a collaborative, coordinative, and milestone-oriented process to handle a case from opening to closure by interacting with the ecosystem and knowledge workers. Case management coordinates knowledge workers, contents, resources, systems, and correspondence to trace the progress of a case to different milestones. The progression of the case is determined and governed by human interactions and by the occurrence of internal and external events, where the process is a non-routine, unpredictive, and ad hoc process.

A case management solution offers case and knowledge workers greater control and the insight to resolve problems more effectively. Case management ensures that the right information is available for decision-making at the right time and in real time.

One can say that effective process management is essential for case management. Case management is nondeterministic because the case flow is dynamically determined at runtime. ACM focuses on managing all the work required to handle a case, regardless of whether it's content-intensive, structured or unstructured, predictable or unpredictable, deterministic or nondeterministic, automated or manual, and so on.

Dynamic case management

Many vendors have various definitions. For some, dynamic case management is a progression from Rigid BPM | Human-centric content-oriented BPM | Social and iBPM (Intelligence BPM) | Case Management.

Dynamic case management is about semi-structured, human-centric, information-intensive, collaborative processes that are driven by events. Dynamic case management enables dynamic changes at runtime. Adaptive case management is about the just-in-time creation of work around the case and processes, with intelligence to learn from the previous case/subcase/work. This means people working on a case should be able to use the subcase/work that is learned by the just-in-time process/case. To most people, adaptive case management and dynamic case management are the same, just defined differently by a different set of people.

Mechanism of adaptive case management

ACM is a novel mechanism of managing work. For me, ACM is about defining a milestone-oriented, state-based, rule-governed, content-outbid, and event-driven case.

For health care, it is a collaborative approach to plan, analyze, define, and then advocate and facilitate an individual's health care needs. The legal industry requires knowledge workers (lawyers, clients, judges, and so on) and their expertise as they drive through advocacy, consultation, and so on, and each individual case has a different life cycle. Also, information and work related to a case need to be assembled as the case progresses. For example, in the legal sector, as a court case progresses, new works are derived that need collaboration with different knowledge workers. Results need to be assembled, which could further lead to a new work identification and so on.

Enterprise Resource Planning (**ERP**) is a superset of processes. ECM is about content, while CRM is about the customer. BPM is about process and process management. There is no process without content and no CRM without communication, collaboration, and processes. Collaboration is not possible without a social BPM. Real-time analytics and transparency are engulfed by intelligent BPM. ACM is an integrated consolidation of ERP, ECM, CRM, social BPM, and iBPM to create a holistic view of the case and it's the customer which is the focus in the case.

ACM targets unstructured processes, where the exact steps and behaviors are not always known ahead of time. Case management is a way to govern and control these unstructured processes. You need rule definition in the form of templates that can be changed at runtime. You need tools to define and modify a process on the fly. You need to add work to the case while the case is executing and so on. Essentially, you need a case management solution.

Work on a case can be performed at discrete places such as an ERP process, CRM, content store, e-mails, manuals, and so on. However, it's the ACM that manages discrete pieces of work to be performed on a case. ACM creates an adaptive ecosystem for a work where a change or addition is acknowledged and adopted in the ecosystem to be adapted by the work.

Process versus case

ACM offers a clear distinction between a process and a case. With a case, to accomplish work and to achieve milestones, many processes might be running in sequence and/or in parallel. BPM will understand and execute these processes as distinct, separate processes being orchestrated by one process, and so on. However, with a case, processes are tightly associated with the case and subcases; hence, cases offer a holistic view.

Case management offerings

Strategies from management, targets from executives, and milestones from process owners should be inline and must be transparent to those who act and execute as well as to those who use them (end users and customers). This transparency can be achieved by knowing what's being moved in real time. Based on real-time analysis, decisions should be taken and actions should be performed by those who are empowered to do so. Above all, the real-time inclusion of customers, process owners, knowledge workers, and ecosystem are brought in focus. ACM is about a real-time and focused empowerment, which brings transparency. Management acquires the full transparency of processes and execution.

ACM is about empowerment. Empowerment comes with focus and transparency, and transparency comes with a socio-collaborative infrastructure. Transparency enables you to monitor which, in turn, increases the focus, and focus is increased by laying milestones and achieving them. Even if BPM empowers participants to act on the task, it's only ACM that empowers knowledge workers and case workers to include resources to reach milestones. It leads to a better customer satisfaction. In an adaptive ecosystem, drill, adapt, transform, optimize, and improve are the key characteristics of adaptive enterprises, and these characteristics are realized by ACM. Stakeholders will have complete visibility and control of their objectives, which are often expressed in key performance indicators. Greater insight translates to the fact that challenges can be identified the moment they arise. This makes the enterprise more proactive to respond to such challenges. Above all, ACM offers holistic work management; this improves the enterprise outcome of work and further translates to increased revenue, effective and better services, and efficient risk mitigation.

The following are some of the offerings of adaptive case management:

- Transparency
- Empowerment
- Optimized and efficient customer experience
- Handling unpredictability

- Adaptive enterprises
- Real-time monitoring
- Greater insight
- Collaborative decision-making
- Participation
- Dynamism
- Holistic approach

The following figure showcases the highlights of adaptive case management:

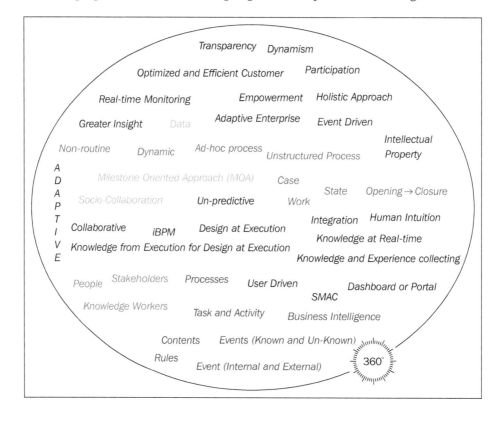

The building blocks of adaptive case management

The following are the building blocks of ACM:

Component	Description
Stakeholders	A stakeholder can be a user/group/role. They can perform actions on the case objects that are part of the case to which stakeholders are related. The behavior of the stakeholders can be defined by the administrators by assigning permissions. Case objects are CASE, COMMENT, DOCUMENT, DATA, EVENT, ACTIVITY, MILESTONE, STAKEHOLDER, and HEADER.
Case/knowledge workers and participants	Case workers, knowledge workers, participants, and so on, can work on the case. Case management offers case and knowledge workers greater control and insight to resolve problems more effectively. Knowledge and case workers are empowered to include resources to reach milestones. With each case, a different set of knowledge workers and participants get associated with the process.
Processes	BPM will understand and execute processes as distinct, separate processes being orchestrated by each process and so on. However, with a case, processes are tightly associated with the case and subcases; hence, cases offer a holistic view.
Tasks and activities	A task and an activity is the work that can be performed in the context of a case. Case tasks and activities can be executed automatically or manually, and they might be mandatory, optional, or conditional. You can implement case activities using human tasks, BPMN processes, or custom Java classes.
Data	Case data and information, case instance data (data objects, comments, and so on), along with case metadata (milestone, stakeholders, outcome, and so on) are stored in a database. Case data also represents the payload of the case, input parameters of the case, and so on.
Content and information	A case contains documents. Case management can be configured to use either a database as the content store or an enterprise content management system as the document store. If you use **enterprise content management** (ECM), then case information is stored mostly in case folders where all the documents related to case instances are stored.

Component	Description
Collaboration	Socio-collaboration is a must for case and knowledge workers to reach a milestone and to identify/modify work/tasks/activities. Collaboration brings human intuition in to the process and improves the overall quality of the case.
Events	An event is an occurrence that impacts the case, which may lead to the addition/deletion/modification of work and tasks, and also defines and decides the progression of the case. ACM allows you to capture events (internal/external) as and when they happen and to act on them as they occur. The more responsive the case management system for the events, the more dynamic the enterprise will be.
Rules and policies	Business rules can be used to control the flow of a case. With Oracle ACM, each case comes with a business rule set and a rule dictionary is generated. Rules can be configured to act on events, milestones, activities, and so on.
Milestones	Milestones are like goals/checkpoints that represent the completion of a deliverable and are indicative, to trace the progress of a case. Milestones are logical checkpoints; the attainment of milestones is defined in the rules, or actions can be performed when a milestone of interest is reached.
Integrations	A BPMN process can be invoked by a case, and BPMN processes can be promoted as case activities. BPMN processes or SOA services can integrate via working on events. A case can raise events and BPMN/SOA can react to these events.
Dashboard or portal	A case dashboard and interface is a must for a collaborative case ecosystem. A user interface allows case workers, knowledge workers, participants, and users to act and work on the case and activities. It also offers a 360 degree view of the case.

The following diagram depicts the building blocks of ACM:

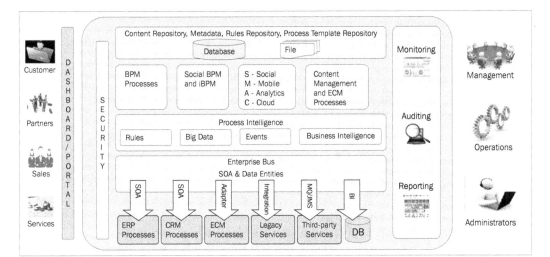

Exploring ACM use case scenarios

The Auto Insurance Claim case is used as the user case scenario to demonstrate case patterns. An **Insurance Claim** case will be created to demonstrate the milestone pattern and other patterns and features, as follows:

1. A customer calls the insurance company's **Customer Service Representative (CSR)** to initiate a claim request. CSR will perform the following actions:

    1. CSR will raise a claim on behalf of the claimant, who is a policyholder with the insurance company.

        ○ CSR will update the **Sensitivity** information (**Expert** or **Regular**).

        ○ If the **Sensitivity** of the case is **Expert**, then an Expert agent is assigned, else a Regular agent will be assigned to the case. Also, the **Service Level Agreement (SLA)** associated with the user task will be different going forward.

        Also, if the case sensitivity is `expert`, the SLA associated with user tasks will take two days; else, it would be seven days.

    2. CSR will initiate the claim case by submitting the **First Notice of Loss (FNOL)**.

    3. Once the FNOL is submitted, the case reaches the FNOL milestone.

2. On reaching the FNOL milestone, a verification activity (`EVerificationTask` or `RVerificationTask`) will be initiated based on the updates from CSR in the earlier step.

    ° In this step, the agent (`Expert`/`Regular`) will review a claimant's policy to ensure that the damaged asset is covered by the insurance policy and that the policy is current.

    ° The agent will also set `fastTrackFlag` to `Yes` or `No`, based on whether the case needs to be fast-tracked or not.

    ° Once the verification activity is completed, the case will reach the Verified milestone.

3. Once the Verified milestone is reached, the service provider needs to be dispatched. The SLA for the service provider's turnaround is based on the **Sensitivity** flag. The service provider will use the loss address to reach the location of the incident if the **Sensitivity** of the case is **Expert**.

4. Once the Verified milestone is reached, the validation activity is initiated and a case manager is assigned to perform the validation. The case manager performs the following actions:

    ° Case validation and checking for any fraudulent activity.

    ° Discussion with the customer and requesting the essential documents.

    ° Defines whether a case needs to be fast-tracked. The case manager will validate the claim, and if it's a valid claim, the case manager will set the **Claim Validated** flag.

    ° Define the settlement (payment/recovery) and communicate with the customer.

    ° Initiating the settlement; to perform the settlement, the case manager will enter the values for a claim reserve, as the claim reserve needs to be performed for both fast-track and regular cases.

The case manager will update the **FaultSubject** field under **Claim | Settlement** to either **Payment** or **Recovery**, based on whether the payment needs to be made to the claimant or recovery needs to be performed from the claimant.

5. Once the settlement is initiated, the case reaches the Validated milestone.

6. On reaching the Validated milestone, a **Customer Acceptance** activity will be raised. One of the features of case management is to involve a customer in decision-making. To do this, and to involve a customer in a collaboration, different socio-collaboration mechanisms can be used.

    A customer's e-mail should be identified from the customer details, and the username should be identified from the customer details as well. For example, a user account will be created in my realm; however, in real time, each customer will have an e-mail account and an actionable e-mail notification will go to the customer. On reaching the Customer Acceptance milestone, the customer receives the documents for customer acceptance. They can perform one of the following actions: either the customer can accept or reject the claim settlement, or optionally, they can upload some supporting documents.

    The inclusion of a customer in the process increases the customer satisfaction level manifold. The customer gets included in the decision-making process and this drives the settlement.

7. Once a customer accepts the claim settlement, they will approve the Customer Acceptance task. Once a task is completed normally, the Customer Acceptance activity gets completed and the case reaches the Customer Accepted milestone; however, if a customer rejects the claim, then the activity (Customer Acceptance) gets faulted and the following activities will happen:

    °   The Customer Rejection event is raised
    °   The case reaches the Customer Rejected milestone

The table in the following screenshot summarizes the use case scenario of the Insurance Claim case:

Event Rule	Milestone Rule	Activity	Stakeholder	Activity Rule	Milestone	Description
⇒ When case started then initiate FNOL activity		FNOL Activity	CSR	When FNOL Activity completes,reach FNOL milestone	FNOL	Project has a FNOL process which contains the FNOL user task. FNOL process is promoted as FNOL activity. User task (FNOL user task) is assigned to CSR role. Case activity rule defines progression of the case. When FNOL Activity gets completed, case reach FNOL milestone.While editing the FNOL task, CSR will set the Sensitivity flag to Expert or Regular.
	If Milestone FNOL reached then initiate Verification Activity	Verification Activity (In Verification Process : If Sensitivity = Expert then Task initiated = EVerificationTask Else If Sensitivity = Regular then Task initiated = RVerificationTask).	Expert Agent or Regular Agent	When Verification Activity completes,reach Verified milestone	Verified	Project has a Verification process which contains the EVerification and RVerification user task.Claim agent verify claimant supplied details, verify policy details and policy status,collecting proof documents and associating documents with the case. Verification process is promoted as Verification activity. Verification activity starts based on activity rule. User task is assigned to agent role. Case milestone rule defines further case progression to Verified milestone.Agent will also set fastTrackFlag to 'Yes' or 'No' based on the fact, if case needs to be Fast Tracked or not.
	If Milestone Verified reached then initiate Validation Activity	Validation Activity	Case Manager	When validation Activity completes,reach Validated milestone	Validated	Project have a Validation process which contains validation task. Validation process is promoted as validation activity. Case manager will validate the claim and if it's a valid claim, case manager will set the flag claimValidated as 'Yes' and would also define the settlement (payment/recovery) and communicating with customer and initiates claim settlement.
	If Milestone Validated reached then initiate Customer Acceptance Activity	Customer Acceptance Activity	Customer	When Customer Acceptance Activity completes,reach Customer Accepted milestone	Customer Accepted	Project contains Customer Acceptance Process and Customer acceptance task. This process is promoted as Customer Acceptance Activity. If customer accepts the claim then activity completes normally and process reaches Customer Accepted milestone. Else activity gets faulted. When faulted, customer acceptance process raises a rejection event which is caught by Rejection Handler Process. Rejection handler process will reassign the case to case manager to further collaborate with customer to check his/her concerns.
				When Customer Acceptance Activity faults,reach Customer Rejected milestone	Customer Rejected	
	If Milestone Customer Rejected reached then initiate Rejection Handler Activity	Reassign case to Case Manager and initiate Rejection Handler Activity	System Admin			On customer rejection, case gets reassigned to the case manager and a rejection handler activity is raised.
	If Milestone Customer Accepted reached then initiate Closure Activity	Reassign case to Case Manager and Rejection Handler Activity				On customer acceptance, case gets processed for closure and all the knowledge workers and particiapnts are notfied to it's status and customer comments and feedbacks.

The building blocks of the Insurance Claim use case

The table in the following screenshot shows the building blocks for the Insurance Claim use case:

Case Data	FNOL (First Notice Of Loss details) Evaluation Decline Claim Appraisal Settlement Close Claim Case	Check InsuranceClaim.xsd schema file to understand the case data definitions. Schema file can be located at – Project → SOA → Schemas
Content & Information	Police Report,Claimant Credit Check Report,Fraud Report, Witness Information Sheet	Configure ECM content store and enable document package at task metadata editor to store and retrieve content documents. We can also associate document from case workspace and tasks.
Milestone	Started FNOL Verified Validated Customer Accepted Customer Rejected	Milestone can be defined at runtime too from case workspace.
Case Activity	FNOL Activity Verification Activity Validation Activity Customer Acceptance Activity Rejection Handler Activity Dispatcher Activity	Processes, Human Tasks etc are promoted as activities.
Stakeholder	CSR Expert Agent Regular Agent Case Manager Customer	Stakeholder can be defined at designed time in JDeveloper and at runtime in case workspace.
Permission	Public/Restricted	
Outcome	Started , Accepted, Rejected, Closed	
Integrations	BPMN Processes, Events, Services	
Event	Dispatch Service & Customer Rejection Event	
Rules and policies	Lifecycle event rule, activity rule and milestone rule	Project contains Insurance Claim Case rule which includes lifecycle, activity and milestone rules.
Dashboard/UI		All the task need to have there user interface. We can create a ADF UI for all the tasks.

Testing the use case

We will walk you through the following steps to execute the Insurance Claim use case:

1. Download the ClaimApps application from the downloadable link in *Chapter 8, Adaptive Case Management*.
2. Deploy the InsuranceClaim project to the web logic server.
3. Log in to **Oracle Business Process Workspace** as the admin user and assign the users to roles (stakeholders) as follows:
   ◦ **CSR Role**: jcooper
   ◦ **Expert Agent**: jstein
   ◦ **Regular Agent**: fkafka
   ◦ **Case Manager**: weblogic
   ◦ **Customer**: achrist

4. Test the `InsuranceClaimCase` service using the `Claim.xml` data file that can be found in the `InsuranceClaim` project itself. Navigate to the following path to find the test data file:

   InsuranceClaim | SOA | testsuites | Claim.xml

5. Use SoapUI or any tool of your choice to initiate a case instance. We can use the **Enterprise Manager** console to initiate the case instance.

6. Choose the **startCase** operation, as shown in the following screenshot, and shift to the XML view for the input arguments:

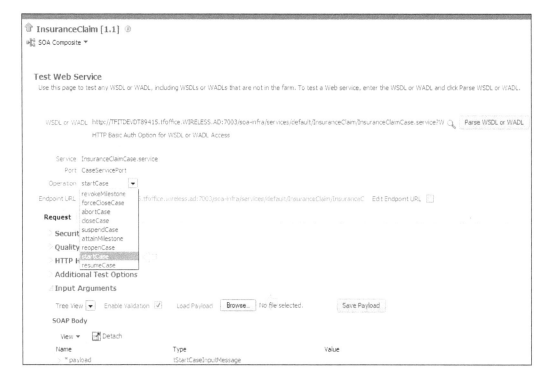

7. Pass the test data from the **Case.xml** file. You can enter a different case ID.

8. Log in to the **Oracle Enterprise Manager** console to check the process flow.

9. Log in to the Oracle BPM workspace in order to perform actions on the case activities and tasks.

A case consists of many activities, and most of the activities have user tasks. User tasks are assigned to roles, and users are assigned to the respective roles. You can follow these steps to log in to the BPM workspace in order to act on a specific activity/task:

1. Log in to the BPM workspace as `jcooper` (CSR) and edit the value and set the **Sensitivity** flag. When the CSR (`jcooper`) clicks on **OK**, the case reaches the FNOL milestone.

2. Log in to the BPM workspace as an Expert agent (`jstein`) if the CSR (`jcooper`) selected the **Expert** value for the **Sensitivity** flag, or else log in as a Regular agent (`fkafka`) if the CSR (`jcooper`) selected the value as **Regular** for the **Sensitivity** flag.

3. While being logged in as an expert agent or regular agent, set **fastTrackFlag** to either `Yes` or `No` based on whether the case needs to be fast-tracked or not. When an agent accepts the task, the case reaches the Verified milestone.

4. Once the Verified milestone is reached, we can note that the Validation task gets assigned to the case manager (`weblogic`). Log in to the BPM workspace as the case manager (`weblogic`) and add documents to the task to perform case manager activities; also, set the **FaultSubject** field to **Payment** or **Recovery**. The case will reach the Customer Acceptance milestone.

5. Log in to the BPM workspace as the customer (`achrist`) and check the settlement details. If the customer is happy with the settlement, they can approve it or else reject it.

   When approved, the case reaches the Customer Accepted milestone and the settlement activity will start.

   When rejected, the case reaches the Customer Rejected milestone and the customer rejection event is raised, which is caught by the customer rejection handler.

We have to create a task form for each of the user tasks. Editing of the values by the users is performed on the task form. For instance, when the verification task is executed, you can log in to the Oracle BPM workspace with the CSR role (`jcooper`). The CSR is expected to edit the claim values and add values in the **Sensitivity** flag as **Expert** or **Regular**. The following diagram shows the placeholder that hosts the **Sensitivity** information.

Once you are finished with editing the claim values, save the task form and then you can perform actions on the task:

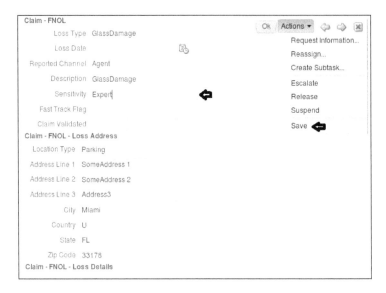

Case stage

Stages are an integral part of a case and are always associated with it. The case stage or phase may or may not be related to a milestone. Similarly, activities can be associated with a phase or stage or with multiple phases or stages. A case will transition from one case stage to another based on the rules that act on milestones, tasks, activities, and events. The following diagram shows the stages that a case passes through while moving from **Opening** to **Closure**:

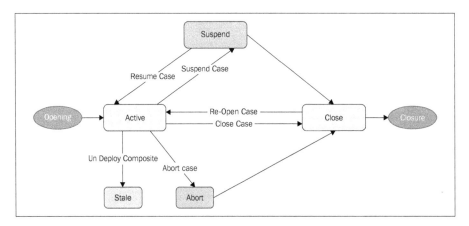

The following table highlights the facts around the Case Stage pattern:

Signature	Case Stage Pattern
Classification	Case Pattern
Intent	Progress a case instance from the Opening stage to the Closure stage.
Motivation	A case's life cycle spans from Opening to Closure; however, a case lives in the different stages/phases in its life cycle.
Applicability	The transition from one stage to another may bring changes in the case and in other integrating and interacting components. For instance, Abort Case will halt the case instance, and closing a case will complete the case instance.
Implementation	A case is exposed as a service; so, the BPMN process or SOA services can invoke the case service to drive the case transition. A case service offers the following operations: • Abort Case • Close Case • Revoke Case • Reopen Case • Start Case • Resume Case • forceClose Case Apart from interacting with case service operations, you can close a case from a case user interface or using APIs.
Known issues	NA
Known solution	NA

In this section, we will walk you only through the Close Case pattern, which deals with closing the case instances. You can use the case service operation to close the case; however, for this example, you can close the case from the BPM workspace case user interface, as follows:

1. Log in to the Oracle BPM workspace (`http://wlsserver:port/bpm/workspace`) as the admin user.

2. Click on **Close Case**; you will be prompted to enter a comment and optionally, you can select **Outcome**, if one exists (**outcomes** are defined in the case editor).

3. Once the case is closed, you can find the comments you entered in the **Audit Trail** section of a case. You can still browse the closed case(s) from the case user interface:

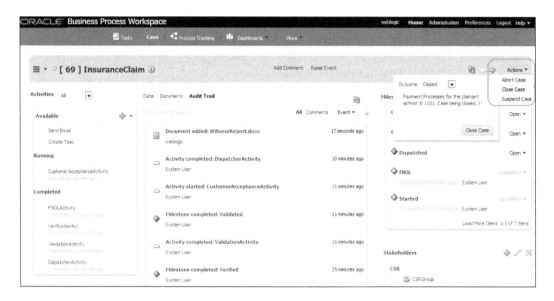

Note that we can abort the case and suspend the case from the **Actions** dropdown. If we suspend the case, the process instance gets suspended. We can resume the case by invoking the **resumeCase** operation on the case service. Similarly, we can abort the case and reopen it too.

Event pattern

The following table highlights facts around the event pattern:

Signature	Event Pattern
Classification	Case Pattern
Intent	An occurrence that impacts the case, which may lead to the addition/deletion/modification of work and tasks, as well as defines and decides the progression of the case.

Motivation	The progression of the case is determined and governed by human interactions and by the occurrence of internal and external events. Dynamic case management is about semi-structured, human-centric, information-intensive, collaborative processes that are driven by events. ACM allows you to capture events (internal/external) as and when they happen and allows you to act on them as they occur. The more responsive the case management system for the events, the more dynamic the enterprise will be.
Applicability	Events are the key components of a case management system. Case management leverages the **Event Delivery Network** (**EDN**) to publish and subscribe to events. The Oracle case management engine raises events and subscribes to events. Oracle Case Management offers the following events: Life Cycle events, Milestone events, Activity events, Data events, Document events, Comment events, and User events. On every case event, business rules are fired.
Implementation	Events occur due to several reasons. Events can be generated when a case instance progresses, when a case reaches a certain milestone, when an activity is triggered, or when an activity is completed or withdrawn. Events can be raised by external systems, by stakeholders, from business rules, or can be explicitly raised. Events offer the best audit trail for the case instance and, moreover, events are used to evaluate business rules. The evaluation of business rules brings progression in the case or leads to a certain milestone or may lead to the initiation of an activity.
Known issues	NA
Known solution	NA

The following diagram shows some of the events used in the **InsuranceClaim** sample project:

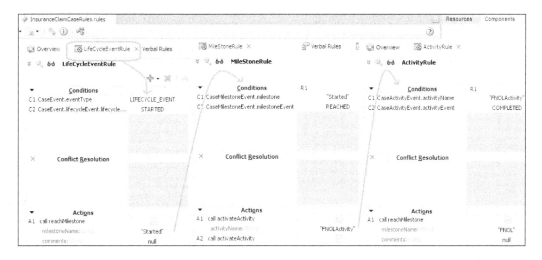

Initiate the case using a service call, case interface, or user interface. When the case instance gets created, the case metadata and case data is inserted into the database. The moment a case instance is initiated, the **case lifecycle** events are raised and all the rules get executed. The rule that is defined to evaluate **case lifecycle** gets fired. If you check the preceding diagram, the **LifeCycleEventRule** business rule gets fired.

LifeCycleEventRule will capture life cycle events and the respective action will be performed. In this case, the **Started** milestone will be reached. The business rule, **MileStoneRule**, acts on the milestone events. On reaching the **Started** milestone, the **FNOLActivity** case activity will get executed. **ActivityRule** showcases the usage of the activity rule. Once **FNOLActivity** (the FNOL case activity) gets completed, then an **FNOL** milestone is achieved by the case. You have witnessed that different types of events can be raised. Events can be anything from case changes, life cycle changes, case milestone changes, and so on. Events can be of the following types:

- Life cycle events
- Milestone events
- Activity events
- Data events
- Document events
- Comment events
- User events

Events are evaluated by the business rules and activities, and a milestone case can be reached based on how rules are defined in those events. Along with the seeded events, we can define custom events (user events). In the `InsuranceClaim` project, we have defined an event and a dispatch service (under **InsuranceClaim | Events**). We can not only configure a rule to raise the event, but also explicitly raise the event from the case user interface. This showcases the dynamism of the case management solution. For instance, if the CSR finds that the Agent (Expert or Regular) has found that the case needs immediate attention at the accident site, they can raise a dispatch service event. This event is caught by the dispatch service to dispatch a team at the site of the accident and various other defined activities:

1. Log in to the BPM workspace as the admin (`weblogic`) user and click on **case workspace**.
2. Click on **Raise Event** as shown in the following screenshot.
3. Select the event, **DispatchServiceEvent**, from the list of user-defined events.
4. Enter a comment, which will appear in the audit trail of the case.

5. Set a permission (public or restricted).

6. Click on **Raise Event** to raise the **DispatchServiceEvent**.

If there is a business rule defined to catch the event, that rule will evaluate to `true` and the defined action will get executed.

This example showcases the seamless integration of an **Event Driven Network** with a case management solution. It also demonstrates the empowerment of the case workers, where it was showcased that case workers can raise events without bringing about a change in the code.

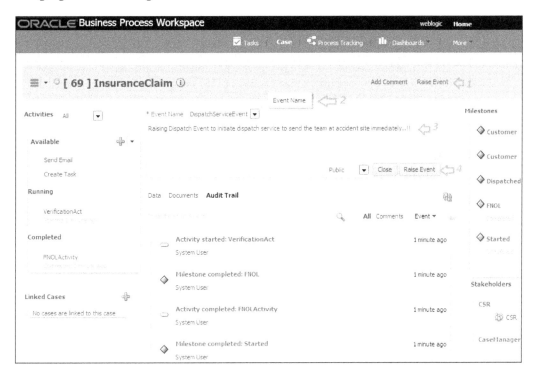

Milestone pattern

Milestones are like goals/checkpoints that represent the completion of a deliverable, and they are indicative factors to trace the progress of a case. Milestones are logical checkpoints; the attainment of milestones is defined in the rules, or actions can be performed when a milestone of interest is reached.

The following table highlights the facts around the milestone pattern:

Signature	Milestone Pattern
Classification	Case Pattern
Intent	A logical indicative of the case's progress.
Motivation	Milestones are like goals/checkpoints that represent the completion of a deliverable and are indicative factors to trace the progress of the case. Milestones are logical checkpoints; the attainment of milestones is defined in the rules, or actions can be performed when a milestone of interest is reached.
Applicability	It's a specific execution point in the case instance. They support a conditional execution of the case flow, tasks, and case activities. Checkpoints can be set to act when certain nominated points in the process execution are reached. Milestones are optional in a case, and they do not bring about changes in the case state. However, they can be used in rules to define and decide the progression of the case flow.
Implementation	Oracle case management offers case components, where milestones are defined. Each case comes with a business rule set and rule dictionary. Milestones are available as a global in the rule dictionary. Case management also offers various events, and one of the primary event sets are milestone events. Business rules in the case can be configured to listen to milestone events. Rules are fired when milestone events are raised in the case management ecosystem. Business logic in the rules can be defined to react when an event of particular interest is received.
Known issues	NA
Known solution	NA

Download the sample case management application, `ClaimApps`, from the download section for *Chapter 8, Adaptive Case Management*. Open the application in JDeveloper. Perform the following steps to check the configuration of milestones and their usage in the business rules:

1. Expand the **InsuranceClaim** project and follow the navigation path to open the case editor for **InsuranceClaimCase**; this case can be found under the path **InsuranceClaim | BPM | Case | InsuranceClaimCase**.

2. Check the general case properties defined for the sample case. You can define the following general properties of the case:

   ○ **Title and category** — Insurance Claim

   ○ **Priority**

   ○ **Milestones and outcomes**

Using the case editor, you can assign outcome values to the case when it is completed. For instance, in a claim case, the outcome when the case is completed can be claim processed, claim recovered, and so on.

3. Click on the green plus (+) icon to add a new milestone in the case editor. Check the milestone being defined for the **InsuranceClaimCase**.

4. Expand the project, **InsuranceClaim | SOA | Business Rules | InsuranceClaimCaseRules**, to open the rule dictionary.

5. Click on **Global** in the rule dictionary and verify that the milestones are listed there.

6. Click on the rule sets to open **CaseEventRule**. The business rule defined here works as follows:

```
If Case == Started, then Milestone reached == "Started"
```

When a case is initiated, the case life cycle event is raised. Whenever an event is raised, the case's business rules are executed. When the correct conditions are met, an action is taken. So when the case's life cycle starts, the case will reach the Started milestone. You can witness this in the business rule's action; there are functions such as `reachMilestone` and `revokeMilestone`, which can be used to define rule actions.

7. Click on **CaseMilestoneRule** in the rule sets. You can witness the usage of milestone events in rule conditions:

```
If Milestone reached == "Started" then initiate FNOL activity.
```

Oracle case management offers milestone events to reason and define the process flow. In this case, if the Started milestone is reached, then the FNOL activity will be initiated.

Perform the following steps to test the scenario:

1. Deploy the `InsuranceClaim` project to the web logic server.

2. Log in to the **Enterprise Manager** console as the admin and click on the deployed `InsuranceClaimCase` service.

3. Choose the **Start Case** operation from the list of operations and pass the input in the XML view in the EM console. You can use SoapUI or any other tool or mechanism to test the service.

4. Pass the test data (`Claim.xml`) and click on **Test Web Service** to execute the service test.

5. You can trace the process flow, which shows the execution of the FNOL user task. The FNOL user task is assigned to the CSR role (jcooper).

6. Verify, from the case editor's stakeholder section, which user is associated with the CSR stakeholder. Log in to the BPM workspace as that user and act on the FNOL user task.

The following screenshot depicts the sequential flow of the activities. When a case starts, the **LifeCycleEventRule** rule gets executed. **LIFECYCLE_EVENT** starts, which will mark the attainment of the **Started** milestone. When the **Started** milestone is reached (as shown with an arrow in the following diagram), **FNOLActivity** (the FNOL activity) gets initiated; **FNOLActivity** is based on the FNOL process that assigns an FNOL user task to the stakeholder. When CSR (jcooper) acts on the tasks, **FNOLActivity** gets completed. When the activity is completed, **ActivityRule** gets executed and a call to **reachMilestone** will bring the case to attain the FNOL milestone, as shown in the following screenshot:

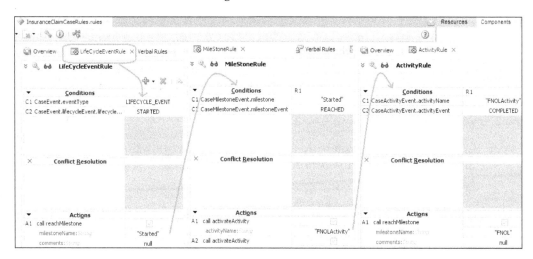

Case interaction pattern

The case interaction pattern highlights the facts around the different processes and service integrations with cases. Interactions and integrations can happen using APIs, service calls, events, and so on. The following table highlights facts around the case interaction pattern:

Signature	Case Interaction Pattern
Classification	Case Pattern
Intent	Integrating the case with processes and services.

Motivation	A case ecosystem where different technology components can integrate.
Applicability	Events are the key components of the case management system. Case management leverages EDN to publish and subscribe to events. The Oracle case management engine raises events and subscribes to events. The SOA service and processes can be configured to subscribe to such events and can integrate with cases.
Implementation	The case management engine can publish/subscribe events to Oracle EDN and a case is exposed as a service; hence, the BPMN process can invoke the case service to integrate with cases. A case service offers the following operations: Abort Case, Close Case, Revoke Case, Reopen Case, Start Case, and Resume Case.
Known issues	NA
Known solution	NA

Localization feature

Localization feature is a must in any BPMN/ACM solution as it offers the flexibility to configure a case to use different languages when it is displayed in the user interface:

Signature	Localization feature.
Classification	Case feature
Intent	Configure a case to use different languages when displaying in the user interface.
Motivation	Case interface to be used by case/knowledge workers and participants following different languages.
Applicability	The following artifacts of a case can be localized: case title, case category, milestone name, outcome, data, user event, stakeholders, and permissions. You can define a display name for all these artifacts, except for the case title and category.
Implementation	Key, value, and translation need to be defined to perform the localization. The case editor has the translation tab to define the following: • Key (the name to identify a key) • Value of the key in the default language • Translation for the target language
Known issues	NA
Known solution	NA

Holistic view pattern

Processes are running across functional, system, and enterprise boundaries. An enterprise needs an end-to-end definition of the case and a unified view of the case. An enterprise wants to be agile and needs a real-time view of the current case status. A real-time view of the case makes enterprises more responsive as and when events happen. The following table highlights facts around this pattern:

Signature	Holistic View Pattern
Classification	Case Pattern
Intent	Offer a holistic 360 degree view of the case instance.
Motivation	As cases run long, a lot can happen over this time and various participants and knowledge workers would have acted and contributed in the due course of time. Hence, a holistic view of the case is required, which ACM offers. ACM offers holistic work management; this improves the enterprise outcome of work and further translates to increased revenue, effective and better services, and efficient risk mitigation.
Applicability	Oracle ACM offers a case user interface that presents a holistic view of the case instance.
Implementation	The Oracle case management user interface can be used to view the details of an open as well as closed case. It provides the flexibility to add comments or initiate events on the case. Working on activities as well as viewing and adding documents and case data are some other events that can be performed via the case user interface. Viewing and adding stakeholders, milestones, and user information can also be performed using the case user interface. A case can be closed and reopened from the case interface too.
Known issues	NA
Known solution	NA

Log in to the Oracle BPM workspace (`http://wlsserver:port/bpm/workspace`) as the admin user and click on the **CASE** interface tab. This will navigate you to the case user interface, shown in the following screenshot:

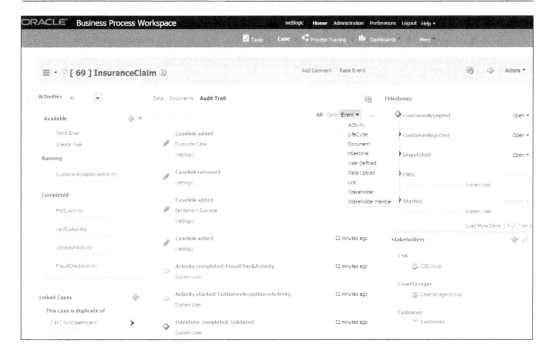

You can perform the following activities though the case interface:

- Browse for the case instance you are interested in. Filter and search for the case instance you are looking for.

- Click on **Add Comment** to add comments to the case, which will be visible in the audit trail.

- You can use the case user interface to **raise events**; however, you can work on the events that are preconfigured using the BPM JDeveloper Studio.

- Activities can be viewed in the left panel of the case interface. **Activities** are categorized based on their state: running, completed, available, and error.

- Activities that are in the **Available** state can be initiated from the case interface.

- The **Audit trail** panel allows you to view case events, participants who acted on the events, and so on.

- The **Data** panel can be used to view and modify the case data.

- The **Documents** panel can be used to view the documents associated with the case instance. Moreover, you can add/upload documents, set permissions for the document, and you can also uncover the users/case workers who uploaded the documents.

- You can view and change the status of the milestones from the **Milestones** panel.

- The **Stakeholder** panel can be used to add new stakeholders. You can also edit the existing stakeholder if the performer has permissions.

Ad hoc feature

Case management is all about handling unpredictable scenarios, unknown events, and dealing with activities that are not predetermined. Hence, we need a solution for the ad hoc inclusion of activities, ad hoc mechanisms to raise events, ad hoc methods to add stakeholders and methods to refer to the subcases in the case, and so on. In this section, we will check the various features of the Oracle adaptive case management 12*c* solution that allow the ad hoc inclusion of stakeholders, rules, activities, subcases, documents, and so on.

The following table highlights the facts around this pattern:

Feature	Ad hoc feature
Classification	Case feature
Intent	The ad hoc inclusion of stakeholders, activities, rules and policies, documents, subcases, and so on.
Motivation	As cases run long, a lot can happen in that time. A case might need new documents for which new knowledge workers need to be added to the task. There might be cases when new ad hoc activities need to be launched, or some of the scenarios need the existing subcases to fulfill a case functionality, or there might be a requirement to change the business rules and policies on the fly when the case is executing.
Applicability	Oracle ACM offers the case user interface, which presents a holistic view of the case instance. Also, it offers the flexibility to perform various ad hoc activities, such as to change or modify a rule/policy, add new rules/policies, define new activities and tasks, add stakeholders, add documents, and so on.
Implementation	The Oracle case management user interface can be used to perform various ad hoc inclusion activities that are covered in the following section.
Known issues	NA
Known solution	NA

Ad hoc inclusion of stakeholders

We can note that Oracle ACM allows you to browse and add users, roles, or groups as stakeholders at runtime. Perform the following steps to add a stakeholder at runtime:

1. Log in to the BPM workspace as the admin user and click on the **Case** workspace.

2. Click on the plus (**+**) sign in the stakeholder section to add new knowledge workers or case workers.

Ad hoc inclusion of activities

Let's assume that somewhere in the case life cycle, if the business feels the need to verify the witness report associated with the case, a witness report verification can be performed by the user (lata). We will create a task at runtime and assign it to the user (lata) to get it verified:

1. Navigate to **Case workspace** | **Activities** and click on **Create Task**.

2. Enter task details (title, assignees, due date, and so on) and click on **Create** to create and initiate the task.

3. Log in as the user (**lata**) and we can find the task in the user's inbox:

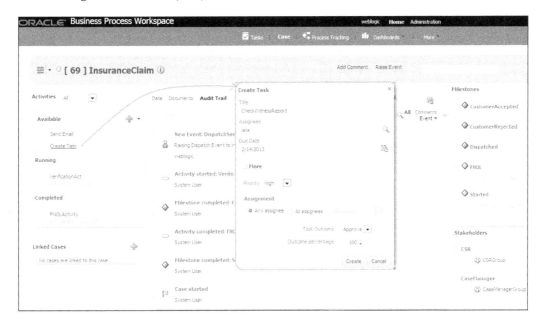

Ad hoc inclusion of documents

We can add documents at various places. Click on a case workspace and go to **Document** to add a document. We can browse for a configured ECM for the document. Extending the case, when the **CheckWitnessReport** task gets assigned to the user (lata), she can associate the witness report with the task and the document will be available in the case.

Association of a case with subcases

A case can depend on another case, a case can be a parent of subcases, a case by itself can be a subcase of another case/subcases, or a case might be a duplicate of some other case. Oracle ACM offers the flexibility to associate a case with **subcases** and other cases. Oracle ACM offers the feature to link cases with other cases and subcases. In real time, an enterprise might have a pool of subcases that can be linked with the current case. For instance, the settlement process is a subcase in the enterprise. When the current case reaches the Customer Accepted milestone, the settlement subcases can be linked with the current case, shown as follows, and settlement subcases will take care of the settlement activities for the parent case:

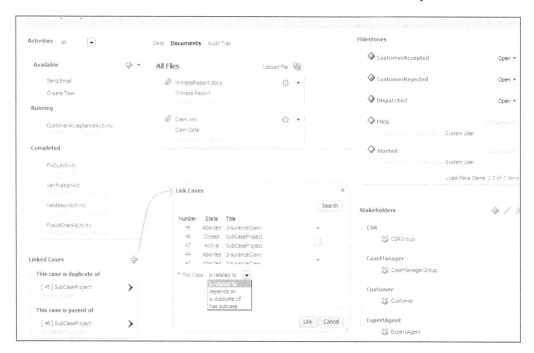

Ad hoc inclusion of rules and activities

When the case is progressing, at some point in the case life cycle, the business decides to perform a check for fraudulent activity on the claimant and their claim request. If we look at the **InsuranceClaim** project, we have **FraudCheckProcess** and **FraudCheckActivity**. However, none of the rules are defined to initiate the fraud check activity. We will now perform an ad hoc inclusion of the activity in the rule that justifies the true dynamism of the Oracle ACM solution.

Log in to the **SOA Composer** application (`http://host:7003/soa/composer/`) as the admin user and perform the following steps:

1. Click on **Create Session** to start an editing session.

2. Expand **SOA-INFRA** and click on **InsuranceClaimCaseRules.rule** inside the **InsuranceClaim** project.

3. Click on **MileStoneRule** and select a decision table.

4. Navigate to **Add action | All function** to call **activateActivity**.

5. Author the rule, as shown in the following screenshot, to call **FraudCheckActivity**.

6. Click on **Save** to save the authored rule as unsaved changes are not published.

7. Click on **Validate** to validate the rule.

8. Click on **Publish** to persist and bring your authored rule into effect.

As we checked in the rule definition, **FraudCheckActivity** gets executed when a case reaches the Validated milestone, as follows:

- Log in to the BPM workspace case manager (the web logic user), edit the rule, and click on **Approve** under the **Actions** pane to approve the user task.

- Trace the process by logging in to the Oracle EM console and check the process trace. We can verify that **FraudCheckActivity** gets initiated.

Summary

We often need a mechanism to handle unpredictable business scenarios, for which case management is the solution. This solution is characterized with unpredictable outcomes, is typically content-driven, usually depends on semi-structured information, and has unpredictable recursive flows.

In this chapter, you have witnessed the milestone pattern, the event pattern, the case interaction pattern, the holistic view pattern, and the case stage pattern. Along with the patterns, we have checked out the ad hoc features of case management that can be viewed as a practical justification to various ACM offerings. While walking through the chapters, you must have realized how empowered knowledge and case workers are. This chapter highlights the ad hoc inclusion of knowledge workers to include human intuition in processes. We have witnessed the realization of some of the ACM offerings through the sample demonstration. We have noted how Oracle ACM integrates seamlessly with SOA, EDN, processes, services, content management solutions, subcases, and so on.

The next chapter is focused on advanced features such as architecture models, value chain models, KPIs, reports, and PAM, which are required for an effective BPMN solution.

9
Advanced Patterns

This chapter discusses an organization's need to capture the context of a business to perform impact and dependency analyses. Also, this chapter highlights how to report on goals, objectives, strategies, and value chains in the organization. We will learn how to create reports on KPIs to view how different components are stitched into the fabric of an organization unit. It also demonstrates how a business architecture model can be used effectively to inline the goals, objectives, strategies, and value chain, which expedite IT development and always keep business and IT in concert. Enumerating process behaviors offers visual representation of a BPMN process that showcases an animated view of your process behavior so that process behavioral patterns can be analyzed even before deploying and publishing the project. The inclusion of a debugger will allow you to identify and fix logical or workflow issues in the process and thus, infuse a preventive mechanism in the process modeling.

The **Process Asset Management (PAM)** section illustrates how process assets can be shared between users who work on different applications and tools and also between different users who work on the same application. PAM infuses business IT collaboration and offers an enhanced method of round-trip between business and IT. This section successfully demonstrates how well, versioning and PAM gel together for an enhanced development and modeling experience for developers and process analysts, respectively. This chapter focuses on methodologies and features around analysis and discovery patterns that make an organization aligned with the goals, objectives, and strategies. It also focuses on creating a collaborative ecosystem for business and IT, and a detailed analysis of PAM and methods to emulate the process behavior. The following methodologies, patterns, and features are covered in this chapter:

- Strategic Alignment Pattern
- Capturing the business context
- Emulating the process behavior
- The debugger feature
- Round-trip and business-IT collaboration

Strategic Alignment Pattern

BPMN needs a solution to align business goals, objectives, and strategies, as well as a solution to allow business analysts and function/knowledge workers to create business architecture models. These business architecture models will then drive the IT development of processes. They will remain inline and align with the organization goals. Oracle BPM 12c offers **Business Architecture (BA)**, a methodology to perform high-level analysis of business processes. This methodology adopts a top-down approach to discover organizational processes, define goals and objectives, define strategies and map them to goals and objectives, and report on BA components. Strategic Alignment is more of a methodology than a pattern. However, it's an important feature for a successful BPMN solution that aligns goals, objectives, and strategies of the organization. The following table highlights the facts around the Strategic Alignment Pattern:

Signature	Strategic Alignment Pattern
Classification	Analysis and Discovery Pattern
Intent	To offer a broader business model (an organizational blueprint) that ensures the alignment of goals, objectives, and strategies with organizational initiatives.
Motivation	A BPMN solution should offer business analysts and functional users a set of features to analyze, refine, define, optimize, and report business processes in the enterprise.
Applicability	Such a solution will empower a business to define models based on what they actually need, and reporting will help evaluate the performance. This will then drive the technological development of the processes by translating requirements into BPMN processes and cases.
Implementation	Using the BPM composer, one can define goals, objectives, strategies, and value chain models. We can refer to BPMN processes from the value chain models. Goals break down into objects that are fulfilled by strategies. Strategies are implemented by value chains that can be decomposed into value chains/business processes.
Known issues	Collaboration and a defined method to collect information.
Known solution	Solution to such a challenge is by including different stakeholders to define such artifacts. Stakeholders include business analysts, systems analysts, the IT department, CEO, CIO, and so on.

Using the BPM composer, we can define models using the following capabilities:

- **Enterprise maps**: In models that showcase key process areas of an organization, Enterprise maps infuse process classification (functional division of processes) and decomposition (business functions of services). Classification is enabled using lanes. Process areas are added to lanes, and each process area is linked to a value chain model.

- **Value Chain Models**: These represent the various stages of the process. A value chain model can be broken down into distinct value chain models or can be linked to business processes. It is the business processes that outline the IT requirements needed to realize the model. We can define KPIs that ensure the tracking of key business information for an organization, within the value chain models.

- **Strategy Models**: This is to define an organization's objectives and goals and also a strategy to achieve them. Strategy Models contain goals (end result of the Strategy Model), objectives (smaller objects or milestones to achieve the organization's goals), strategy (plans to achieve an objective), and value chain (how a strategy is implemented by referencing other value chains or BPMN processes).

 We will use the Loan Origination application and Loan Origination project from *Chapter 6, Correlation Patterns*. Download the Loan Origination project from the `Correlation` directory. You can deploy the Loan Origination project as it is and start executing the samples given in this chapter.

Perform the following steps to create enterprise maps:

1. Log in to the BPM composer application at `http://host:7003/bpm/ composer`. We will create an enterprise map for a new project.

2. Click on **ALL** and **+** (pointed to as **1** in the following screenshot) to create a process space.

3. You can select a process space that already exists or create a new process space. Process spaces group related BA and BPM projects.

4. Enter the name of the process space as `MyBPMProjectSpace`.

5. Click on **Save** to save the process space. By default, a space is a private space.

6. Click on **Edit** (as pointed to by arrow **3**) to add participants to the process space.

7. Click on **Enterprise Map** on the welcome page under **BA Project**.

8. Enter the enterprise name as MySocialBankEnterpriseMap.

9. Select the process space that we just created, that is, **MyBPMProjectSpace**.

10. Enter a name for the project as MySocialBankProject, as shown in the following screenshot, and provide a description for the map.

11. Click on **Create** to create a BA Enterprise map project.

The Enterprise map editor will open up. You can add new lanes and process areas; by default, 12c offers core, management, and support lanes. We can drag-and-drop the lane and process area components from the component pallet to the map editor to add a lane or process area by performing the following steps:

1. Drag-and-drop **Process Area** from the component pallet to create a process area into the **Core**, **Management**, and **Support** lanes.

2. Click on the pencil icon to edit it. This will open the **Properties** page. Enter a name and save your activity.

3. Enter the name of the process area and a description, and click on **OK**.

4. Save your work by clicking on the **Save** icon, as pointed to by an arrow at the top of the window, in the following screenshot.

5. Create a lane structure with process area, as shown in the following screenshot:

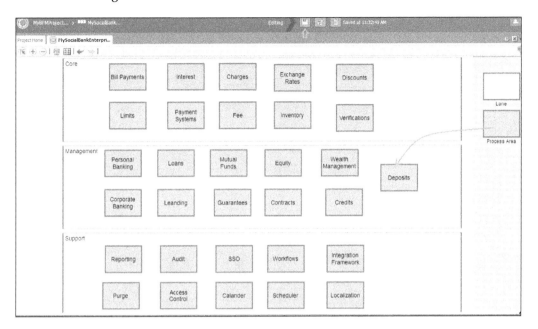

The Value Chain Model

Perform the following steps to create a Value Chain Model and associate the BPMN process to it:

1. Navigate to **Value Chain Model** in the project, as shown in the following screenshot, and click on **New** (**+**) to create a Value Chain Model.

2. Enter the name of the Value Chain Model as MySocialBankValueChain; then, enter a description and click on **Save**, as shown in the following screenshot. Remember to select a process space for the Value Chain Model. We are performing this step to create a master Value Chain Model.

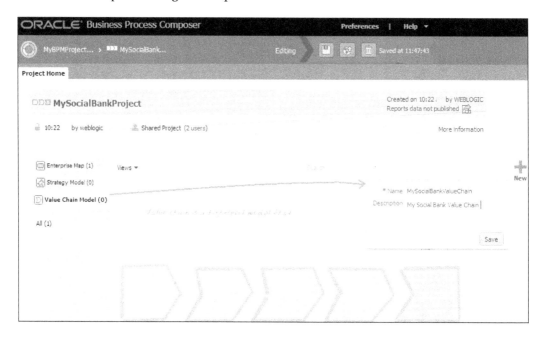

3. Drag-and-drop a chain step into the Value Chain Model editor, and click on **Edit** to enter the names of the chain steps (Loan Origination and Payments). This will create a master Value Chain Model.

4. Navigate to the project space, click on **Value Chain Model** again in the project to create another Value Chain Model, and name it as LoanOriginationValueChain. This will create a child Value Chain Model. We will link this child model to the BPMN process.

5. Drag-and-drop a chain step into the Value Chain Model editor, shown in the following screenshot, and click on the **Edit** (pencil) icon to enter the name of the chain step (for **Validation**, **Underwriting**, and so on). This will create a child Value Chain Model that will refer to the BPMN process.

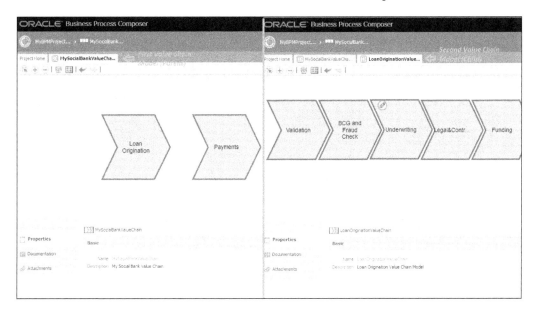

6. In the child Value Chain Model, click on **Validation chain step** and go to its **Properties** page.

7. In the **Properties** dialog box, under **Links**, click on the browse icon beside the **BPM or Value Chain** section. This will open the **Link** dialog box.

8. Choose **LoanOriginationProject** and click on **Next**.

9. Then, choose **LoanOriginationProcess** and click on **Finish**.

 We just associated the BPMN process with the Value Chain Model.

Perform similar steps with other chain steps (**BCG**, **Underwriting**, and so on) to associate them with the **Fraud Check** process. The preceding process is demonstrated in the following screenshot:

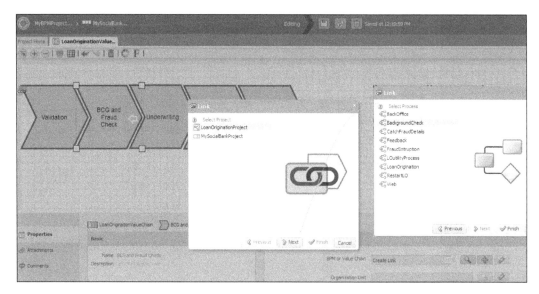

10. Save the edition and publish the changes.

11. Navigate to the primary Value Chain Model named **MySocialBankValueChain**. We will now link the primary Value Chain Model to the child Value Chain Model.

12. Click on the **Loan Origination** chain step and go to its **Properties** page.

13. Click on **Links** as shown in the following screenshot.

14. Select **MySocialBankProject** and click on **Next**.

15. Choose the **LoanOriginationValueChain** child Value Chain Model and click on **Finish**.

    This establishes a master-child Value Chain relationship between the Value Chains we defined earlier. The preceding process is demonstrated in the following screenshot:

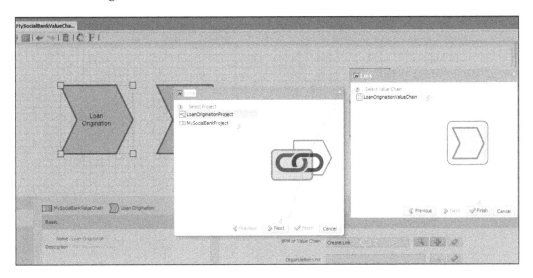

In this section, we defined the master and child Value Chain Models, and associated them to define the relationship. We also associated a value chain model with BPMN processes.

The Strategy Model

In this section, we will create a Strategy Model and link the goal to the objectives. We will then link objectives to strategy and strategy to Value Chain references, as shown in the following screenshot. Goals break down into objects that are fulfilled by strategies. Strategies are implemented by Value Chains; these strategies can be decomposed into value chains/business processes. Create a Strategy Model for the organization using the following steps:

1. Click on a Strategy Model in the **MySocialBankProject** project.

2. Enter the name and details for the Strategy Model named **MySocialBankStrategyModel**. This will open the model editor.

3. Drag-and-drop the goals, objectives, and strategy, and name them as shown in following screenshot:

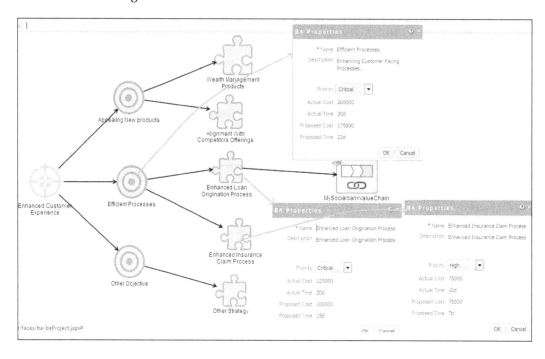

4. Click on the processes objective, that is, **Efficient Processes**, and go to its properties page, as shown in preceding screenshot.

5. Choose **Priority** as **Critical**, and give appropriate values for **Actual Cost**, **Actual Time**, **Proposed Cost**, and **Proposed Time**.

6. Click on **OK**, and save it to retain the changes.

7. Similarly set properties for other objectives too.

8. Link the goal to objectives and objectives to strategies, as shown in the preceding screenshot.

We will now create a value chain reference by performing the following steps:

1. Drag-and-drop a Value Chain reference to the canvas.

2. Enter the name as MySocialBankValueChain and provide a description.

3. Browse for the Value Chain links, select the Value Chain named **MySocialBankValueChain**, and click on **Finish**.

Mapping goals to an organization

We are now going to map goals to the fictitious organization unit, **MySocialBankOrganization**. All the assets (objectives, strategies, and Value Chain Models) that are linked to the goal will automatically get linked and grouped for this organization unit. Perform the following steps to map goals to the organization:

1. Go to the project's home page, create an organization unit named `MySocialBankOrganization`, and save it.

2. Go to **Strategy Model**, visit the properties of the goal, and assign the organization unit to the goal.

Defining KPIs in a BPMN project

In this section, we will define the KPIs that will help an organization track its performance against the objectives that are set. **LoanOriginationProject** already contains the measurements defined for loan amount. If we check the process in the BPM composer, we can find the measurements under **Business Indicators**. We will now define the **KPIs** section, shown in the following screenshot, for the business indicators:

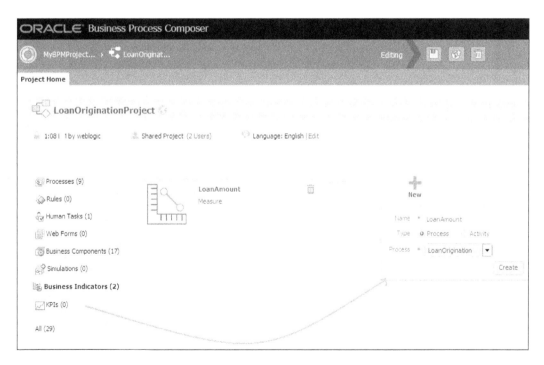

Perform the following steps to define the KPI:

1. Click on **KPIs** and then on the plus (**+**) icon to create the KPI.
2. Enter the name of the KPI as `Loan Amount`, as shown in the preceding screenshot.
3. Click on **Create**. This will open the KPI's edit page.
4. Enter the KPI details as shown in the following screenshot.
5. Enter the display name, and choose the **LoanOrigination** process.
6. Select the **LoanAmount** business indicator.
7. Define **Target Type** as **Range** and enter the range values.
8. Let **Operation** be set to **Total** and **Time Range** to **Last 365 days** (that is, the whole year).

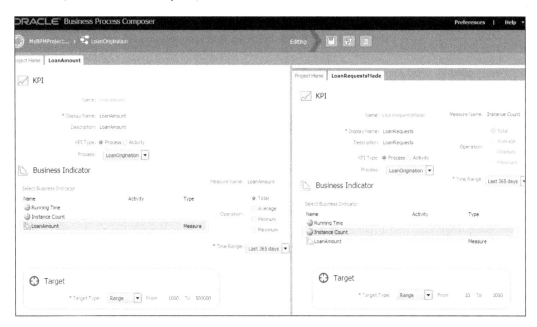

9. Similarly, define a KPI based on the seeded business indicator, **Instance Count**, and name the KPI as `LoanRequests`

10. Save the changes and publish the project.

Defining KPIs in a BA project

We just defined the KPIs in a BPMN project. Now, we will define KPIs in a BA project. We will define the range for the KPIs, and this way, we can visualize the impact of business indicators on our process, with the real values that we defined. KPIs can be manual KPI (to plug a known value), rollup KPIs (to aggregate child KPIs), and external KPIs (to include KPIs from external applications).

Defining KPIs in a child Value Chain Model

We can define KPIs on a Strategy Model and on Value Chain Models. In this section, we will define KPIs on the child Value Chain Model that we created earlier.

KPIs in the Value Chain Step level

Perform the following steps to create KPIs on the Value Chain step level:

1. Navigate to the BA project, **MySocialBankProject**, and click on **Value Chain Model**.

2. Select the child Value Chain Model named **LoanOriginationValueChain**.

3. Right-click on the chain step, **Validation**, and select **KPIs**.

4. Click on the plus (+) sign to create two manual KPIs, as shown in the following screenshot.

With manual KPIs, we are able to plug in known values for the number of loans processed and rejected. The following screenshot demonstrates the creation of manual KPIs:

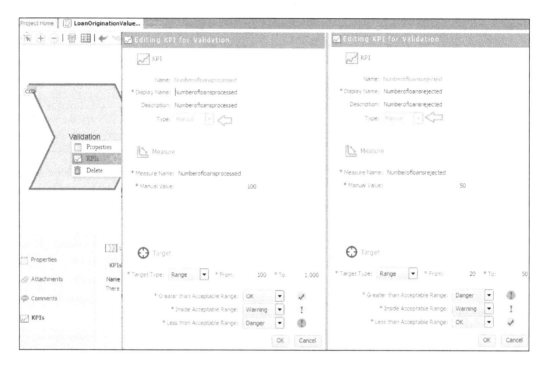

Now, we will create rollup KPIs, which allow us to rollup the number of loan requests and the amount mentioned in loan requests from the underlying BPMN project. Click on the plus (+) sign to create two rollup KPIs, as shown in the following screenshot. As we witnessed, rollup KPIs are based on the available KPIs from the business process, as depicted in the following screenshot:

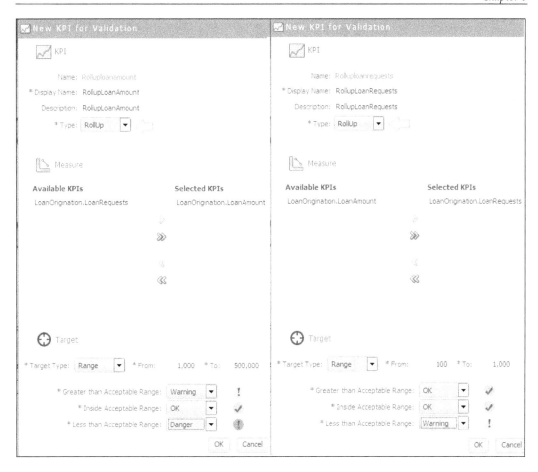

KPIs in the Value Chain Model level

Perform the following steps to create KPIs on the Value Chain Model level:

1. Double-click on the Value Chain Model grid in the background. We will be at the **LoanOriginationValueChain** model level.

2. Click on **KPIs** and then on the plus (+) icon to define a KPI. The following screenshot shows how to define a KPI for **LoanOriginationValueChain**:

Defining KPIs in the master Value Chain Model

In this section, we will define KPIs on the master Value Chain Model that we created earlier.

KPIs in the Value Chain Step level

Perform the following steps to create KPIs in the Value Chain Step level:

1. Navigate to the BA project, **MySocialBankProject**, and click on **Value Chain Model**.

2. Select the master Value Chain Model, **MySocialBankValueChain**.

3. Right-click on the **LoanOrgination** chain step and select **KPIs**.

4. Click on the plus (+) sign to create two manual KPIs, **TotalLoanRequests** and **TotalLoanAmount**, as shown in the following screenshot.

5. Save and publish the changes.

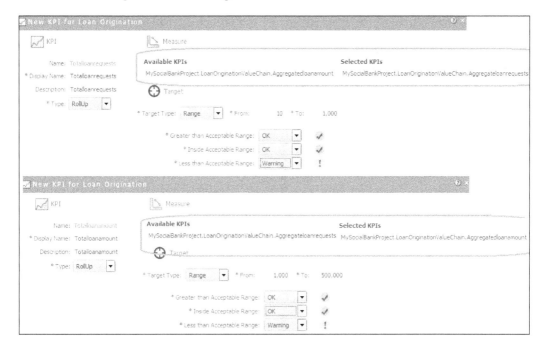

KPIs in the Value Chain Model level

Perform the following steps to create KPIs in the Value Chain Model level:

1. Double-click on the Value Chain Model grid in the background. We will be at the **MySocialBankValueChain** model level.

2. Click on **KPIs** and then on the plus (+) icon to define a KPI.

3. Define one KPI, Volumeofloanrequests, which is of the **Rollup** type by selecting **Loanorigination.Totalloanrequests** from the list of available KPIs. Define it with the same range as the **Totalloanrequests** KPI.

4. Define another KPI, Grandloanamount, which is of the **Rollup** type by selecting **Loanorigination.Totalloanamount** from the list of available KPIs. Define it with the same range as the **Totalloanamount** KPI.

5. Save and publish the changes.

6. Release the lock.

7. Deploy the BPMN project from the BPMN composer if it's not already deployed.

You can create a simple Loan Origination process in the composer with a Start Message Event and two business indicators defined as the measurement marks. Alternatively, we can use the Loan Origination project from the `Correlation` folder available in the downloadable code of *Chapter 6, Correlation Patterns*. Until this level, we defined KPIs for the child and master value chain steps and models.

Publishing report data

Before we generate a report, we have to publish the report data. Perform the following steps to publish the report data and generate reports:

1. Go to the main menu and click on **Publish report data**. A message dialog will appear with the published details.

2. To generate a report in the main menu, navigate to **Reports | Business Architecture | Impact Analysis Report | Value Chain** (the value chain report will help us understand how goals, objectives, strategies, value chains, and processes are linked).

3. Click on **Viewpoint** and select **By Organization Unit**, as we want to generate reports based on the organization unit.

4. In the following screenshot, we can see that goals are listed inside the organization units. Objectives are linked to the goals. Similarly, strategies are bound to respective objectives, and processes are linked to the Value Chain Model.

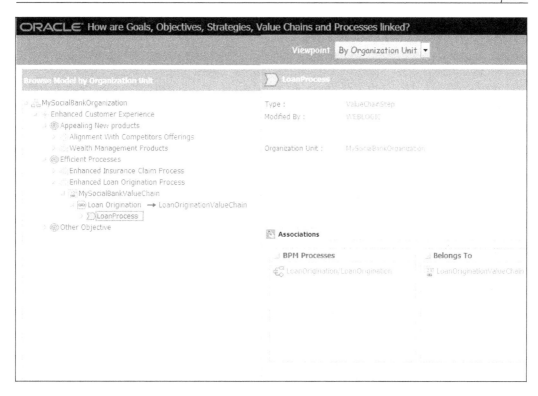

As we can see, the Impact Analysis report used the published data stored in the BPM repository, and these reports showcase properties and hierarchy of BA components. We can also run the Process Critical report, where values will come from the KPIs that we just created. We can drill into the report and click on the text inside the value chain model. Using BA, we modeled the processes within an organization and defined goals, objectives, and strategies. We can use reports to view how different components are stitched in the fabric of an organization unit. These reports will help us in knowing the following:

- What our goals are
- How goals and objectives are fulfilled by strategies
- How goals, objectives, strategies, and value chains are linked
- How goals, objectives, strategies, value chains, and processes are linked

Capturing the business context

Organizations need process documentation that helps them perform Impact and Dependency analysis. Using the BPM 12*c* composer, we can document the process at various levels such as project, process, and activity levels, and generate reports for the analysis of business requirements, issues, challenges, and so on. There are various documentations defined at discrete document levels as shown in following table:

Document level	Documentation	How it's defined?	When it's used?	Where it's used?
Project	Project description (helps distinguish between different projects)	When a project is created, we can enter it's description	When projects are enlisted in the space	Detailed Business Process Report
	Role description	Below the role in the narrative view	Role description	Detailed Business Process Report
Process	Process description (it explains the title and helps distinguish between different processes)	When a process is created, we can enter its description in the general tab in process properties or below process name in the narrative view	When process are enlisted in the space.	• Detailed Business Process Report • Business Requirements Report • Process Properties Report
	Process documentation (links can be added to check information duplicity, and the documentation type will help us define whether document visibility is for end user or internal user)	Can be added in the narrative view or documentation properties in the process properties, (it's shown in the following screenshot)	Add information to the process when information does not exist elsewhere.	• Detailed Business Process Report • Business Requirements Report

Document level	Documentation	How it's defined?	When it's used?	Where it's used?
	Process links (link description helps in removing the confusion when information is generic in various components)	Link tab in the business properties	To determine if a link contains the appropriate document, we can add information to links, which is then added to activities, processes, requirements, activity documentation, and process documentation.	• Detailed Business Process Report • Business requirements report
	Requirements (this feature allows tracking status, priority, and challenges of the requirements of a process.)	Business properties (it is shown in the following screenshot)	Requirements allow us to set the business context. We can add multiple requirements. Downstream we can sort them by date, status and so on.	• Detailed business process report • Business requirements report
	Process notes (they are like sticky notes)	Drag-and-drop notes from the component pallet to the process graphic	While editing and creating a process, notes are useful to establish collaboration.	Not visible
Activity	Activity description	In the graphic view at activity business properties or narrative view	Brief expansion of the activity name	• Detailed Business Process Report • Business Requirements Report • Human Tasks versus Process Report • Services versus Process Report
	Activity links	Business properties as shown below; multiple links can be added	Can be added to activities, processes, requirements, activity documentation, and process documentation. You can enter name, description, and select the URL of the link with the correct format, as shown in the following screenshot.	• Detailed Business Process Report • Business Requirements Report

Document level	Documentation	How it's defined?	When it's used?	Where it's used?
	Activity documentation	Can be added at narrative view or documentation panel	To add relevant information to the activity. Documentation type will help us define whether document visibility is for end user or internal user.	• Detailed Business Process Report • Business Requirements Report
	Activity comments	Add through business properties	Use comments to record information. They appear in various reports as they are permanently attached with the activities.	• Detailed Business Process Report • Business Requirements Report • Issues and Comments Report
	Activity notes	Drag-and-drop the activity note from the component pallet to process graphic	Helps in collaboration. They are like sticky notes and are not permanent; they should be used as reminders.	Not available
	General	In the **General** tab under business properties	It facilitates process improvement and discovery. It helps tack the cost and time required to perform the activity.	• Detailed Business Process Report • Business Requirements Report

Document level	Documentation	How it's defined?	When it's used?	Where it's used?
	Issues	The **Issues** tab in business properties	• It facilitates process improvements, testing, and discovery. Issues can be sorted based on severity, date, priority, and resolution status. • It facilitates the tracking of issues, such as severity, priority, and resolution status, that are associated with activities	• Detailed Business Process Report • Business Requirements Report • Issues and Comments Report
	RACI (Responsible Accountable Consulted Informed)	The **RACI** tab in business properties tracks those who are responsible, accountable, consulted, and informed on an activity	Facilitates process improvements, testing, and discovery to ensure that proper roles are associated with the activity	The RACI report

The following screenshot showcases the **Narrative** view, **Documentation Type**, **Links**, **Requirements**, and an activity's **RACI** properties:

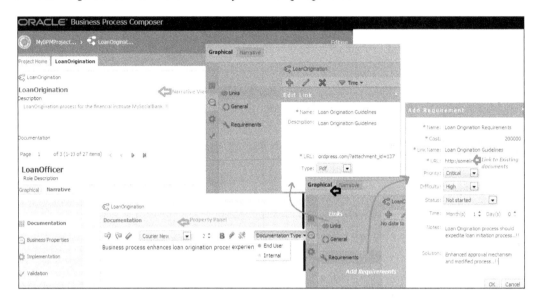

Save and publish the information to the BPM repository. We can now generate reports by clicking on the main menu in the application's welcome page and selecting **Process Report** from the drop-down list. We can generate various report types, as shown in the following screenshot. Select the report type and output format, and the respective report will be generated.

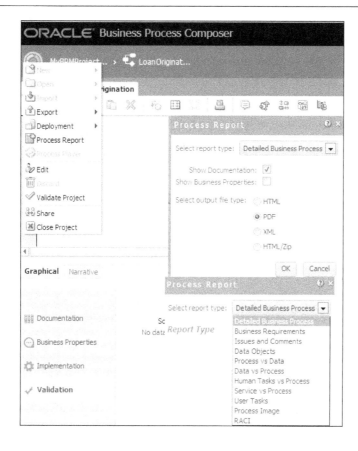

Emulating Process Behavior

The following feature table highlights the facts around Emulating Process Behavior feature:

Feature	Emulating Process Behavior
Category	Analysis and Discovery Pattern
Intent	Facilitating process designers with the creation of test and revise processes without saving and deploying the process.
Motivation	Visual representation of a BPMN process, which showcases an animated view of your process behavior so that process behavioral patterns can be analyzed even before deploying and publishing the project.

Applicability	Process player does not require that you either deploy or publish the project to visualize the changes. Technically, the Oracle BPM composer will validate the project and will deploy the draft version of the BPM project to a player partition in BPM's runtime environment.
Implementation	In a BPMN process, the process player will emulate the runtime behavior of User Tasks, Message Send Tasks, Send Events, Timer Events, Call Activities, End Events, and other activities.
Known issues	NA
Known solution	NA

Enabling the process player is a two-step process. First, the process player needs to be enabled, and second, we need to map the role defined in the process to the user or group in the organization's infrastructure.

While enabling the process player, we need to provide the SOA administrator credentials, because the BPM composer uses them to deploy the draft version of the project to runtime player partition and to perform tasks on the process instance as different users. Any user with edit privileges can run the process player. Perform the following steps to access edit privileges:

1. Log in to the Oracle BPM 12c composer application.

2. Go to **Administrator view** in the application's welcome page.

3. Select **Process Player** and enter the SOA admin user name and password.

4. Click on **Save**, and we will receive a message saying that the SOA admin credentials were successfully configured.

Now, we will map the role defined in the process with the user/group defined in organization infrastructure as this facilitates the emulation of process behavior in a real-world situation.

The following screenshot showcases the **Administrator view** and enables the process player by supplying the SOA admin credentials. It also shows the **Modular view** to start the process player by mapping the role with the user and selecting the process to analyze:

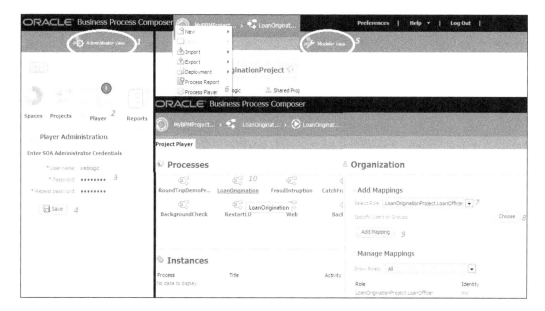

A process role (all the roles defined in the process) must be mapped to at least one user/group each. Select a process from the list of processes; for example, select the **BackOffice** process. BPMN will start deploying the process to a runtime player partition as shown by number **2** in the following screenshot. It will open a web service test client.

Select the operation (for example, **startBO**) and enter the request parameters. We can pass security details if required by the process. Policies can also be associated if required. Clicking invokes the initiation of the process instance. When a process starts, you can find the process emulation behavior shown by number **8** in following screenshot:

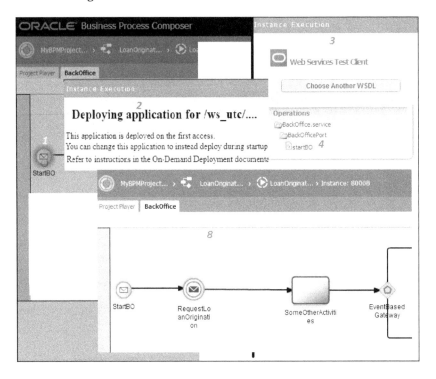

When the process reaches the end event, we can click the drill-up icon to end the process emulation. This will end the process instance, and the process player will delete the process instance.

The Debugger feature

The following feature table highlights facts around the Debugger feature:

Feature	BPM Debugger
Category	Analysis and Discovery Pattern
Intent	To identify and fix logical or workflow issues in the process.
Motivation	It's a preventive approach to know in advance various challenges in the logical and process flows. The Debugger feature allows us to track the BPMN process, inspecting process instance attributes, drilling into data objects, watching correlation keys and conversations, and, above all, allowing us to inspect the message values sent from and returned to the BPMN components.

Applicability	Processes logical thread while executing and activates various frames that contain sets of data values which represent process data objects and attributes. The BPMN process, subprocess, callable subprocess, and event subprocess are data-declaration containers. When a process starts or enters one of these containers, a new frame is created. The debugger will then build a stake of frame based on how these containers are nested in the process. The debugger basically creates a model out of the stake frame, where this model offers data visibility and enables access to data in the BPMN process.
Implementation	Implementation is based on breakpoints. We define breakpoints in the BPMN process, and these are the points where the process will stop. This stoppage will allow monitoring of values in the BPMN process variables. These values will help analyze any potential problems in the process logic or process flow.
Known issues	NA
Known solution	NA

Perform the following steps to enable debugging in the BPMN process:

1. Expand the Loan Origination project, and open the Loan Origination process.

2. Right-click on any of the BPMN process components on which we want to set a break point.

3. Select the Toggle breakpoint (a red dot will appear on the component, as seen in the following screenshot):

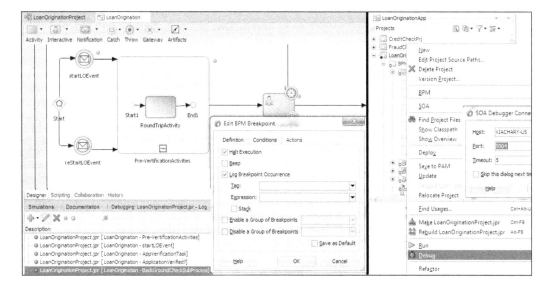

4. We can navigate to **JDeveloper** | **Window** | **Breakpoint**, and this will enlist all the break points defined in the process. We can edit their behavior as shown in the preceding screenshot.

Perform the following steps to attach a BPM project to the debugger:

1. Right-click on the project.
2. Select **Debug**; this will open the **SOA Debugger Connection Settings** dialog box.
3. Enter the debugger's host and port, and click on **OK**.
4. Select the option to deploy the project to the application server.
5. The composite editor and debugger windows will appear; we can run the BPMN process step by step and analyze the values at various breakpoints.

Round Trip and Business-IT Collaboration

The following feature table highlights facts around Business-IT Collaboration feature:

Feature	Round Trip and Business-IT Collaboration
Category	Process Collaboration
Intent	Facilitating storing and sharing of business process assets and business architecture assets.
Motivation	Common storage for process assets and business architecture assets. Sharing of assets between process developers who work on the BPM studio and process analysts who work on composer application.
Applicability	PAM supports collaboration (allowing multiple users to work on the same project at the same time), versioning (allowing the existence of multiple versions of the same asset), security and access control (providing secure access control of the business assets), life cycle (flexible life cycle model), reporting (detailed report of business assets), conflict resolution, difference and merge (viewing the difference between different versions of the asset, resolving conflict, and merging the changes), and backup and recovery (the ability to roll back to a stable version in case of error/bugs).

Implementation	Oracle BPM 12*c* uses PAM to store and share business process assets and business architecture assets. PAM infuses the sharing of assets between process developers who work on the BPM studio and process analysts who work on a composer application.
Known issues	NA
Known solution	NA

Working with PAM is a multistep process, which is as follows:

1. Open JDeveloper 12*c* and navigate to **Window | Process Asset Manager Navigator** to connect with a PAM server.

2. Enter the connection name as `MyPAMConnection`; also, enter the admin username and password of the asset manager server, and click on **Next**.

3. Enter the location of the asset manager, that is, the server and port.

4. Test the connection and save the PAM server connection configuration, as shown in the following screenshot:

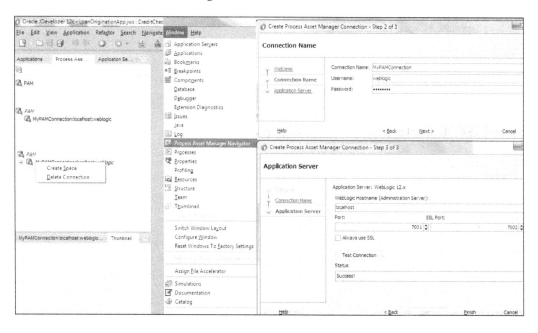

We can create a process space from JDeveloper too. However, let's take a round trip to the process composer to perform other activities. We will use JDeveloper 12*c* to modify a process in the Loan Origination project. Then, we will open the same project in the process composer to share it with other users to perform further modeling. When composer users perform the changes, JDeveloper users will be able to merge them and continue with the development.

Remember that the lock feature prevails when we want to save the asset into PAM. If the asset is locked by another user or the same user in JDeveloper/composer, the asset cannot be saved until it is unlocked by the other user.

If the asset is already updated by another user or another application or if there is an updated version of the project in repository, we need to first update our local copy and then save it.

Open the Loan Origination application in JDeveloper12*c* and expand the Loan Origination project. Then, perform the following steps:

1. Open the Loan Origination process and add an activity named `RoundTripActivity`.

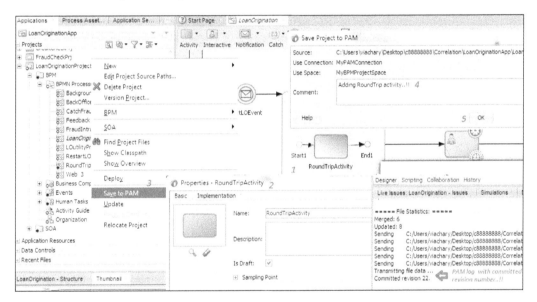

2. Select the **Is Draft** checkbox to let the activity be in the draft mode.

3. Right-click on the project and select **Save to PAM**.

4. Enter a comment in the **Save Project to PAM** dialog.

5. Click on **OK**.

6. Check the **PAM log**, and we can witness the PAM commit status and the new **revision number**.

In this exercise, we added a new activity in the Loan Origination process. We can now log in to the Oracle BPM composer to check the Loan Origination process model to verify the change.

We will share the project with two users using the following steps; you can share it with any two users defined in the LDAP or embedded LDAP (myrealm):

1. Go to the application's welcome page and click on **Edit** on the process space to which your project belongs.

2. Specify the user and select a role (**Owner, Editor,** or **Viewer**). Let the users (RIVI and LATA) be editors.

3. Click on **Share** to share the assets with the users (RIVI and LATA) who are in the editor role.

4. We can witness the users as **Team** in the project space, as shown in the following screenshot:

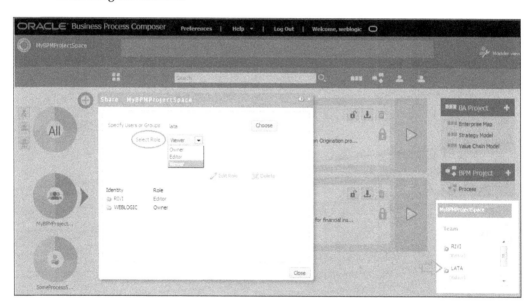

Open the Loan Origination project in three different browsers by logging in as, weblogic, rivi, and lata users and perform the following steps. If the project is already locked by the weblogic user, it needs to be unlocked by the weblogic user to allow the rivi or lata user to perform editing. Otherwise, they would be in the viewing mode.

1. Log in to the BPM composer as weblogic.

2. Open the Loan Origination project (at this stage, `weblogic` is editing the project). Close the project, as shown in the following screenshot:

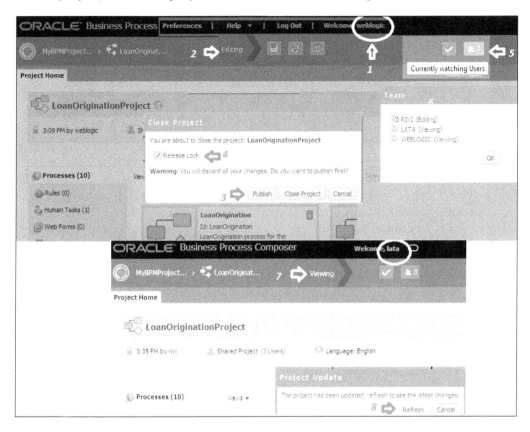

3. The **Close Project** dialog will ask to **Release Lock** and recommend that you publish any unpublished changes. Click on **Publish** to publish the changes made by `weblogic` into the BPM repository.

4. Check the **Release Lock** box to unlock the project so that other users can open it in editing mode.

5. As we logged in to the BPM composer in other browsers with users `rivi` and `lata`, allow user `rivi` to start editing the project.

6. Navigate back to the browser in which we are logged in as `weblogic`. Click on the team–sharing logo in the application's welcome page as pointed by number **5**.

7. The **Team** dialog will appear; this will showcase which user is performing what function and how the asset is shared between the team. We can witness that `rivi` is performing editing, and `weblogic` and `lata` are viewing the project.

8. Go to the third browser where we logged in as user `lata`. As `weblogic` has published its changes, asset is modified in the repository, and hence, the user `lata` will be prompted to refresh the project to view the latest changes.

This exercise shows how collaboration between different users and between applications and the JDeveloper tool can be facilitated quickly and efficiently. If there are new published changes, the viewing users are notified by a request to refresh their view. If a user wants to close the project and there are unpublished changes, then they will be promoted to publish these changes, as shown in the following screenshot. Lock-unlock is another feature that allows effective sharing of assets between a team. Perform the following steps to demonstrate the round-trip process:

1. Log in to the BPM composer as user `rivi`, open the Loan Origination project, and click on **RoundTripDemoProcess**.

2. Edit **RoundTripDemoProcess** by adding two new activities in the draft mode, as shown in the following screenshot:

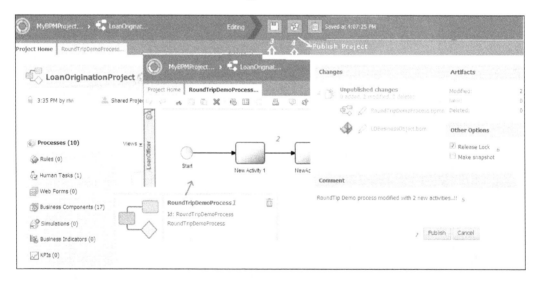

3. **Save** the asset.

4. When we click on **Publish**, the **Publish Project** dialog appears.

5. Enter comments while publishing the changes.

6. We can either select **Make snapshot** and/or select **Release Lock** to unlock the project

7. Click on **Publish** to publish the changes to the repository.

Open JDeveloper and make changes to **RoundTripDemoProcess**. These changes made by a user in JDeveloper are different from the changes made by a user in the BPM composer. We are trying to demonstrate the difference and merge in this section by performing the following steps:

1. Right-click on the project in JDeveloper.

2. Expand **Versioning** to click on update.

3. We will try to update the asset definition.

4. Click on **Yes** in the dialog; this prompts for the changes to be saved, as shown in the following screenshot:

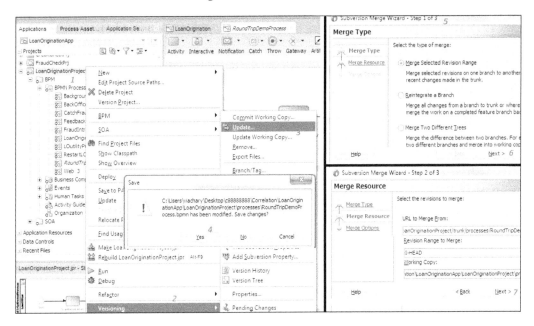

5. Updating the process will open the **Subversion Merge Wizard** dialog. Select **Merge Selected Revision Range** to perform the merge.

6. Click on **Next**.

7. In the next dialog box, click on **Next** again.

8. The wizard showcases **Conflicts**, as shown in the following screenshot. Then, click on **Finish**.

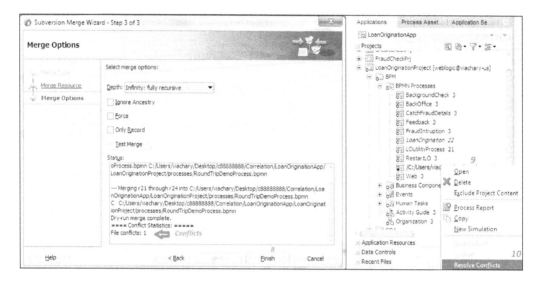

As a project has conflicts, we will try to resolve the conflicts by performing the following steps:

1. Right-click on the project and select **Resolve conflicts** (steps **9** and **10** in the preceding screenshot).

   This will open a visual difference and merge screen. We can do this for every file that has conflicts. We can then click on **Save and Complete Merge**, as shown in the following screenshot, when all conflicts are resolved:

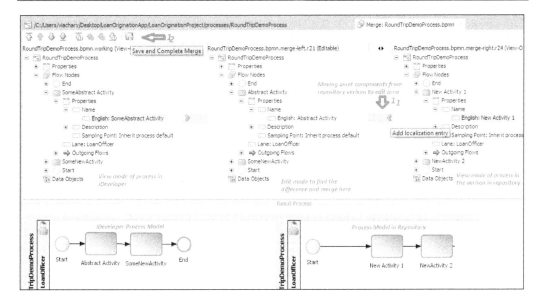

2. When all differences are sorted and merged in the editable section, add a localization entry, from the section on which you want to bring the change, to the editable area (step 11, in the preceding screenshot).

3. Click on **Save and Complete Merge** (step 12 in the preceding screenshot). This will showcase the result process.

As we can check in the preceding screenshot, the left-hand side window shows the JDeveloper process, and the right-hand side window shows the process after the conflicts are resolved. As we saw in the preceding sections, PAM and SVN were used interchangeably. We have the flexibility to choose between the features of PAM (update, save and resolve conflict, and resolution functionality) and the SVN versioning features (update, remove, merge, lock, unlock, switch, and so on). For example, you can use the save action of PAM to publish a project, or you can use the SVN commit action.

Summary

The Strategic Alignment pattern in the Analysis and Discovery pattern category demonstrated features to analyze, refine, define, optimize, and report business processes in the enterprise. This pattern highlighted how IT development and process models can be aligned with organization goals. While performing alignment, we learned about enterprise maps, Strategy Models, and Value Chain models. We discovered how models are created and linked to an organization. We learned how to define KPIs in processes and Value Chain models.

The chapter also offered a detailed description on publishing report data, and creating impact analysis reports and critical reports. Capturing business context shows the importance of documentation in the process model phase. Different document levels and their methods of definition were discussed along with their usage. Further, we learned how to create different reports based on the information we documented in the process, such as RACI reports. The process player's demonstration showcased how process behavior can be emulated in a visual representation that allows designers and analysts to test and revise the process without deploying it.

While doing so, we learned how to navigate in various modes, mapping users to roles and running process instances to analyze process behavior. We also learned how to set breakpoints and enable debugging in the BPMN process. Round-trip and business-IT collaboration facilitated storing, sharing, and collaborating on process assets and business architecture assets. While doing so, we witnessed PAM and subversion and also learned versioning, save/update/commit, difference and merge, and various other activities, which empower developers and analysts to work in unison.

Installing Oracle BPM Suite 12*c*

This appendix introduces you to the installation of Oracle BPM suite 12*c*.

Installing JDK

Download JDK from the following URL, which is from official site of Oracle. Make sure that you download a JDK higher than 1.7.0_15, as Oracle BPM 12c requires JDK 1.7.0_15 and higher:

`http://www.oracle.com/technetwork/java/javase/downloads/index.html.`

After clicking on the preceding link, the **Java SE Development Kit 7u60** window opens as shown in the following screenshot:

Java SE Development Kit 7u60		
You must accept the Oracle Binary Code License Agreement for Java SE to download this software.		
Thank you for accepting the Oracle Binary Code License Agreement for Java SE; you may now download this software.		
Product / File Description	File Size	Download
Linux x86	119.67 MB	jdk-7u60-linux-i586.rpm
Linux x86	136.95 MB	jdk-7u60-linux-i586.tar.gz
Linux x64	120.97 MB	jdk-7u60-linux-x64.rpm
Linux x64	135.77 MB	jdk-7u60-linux-x64.tar.gz
Mac OS X x64	185.94 MB	jdk-7u60-macosx-x64.dmg
Solaris x86 (SVR4 package)	139.43 MB	jdk-7u60-solaris-i586.tar.Z
Solaris x86	95.5 MB	jdk-7u60-solaris-i586.tar.gz
Solaris x64 (SVR4 package)	24.64 MB	jdk-7u60-solaris-x64.tar.Z
Solaris x64	16.35 MB	jdk-7u60-solaris-x64.tar.gz
Solaris SPARC (SVR4 package)	138.73 MB	jdk-7u60-solaris-sparc.tar.Z
Solaris SPARC	98.57 MB	jdk-7u60-solaris-sparc.tar.gz
Solaris SPARC 64-bit (SVR4 package)	24.04 MB	jdk-7u60-solaris-sparcv9.tar.Z
Solaris SPARC 64-bit	18.4 MB	jdk-7u60-solaris-sparcv9.tar.gz
Windows x86	127.91 MB	jdk-7u60-windows-i586.exe
Windows x64	129.65 MB	jdk-7u60-windows-x64.exe

Install JDK, set JAVA_HOME, and update the environment variable with JAVA_HOME.

Installing BPM suite

To install the BPM suite, perform the following steps:

1. Download Oracle BPM Suite 12c from OTN or Oracle product downloads for BPM 12c at http://www.oracle.com/technetwork/middleware/bpm/downloads/index.html.

2. Save the download file and unzip it to a local directory.

3. Open the command prompt with admin privileges, and run the following command to begin the installation:

```
Java -jar fmw_12.1.3.0.0_bpm_quickstart.jar
```

The preceding command line is entered into the command prompt as shown in the following screenshot:

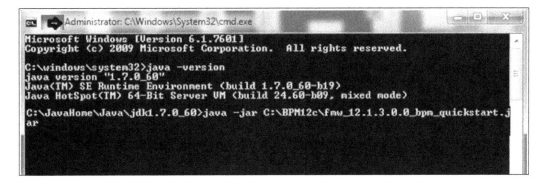

4. This will start the extraction of the file and will essentially start the installation. The following screenshot shows you the **Welcome** page of the installer window:

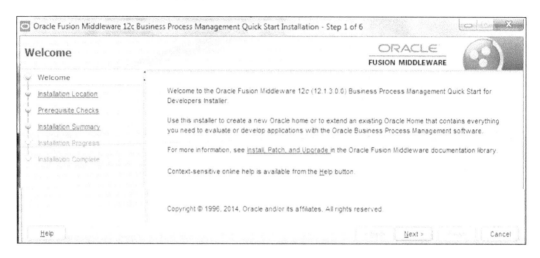

5. Click on **Next**.

6. Enter the installation location that will be the Oracle home. It checks for the operating system and Java version (JDK 1.7.0_15+ is expected).

7. Verify the installation summary, and click on **Install** to begin the installation. Then, click on **Next**.

8. The **Installation complete** screen shows you the installation summary. You can check/uncheck the **Start JDeveloper** checkbox if you want to start/not start the JDeveloper after the installation.

9. Click on **Finish** to complete the installation process. The installed files can be viewed as follows:

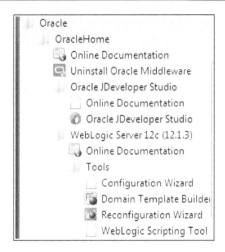

Configuring the default domain

Perform the following steps to configure the default domain:

1. Launch JDeveloper.
2. Allow for the visibility of **Application Servers** by navigating to **Window** | **Application Servers**.
3. Start the integrated WebLogic server as shown in the following screenshot:

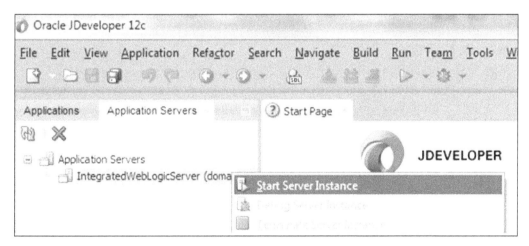

4. This will launch the domain creation dialog box.

5. Create the default domain with all the details, as shown in the following screenshot:

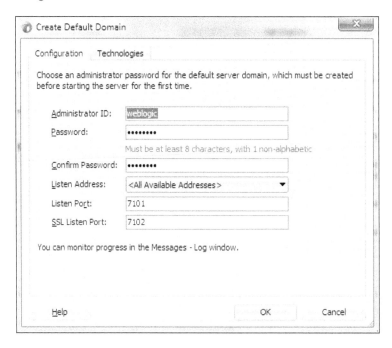

6. We can enter a password of our choice and the ports as we want to define them. Click on the **Technologies** tab to review the technologies that will be configured.

7. Click on **OK**.

8. JDeveloper will be using the derby database. Once you get the message that the server has started, in the JDeveloper log, as shown in the following screenshot, you can log in to the console and verify the configurations:

9. Log in to the WebLogic console at `http://localhost:7101/console` using the `weblogic` username and the password that you entered while configuring the domain.

10. Navigate to **Deployments** to verify the BPM Composer application, BPM Workspace application, and EM.

11. Log in to the workspace at `http://localhost:7101/bpm/workspace`, and verify the case workspace UI and other features.

12. Navigate to **myrealm | Users and Groups** and verify the users. We will find only three users available.

Enabling the demo user community

To include other users and build a hierarchy, perform the following steps:

1. Log in to WebLogic console and navigate to **Deployments**. On the summary page of **Deployments**, click on **Install**.

2. Browse `SOATestDemoApp.ear` to install the demo community by clicking on the **upload your file(s)** link as shown in the following screenshot, and click on **Next**:

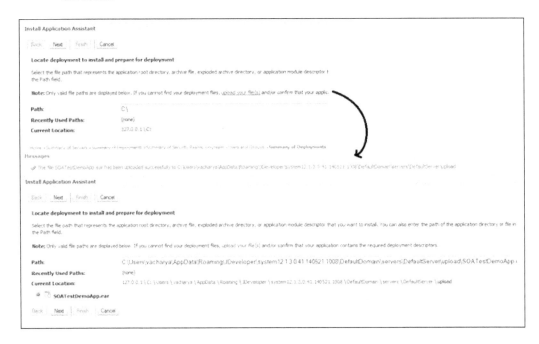

3. Click on **Next** and select the option to install the deployment as the application.

4. On the **Optional Settings** page, click on **Next**.

5. In the installation assistant, review the page, click on **No, I will review the configuration later.**, and click on **Finish**.

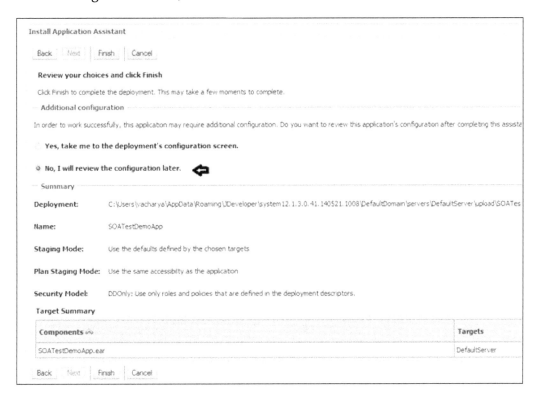

6. Log in to `http://localhost:7101/integration/SOADemoCommunity/DemoCommunitySeedServlet`.

7. Click on **Submit** in order to seed the demo community. The following screenshot shows you the **Seed Demo Community** page:

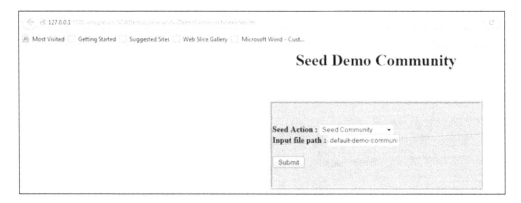

8. Once done, come back to the WebLogic console, navigate to **myrealm | User and Groups | Users**, and verify the new users that have been created.

9. Stop the default domain.

10. Click on the Terminate icon to stop the integrated weblogic.

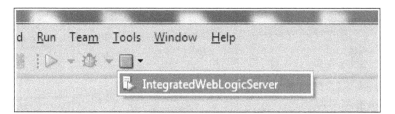

Custom domain creation

The default domain installation comes with JavaDB (derby DB); however, if you are looking for a complex domain structure and want to install the product suite on a database, perform the following steps:

1. Install the database (XE or Oracle 11g) (*I'm not covering the database installation here*).

2. Open the command prompt with admin privileges, and navigate to the `ORACLE_HOME/oracle_common/bin` directory.

3. Run `rcu.bat`, as shown in the following screenshot. This will start the repository creation script.

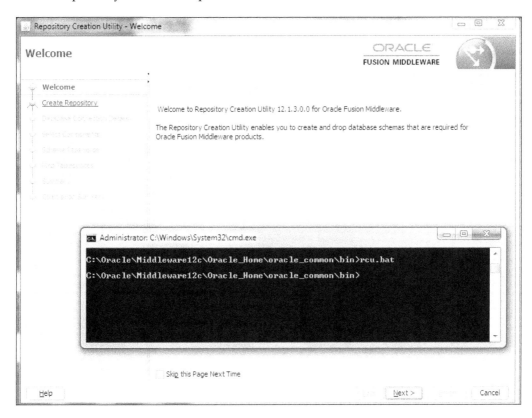

4. On the RCU creation welcome page, click on **Next**.

5. As shown in the following screenshot, choose **System Load and Product Load** if you have DBA privileges, and click on **Next**. You can use the same screen to drop the repository, if required.

6. Enter the database details as shown in the following screenshot, and click on **Next**:

7. In the **Select Components** window, enter a schema prefix for the components that we are going to install:

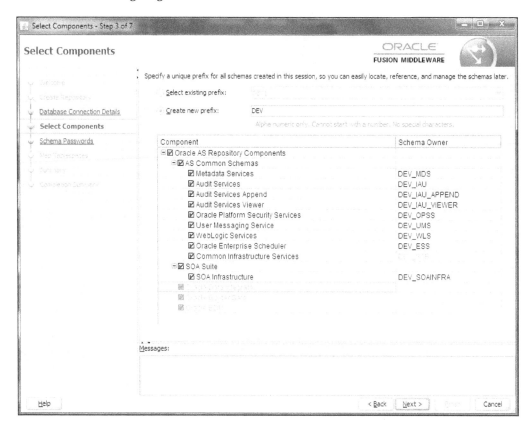

8. Click on **Next**; once the prerequisites are checked, click on **OK**.

9. Enter the schema password.

10. Enter the values for the custom variable. As this is a standard installation, let the default values be selected. Click on **Next**.

11. In the **Map Tablespaces** window, click on **Next**. This will create tablespaces in the database.

12. The **Summary** window will showcase the component, schema, and tablespace. Click on **Create** to create and load the components.

13. The **Completion summary** window, as shown in the following screenshot, will show you the completion status and will also allow you to click on the respective logfiles of the components:

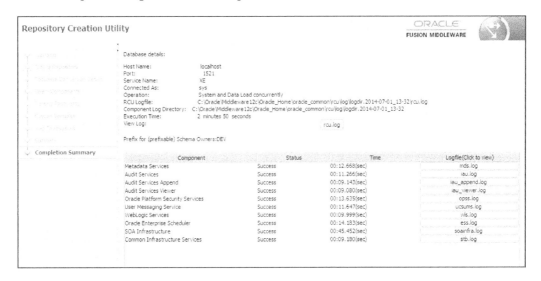

The BPM/SOA configuration

Perform the following steps to configure BPM 12*c*:

1. Open the command prompt with admin privileges, and navigate to ORACLE_HOME/oracle_common/common/bin.

2. Start the configuration process with the config.cmd command, as shown in the following screenshot:

3. This will start the creation wizard.

4. Enter the name for the domain if you want to create a new domain. Also enter the location of domain home, as shown in the following screenshot, and click on **Next**:

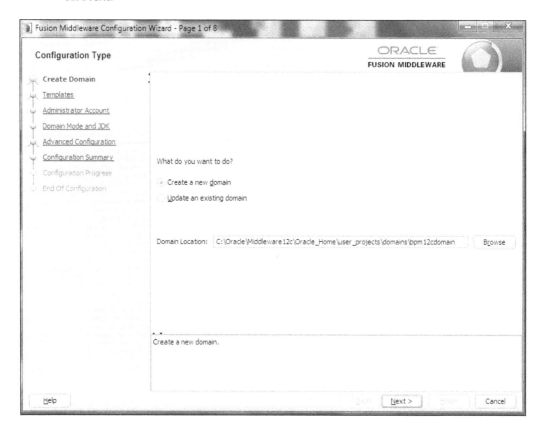

5. In the **Templates** window, as shown in the following screenshot, select the templates for the components you need to configure, and click on **Next**:

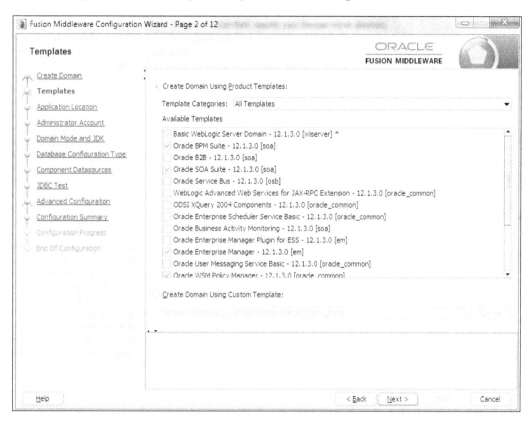

6. The **Application Location** window will enlist the domain, domain location, and domain home; click on **Next**.

7. Enter the domain password in the admin account dialog, and click on **Next**.

8. For **Domain Mode**, select the **Development** mode and the JDK that we used; the installation will be listed as a hotspot. However, we can select the **Production** mode, as shown in the following screenshot, when setting a PROD environment. Click on **Next**.

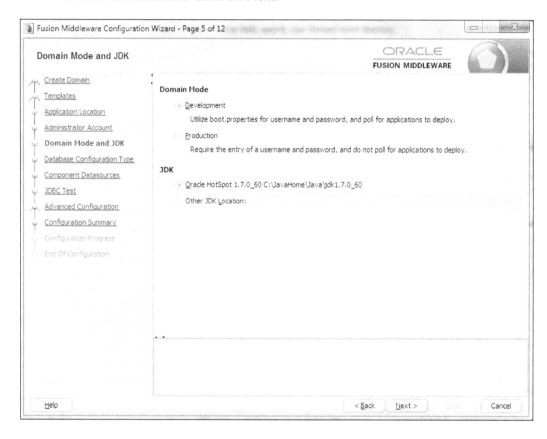

9. Select **Manual Configuration** in the database, and click on **Next**.

10. Enter the DB service name, host, port, schema, and schema password, as shown in following screenshot, and click on **Next**:

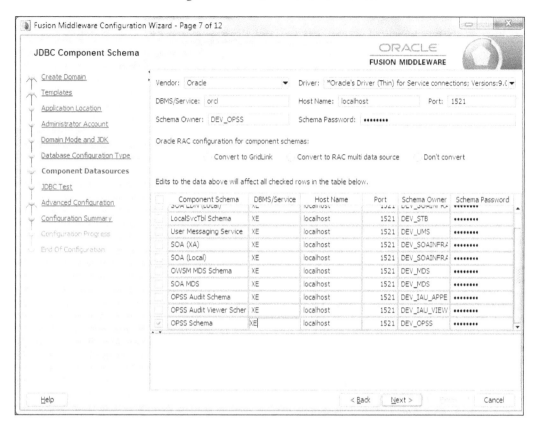

11. The JDBC test will perform the data source connection testing; once it is successful, click on **Next**.

12. The advance configuration allows for the **Administration Server**, **Node Manager**, **Managed Servers**, and **Cluster and Coherence** configurations. Click on **Next** if you want the default topology configuration.

13. The **Configuration Summary** window will enlist the configuration that you have defined. Click on **Create** when you are satisfied.

14. The **Configuration Progress** window will guide you through the percentage of the domain configuration that is in progress. Once this is completed, click on **Next**.

15. The **Configuration Success** page will show you the configuration success message. The domain location and admin console location will be enlisted. Click on **Finish**.

16. We can use following lines of command to start the weblogic server and the managed server, respectively:

    ◦ `startWebLogic.cmd`

    ◦ `startmanagedWebLogic.cmd`

17. We can use the following command to stop the weblogic server and the managed server, respectively:

    ◦ `stopWebLogic.cmd`

    ◦ `stopmanagedWebLogic.cmd`

18. Use following links to log in to the WebLogic console and EM console, respectively:

    ◦ `http://administration_server_host:administration_server_port/console`

    ◦ `http://administration_server_host:administration_server_port/em`

Summary

The walk-through provided by this appendix will help us install the Oracle BPM 12c environment. This will facilitate in deploying and testing the sample applications delivered with this title. This document facilitates the quick-start installation of Oracle BPM 12c, and it also demonstrates the creation of complex domains and executing schema and domain creation. It also helps us provision the demo community on our installed environment.

Index

A

Activities 281
Adaptive Case Management (ACM)
  about 321-324
  benefits 325, 326
  highlights 326
  use case scenarios 330-332
Adaptive Case Management (ACM),
      components
  activity 327
  case 327
  collaboration 328
  content and information 327
  dashboard 328
  data 327
  events 328
  integrations 328
  knowledge workers 327
  milestones 328
  participants 327
  policies 328
  portal 328
  processes 327
  rules 328
  stakeholder 327
  task 327
ad hoc feature
  about 348
  applicability 348
  association of case, with subcases 350
  facts 348
  implementation 348
  motivation 348
ad hoc inclusion, of activities 349
ad hoc inclusion, of documents 350

ad hoc inclusion, of rules and activities 351
ad hoc inclusion, of stakeholders 349
ad hoc routing pattern, facts
  about 173
  applicability 173
  classification 173
  exploring 173, 174
  implementation 173
  intent 173
  motivation 173
  signature 173
advance conversation 208
Allocated-Error Exception Handling
      pattern
  about 287
  scenarios 288
Allocated Exception Handling pattern
  about 285-289
  Allocated-Complete pattern 285, 286
  Allocated-Error pattern 285-289
  Allocated-Terminate pattern 285-289
  applicability 285
  Boundary Catch Event, modifying 289
  classification 285
  implementation 286
  intent 285
  motivation 285
  signature 285
allocated state, business process 283
Allocated state External Exception
      Handling pattern
  about 304, 305
  cases 306, 307
  implementing 306, 307
Allocated state error 304

Allocated-Terminate Exception Handling pattern
about 289
process flow trace, checking 289
application roles 133
approval group list builder pattern
about 143
serial routing pattern, configuring with 159
used, for parallel routing pattern configuration 152
using, with single routing pattern 166
approval groups
URL 134
AppsVerify-BC, input parameter 290
AppsVerify-BE, input parameter 291
AppsVerify-BT, input parameter 291
arbitrary cycle pattern
about 72, 73
applicability 72
exploring 73-75
functionality 76
implementation 73
intent 72
motivation 72
signature 72
assigned state, business process 282
asynchronous interaction pattern
about 211
asynchronous process and service interaction, with Receive Task 219
asynchronous process and service interaction, with Send Task 219
boundary event, enabling on Receive Task 221
boundary event, enabling on Send Task 221
external services interaction, enabling 217, 218
asynchronous process
implementing, with Receive Task as start activity 222-224
interaction, Catch Events used 213-215
interaction, Message Throw used 213-215
asynchronous process and service
interaction, Receive Task used 219-221
interaction, Send Task used 219-221

asynchronous request-response (request-callback) pattern, asynchronous interaction pattern
applicability 212
classification 211
implementation 212
intent 211
known issues 212
known solution 212
motivation 212
signature 211
asynchronous request-response (request-callback) pattern, web service pattern
about 87
applicability 87
BPM Process as a Service, exposing 88-90
implementation 88
intent 87
known issues 88
known solution 88
motivation 87
asynchronous service
interacting with, Catch Events used 216
interacting with, Message Throw used 216
automatic correlation 242

B

BackOffice process 202
BA project
KPIs, defining in 365
Boundary Catch Event
modifying, from interrupting to non-interrupting 289-291
boundary event
enabling, on Receive Task 221
enabling, on Send Task 221
boundary event based activity correlation
working 277
boundary event, embedded subprocess interaction pattern
interrupting 234
interrupting event 236
interrupting timer boundary event configuration 235

non-interrupting event 236
BPM
  about 9, 324
  configuring, steps for 407-412
  flow control pattern 10
BPM composer
  used, for defining models 355
BPM events
  URL 202
BPMN process
  debugging, enabling 382, 383
BPMN process modeling
  versus human task modeling 139
BPMN project
  KPIs, defining in 363, 364
BPM process
  exposing, with Receive Task operation 97
  exposing, with Send Task operation 97
BPM project
  attaching, to debugger 383
BPM suite
  installing 394-396
Business Architecture (BA) 354
business catalog, synchronous
          request-response pattern 226
business context
  capturing 372-376
  document level 372
business exception 281
business process
  initiating, through event 105, 106
Business Process Management. *See* BPM
business process state
  about 281
  allocated 283
  assigned 282
  invoked 283
  reallocated 283
  started 283

C

cancel activity pattern
  about 275, 276
  applicability 275
  classification 275
  implementation 275

intent 275
known issues 275
motivation 275
testing 277, 278
cancel instance pattern
  about 258, 259
  applicability 258
  classification 258
  components 259, 260
  correlation definition, checking 261
  implementation 258
  intent 258
  motivation 258
  restart instance pattern 262
  signature 258
  testing 261, 262
cancel interaction pattern
  applicability 345
  implementation 345
  intent 344
  motivation 345
cancellation patterns
  about 80
  cancel multi-instance task pattern 80
canceling discriminator pattern 46, 47
canceling partial join pattern
  about 47, 66
  applicability 66
  classification 66
  implementation 67
  intent 66
  motivation 66
  signature 66
cancel multi-instance task pattern
  applicability 81
  classification 80
  implementation 81
  intent 80
  motivation 81
  signature 80
  testing 81
case
  about 322, 323
  versus process 322, 325
case interaction pattern
  about 344
  facts 344

case management 321-323
case stage pattern
  about 336
  applicability 337
  facts 337, 338
  implementation 337
  intent 337
  motivation 337
Catch Events
  used, for asynchronous process
      interaction 213-215
  used, for asynchronous service
      interaction 216
CatchFraudDetails process 204-206
CBE 300
child Value Chain Model
  KPIs, defining 365
  KPIs, defining in Value Chain
      Model level 367
  KPIs, defining in Value Chain
      Step level 365, 366
collaborative communications
  reasons 201
complex gateway
  discriminator pattern,
      implementing with 43
  partial join pattern, implementing with 43
complex synchronization pattern
  about 45, 46
  canceling discriminator pattern 46, 47
  canceling partial join pattern 46, 47
complex task pattern 135
components, cancel activity pattern
  event gateway 260
  event subprocess 259
conditional parallel split and
      parallel merge pattern
  about 32
  antipattern 35
  working with 33, 34
conditional sequence flow 12
Connection Factory
  about 120
  creating 121
connection pool
  configuring 122, 123

content access policy and task actions
      feature, facts
  about 196
  applicability 196
  implementation 197
  intent 196
  known issues 197
  known solution 197
  motivation 196
Continue Execution Exception Handling
      pattern
  about 299, 300
  applicability 300
  CBE 300
  classification 299
  implementation, scenarios 300
  intent 299
  motivation 299
  signature 299
  testing 301, 302
conversation pattern
  about 207-211
  advanced conversation 208
  applicability 207
  classification 207
  default conversation 208
  implementation 208
  known issues 208
  known solution 208
  motivation 207
  scoped conversation 208
  signature 207
conversations, types
  define interface 211
  process call 211
  service call 211
  use interface 211
correlation behavior 249, 250
correlation definition
  configuring 247-249
correlation keys
  about 244
  defining 247-249
correlation mechanism
  about 242
  correlation behavior 249

correlation definition,
    configuring 247-249
correlation keys, defining 247
correlation properties, defining 246
correlations, types 242
environment, configuring 244
correlations, components
    correlation keys 244
    correlation property 243
    correlation property alias 244
    correlation set 244
correlations, types
    automatic correlation 242
    payload/message-based correlation 243
CreateApprovalGroupList function 146
CreateJobLevelList function 146
CreateManagementChainList function 146
CreatePositionList function 146
CreateResourceList function 146
CreateSupervisoryList function 146
custom domain
    creating 402-407
Customer Acceptance activity 331
**Customer Service Representative
    (CSR) 114, 329**

D

deadline
    about 182
    applicability 182
    classification 182
    implementation 182
    intent 182
    motivation 182
    Participant Level Deadline 185
    task level deadlines 183
Debugger feature, facts
    about 381-383
    applicability 382
    category 381
    feature 381
    implementation 382
    intent 381
    known issues 382
    known solution 382
    motivation 381

default conversation 208
default domain
    configuring, steps for 397-399
demo user community
    enabling 399-402
discriminator pattern
    about 40
    implementing, with complex gateway 43
    structured discriminator pattern 41
dispatching pattern
    about 170
    LEAST_BUSY task, configuring 170
    MOST_PRODUCTIVE, configuring 170
    ROUND_ROBIN, configuring 170
document level, business context
    activity 373-375
    process 372, 373
    project 372
do-while loop
    demystifying 70, 71
    scenario, testing 71, 72
    structured loop functionality 72
driver attributes, notification
    configuring 193, 194
driver properties, notification
    configuring 193, 194
duration deadline, task level deadlines 183
**dynamic assignment,
    task assignment pattern 141**
dynamic case management 324
**dynamic partial join,
    for multiple instances pattern**
    about 67
    applicability 67
    classification 67
    implementation 67
    intent 67
    motivation 67
    signature 67
    working with 68

E

ECM 324
e-mail
    used, for one-way invocation pattern
        implementation 102

Email Start Pattern
applicability 102
implementation 102
intent 102
known issues 102
known solution 102
motivation 102
embedded subprocess 227
embedded subprocess interaction pattern
about 232
applicability 233
boundary event, interrupting 234, 235
characteristics 233
classification 233
implementation 233
intent 233
known issues 233
known solution 233
motivation 233
signature 233
Emulating Process Behavior feature
about 377-381
applicability 378
category 377
feature 377
implementation 378
intent 377
known issues 378
known solution 378
motivation 377
end cases, Internal Exception
Handling pattern
complete 309
error 309
terminate 309
end states, Allocated state External
Exception Handling pattern
JExternal-Complete 308
JExternal-Error 308
JExternal-Terminate 308
end states, Internal Exception
Handling pattern
Internal Complete Exception
Handling pattern 310
Internal Error Exception
Handling pattern 311

Internal Terminate Exception Handling
pattern 311
enterprise content management, for task
documents
about 197, 198
applicability 197
classification 197
implementation 197
intent 197
motivation 197
enterprise maps
about 355
creating 355
Enterprise Resource Planning (ERP) 324
environment, correlation mechanism
configuring 244, 245
error assignee feature, facts
applicability 191
classification 190
implementation 191
intent 190
known issues 191
known solution 191
motivation 190
escalation feature
applicability 187
classification 187
implementation 187
intent 187
known issues 187
known solution 187
motivation 187
URL 189
escalation pattern
about 171
escalating, ways 172
URL 172
Event Definition Language (EDL) 236
Event Delivery Network (EDN) 236
event-driven interaction pattern
about 236-238
applicability 237
components 236
event producer component 237
implementation 237
intent 237
known issues 237

known solution 238
motivation 237
scenario, defining 238, 239
signal catch event configuration 238, 239
event gateway 260
event pattern
applicability 339
classification 338
implementation 339
intent 338
motivation 339
signature 338
events
about 339-341
types 340
event subprocess 229, 259
exception
about 279
business exception 281
classifying 280
external triggers/process exceptions 281
system exceptions 280
timeout/deadline exceptions 281
exclusion feature, facts
applicability 190
classification 190
implementation 190
intent 190
motivation 190
exclusive choice pattern(exclusive choice
and simple merge pattern)
about 16, 17
elucidating 22
overview 21
use case 19
working with 18-21
exclusive choice pattern,
decision mechanisms
data 17
events 17
expiry feature
about 186-189
applicability 187
classification 187
implementation 187
intent 187

known issues 187
known solution 187
motivation 187
explicit termination pattern
about 79
applicability 79
classification 79
implementation 79
motivation 79
signature 79
working 79
external services interaction
enabling 217, 218
External Trigger-N 318
External Trigger-O 318
external triggers 318
external triggers/process exceptions 281

F

Feedback process 204-206
First Notice of Loss (FNOL) 329
flow control pattern, BPM
about 10
complex synchronization pattern 45, 46
conditional parallel split and
parallel merge pattern 32
discriminator pattern 40
exclusive choice pattern 16, 17
multichoice pattern 22, 23
multimerge pattern 36-38
parallel split pattern 28
partial join pattern 40
sequence flow pattern 10, 11
synchronization pattern 28
synchronizing merge pattern 22, 23
use cases, executing 14, 15
Force-Complete Exception Handling pattern
about 295
applicability 295
classification 295
implementation 295
intent 295
motivation 295
signature 295

force completion/early completion
        pattern, facts
    about 179
    applicability 179
    classification 178
    Enabling Early Completion in
        Parallel Subtasks option 180
    implementation 179
    motivation 178
    signature 178
Force-Error Exception Handling pattern
    about 293, 294
    applicability 293
    classification 293
    implementation 293
    intent 293
    motivation 293
    signature 293
Force-Error Execution Exception
        Handling pattern
    about 303, 304
    Allocated state External Exception
        Handling Pattern 304
    applicability 303
    classification 303
    implementation 304
    intent 303
    Internal Exception Handling pattern 309
    known issues 304
    known solution 304
    motivation 303
    Reallocated Exception
        Handling pattern 313
    signature 303
Force-Terminate Exception
        Handling pattern
    about 292
    applicability 292
    classification 292
    implementation 292
    intent 292
    motivation 292
    signature 292
Force-Terminate Execution
        Exception Handling pattern
    about 302, 303
    applicability 302

classification 302
    implementation 302
    intent 302
    motivation 302
    signature 302
function-based derivation, task assignment
        pattern 142
FYI approver pattern
    using, with job level list builder pattern 167
    using, with name and expression list
        builder pattern 167
FYI routing pattern 140
FYI task pattern 135

G

groups 133
group task pattern 135
guaranteed delivery pattern
    about 117
    applicability 118
    classification 118
    implementation 118
    intent 118
    known issues 118, 119
    known solution 119
    motivation 118

H

hierarchical list builder pattern
    about 144
    job level 145
    management chain 144
    position 145
    supervisory 145
holistic view pattern
    about 346
    applicability 346
    facts 346
    implementation 346
    intent 346
    motivation 346
    signature 346
human task
    about 131, 133
    participants 133
    user task patterns 135

human task, features
about 132
content access policy 196, 197
deadline 182
error assignees 190
escalation 186
exclusion 190
expiry 186, 187
notification 192
renewal 187
request information feature 175
reviewer 190
task actions 196, 197
human task initiator pattern
about 113
applicability 113
classification 113
implementation 113
loan origination, via human task form 114
motivation 113
process, testing 116, 117
human task modeling
versus BPMN process modeling 139
human task patterns
about 132
ad hoc routing pattern 173
complex task 135
dispatching pattern 170
escalation pattern 171
force completion pattern 178
FYI task 135
group task 135
initiator user task 135
list builder pattern 142
management task 135
milestone pattern 136
Notify/FYI pattern 166
parallel routing pattern 147
reassignment and delegation pattern 177
routing pattern 139
routing rule pattern 180
rule-based reassignment and
    delegation pattern 172
serial routing pattern 158
single routing pattern 165
task aggregation pattern 167

task assignment pattern 140
user task 135

I

implicit termination pattern
amalgamating, in process flow 78, 79
applicability 78
classification 78
implementation 78
intent 78
known issues 78
motivation 78
signature 78
incoming sequence flow 11
initiator user task pattern 135
Insurance Claim case
about 329
building blocks 332
testing 333-335
interaction patterns
demonstrating, by use cases definition 202
Internal Complete Exception
    Handling pattern 310
Internal Error Exception Handling pattern
possibilities 312
reallocated scenario 312
restarted scenario 312
restarted scenario, testing 312
Internal Exception Handling pattern
about 309
implementing 309
pattern categories 309
Internal Terminate Exception
    Handling pattern 311
Inter Process Communication (IPC). *See*
    interaction patterns
interrupting event 234, 236
interrupting timer boundary
    event configuration
demonstrating 235
Invoked Exception Handling pattern
about 296
activities 296
exception handling, categories 297
invoked state, business process
about 283

call activity 284
catch event 283
Message Throw Events 283
Receive Task 283
Send Task 283
service task 283
Invoked State Exception Handling pattern
about 297-299
applicability 297
challenge 299
classification 297
implementation 298
intent 297
known issues 298
known solution 298
motivation 297
scenario, testing 298
signature 297

J

Java Message Service (JMS) 85
JDK
installing 393, 394
JExternal-Complete state 308
JExternal-Error state 308
JExternal-Terminate state 308
JMS adapter
configuring 123
JMS module
creating 121
JMS queue
creating 122
JMS resources
Connection Factory, creating 121
connection pool, configuring 122, 123
creating 120
JMS adapter, redeploying 123
JMS module, creating 121
JMS queue, creating 122
JMS server, creating 120
JMS subdeployment, creating 121
JMS topic, creating 122
JMS server
about 120
creating 120

JMS subdeployment
creating 121
JMS topic
creating 122
job level list builder pattern
about 145
FYI approver pattern, using with 167
participant list, modifying with list
    modification 162
participant, substituting with list
    substitution 162, 163
serial routing pattern,
    using with 160-162

K

KPIs
defining, in BA project 365
defining, in BPMN project 363, 364
defining, in child Value Chain Model 365
defining, in master Value Chain Model 368

L

lane participant list builder pattern
about 143
parallel routing pattern, using with 153
LEAST_BUSY task 170
list builder pattern
about 142
applicability 142
classification 142
hierarchical list builder 144
implementation 142
intent 142
motivation 142
nonhierarchical list builder patterns 143
rule-based list builder 145
signature 142
loan origination process
about 203
initiating, over e-mail 103, 104
initiating, over event 107-110
initiating, over JMS' Queue/Topic 119
initiating, over multiple
    event occurrence 111, 112
testing, for restarting loan 263, 264
via human task form 114-116

loan origination BPM process
consumer process, creating 124, 125
initiating, via queue 119
JMS resources, creating 120
message, pushing to queue 126, 127
publisher process, creating 124
publish-subscribe pattern,
    Topics used 127, 128
localization feature
applicability 345
implementation 345
intent 345
motivation 345
local synchronizing merge pattern 27

M

management chain list builder pattern
about 144
parallel routing pattern,
    using with 156, 157
using, with single routing pattern 166
management task pattern 135
master Value Chain Model
KPIs, defining in Value Chain
    Model level 369, 370
KPIs, defining in Value Chain
    Step level 368, 369
message-based correlation pattern
about 250
applicability 251
characteristics 252
implementation 251
intent 250
motivation 250
testing 256-258
working 252-256
Message Throw
used, for asynchronous
    process interaction 213-215
used, for asynchronous
    service interaction 216
MI
demonstrating, with prior runtime
    knowledge pattern 55, 56
dynamic partial join functionality 69
static partial join pattern, working 66

working, with prior runtime knowledge
    pattern 57
milestone pattern
about 136, 137, 341
applicability 136, 342
BPMN process,
    versus human task modeling 139
classification 136
facts 342
implementation 136, 342
intent 136, 342
motivation 136, 342
sequence flow, modeling 137, 139
signature 136
**MI, without prior runtime
    knowledge pattern**
about 58
applicability 57
classification 57
implementation 58
intent 57
motivation 57
signature 57
use case, testing 60, 61
working 58, 59
model definition, capabilities
enterprise maps 355
Strategy Model 355
Value Chain Model 355
MOST_PRODUCTIVE task 170
multichoice pattern
about 22, 23
demonstrating, with OR gateway 23, 24
working with 26
multi-instance subprocess
about 227
executing, with prior design-time
    knowledge pattern 51-54
multimerge pattern
about 36-38
exploring 38, 39
multiple instances pattern
dynamic partial join 67
static partial join patterns 62
**multiple instances, with prior design-time
    knowledge pattern**
applicability 50

classification 50
demonstrating 55, 56
implementation 50
intent 50
motivation 50
signature 50
working 57
multiple instances, with prior runtime
knowledge pattern
about 54
applicability 55
classification 55
implementation 55
intent 55
motivation 55
multiple operations, for BPM Process
exposing, steps 94-97
multiple start events 128

N

name and expression list builder pattern
about 143
FYI approver pattern, using with 167
participant identification type,
application role 159
participant identification type, groups 159
participant identification type,
users 158, 159
using, with single routing pattern 166
nonfunction-based derivation,
task assignment pattern 142
nonhierarchical (absolute)
list builder patterns
about 143
approval groups 143
lane participant 143
name and expression 143
parametric role 144
non-interrupting event 234, 236
notification
about 192, 193
applicability 192
attributes, configuring 193, 194
classification 192
definition, configuring 194, 195

driver properties, configuring 193, 194
implementation 193
intent 192
motivation 192
Notify/FYI pattern 166

O

one-way invocation pattern
about 99
implementing, e-mail used 102
implementing, timer used 100, 101
one-way invocation pattern
implementation, with e-mail
flow, testing 105
loan origination request,
initiating 103, 104
Oracle BPM Suite 12c
URL 394
Oracle BPM workspace
URL 337
organizational roles (parametric roles) 134
outgoing sequence flow 11

P

PAM
about 353
working with 384
parallel routing pattern
about 140, 147
applicability 147
classification 147
configuring, with approval group list
builder pattern 152
implementation 147
intent 147
motivation 147
use cases, testing 147
used, for creating participant type 148-151
used, with lane participant list
builder pattern 153
used, with management chain list builder
pattern 156, 157
used, with rule-based list builder 154, 155
parallel split pattern 28
parametric role list builder pattern 144

partial join pattern
  implementing, with complex gateway 43
  structured partial join pattern 42
  testing, for failure complex gateway 44
  testing, for success complex gateway 44, 45
participants, human task
  groups 133
  organizational roles (parametric roles) 134
  roles 133
  users 133
payload/message-based correlation 243
peer subprocess 228
persistent trigger pattern
  applicability 77
  classification 77
  implementation 77
  intent 77
  motivation 77
  signature 77
point-to-point (PTP) model 120
position list builder pattern
  about 145
  using, with serial routing pattern 163
prior design-time knowledge pattern
  used, for executing multi-instance
      subprocess 51-54
  using, with multiple instances 50
prior runtime knowledge pattern
  MI, demonstrating with 56
  MI, working with 57
  using, with multiple instances 54
process
  about 321
  versus case 322, 325
Process Asset Management. See PAM
process data objects (PDOs) 219
Process-Level Exception Handling pattern
  about 314
  implementing 315-317
  testing 317, 318
publish-subscribe pattern
  about 105, 106
  applicability 106
  implementation 107
  intent 106
  known issues 107
  known solution 107

loan origination,
    initiating over event 107-110
  motivation 106

Q

query pattern
  about 268
  applicability 269
  classification 268
  implementation 269
  known issues 269
  motivation 268
  testing 270-272
  QuerySubprocess configuration,
    checking 269, 270
Queue 120

R

RACI (Responsible Accountable
    Consulted Informed) 375
Reallocated Exception Handling pattern 314
reallocated state, business process 283
Reassigned Exception Handling pattern
  about 284
  applicability 284
  classification 284
  implementation 284
  intent 284
  motivation 284
  signature 284
reassignment and delegation pattern
  about 177
  applicability 177
  classification 177
  implementation 177
  intent 177
  motivation 177
  signature 177
Receive Task
  boundary event, attaching on 221
  used, for asynchronous process and service
    interaction 219, 220
Receive Task, as start activity
  asynchronous process,
    implementing with 222-224

reminder, task level deadlines 183
renewal feature
  about 187
  applicability 187
  classification 187
  implementation 187
  implementing 188, 189
  intent 187
  known issues 187
  known solution 187
  motivation 187
report data, Strategic Alignment pattern
  publishing 370, 371
request information feature
  about 175
  applicability 175
  classification 175
  implementation 175
  motivation 175
request-response pattern
  applicability 90
  implementation 91
  intent 90
  known issues 91
  known solution 91
  motivation 90
  service message interaction pattern,
    modifying 91, 92
response type 165
restart instance pattern
  about 262
  loan origination process, testing 263, 264
  restart scenario, testing 264-266
restart scenario
  testing 264-266
reusable processes interaction pattern
  about 229
  applicability 230
  characteristics 230, 231
  implementation 230
  intent 230
  known issues 230
  known solution 230
  motivation 230
  use case scenario 231, 232
reusable subprocess 228
reviewers feature

applicability 191
classification 190
implementation 191
intent 190
known issues 191
known solution 191
motivation 190
roles
  about 133
  application roles 133
  approval groups 134
  swimlane roles 134
ROUND_ROBIN task 170
round trip and business-IT collaboration
  about 383-391
  applicability 383
  category 383
  demonstrating 388, 389
  feature 383
  implementation 384
  intent 383
  known issues 384
  known solution 384
  motivation 383
routing pattern
  applicability 139
  classification 139
  FYI 140
  implementation 140
  intent 139
  motivation 139
  parallel 140
  serial 140
  single approver 140
routing rule pattern
  about 180, 181
  applicability 180
  classification 180
  COMPLETE action 181
  ESCALATE action 181
  GO_FORWARD action 181
  GOTO action 181
  implementation 180
  intent 180
  motivation 180
  PUSHBACK action 181
  signature 180

rule-based assignment,
    task assignment pattern **142**
rule-based list builder
  about 145, 146
  CreateApprovalGroupList function 146
  CreateJobLevelList 146
  CreateManagementChainList function 146
  CreatePositionList function 146
  CreateResourceList function 146
  parallel routing pattern,
      using with 154, 155
  using, with serial routing pattern 165
rule-based reassignment
    and delegation pattern
  about 172
  applicability 172
  implementation 172
  intent 172
  motivation 172

S

scenario, event-driven interaction pattern
  defining 238, 239
scoped conversation 208
Send Task
  boundary event, attaching on 221
  used, for asynchronous process and service
      interaction 219-221
sequence flow pattern
  about 10, 11
  elucidating 14
  working with 12, 13
sequence flow pattern, categories
  incoming sequence flow 11
  outgoing sequence flow 11
sequence flow pattern, types
  conditional sequence flow 12
  default/unconditional sequence flow 12
serial routing pattern
  about 140, 158
  applicability 158
  classification 158
  configuring, with approval group list
      builder pattern 159
  configuring, with supervisory list builder
      pattern 164, 165

implementation 158
intent 158
motivation 158
signature 158
using, with job level list-builder
    pattern 160-162
using, with management chain list builder
    pattern 160
using, with name and expression list
    builder pattern 158
using, with position list builder pattern 163
using, with rules list builder pattern 165
Service Level Agreement (SLA) 221, 329
single approver routing pattern 140
single routing pattern
  about 165
  using, with approval group list
      builder pattern 166
  using, with management chain list builder
      pattern 166
  using, with name and expression list
      builder pattern 166
SOA
  configuring, steps for 407-412
stakeholders 327
started state, business process 283
static assignment, task assignment
    pattern 141
static partial join patterns, for multiple
    instances pattern
  about 62
  applicability 62
  classification 62
  intent 62
  motivation 62
  signature 62
  use case, testing 64, 65
  working on 63
Strategic Alignment pattern
  about 354-356
  applicability 354
  classification 354
  goals, mapping to organization 363
  implementation 354
  intent 354
  known issues 354
  known solution 354

KPIs, defining in BA project 365
KPIs, defining in BPMN project 363, 364
motivation 354
report data, publishing 370, 371
Strategy Model 361, 362
Value Chain Model 357-361
Strategy Model
about 355
creating 361, 362
structured discriminator pattern 41
structured loop functionality 72
structured loop pattern
about 69
applicability 69
classification 69
do-while looping 70
implementation 70
intent 69
motivation 69
signature 69
while-do looping 72
working with 70
structured partial join pattern 42
structured synchronizing merge pattern 26
subdeployment resource 120
subprocess 232
subprocess interaction patterns
about 227-229
embedded subprocess 227
event subprocess 229
multi-instance subprocess 227
peer subprocess 228
reusable processes interaction pattern 229
reusable subprocess 228
supervisory list builder pattern
about 145
using, with serial routing pattern 164, 165
suspend activity pattern
about 274
applicability 274
classification 274
implementation 274
intent 274
motivation 274
suspend process pattern
about 272-274
applicability 272

classification 272
implementation 272
intent 272
motivation 272
signature 272
swimlane roles 134
synchronization pattern 28-31
synchronizing merge pattern
about 22, 23
demonstrating, with OR gateway 23, 24
local synchronizing merge pattern 27
structured synchronizing merge pattern 26
working with 26
synchronous request-response pattern
about 224
applicability 224
business catalog 226
demonstrating 225, 226
implementation 225
intent 224
known issues 225
known solution 225
motivation 224
signature 224
system exceptions 280
system-level exception
        handling pattern 318

T

task aggregation pattern
about 167, 170
routing pattern 168, 169
staging 168, 169
task assignment pattern
about 140
applicability 141
classification 140
dynamic assignment 141
function-based derivation 142
implementation 141
intent 140
motivation 140
nonfunction-based derivation 142
rule-based assignment 142
signature 140
static assignment 141

task level deadlines
  about 183-185
  duration deadline 183
  reminder 183
  warning 183
timeout/deadline exceptions 281
timer
  used, for one-way invocation
      pattern implementation 100, 101
timer boundary events
  interrupting event 234
  non-interrupting event 234
timer start pattern
  applicability 99
  implementation 99
  intent 99
  known solution 99
  motivation 99
Topic 120
transient trigger patterns
  applicability 77
  classification 76
  implementation 77
  intent 76
  known issues 77
  known solution 77
  motivation 76
  signature 76
trigger patterns
  about 76
  persistent trigger 77
  transient trigger 76

U

update task pattern
  about 266, 267
  applicability 266
  configuration, checking 267, 268
  functionality, demonstrating 268
  implementation 266
  intent 266
  motivation 266
  signature 266

use cases, parallel routing pattern
  testing 147
**use case scenarios, Adaptive
      Case Management (ACM)**
  about 330-332
  Insurance Claim 332
**use cases, for interaction
      pattern demonstration**
  BackOffice process 202
  CatchFraudDetails 203-206
  Feedback process 203-206
  loan origination process 203
User Messaging Service (UMS) 103, 193
users 133

V

Value Chain Model
  about 355
  creating 357-361

W

web service pattern
  about 86, 87
  asynchronous request-response
      (request-callback) pattern 87-90
  BPM process, exposing with
      Receive Task operation 97
  BPM process, exposing with
      Send Task operation 97
  challenges 86
  multiple operations, enabling 94-96
  request-response pattern 90, 91
  Receive Tasks, implementing 97, 98
  Send Tasks, implementing 97, 98
while-do loop
  demystifying 72

Thank you for buying
Oracle BPM Suite 12*c* Modeling Patterns

About Packt Publishing

Packt, pronounced 'packed', published its first book "Mastering phpMyAdmin for Effective MySQL Management" in April 2004 and subsequently continued to specialize in publishing highly focused books on specific technologies and solutions.

Our books and publications share the experiences of your fellow IT professionals in adapting and customizing today's systems, applications, and frameworks. Our solution-based books give you the knowledge and power to customize the software and technologies you're using to get the job done. Packt books are more specific and less general than the IT books you have seen in the past. Our unique business model allows us to bring you more focused information, giving you more of what you need to know, and less of what you don't.

Packt is a modern, yet unique publishing company, which focuses on producing quality, cutting-edge books for communities of developers, administrators, and newbies alike. For more information, please visit our website: www.packtpub.com.

About Packt Enterprise

In 2010, Packt launched two new brands, Packt Enterprise and Packt Open Source, in order to continue its focus on specialization. This book is part of the Packt Enterprise brand, home to books published on enterprise software – software created by major vendors, including (but not limited to) IBM, Microsoft and Oracle, often for use in other corporations. Its titles will offer information relevant to a range of users of this software, including administrators, developers, architects, and end users.

Writing for Packt

We welcome all inquiries from people who are interested in authoring. Book proposals should be sent to author@packtpub.com. If your book idea is still at an early stage and you would like to discuss it first before writing a formal book proposal, contact us; one of our commissioning editors will get in touch with you.

We're not just looking for published authors; if you have strong technical skills but no writing experience, our experienced editors can help you develop a writing career, or simply get some additional reward for your expertise.

Oracle SOA Suite 11*g* Performance Tuning Cookbook

ISBN: 978-1-84968-884-0   Paperback: 328 pages

Over 100 recipes to get the best performance from your Oracle SOA Suite 11*g* infrastructure

1. Tune the Java Virtual Machine to get the best out of the underlying platform.

2. Learn how to monitor and profile your Oracle SOA Suite applications.

3. Discover how to design and deploy your application for high-performance scenarios.

4. Identify and resolve performance bottlenecks in your Oracle SOA Suite infrastructure.

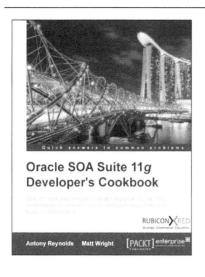

Oracle SOA Suite 11*g* Developer's Cookbook

ISBN: 978-1-84968-388-3   Paperback: 346 pages

Over 65 high-level recipes for extending your Oracle SOA applications and enhancing your skills with expert tips and tricks for developers

1. Extend and enhance the tricks in your Oracle SOA Suite developer arsenal with expert tips and best practices.

2. Get to grips with Java integration, OSB message patterns, SOA Clusters, and much more in this book and e-book.

3. A practical Cookbook packed with recipes for achieving the most important SOA Suite tasks for developers.

Please check **www.PacktPub.com** for information on our titles